Swami Satyananda
Saraswati

Volume V

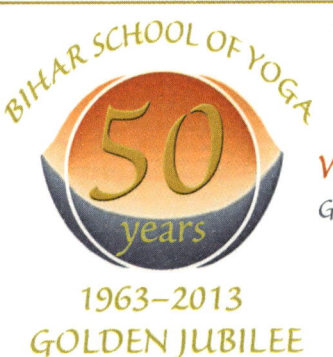

WORLD YOGA CONVENTION 2013
GANGA DARSHAN, MUNGER, BIHAR, INDIA
23rd–27th October 2013

BIHAR SCHOOL OF YOGA
50 years
1963–2013
GOLDEN JUBILEE

Teachings of
Swami Satyananda Saraswati

Volume V

*A compilation of talks and satsangs given by
Swami Satyananda Saraswati during his Australian and
New Zealand tour from November 1983 to April 1984.*

Yoga Publications Trust, Munger, Bihar, India

© Bihar School of Yoga 1986, 2013

All rights reserved. No part of this publication may be reproduced, transmitted or stored in a retrieval system, in any form or by any means, without permission in writing from Yoga Publications Trust.

The terms Satyananda Yoga® and Bihar Yoga are registered trademarks owned by International Yoga Fellowship Movement (IYFM). The use of the same in this book is with permission and should not in any way be taken as affecting the validity of the marks.

Published by Bihar School of Yoga
   First edition 1986

Published by Yoga Publications Trust
   Second edition 2013

ISBN: 978-81-85787-06-0

Publisher and distributor: Yoga Publications Trust, Ganga Darshan, Munger, Bihar, India.

Website: www.biharyoga.net
         www.rikhiapeeth.net

Printed at Thomson Press (India) Limited, New Delhi, 110001

Dedication

*In humility we offer this dedication to
Swami Sivananda Saraswati, who initiated
Swami Satyananda Saraswati into the secrets of yoga.*

Content

Satyananda Ashram, Mangrove Mountain, Australia
1. Inaugural Speech — 1
2. Satsang — 8
3. Satsang — 19
4. The Ancient Tantric Tradition and Modern Science — 30
5. Kriya Yoga — 38
6. Satsang — 42
7. Satsang — 54
8. Satsang — 69
9. Satsang — 79
10. Introduction to Advanced Kriya Course — 85
11. Satsang — 94
12. Mantra Yoga — 103
13. Satsang — 109
14. Satsang — 119
15. Satsang — 130

Manly Ashram, Australia
16. Awakening the Inner Experience — 144

Satyananda Ashram, Mangrove Mountain, Australia
17. The Inner Christmas — 155

18. My Early Life	162
19. Interviews	173
20. Shivalingam	194

Kuranda Ashram, Australia

21. Meditation: A Tool for Man's Higher Evolution	205
22. The Practices of Yoga	214
23. Satsang	224

Rocklyn Ashram, Australia

24. Inauguration of an Ashram	239
25. Satsang	249
26. The Philosophy and the Practices of Tantra	262
27. Purpose of Ashram Life	279

Satyananda Ashram, Mangrove Mountain, Australia

28. Radio Interview	287

Gosford Ashram, Australia

29. Dhyana Yoga	290

Brisbane Ashram, Australia

30. Radio Interviews	302
31. Dealing with the Mind	309
32. Satsang	319
33. Expansion of Mind	331

Gold Coast Ashram, Australia

34. Awakening the Evolutionary Energy	343

Lillian Rock Ashram, Australia

35. The Supreme Yoga	359

Nimbin, Australia
36. How to Meditate   374

Bellingen Ashram, Australia
37. Indirect Method of Meditation   390

Newcastle Ashram, Australia
38. The Systems of Yoga   396

Taree, Australia
39. Yoga Research and Meditation   410

Perth, Australia
40. Satsang   421

Auckland, New Zealand
41. Karma Sannyasa Initiation   436
42. Methods for Awakening Higher Consciousness   439

1

Inaugural Speech

Satyananda Ashram, Mangrove Mountain, Australia, 18 November 1983

This year, 1983, I made a great change to my responsibilities. On January 19th, I withdrew from my official and active participation with Bihar School of Yoga, of which I was president for twenty years. Since then I have undertaken a long travelling scheme.

I have experienced that my life is divided into cycles of twenty years. For twenty years I was at home with my people. For twenty years I was a sannyasin, a disciple. For twenty years I was a founder, an administrator and a teacher, and that makes my sixty years. For the next twenty years, I will be moving dispassionately, without working for any organization, sect or system, and with Australia today I begin that twenty year cycle.

I will come back to India from time to time, as I come back to Australia, Greece, Italy, France, England or America, but most of my time will be spent moving around the world and aiding the great uprising of yogic consciousness that is already taking place in every heart and in every being throughout the world. I must nourish and help that awakening.

In search of the self
Today, for the first time, scientists and intellectuals have understood and begun to heed the warnings of great thinkers

of the past who said that the Western world in particular and the modern, technological world in general did not have a foolproof culture, society, philosophy or even religion.

As man is a seeker, you cannot deceive him for all time. He is an adventurer, as he has always tried to search for the purpose of life on this plane. Maybe for some years we don't think about it. We spend our time eating, drinking and merrymaking. Everybody does it, but there comes a moment when the awakening begins from the depths of our consciousness and we begin to question our existence. Why do I exist? Where have I come from? Where shall I go?

The simplest but not the exact answer is: from God we come, to God we go. The exact answer is complicated. It is a technical answer. At the same time, if we want to realize our real personality, our real self, we have to work very hard. Now, people everywhere are searching and asking what the reality is. With the philosophy and science of yoga, they have come to a greater understanding about their own self.

When people begin to meditate and look within themselves, they are able to transcend the external mind, the external experiences, and even the very stuff of their existence called the ego. They then begin to realize that this body, this name, this nationality which I hold, this empirical definition, is not the ultimate explanation, not the ultimate definition. I am something more than what I have been thinking about myself. All along I have been thinking, I am a man, I am a human being, I am different from animals, but this is not true. I have been thinking that I am white, black, yellow, mixed, this or that, but these are merely the definitions of this external appearance.

For example, you have a car. Maybe it is Japanese, American, French or Australian. Is that the definition of the passenger? Is the passenger also Japanese, American, French or Australian? Well, in this case the passenger is Australian, using a Japanese car. In the same way, how can you say that this body is the ultimate definition of yourself, whatever this body may represent: name, form, nationality, religion, culture, civilization and so forth?

If you go beyond this body, then comes the mind and its vrittis. Is the mind your definition? Is happiness, unhappiness, love, hatred, agony, joy, past, present and future your definition? These experiences which I have had, which I am having in this life – do they belong to me? When the shock absorber of the car is broken, does anything happen to the driver? No. These diverse, conflicting experiences which break my body, my personality and my mind throughout life do not belong to me. I am not this.

Beyond the body and mind
Like this, if you go on analyzing and trying to understand, you will find that the deeper you go in dhyana, the deeper you go within your own self, within the dimensions of total equanimity and samadhi, all that you have been thinking, all that you have been experiencing about yourself does not exist. There you are a different person altogether. The experience of that 'I' and the experience of the present 'I' are different.

The experience of this present 'I' is covered by notions of duality and multiplicity; there is no unity. As long as you have the experience of the present 'I', you cannot experience unity. You can only experience duality, and therefore conflict. Multiplicity and diversity do not bring unity. Unless you experience unity, you cannot experience love. Love is a much misused, abused word.

Love is the greatest, the highest experience in life. But you have never experienced it, have you? The saints have said, "Love is God." What they meant was not the lower form of love which we know, but that experience which is a result of unity, born of the experience of the self, when you have become completely devoid of the lower ego.

This experience of *aham*, the cosmic 'I', emerges when you go deeper and deeper into your own self, not into your own body, mind or personality, but into your own self. This self is not confined to this body even as energy is not confined to one particular point. Energy is universal. Spirit, *atma*, the cosmic self, is universal.

By mistake, by wrong notion, you identify that self with this body because you know this body as your self; but the spirit, the atma, the cosmic self, is not confined to this body. It is not in the body. It is beyond the body. It is a mistake to say it is in the body. The body is in the self because the body is limited and the cosmic self, the atma, is not limited.

The cosmic self is the finest experience of human life. It is the ultimate experience, and therefore we call that experience *atma jnana*. You may have read about it in many of the books on philosophy. *Atma* means cosmic self, infinite self, real self, total self; not the little self, the egotistical self, the physical or mental self. *Jnana* means awareness, knowledge, experience. When you experience that cosmic self, it is called atma jnana. This is the ultimate of yoga.

Start from where you are

It is this destination which we have to reach sooner or later and it is to achieve this greatest experience of life that, throughout the world, hundreds and thousands of people, irrespective of their religions, faith and political ideologies, are working. And they have found that the system of yoga is a very disciplined system.

The system of yoga is rooted in tantra. It is not rooted in religion. Therefore, it considers that everybody can have this experience. Religions have their own do's and don'ts. If you tell lies, if you drink champagne, if you go to many women, you can't get it. Tantra, however, says that nothing can bar you from having this experience. Tantra never says what you should do and shouldn't do. It says do whatever you like, it matters very little.

The important point that tantra emphasizes is that if you want to reach Delhi from Sydney, you don't have to go via Honolulu, San Francisco and New York. If you want to go from San Francisco to New Delhi, you don't have to go via Sydney. In the scheme of evolution, you are standing at a particular point. You start from there. Do not try to jump onto another's platform and start your journey from there – you will make a mistake.

Everybody has his own karma, his own personality, his own desires, passions, idiosyncrasies and infirmities. Everybody is not strong and cannot bear the brunt of penance and austerity. Many times we want to have a high experience, but at the same time the fabric of our existence is so flimsy, so weak, that we succumb to the ordinary desires of life. We are not able to live without sense gratification, attachments, addictions.

Now, what happens to this man? Can he realize his own self or not? Can he experience his highest consciousness with all the idiosyncrasies of his life, or is it necessary that he has to become a puritan? Tantra is very clear on this point. It says, 'Whatever you are, go ahead, practise yoga, and in time you will find that you have transcended your external self.'

An intimate experience

A debauchee, a criminal, a thief, a robber, a smuggler, an Indian, an Australian, a virtuous man, a compassionate man, all these external qualifications or disqualifications do not belong to the self. That self, that atma, which you have to experience, is beyond all these external definitions. These external limitations and references do not taint this effulgent, spiritual consciousness, which you are.

The only qualification regarding the self is that you have to experience it. Knowledge is not enough. I am now talking about the self; this is called knowledge. You are receiving it; you are understanding it through your intellect, but this is not experience. Experience is intimately personal. It doesn't involve a teacher, a scripture, a priest, a dictum or a sermon.

You have suffered sometimes in your life. This is your personal experience. You know what it is and if I ask you to explain that suffering to me, you can do it. But if I have not suffered, I cannot understand it. In the same way, if I tell you what atma jnana is, what brahma jnana is, you will not understand it because you do not have that intimate experience. An intimate experience is not the subject matter of intellect, mind and emotion. No. Intimate experience is a quality of innermost consciousness and it is to that point that yoga should take you.

The correct sadhana

If you find that one path of yoga is inadequate, do not criticize it. Add another type of yoga to it. Supposing you are practising ajapa japa and it has not been giving you any intimate experience of transcendence, do not criticize this practice; add a special pranayama practice to that. This is how you have to try to break the barrier of the limited self.

Scientists launch rockets. These rockets go at a terrific speed intended to counteract the force of gravity. If the speed is not sufficient, it will not be able to counteract the gravitational force and the rocket will not go beyond the sphere of gravity. In the same way, there is a law of gravity with this empirical self. You want to get out of it. You want to transcend the body. You want to transcend the mind. You do so for some time and then again you come back.

This gravitational force related to the body, to the mind and senses is known as maya. On account of this force, most of us are not able to go beyond name and form. We are not able to go beyond time, space and object. We are able to transcend certain things to some extent. We go up and then we fall back down. We have to find out the sadhana, the practice for this transcendence.

The destination of yoga

So this is the beginning of my twenty year program, which I begin from Australia today. I'll be here for a few months and then I will go to Europe, America and many other places. For the next twenty years I'll mostly be travelling, meeting the people, and I will tell them the real purpose of yoga, the destiny of yogic practices. And if I find that some people are able to handle that experience and are ready for it, I can help them.

There are gurus throughout the world who have the capacity to awaken spiritual experiences, but the problem is most sadhakas are not able to handle those experiences. Therefore, the gurus go slowly. I want to tell all of you to work with greater sincerity. You are working very hard and that brings you here, but there is no complacency on this path.

A vision of the destination has been given to you and I have also told you what you should forget, what you should transcend, what you are experiencing at the moment, which experience you must cease to experience and which experience you must experience. The little I, the limited I, must be forgotten, but to forget the little I is not enough. You do that in deep sleep as well. When you go into deep, profound sleep, you are not aware of that I. The little I becomes dormant for the time being, it hibernates.

However, I'm not asking for hibernation or dormancy. You have to transcend the little I completely and the cosmic I has to emerge. For that, the change you have to effect is the inner one, not the external one. With this note, I begin my new twenty year scheme. I'm sure that, with the good wishes of everybody here, I'll be able to tell people more and more about the destiny which yoga has to fulfil in respect to mankind as a whole.

2

Satsang

Satyananda Ashram, Mangrove Mountain, Australia, 19 November 1983

If man's essential nature is infinite, how did we ever become finite beings?
This is a question which I am not able to answer, because how does infinite become finite? Finite can experience infinite by dissolving its finite nature, but the question is, how does infinite become finite? This is something which I am not able to answer.

From time to time, many prophets have come, avatars or incarnations have come, and it is said that they were finite manifestations of the infinite. I have not been able to reconcile or understand how it happens; I don't even believe that such things can happen.

I believe that man can grow, I can grow, you can grow. We can become intuitive, our minds can give very precise decisions. I may be known as a prophet or a saint. I may be declared as an avatar in the course of time if I have grown or if I have evolved my spirit. I personally feel that there is no process of infinity becoming finite.

Is it necessary or essential to accept the guru for one's spiritual path or can we achieve the same things relying on God or the self?

We can depend on God for spiritual guidance, for blessings, for a good future, for good health, for each and everything, but remember, this is intellectual dependence. When we say, "I depend on God," it is an intellectual concept. Most of us who talk about God, who think about Him, merely remain on the intellectual plane and don't come to the zenith of experience. For us, God is not a reality. At this moment of our evolution, God is a philosophy, and philosophy is always intellectual; it is never intimate.

I can vividly bring before you the picture of a fight between a tiger and a hunter. The hunter goes into the jungle with a rifle and he confronts the tiger. The tiger roars and jumps at him with terrible anger. The hunter is afraid but he has to fight for his life. Now, I am describing this fight between the tiger and the man, but can you have a real experience of this event? No, you could experience it only if you were a hunter facing the same situation.

In the same way, all talks about God are philosophical, they are intellectual. God is very far from our intimate experience and therefore we do not get proper guidance from Him. It is not to deny God's greatness, but we are deaf and blind to it. To a blind man, the sun exists philosophically, but not really.

Therefore, guru is someone with whom our relationships are not merely intellectual, they are actual. He can feed us with proper knowledge, according to our limitations. Sometimes the language of the divine is beyond our mental understanding. It is symbolical and we don't understand it. However, we can understand guru and, at the same time, guru can understand us. He knows out limitations, our difficulties and our inabilities because he is one like us and he has been through this point of evolution where we are today.

In order to accept a mantra, you must accept a guru. In order to get lessons on spiritual life, you must find a guru for yourself. When you have gone beyond, then you can have the intimate experience and when you have the intimate experience, then you can hear the divine voice. The voice of God is not like the voice of man. It is not English, I can definitely tell you. It is not Sanskrit, it is not Italian, it is not Greek. The voice of God is not in the form of sound.

If God speaks in English, you can hear and you can understand. If He speaks in Greek, you can record what He says and go to some Greek swami and ask him to translate it. Every sound, every instruction that is given to us has a frequency; even the mental sound has a frequency. When I whisper, it has a frequency, but the divine voice has no sound frequency. If a voice has no frequency and it just tells you that your mantra is *Om Namah Shivaya*, how will you hear it? Your ears, your mind and your eyes must be tuned to that frequency, but they are not.

Therefore, although divine blessings are tangible, real, intimate, absolute and eternal, we have to wait until we are able to attune ourselves to that voice of silence. The transcendental voice is known as the voice of silence. When the mind slips, when the self drops, then duality ceases, and when nature does not exist any more for you, then the voice of God is heard. It is written in many books and it is said in all the sermons of saints, sadhus and realized people.

So, it is absolutely incorrect to say that with this particular dimension of experience, with this duality, with this ego, with this finite mind, you can attune yourself to the infinite. You may say, "Yes, it is possible. God is all-knowing and He will make me hear Him." But I say, "No, He will not do it." There is *dharma*, cosmic law, and God is the creator of that law. He moves by that cosmic law. If that was not the case, then everybody in this world would have heard that divine whisper.

Even the saints and sages, the most virtuous of people, have missed it. The people who were absolute incarnations of goodness have missed it, but an ordinary person who has been able to transcend the borders of duality, multiplicity and diversity could hear the voice of the divine easily. Ramakrishna Paramahamsa was illiterate. All the disciples of Christ were illiterate. Many of the saints we talk about in all parts of the world were illiterate, but they have been able to transcend, to jump over their mind. They have been able to stop their mind, switch off the ego, break through the barrier, until they reached a point where the diversity, the multiplicity, was completely destroyed, where they totally and completely died. They did not exist. During that particular moment of total death, the voice of the divine was heard.

If you have reached that point, you definitely do not need the guru, because you are the guru. But if you do not have that experience, please do not be duped by the intellectual wall of defence and say that you do not need a guru. You need a guru for your spiritual path. You need a guru for your academic path. You need a guru for each an every branch of learning.

When I'm in your presence, instead of being inspired by you, my mind keeps on thinking of my negative qualities. Is this good or bad?

Very good! I was suffering from constipation for one full week. I went to the doctor and he gave me a purgative. I went to the toilet twelve times. At midday I went back to him and said, "Doctor, I asked you to relieve me of constipation. I did not ask you to make me purge so many times. It's horrible, it's painful, it's exhausting."

The doctor looked at me with a medical smile and said, "Look here, both the constipation and purging are interrelated affairs." Similarly, meeting the guru with loaded and constipated emotions and mind, and then feeling and facing and confronting the negativity of mind are both interrelated. On the other hand, if you had nothing but good stuff in your mind, you would have experienced that, but you had nothing but negative stuff and so you are experiencing that.

Guru's presence and association act as a purgative, an eliminator, a destroyer and dispeller of ignorance. What is the literal meaning of guru, do you know? *Guru* does not mean a master, it does not mean a teacher. It means dispeller of ignorance, of darkness. It is a combination of two syllables: *gu* means 'dispeller' and *ru* means 'darkness'. What does dispeller mean? Eliminator or remover of the constipation, the negative tendencies of the mind that have been accumulated by you decade after decade.

Guru does not only dispel the negative ideas; that is just something which happens at the beginning of our relationship. Later on, in meditation you may experience horrible visions. Then you will come to the guru again and say, "You taught me meditation, but I'm having nightmares." Even at the time of kundalini awakening, you will have fears and passions. You will say, "Guru, you taught me to awaken kundalini and I was living a very good life before that. I had nothing in my mind. But since the awakening, from morning to night, I just have one idea in my mind all the time – sex, sex, sex; the unbroken idea of sex in my mind." That is one effect of our relationship.

You must understand that the relationship between disciple and guru is not like the relationship between a young boy and girl. When they look at each other, they forget everything. They are so happy, roaming through the flowers, flying with the wind, thinking of the clouds. It's not like that. You have to face reality because you have admitted one item into your life which will instigate the process of elimination. Elimination of filth from the body, elimination of filth from the mind, elimination of filth from the emotions, elimination of filth from the philosophical attitude, elimination of the filth from your entire being. Then how do you expect love and romance between us?

What is the value of kriya yoga? Is it a good practice for householders?

Kriya yoga is a practice from the tantric tradition. Therefore, it is especially meant for those who are enmeshed in this world.

It is said that awakening of kundalini by various yogas and other religious practices is very difficult because one has to have perfect self-discipline and undergo rigorous austerities. There are so many do's and don'ts. Therefore, in the tantric tradition, they evolved a series of practices which were intended for the proper development, growth and evolution of this great energy in every being.

There are many practices which are intended to develop the intimate experience, the highest experience, but there is one difficulty, that is controlling the mind. Every yoga practice, every religion and mystic science emphasizes that the mind be controlled first. You know how difficult it is to face your life, your family, your friends, your society, etc. Many times your mind gets disturbed for nothing. Then, when you try to meditate or pray, when you retire into seclusion, when you observe silence, when you visit sacred places or read the scriptures, you find that your mind is affected by the events which have already taken place.

You may try very hard, but you will not be able to create the necessary balance of mind, continued balance. You can force your mind for some time, but you cannot compel the mind to remain quiet and tranquil, constantly and consistently for weeks, months and years. If you have attained mental balance for about a week, it is not enough. Mental control, mental equilibrium must become stabilized. Can this happen in the life of an ordinary householder? No. There may be one out of millions who is able to accomplish this great task of stabilizing the mind for years.

Many times we try to balance the mind by means of suppression or through intellectual rationalization, which is not enough. Therefore, the tantric yogis began to think about this and they ultimately came to one conclusion. That is, even without controlling the mind, without facing the mind or without trying to balance the mind, it is possible to evolve. This is an entirely new concept in spiritual life. Few people have imagined this.

When we undertake some spiritual practices or religious practices and go to the gurus, the first thing they tell us to do is control the mind, but the seers of kriya yoga said it is not necessary. Let the mind do what it wants and you go on practising your kriyas. In the course of time, the evolution of consciousness will take you to that height where the mind will no longer trouble you.

After all, mental control is a concept, mental wandering is also a concept. You are sensitive and you are worried about it. You are overconscious of the mind and therefore you are tormented by the awareness of your mind. If this awareness can be helped, if your sensitivity can be balanced, then whatever is happening in the mind does not matter.

The realm of the mind and the realm of matter are not the same. We are all sitting quietly here in the assembly hall and outside there may be a few children shouting and making a lot of noise. That does not disturb most of us, but if someone is particularly allergic to them, then his mind will be disturbed. Not because he hears them shouting, but because he feels these rascals outside are shouting.

That is exactly what happens with you and your mind. You are not hearing the shouts of those rascals, but you are allergic and that allergy has been put into the mind by religion. Religion is responsible for the guilt, shame and complexes in us. Often people say to me, "Swamiji, when I sit for meditation, my mind wanders so much." This is also a complex. Stop fighting with the mind. It is dangerous. That is why most of the people who go to the mental hospitals are those who are extremely religious.

In religion, there is a process of conflict, creating conflict, developing conflict. This conflict which is raised in the mind by religion is between myself and myself. Who controls the mind? The mind controls the mind. Who is wandering? The mind is wandering. One part of the mind becomes the dictator and the controller, and the other part becomes the victim. Thereby you create an antagonism in your personality and this antagonism creates a split. If this split becomes wider and wider, then it is called schizophrenia.

Religion, ethics and morality are responsible for this problem. The people who are less aware of ethics and morality have fewer mental problems. They are very good and happy-go-lucky people. It is only those who are extremely religious that think this is good, that is bad, this is Satan, that is evil. Good God! This type of thinking creates a vicious atmosphere within the various abilities, faculties and dimensions of your own mind.

Therefore, the first thing that you are told in kriya yoga by your teachers is, please do not worry about the mind. If at all this mind is shouting, it is not shouting here, it is shouting elsewhere. You are not listening; you are just feeling, and by this you are not creating any problem for the mind.

Many people who want to be spiritual begin to create a problem for the mind and thus they create a problem for their own self. Now, what to do? Why do you want to control the mind? In order to be able to meditate, to concentrate on your ishta devata or on your symbol. That is precisely the reason why you feel that the mind is a great disturbance to you and to your practice, but you can completely bypass the mind.

I am not a devotee of ganja and I am not asking you to take it either, but I am giving you a very gross example. After taking a few puffs of ganja, what happens to the mind? The brainwaves slow down from beta to alpha to delta. As the brainwaves change, suddenly you begin to feel calm and quiet. What happened to your mind? You didn't fight with your mind. Here you tackled the mind as a gross substance by infusing some sort of hallucinogenic drug and consequently the chemical properties of the gross body changed. The heart slowed down, oxygen adjusted itself, brainwaves changed, etc. Is it not possible to arrive at the same stage through kriya yoga?

This is exactly what is accomplished by the various practices of kriya yoga, particularly vipareeta karani mudra, khechari mudra, moola bandha, etc. These practices control the nervous system. They equalize the pranic force. They balance the pranic impulses going into the brain through the right and left nostrils. They also create a balance between the sympathetic and parasympathetic nervous systems.

More than that, they help you to attain that state of peace and tranquillity without beating, kicking and abusing the mind, without criticizing or doing anything with the mind, just by introducing certain unused chemicals into the system. One of these chemicals is known in yoga as *amrit*, ambrosia or nectar. In all the ancient books on mysticism, Occidental and Oriental, you have references to this nectar, but they have not said anything more about it.

However, yoga has said it. At the top back of the head, there is an important centre called *bindu*. A tiny gland is situated there which is known as the seat of nectar. The practice of khechari mudra stimulates that centre and the nectar begins to flow. When this nectar begins to flow and is assimilated by the body, every part of the body as well as the mind becomes calm, quiet and tranquil. Khechari mudra is a part of hatha yoga and kriya yoga. In hatha yoga, the yogis elongate the tongue by certain methods and insert it into the nasal orifice. Then the nectar begins to flow.

When you practise moola bandha, you contract the area between the sexual organ and the anus. When you control this area, which is related to the excretory, urinary and reproductive systems, then you have an immediate effect on the nose. There are hundreds of nerve fibres which emanate from the nose and are directly connected with mooladhara chakra. As soon as you practise moola bandha, ida and pingala nadis immediately change their rhythm and both nostrils begin to flow.

When both nostrils begin to flow, automatically there is peace, calmness and tranquillity. Then you don't feel your mind and you don't worry about it. When pingala nadi, the right nostril is flowing, the *karmendriyas*, the motor organs, are stimulated. When ida nadi, the left nostril is functioning, the sensory organs are stimulated. When both nostrils are flowing equally, then neither prana nor mind is disturbed. At that time, the spirit wakes up.

This is the simple philosophy of kriya yoga. The right nostril represents *prana*, the life force. The left nostril represents *chitta*, the mind. In ordinary meditation, you are trying to control the mind without having any control over the nadis. Mind is not an idea, a philosophy, a mythological substance. Mind is a reality. At one point or level, the mind is a gross reality and at another point it is a subtle reality.

Just as the electrical flow through these cables is a reality, in the same way, in your physical body there are thousands and thousands of channels through which one form of energy flows and that form of energy is known as chitta, the mind. Now you understand that you are fighting with a thought, with an idea, when you are trying to control the mind. You are not controlling the mind. You are simply fighting with yourself.

I am not against controlling the mind, but I am telling you very clearly, controlling the mind is controlling the energy flows in the physical body, which you cannot do, because this energy is alive, it is perennial, it is a force. You can't stop it. If you want to stop it, then you will have to do it by the practices of kriya yoga. Practices which are predominantly ethical, moral and religious can only make your mind ill and sick. Therefore, the practices of kriya talk about khechari mudra and moola bandha.

There are six psychic centres located in the spine called *chakras*. These chakras are important junctions through which the energy is distributed. Just as you have junctions for electricity, in the same way, these are the junctions from mooladhara chakra to ajna chakra. If you can create *nada* or sound vibration in these junctions, then these chakras become active. When these chakras become active, they develop a psychic field. They develop psychic awareness. They develop forms and images and sounds. With the emergence of these forms and sounds your mind becomes balanced; the energy flow through the thousands and thousands of nerves in the body is absolutely balanced. This is accomplished by the practices of kriya yoga.

There is another important aspect you have to remember. On this planet there are two poles of energy, the south pole and the north pole. Australia is closer to the south pole. There has to be a polarity between these two energies. These two forces act opposite to each other. That is their initial behaviour. In the same way, in the human body, the upper base is sahasrara chakra, like the north pole, and the lower base is mooladhara, like the south pole.

These two poles of energy are absolute realities. On the earth you have the macrocosmic aspect of these two energy poles: the north and south pole, and in the individual there is the microcosmic aspect. These two energies are also known as Shiva and Shakti, positive and negative, time and space, plus and minus. Now, these two poles of energy have to be brought together.

Therefore, don't talk about the mind, don't talk about mental control. If there is any such thing as mental control, it will happen by itself. You should engage yourself with the game of energy. Kundalini shakti is at the base; Shiva is at the top, they should be united with each other. Shakti should be aroused with the help of the kriyas and when a little bit of awakening takes place, then where is the mind, where is the mental turbulence?

Do you ever feel mental turbulence in profound sleep? An ordinary change called sleep takes you away from your mental problems. Imagine if you are able to go a little bit higher in the field of awakening of kundalini; not absolute awakening, but on your way. How would you feel the troubles of your mind? Therefore, the value of kriya yoga is that it gives you a spiritual path without fighting with yourself.

3

Satsang

Satyananda Ashram, Mangrove Mountain, Australia, 20 November 1983

How does one cultivate faith?
Faith is an inherent quality. You don't have to cultivate it; you have to discover it. *Prana* or life force is inborn. You don't have to cultivate it; you have to realize it. Man is born with life, with consciousness and with faith. In the course of his evolution, he has become aware of life. You know you have life, you know you have a mind, you know you have consciousness, although you don't know much about them. In the same way, you will have to discover that you have faith.

Belief can be learned, cultivated, indoctrinated, structured and destroyed, but not faith. In yoga, faith is called shraddha. *Shraddha* means 'the basis of truth'. There is a basis of truth in everybody which is a part of their being; they are born with it. This shraddha or faith has to be realized. In order to realize this faith, it is very important to cultivate a greater closeness, a deeper relationship and a better understanding with someone who can help you to realize it. God, guru and your concept of a divine being, are the three things which can help you to rediscover that faith.

How does one recognize one's guru?
How do you recognize that a boy or a girl is for you? You have an emotional personality and thereby you realize it. In the same way, you have to develop the spiritual vision in order to realize your guru. Your spiritual area of awareness should be developed. First you must have satsang, study the lives of saints, think about the self and the deeper layers of your personality. Then you should try to understand that there are things beyond this universe, beyond this limited perception and then a time comes when the guru is realized by you.

What is the place of prayer in yoga?
Prayer is a way to meditation. If you can pray in silence, with your heart, with your feelings, with the totality of your awareness, then it will automatically awaken the deep-rooted energy in you. Prayer is a yoga by itself. Of course, most of us do not know how to pray. We pray from the book, but prayer is the language of the soul. It is a expression of the heart. It has no written language. It is a feeling.

Of course, there are written prayers and you can repeat them or sing them over and over again but those repeated prayers will not necessarily transport you to a higher dimension or higher realm every time you say them. Many times this type of prayer is just mechanical. That is why millions and millions of people who pray every day only progress to a small extent; they don't go very far.

When you retire into seclusion and maintain silence of body and mind, then the prayer should be expressed without language, in the form of feeling, in the form of awareness. Definitely, that is a yoga by itself and it can awaken kundalini shakti.

Is it possible to maintain self-awareness and high energy while living with a partner who does not practise yoga?
It is always possible to maintain a high level of awareness and energy in the home, even if the people close to you are not

concerned, even if they do not care, but you will have to make a change in your attitude. In the West there is a peculiar way of thinking, "If I am a Christian, my wife should also be a Christian. She has to believe as I do." Of course, this attitude is not always prevalent, but it usually is.

If the husband practises yoga and the wife doesn't, there is a problem. At least, the husband feels that because she doesn't practise, something must be wrong and he is always trying to make her do it. If the wife practises but the husband does not, she feels the same way. If that is the feeling in your home, then of course you can't maintain a very high level of energy or awareness. Therefore, it is better to be concerned only with your own practice.

It is not possible that both partners should share the same philosophy, the same religion, the same spiritual views or the same outlook regarding life. That is what we are taught in India. The Hindus particularly believed that everybody has his own set of karmas, his own level or range of evolution. The husband or wife may be sattwic and the partner rajasic, but it does not matter because she has her own karma and he has his. She may believe in divine incarnations and worship idols while her husband thinks there is no God at all, but he does not interfere with her religious faith and she doesn't interfere with his nihilistic attitude, because this is his point of evolution and that is hers.

Although husband and wife come from the same society, they are not at the same point of spiritual evolution. Therefore, if you are practising yoga and your partner is not, do not worry about it, do not try to change it, do not wish for anything else. If your partner practises yoga, well and good. If not, let him or her follow their own evolution, their own karma, their own destiny. Thereby, you will maintain peace and harmony in the home and establish a high level of energy.

In my family, my parents had totally different beliefs. My father was following a Hindu sect called Arya Samaj, which is more or less like the Protestants in Christianity. He believed in that implicitly and he never went to temples where idols were worshipped. He never thought of God as one having a form. He did not read many scriptures either. He just believed in the Vedas, that was all. Everything else was unnecessary for him. The only mantra he would chant was Gayatri because that was from the Vedas. He did not chant other mantras like *Om Namah Shivaya, Sri Ram Jai Ram*. His argument was that Rama was a man, so how could he worship him as God? Rama had a wife; God has no wife.

My mother, on the other hand, was a devout Hindu. On Monday she would go to the Shiva temple, on Tuesday to the Hanuman temple and on Friday to the temple of Devi. Throughout the week, she visited all the temples and always observed the traditional fasting days on the eleventh day of the fortnight, the full moon, the dark moon, etc. Even though my parents had totally different views, they never crossed each other. She had her own way of thinking and he had his.

As for myself, in my early years, up to the age of eighteen or nineteen, I was an out and out atheist, an honest atheist. I thought that God was created by shrewd politicians and that religions were created to facilitate army movements. Before sending in the army, you send in your clergymen for twenty years to get the ground ready. I still believe this, and they have succeeded everywhere except in India. Whenever a religious ceremony was being performed in my family, I would go out.

I didn't want to hear *Om Namah Shivaya* and all those things. Although we often sat together, my father never admonished me for my attitude. We didn't discuss it at all. Once, one of my nearest relatives died. When someone in the family dies, usually there is no food in the kitchen. Everybody has to fast. So my brother, my sister and myself took a few rupees, went out to the hotel and ate a nice curry while everybody was fasting. When we came back, nobody asked us whether we had eaten or not. It was only after a few days that my father wanted to know where we were on the day that our relative had died. I said we went to the hotel.

You see, we must remember that although the four, five or six family members may belong to one religion, one race, one blood line and one ancestral line, as far as karmas are concerned they are entirely different. The family is only an assemblage of many heterogeneous parts, like in a motor car. And, therefore, in order to maintain a high level of awareness, you should not worry at all about what your partner believes in and what he doesn't believe in. This is the best way of maintaining peace in the family.

By karma, by temperament, by one's own evolution, everyone has a different state of mind. You don't believe in what I believe in and you shouldn't compel me to believe in what you believe because my state of mind and your state of mind are different. Therefore, in spiritual life, if your husband or your wife doesn't believe in yoga but you do, it's quite all right.

You must know how to live with one another. Harmony does not mean total uniformity. Harmony can be achieved in opposite, difficult and conflicting stages also. Harmony is an outcome of perfect understanding. That's the reason why in the West, husband and wife are not able to live together for a lifetime. There are a lot of difficulties and these are not because she is different to you. It is because you want both to be the same – that's the mistake.

Let an atheist wife live with a theist husband. Let a socialist wife live with a pacifist husband. Let a Protestant husband live with a Catholic wife. Let a Christian husband live with a Hindu, brahmin wife. Both of them should try to understand that he is an outcome of his karma and she is an outcome of her karma, and both have to live together and work out their differences.

In a piano, sitar or violin, there are different strings and they produce sounds at different pitches, but if all the strings were to produce only one pitch or one note, what horrible music that would be, and that is Western music. It is not the music of light, because both strings are saying 'sa'. One must say 'sa' and the other 'ta'. Then there is music.

I have come here as a layperson with little experience of ashram life. Can you please tell me what the ashram is and what it can offer me?

Ashram life, the ashram tradition, is the most ancient tradition. It is a place where you can expose your personality to utter simplicity. Of course, this ashram in Mangrove Mountain is unique. There are many places in the West, in Australia, even in India, which are known as ashrams, but they are not. This place is an ashram and it offers a simple life where you can expose yourself to the best possible extent.

A place where you make spiritual effort is called *ashram*, where you live with a lot of people, sharing everything with them, knowing each other and trying to understand that you are not the only sufferer in this great world. Everybody is toiling more or less along the same lines. We are co-travellers, but we never knew one another.

The atmosphere of the ashram is charged with spiritual vibrations created by the system, by the discipline, by the good thoughts and by the spirituality of people who visit the ashram from time to time. Therefore, in the ashram we try to live in a way which contributes to the peaceful vibrations. There should be regular classes on yoga, meditation, kirtan and a free atmosphere. Then the ashram life improves your spiritual destiny and spiritual personality.

In India we have many ashrams in calm and quite places like Rishikesh, where people go from every part of the country and spend some time with their guru or their fellows. There they make themselves completely free from the type of life they have been leading so far. Diet is changed, lifestyle is changed. You can't expect and you shouldn't expect the same comfort and luxuries which you were having at home. A change in lifestyle by living in the ashram is for the better.

Once, about two years ago, some people came to see me. They wanted to make an ashram in Australia. I said, "It's a good idea; have about twenty or thirty acres of land." They said, "But we want to have a little more comfort there." Here they did not find comforts like hot water, separate rooms, or television. I told them, "If you are making an ashram like a motel, then you had better call it Satyananda Motel. Don't call it an ashram because in an ashram the richest and the poorest must throw away those distinction which they have superimposed on themselves. You can have a motel, a bathtub, a mirror, television, a fridge with a few bottles inside. Then more people will come and none will go and none will grow."

So you have come to an ashram for the first time. Spend your time in practices as long as you are here and if you have some time left, then go to the garden and work with the swamis who are growing vegetables, trees and flowers. Try to do some sort of selfless service. It will give you peace of mind and it will give us a lot of nice, fresh vegetables.

When you go back, try to take this ashram with you in your lifestyle. Even if you are not able to create a prototype ashram there, do take a few important items which you think you can use in your place. If every home can incorporate a little from the ashram life and if the simplicity and the serene atmosphere of the ashram can be taken back to your home, I think your home can also become a mini-ashram and you will be the guru there.

Is anyone eligible to take full sannyasa? What do you have to do or be?

If you consider sannyasa as a part of a great organization, religious or occult, then there will have to be some qualifications. If you fulfil certain qualifications, then you become a professor or bishop, but if you consider sannyasa as a personal choice made by an individual for his spiritual salvation or his spiritual upliftment, then no external qualifications are necessary. The only qualifications are absolutely personal. Am I sincere? Do I want it? Am I taking sannyasa for my spiritual upliftment? Then, in that case, the minimum possible qualifications are sufficient for taking sannyasa.

What is sannyasa? *Sannyasa* literally means complete dedication. Now, everybody has to understand what dedication means. If you just say, "I am dedicated," it is not enough.

If you just say, "I want to give everything to you," that is not enough. What do you dedicate and how? As an individual, as a human being, you have emotions, intelligence, memory, speech, strength, good health, resources, friends, society. This is your wealth; this is your money. Are you using this or are you squandering it for yourself? Then one day it comes to your mind, "Hey, what am I doing? Let me use what I have for a definite purpose."

That is your sankalpa. So from that day, your thoughts, your energy, your mind, your prana, your day, your night, your eating, your sleeping, your friends, everything is utilized for that purpose. That is the exact literal meaning of sannyasa. That is why sannyasins don't get married. If you have a wife, you have to look after her. That means you have to give her your mind, your money, your love, your support and so many things that are your wealth. For that purpose there is celibacy in sannyasa.

Sannyasa is one of the oldest orders. It has nothing to do with monks. Monks and priests are a different order. Do not confuse sannyasa with the traditions of monks. In the ancient Greek civilization, there was a tradition of monks and the word monk is derived from the word mono, which means single, one. Sannyasa is not becoming a monk. Many times when I went to Europe in the past, I was introduced to the assemblies and conferences as Swami Satyananda, a Hindu monk. I said, "I do not want this monkish business. I'm not a monk, I'm a sannyasin."

A sannyasin is one who has totally dedicated himself to the purpose of self-awareness, *atma jnana*, self-knowledge. To discover yourself, who you are, is the purpose of sannyasa. Right now, we think, "I am Swami Satyananda, that is enough." No. I am not Swami Satyananda. I am not just this name, this form, this mind, this prana, these senses. I am the self. Who is that self? Is he light? Is he power? Is he wisdom? Is he shoonya? What is he? Does he exist at all?

In order to discover one's real nature, in order to go beyond the body, the mind and the senses, in order to understand the relationship of the atma with the total, you need to completely divert all your mental, psychic, emotional and physical resources to that end. Then you take sannyasa and when you take sannyasa, you have to make certain rules for yourself. You cannot just be lenient and licentious.

I don't say that sannyasa is a means of suppression, but those who have desires and passions, who have violence and vehemence, should not take sannyasa. Maybe a sannyasin can divert his mental resources here and there a little bit, but not totally. Through his mind, body, senses and emotions he is aware of just one target. It is these people who take sannyasa and follow the path, setting certain rules and regulations for themselves.

Sannyasa has absolute and total relevance in relation to guru. If you have no guru, you are not a sannyasin. Offering oneself, dedicating oneself, giving up oneself for somebody, is the inner spirit of sannyasa. If you have to dedicate yourself and become a sannyasin, then there must be someone to whom you are dedicated. Therefore, guru is the best person to whom dedication is made. This is one aspect of sannyasa.

It is out of absolute devotion that you dedicate yourself. If you don't have devotion, I don't think that you can be dedicated. Dedication presupposes total and absolute devotion. People have become martyrs in history. Many people have sacrificed their life for the sake of something. Why? It is only out of devotion, total dedication, that you become a martyr or you sacrifice yourself.

In the same way, if you love someone, it is because you are devoted to him. You serve a community, a country, a person. What for? Because you are devoted. Sannyasa is an outcome of total devotion to someone. If you lack that total devotion to someone, then you are a monk and not a sannyasin. You are a renunciate, a recluse, and all these are selfish people because they are devoted to none. This is the first aspect of sannyasa.

Another aspect of sannyasa is perfect endowment. Before you take to sannyasa, your body, your mind, your senses, your ambitions, your aspirations, your emotions and your faculties are all directed towards the pleasures of the self, because you consider them to be yours. But once you take sannyasa, everything is booked, everything is directed towards one cause. You cannot appropriate any of your faculties or resources for your own pleasure; that would be misuse. Therefore, a sannyasin is one who has created a perfect endowment, a trust of all his physical, mental, intellectual, emotional, social and economic resources.

All these resources are directed for one purpose, and that purpose is fulfilling the guru's order. Whatever guru decides for you, you do it. If he is asking you to retire into caves and meditate for twelve hours a day, do it. All the energies must be directed and focused towards the fulfilment of that command of your guru. If guru wishes you to work in the garden, in the farm, in the kitchen, in the office, or in the classrooms, do it. Use all your energies, direct all your energies for the fulfilment of that particular command of your guru. Thereby, you become free of ego. This is the spirit of sannyasa.

Therefore, sannyasa is a very difficult path to follow from this point of view. I am not discouraging anyone; I can give sannyasa to everybody. It would be easy if sannyasa meant merely donning the robes. It would be easy if it meant merely changing your name and your tradition, and much easier if it was just changing your religion. It's the easiest thing in the world to change your religion; you just change the certificate, that's all.

If going into seclusion or living in caves was the meaning of sannyasa, then you could do it without much difficulty. If sannyasa was taking only one meal a day before noon, even that you could do. If sannyasa was living with the minimum requirements for life, that also you could do. But surrendering, submitting oneself totally before another being, maybe your guru, and accepting all he says is very difficult, because it is a question of humbling your own ego, and submission of ego is very difficult.

As such, if you want sannyasa as a tradition of monks, then there are other rules, but if sannyasa has to do with guru and discipleship, then it is very difficult. However, I think those who are inclined to take sannyasa proclaim their independence in life, move around as free persons as a part of the classless society or the casteless society. If a sannyasin is a person without any bondage, then I think that many people are qualified to take sannyasa.

4

The Ancient Tantric Tradition and Modern Science

Satyananda Ashram, Mangrove Mountain, Australia, 20 November 1983

In the last century scientists and leaders in every field taught us that we were living in a world of gross substance. For them, the whole earth was made up of minerals, of gross elements, and man was a compound of flesh, blood and bones. In the scheme of evolution, man stood at the top according to the Darwinian school. That is how everything was set up: society, laws, philosophy, religion, government and also education. They could not penetrate beyond the gross. They could not even accept that there was anything beyond it.

In fact, there were many myths and sayings which were related with the more subtle aspects of life, but during the last century scientists began to criticize all these beliefs and views. In the West, at most, scientists accepted religion to some extent, not because they believed in it, but because they needed it for their own survival. Otherwise, they thought they also would face the fate of the early scientists. However, in the last hundred years, science has changed and physics has almost become metaphysics. Now they are talking about the same thing which tantra used to say many thousands of years ago.

The earliest tantric tradition which historians can now find from the archaeological remains is six to seven thousand years old. It was related to the Harappa and Mohenjodaro civilizations which existed at the north-western frontiers of India, in the present Pakistan. This does not mean that tantra is only five thousand years old. It means that a thriving culture, based on tantric concepts, rituals and philosophy, was existing on a prosperous scale at least that long ago. But it is probable that other tantric civilizations existed all over the world, even further back in time to the beginning of man's existence. Of course, I am not going to go into the historical details of tantra because that doesn't serve our purpose.

The concept of creation
The tantric philosophers who preceded Lord Buddha, Christ, Mohammed and even Moses, Socrates, Aristotle and Plato used to say just one thing, which you should bear in mind. Everything that is visible or invisible is nothing but an expression of *shakti* or energy. This was the dictum, the conclusive statement made by the tantric philosophers many thousands of years ago.

What are the scientists talking about today? Exactly the same thing in terms of atoms, protons, molecules, electrons, photons, etc. If you arrange them, there is a goat; again rearrange them and there is a man. The external or the gross forms are just different proportions of energy. This is not a joke, of course I can't say scientifically which proportions make a man and which make a goat. That is immaterial, but what is important is that everything, each and every substance in existence, living or not living, moving or not moving, visible or not visible, is a compound of the forces of energy. Basically, when you look carefully, you come to the conclusion that at the source, everything is the same.

The source of all human beings, animals, insects, vegetables, minerals is one and the same. Each and everything has emanated from one nucleus. We should understand the meaning of nucleus because we are living in a nuclear age. The entire creation has one nucleus, not two. The whole universe is like a proto-matter, like an egg. The upper pole and the lower pole are two separate poles of energy. One is called the positive pole and the other is the negative pole.

In tantra you call them shiva and shakti, and in physics, time and space. Time is one pole of the matter and space is another. Time and space are two separate dimensions of energy and they have to be united. When time and space come together, they travel from opposite directions towards the centre and they meet at the nucleus. What is that nucleus? In physics it is called the centre of matter, the point from which the object becomes manifest. Thus, you must have studied about the three aspects of creation – time, space and object; time, space and matter.

These are the three categories of this universe. Whatever you see – the sun, moon, stars, solar galaxies, constellations, clouds, seas, mountains – are all composed of these three factors, time, space and matter. When time and space meet at the nucleus of matter, there is an explosion. This explosion throws off millions and trillions of nebulae into the physical universe. These nebulae later become the stars and your earth is one of those nebulae.

This has been happening in the external world for millions and millions of years and it will continue to happen for eternity. The same thing happens in us when we are practising concentration and meditation. Meditation is not just a psychological exercise. Many of you are teachers; you like to do research in psychology and you begin to think that meditation is a psychological exercise. It is not true. In meditation, you are handling the energy forces. When you are concentrating on a flame, on a point, on your guru, on a cross, on a shivalingam, on your heart centre or eyebrow centre, what exactly is happening is that time and space are coming closer.

Please think about it. What is time and what is space? You have never thought about it because you have no time to think about time. Time is a concept of the mind and you live within it. It is not only the gross time, one hour, two hours, three hours. Time is related to object and object is related to time and both are related to space. Time, space and object are interrelated and that is called creation. Now, our scientists have come to the same conclusion, that is, the whole of creation, matter, minerals, vegetable kingdom, oxygen, hydrogen, etc., seen and unseen, are nothing but a consequence of the union between time and space, or between the positive and negative poles of energy.

It is a very simple thing to understand. How was I born? My father and mother met with each other. Nobody can deny this. Is there anybody here who was born without union? The union between male and female components, between the positive and negative physical components, brought me into existence, brought you into existence, brought everything into existence. Every dog, every donkey, every man was born through the union between the two opposite poles. Man and woman, male and female, represent two opposite poles of nature and energy. They are not the same. Physically they look the same except for a few basic differences, but from the point of view of energy they are not the same at all.

Male represents positive energy and female represents negative energy. Therefore, both of them represent time and space and when they meet, in the form of sexual union, in the form of emotional union, they create a connection, a contact between time and space, and then an object is created. This happens with everything in this world and therefore we come to one conclusion, that creation is the result of a union of positive and negative forms of energy.

Going further, when you meditate, you are again creating another union. At the cosmic level, union took place between time and space. At the human level, union took place between my mother and my father. Now in meditation, the union takes place between mind and prana, the mental force and the vital force. These two forces in our body are represented by ida and pingala nadis, sun and moon, Shiva and Shakti. In cosmic parlance Shiva and Shakti are responsible for the myriad forms of creation and again in human life, the male is Shiva and the female is Shakti. Their union brings us into existence.

A matrix of energy

It is said that not only the body and mind, but this whole vast universe can be turned into energy at any time. Matter is one gross manifestation of energy. We should not see basic differences between matter and energy. Well, I don't have to go to the famous equation of Albert Einstein – you know that $E=Mc^2$. This is a very recent equation, but what I am talking about in tantra is the same thing. The tantric philosophers also believed and said that matter is one state of energy, and energy is one state of evolution of matter.

Therefore, from the scientific point of view and also from the tantric and yogic point of view, we must come to one conclusion, understanding and realization, that we are not just a compound of flesh, blood and bones. Every thought, every action and every feeling is charged with energy. I'm talking into the microphone and you can hear my voice somewhere from the sound box. It is electrically charged. If that is electrically charged, why not my voice also? How can you say that the voice is nothing but a consequence of friction between one organ and another? This is a very gross explanation.

We will have to understand each and every action, each and every expression, each and every thought in terms of this electromagnetic force. The scientists have come this far and realized that even this atmosphere which you see between yourself and myself is not just air. There is an electromagnetic field which connects you and me and everything together. This means that each and every speck of creation is nothing but a matrix of energy, *shakti*.

We can call this energy, electron, proton, photon or anything we like. It makes no difference. But definitely, we have to bear in mind that in the last century we were not at all prepared to believe what we know about ourselves today and what we are taught in modern psychology. We are not just gross emotions; we are not just mud and filth; we are not just a product of the sin of our parents. If my father has gone to my mother, he hasn't committed a sin, and I am not an outcome of sin. I am an outcome of the blossoming of love and the feeling of unity that must have taken place between my father and my mother. Do you agree?

I don't think I was born as a consequence of their union in the state of depression. I imagine my father at that time must have been about twenty-five and my mother twenty. They must have been in the prime of their youth, hot in emotion, hot in thinking, and they must have been thinking of the stars, of flowers, of beautiful things. They must have been talking poetry. I must have been born out of those circumstances, not out of a criminal, sinful and depressive attitude of my parents.

If we have this faith in us that we are something more than gross matter born of sin, we can further resolve to transform this physical body into a spiritual substance; it can be done. They say that Christ went directly to heaven. Many people say it's not possible because there is no heaven. Perhaps they have gone to Mars or somewhere, but I believe it can happen. The body can just disappear.

Conversion into light

Once there lived a great lady saint known as Mirabai. She was a princess of a western Indian state called Rajputana near Udaipur. When she was six years old, a swami came to the palace and gave Mira an idol of Sri Krishna. She always kept it with her and in time she began to believe that she was married to that idol. Everyone thought she had gone crazy. It is alright to feel for some time that you are married to an idol, but when you are twenty-five and you are still thinking that you are married to a statue, something is wrong.

According to the customs of the society, she was forcibly married to the prince of Chittor, which was a powerful state at that time. Even after her marriage, she continued to think that she was married to Sri Krishna. She used to say, "My husband is Krishna and no other." She refused to have any relations with the king. She said, "No, you are not my true husband."

So, he thought perhaps she was having an affair with somebody else and that was why she wouldn't have anything to do with him. One day he was informed that Mirabai was talking to someone in a closed room and his suspicion became very strong. He also overheard the whispers. So he broke open the door, but there was nobody there because she was talking to herself. The Krishna which she loved was her own self projected in the statue of Sri Krishna.

Finally, when she could not stay in the palace any longer, she left Chittor and came to Vrindavan, where she became a great saint. At the time of her death she did not lose her body, she did not die as we do; she entered into a temple near Mathura and converted herself into light.

The same thing happened to Christ, to Chaitanya Mahaprabhu, and it must have happened to many more saintly people about whom we hear stories which seem to be so impossible. However, if only your attitude is very high, if your mind is not functioning on a lower level, then such instances are not impossible. If your mind is strongly rooted in the deeper, higher and real self, then matter and energy are not separate substances for you. They are one and the same.

Two basic traditions

When a scientist looks at matter, he realizes the energy in it. He sees energy in the different elements of which the matter is composed. In the same way, the tantric philosophy deals with the matters of creation, of existence, of metamorphosis, of transmigration, etc., but finally it says that everything in this universe is only the formation, reformation, reduction, reorganization and manifestation of one shakti, and from one nucleus everything is born.

The multiplicity, the diversity, the duality is in the matter, but it is not the basic substance and this is what I have tried to convey to you here. I hope you will reflect more deeply on this, because as an intelligent human being you have your own questions and these questions cannot be answered by conventional religions and philosophies, no matter where they come from. There are only two basic traditions that can give you an answer. One is modern science and the other is the ancient tantric philosophy.

Recently, these two traditions have started coming together, correlating the facts, agreeing with each other and interpreting each other. Tantra is interpreting science and science is interpreting tantra. The dangers in both are the same. Science can be misused and the practices of tantra, even when they are sincerely and diligently practised, can be misused and abused.

After all, what are you going to do with the mental powers, with the energy which you will gradually receive through the practices? Have you ever thought about it? Mostly they will be misused. Therefore, side by side with your practices, whatever you are doing, you must try to spiritualize your mind and your life so that this energy will not be misused.

5

Kriya Yoga

Satyananda Ashram, Mangrove Mountain, Australia, 21 November 1983

Kriya yoga is a combination of many practices. It is related to hatha yoga in general and to the tantric tradition in particular. In the ancient scriptures or books on tantra, you find many references to kriya practices. All of them are not explained together. In *Maha Nirvana Tantra*, the tantra of the great liberation, you find references to six important kriya practices. Similarly, in the other tantric texts, the practices of kriya yoga are mentioned here and there.

In these tantric texts, the practices of kriya yoga are described in a very symbolic manner. With the help of my guru, I was able to decipher and explain these kriyas further. In fact, when you practise kriya yoga, you do not consider this body as a compound or a combination of flesh, blood, bone, marrow, etc., which is what you are taught at school. The basic philosophy and concept of kriya yoga in particular and yoga in general is that this body is a field of energy.

Three forms of energy

What do we mean by energy field? This physical body which appears to be fleshy, gross and physical is not so in reality. It has a field of energy, which is not a philosophical, psychological, mythological or symbolic concept. When we talk about energy, we are not talking about an idea, we are talking about the flow of a current. What is energy and what is the definition of energy in relation to the body and mind?

This physical body is three forms of energy. One is mental energy, which can be measured with the most sophisticated instruments today. Another is pranic energy or vital energy, which can also be measured by scientific instruments. The third energy is known as spiritual energy and nobody has yet measured that. These are the three forms of energy.

Out of these three energies, the first two function regularly in the body. In yoga they are know as ida and pingala, in tantra as Shiva and Shakti, and in modern science as time and space. The changes which occur in the level of these two energies during the practices of yoga are now being measured by researchers. Beside these two energies, there is the third energy called spiritual energy, or in yogic terms *sushumna*. This energy has to be awakened, and to awaken it is the prime purpose of kriya yoga.

Mental energy is already functioning. It is manifest as you know. Without mental energy both you and I could not think, our sense organs could not function. The pranic energy is also functioning and that is why we are alive, food is being digested, we are walking and talking, the motor organs are functioning.

The third energy, however, is not in action. It is dormant. It exists in everyone, but it is absolutely quiet, sleeping in eternal sleep. That force is called kundalini shakti. Some scholars prefer to call it primordial energy or evolutionary energy. That energy is the basis of your spiritual consciousness, your spiritual awareness.

The quality of awareness

Spiritual awareness and sensory awareness are two important terms. What is sensory awareness? You can see, hear, taste, touch and smell. This is called sensory awareness. You can dream, think a thought, feel emotions such as fear, passion, depression, elation, delight, joy, happiness, etc. This is called external awareness. All of us live in the field of external awareness except those who are idiots.

Some people have keen external awareness and others have feeble external awareness. This external awareness is very contradictory. It always moves and exists in paradox. That is why you are unhappy. There is nothing wrong with the world, with your wife or husband, with your job or with anything, but because this external awareness is imperfect, it is limited, you become unhappy with life. In order to overcome unhappiness, to transcend the limitations of external emotions, you will have to change the quality of your awareness.

To change the quality of awareness, what do you have to do? Side by side with external awareness, you will have to develop inner awareness. What is inner awareness? In external awareness, you are aware of objects, etc., but when the inner awareness grows, one begins to know that this external awareness has a source somewhere else.

Inner completeness

The source of happiness which you think you get from your family is not from the family but from somewhere else, although you don't know it. The delight which you get from sense objects is not from the sense objects but from somewhere else. It is called the source of joy and delight, *ananda*. Kriya yoga must become a tool, an instrument in the hands of the practitioners to tap this source.

Unless the awakening of sushumna takes place, unless this spiritual awakening takes place, man will not be complete, no matter how much morality you practise or how many ethics you have. You may be the most virtuous man on the face of this earth, you may be the best and most compassionate, the most charitable and truthful person, but please remember that unless inner awakening takes place, all these external things will not give you delight and total completeness.

Therefore, kriya yoga should be practised in order to open the source of inner happiness and inner completeness. The great field of energy which you are should be united with the greater field of energy. We are the microcosmic field of energy, not the total field of energy. These kriya yoga practices are very important for you to learn. They will enable you to go a long way in your life and bring you closer to yourself.

6

Satsang

Satyananda Ashram, Mangrove Mountain, Australia, 22 November 1983

If one is a householder and has no guru, how does one decide upon a sadhana? Is it just what feels best to you, or can you get advise from other sources?

If you want to practise sadhana, even without a guru, you can. First of all, you must remember that asana and pranayama, the practices of hatha yoga, can be learned from a yoga teacher. He may not be your guru. When you practise asana and pranayama, you are actually doing something for your spiritual life; you have started.

Then you should read books on the practical side of sadhana and your awareness will become deeper. By and by, you will become familiar with some of the practices like awareness of the breath, chanting of the mantra *Om*, feeling the mantra *Soham* in the psychic passage, or other spiritual practices. By this time, if you are an aspirant and if you are searching, you will definitely find a guru.

I've reached the crossroads and it feels like a tunnel. I'm at one end and the pull through is like a strong suction. All I desire is to devote the rest of my life to your cause, yet I cannot reconcile myself to living in an ashram. I've no desire to create any more karma, having experienced many

things in my present life. I realize all that is worthwhile is to serve you only. In what direction do I go?
It is very important that you should live in the ashram. Ashram life is not a comfortable life and therefore you should live it. By living in the ashram, you will be exhausting your karmas at a greater speed and when you are able to live in the ashram, even with difficulties, inconveniences, disturbances, distractions, obstacles and so on, then you will have a strong mind and a strong and clear perception. After that, you should go out and enlighten the people about the inner, higher, sublime life in yoga, or through yoga practices.

I am considering taking sannyasa. How important is it to have parental permission or approval?
I don't know about the condition in this country, but in India it is necessary to have the permission of parents because there the society is very strong and the link or bond between parents and children is also very strong. It is always good to give respect to the elders, to have their permission or to inform them, because after taking sannyasa you have to be able to convince all these people and more about yoga, spiritual life and so on.

So why not start with your parents? First convince them with sweetness, intelligence, commonsense and total union with them, and remember, you can only convince them if you have convinced yourself. I am sure about it. If you have not convinced yourself, you cannot convince your parents and if you can't convince your parents, you have not convinced yourself.

If you have not convinced yourself, please do not take sannyasa. Sannyasa is an absolute decision. It is a realization, an understanding. It is not yet another path for you to escape from the thraldom of existence. So you have to convince yourself, then you can convince your parents. Welcome! You can take sannyasa anytime that I'm ready to give.

We hear a lot about expressing one's personal karma or going with the flow so to speak. How does one know

that this perceived personal karma is not an intellectual invention?
When you practise tantra, yoga, kriya or any such thing, then there is an automatic expression of karma in the mental field. Thereby, expression is not intellectual. It is real, it is actual.

What is the cause of uncertainty and indecision in one's life? Can regular spiritual practices help eradicate this problem?
Concentration of mind is necessary to overcome uncertainty and indecision. When you practise concentration of mind, then your mental forces begin to be unified and your confidence increases. Your willpower becomes stronger and the gap between the two areas of the mind which has been causing conflict is unified.

I often feel tension or nervousness in my stomach for no apparent reason. Could this be blocked energy?
This is on account of an imbalance in manipura chakra. You must therefore try to practise those things in which prana and apana, the two forces of prana, are united in manipura, the navel centre. This can be done through the practice of uddiyana bandha, which is very good for working out the tensions due to an imbalance in pranic and apranic forces.

We are a very varied group. How is it that the one kriya course is suitable for us all?
The practices of kriya yoga are highly developed forms of hatha yoga and they have been designed for those people who belong to a particular category or class of existence. We are a varied group, no doubt, but there is something which we can start with. For example, we can all practise vipareeta karana mudra because everybody is wasting their energy. The wear and tear in the body is taking place at a great rate. Therefore, vipareeta karani mudra is an important method of conservation and sublimation of this energy which is necessary for all. The other practices of kriya yoga are designed for a

group of people who have come through the practices of hatha yoga, pranayama, mudra and bandha and so are capable and qualified to practise them together.

Can a householder attain the highest state of spiritual consciousness through regular practice of kriya? To achieve this, does one need to abstain from all intoxicants, specifically alcohol and marijuana?
There are two ways to experience the inner consciousness. One is a direct path, a shortcut; the other path is long and circuitous but sure. A householder can reach the highest experience of the self. He is designed for this and this is his destiny, but the practices which he has to take up will be different from those of a sannyasin who has renounced, who abstains.

So far as the use of alcohol and marijuana is concerned, there can be no two opinions about it. They destroy the powers of the mind and consciousness and interfere with the experiences of natural evolution. As far as I know, marijuana does induce a state of mind in which you can experience some visions, images and depth of ideas, but that is not on account of expansion of consciousness.

The experiences which one gets by the use of marijuana are not because one has expanded one's consciousness. It is because an imbalance, a lack of equilibrium has been created in the sympathetic and parasympathetic nervous systems. As a result of this imbalance, the central nervous system undergoes a change in the level of expression and in the level of experience. A lot of experiments have been done on it.

For those who want to awaken kundalini, who want to increase and amplify the inner force, who want to dynamize their willpower, to conserve, divert and sublimate the *shakti* or energy, the first thing to do is to refrain from all those habits which dull the mind or which create depression in the nervous system, or stimulate the brain or the nervous system for a certain period of time.

In yoga and tantra, there are certain sects which do use these things, but they are only for highly evolved sadhakas.

That particular branch or practice of tantra is not meant for beginners. So householders must practise their kriya yoga and maintain purity of body, purity of the nervous system, a strong heart, strong brain and strong body.

What is the significance of the deity, mantra, ishta and number of petals that each chakra represents? On awakening the chakra, does one perceive it exactly as represented, or does the experience differ from person to person?

In kriya and kundalini yoga, we are told that we have six chakras: mooladhara, swadhisthana, manipura, anahata, vishuddhi and ajna. Above that is bindu, but it is not a chakra and sahasrara is also not a chakra. *Chakra* means circle, anything that is round. Usually chakra represents the revolution of energy. Anything in which there is revolution of energy is called chakra.

Each chakra is represented by a lotus with a certain number of petals. These petals symbolize the expression and outlet of energy. From each chakra, energy is distributed to various parts of the body. *Ida* is the mental energy and *pingala* is the pranic energy. These forms of energy are like positive and negative lines. When they come together, they produce an action. If the positive and negative lines are separated, then action does not take place, the light will not burn, the microphone will not work and so on.

Ida and pingala nadis represent mental and pranic energies and these energies are distributed throughout the body. For example, mooladhara chakra is the distribution centre for the reproductive, excretory and urinary systems. In the same way, from swadhisthana chakra onwards, the various chakras are distribution centres to different organs of the body, like the digestive system, liver, pancreas, etc. It is exactly like the sympathetic and parasympathetic nervous system. They feed various organs in your body with impulses. Therefore, the petals in these lotuses indicate the distributing channels.

The seed mantra which is indicated in each and every chakra represents the dormant energy. The seed letters are called *bija mantra* and they are *Lam, Vam, Ram, Yam, Ham, Om*. Each mantra represents one *tattwa*, one element. In the structure of creation, everything is composed of the five elements: earth, water, fire, air and ether. These five elements are known as primordial elements. In yoga and tantra they are known as the *pancha tattwa*. Permutation or combination of these elements brings all matter into existence, brings creation into existence.

Each chakra has one letter which represents the predominating tattwa. Mooladhara, for example, is predominantly earth element and therefore its mantra is *Lam*, representing the sound waves which symbolize earth. These five elements have different frequencies, densities, waves, vibrations and colours. Therefore, each and every tattwa or element is represented by one sound wave. As you know, the basis of all matter, the origin of the entire creation is sound. Sound is the most subtle force.

In tantra this sound is known as *nada*. Even in the Bible it says, "In the beginning was the word." Here the word implies sound. This sound can be manifested in the form of waves. You have various ranges of sound. I am speaking, this is also sound but it is gross. Its frequency is low and its velocity is high. It has speed. It has colour. Each and every letter that we pronounce is a sound and that sound has inherent frequencies, velocities, colours, densities, vibration, modulations, etc. Therefore, bija mantras represent the inherent elements of each chakra.

The various deities of these chakras represent the subtle form. Remember one important thing: there is a gross form and a subtle form of all matter. This body is your gross form, not your subtle form. Your subtle form is different. A flower, plant or tree in the gross form is exactly as you see it. That gross form is visible to your senses. It also has a subtle form and that is not exactly like the flower that you see, but different. That subtle form cannot be seen through the senses, but only with the subtle mind.

These different deities related to each and every chakra are the subtle forms, the transcendental forms or the psychic forms of the force inherent in that particular chakra. Each and every chakra is a cycle of force in revolution and it has a form that is symbolized by these deities which you come across during your studies in kundalini yoga.

Is there any conflict between yoga and Christianity?
If there is any conflict, it is between Christianity and modern science. These two will never meet. The basic concepts of modern science and the basic concepts of Christianity are completely different. Take, for example, cosmology, the evolution of creation and life. Christianity says that creation took place in six days, but science says it took place over billions and billions of years. So, if you are trying to find out if there is any conflict, you should first try to find out if there is any conflict between Christianity and science.

If there is any conflict between yoga and Christianity, it is not in the basic tenets, principles or doctrines, but in our own understanding of them. We are different and so we think differently. Our philosophies, concepts, visions, assessments and values are different, but basically there is no difference.

Christ was not Christian. He was not Roman Catholic. He was not Protestant. He did not belong to the Anglican Church, nor did he establish the Vatican. He was born a Jew and he died a Jew. His disciples believed in him, so they called Christians followers of Christ. Supposing my disciples believe in me. They will be called followers of Satyananda, and afterwards they will establish Satyanandity.

This is what happens. Christ did not preach a religion. Buddha did not preach a religion. Mohammed did not preach a religion. I don't preach a religion, but my disciples are going to make my teaching a religion. Not now but maybe after five hundred years or so, they will hold conventions and write canons. They will do it all in my name and then they will say, "Swami Satyananda will reappear."

Today people say that Christ will reappear. I hope he does not, for if he does, first of all he is going to attack your established systems. He is going to tell you what you are doing is all wrong, just as he did two thousand years ago in Israel, for which he was crucified. This time he will not be crucified; he will be executed. Someone will definitely shoot him, because great saints like Christ know the truth. They speak the truth and we don't want to hear it. We just say that he will come, but remember, if we are to survive with all our hypocrisies, he should not come again. It's dangerous, like a policemen appearing amongst criminals.

Christ was divinity personified. There was nothing except divinity in him. You can say he represented total illumination, no dark force remained in him. He was a yogi, a saint, a bhakta, a karma yogi, a kriya yogi and a jnana yogi of the highest order because he represented divinity, not this lower empirical self.

During his lifetime all his teachings represented truth, so much so that when the soldiers wanted to arrest him, they needed someone to tell them who this Christ was. If the police were to come for me, they would know me easily, but Christ always remained anonymous, confined in deep meditation. There are a few stories told about his miracles, that's all. He was not a man of hotel, bottle and bill.

He lived within himself and with his disciples. This is one of the basic traits of the nature of yogis. They always remain in silence, in seclusion, away from the teeming crowd, and that is how he lived. So it was very difficult for the soldiers to find out who Christ was. Judas had to tell them, he had to point Christ out to them.

This great man did not preach the religion that you follow today. He only taught how to hear the inner voice, how to see the inner beauty, how to hear the inner music and how to see God or feel the presence of He who is the innermost being, the highest inner experience. This is what he taught.

Therefore, the teachings of Christ and yoga go together. There may be a conflict between Christianity and yoga which you have to find out, but definitely there is no conflict, no difference, between what Christ taught and what yoga is trying to teach.

How can I best use the kriya energy for the benefit of mankind?

First of all, you must utilize the energy of kriya for the betterment of your inner experience. You can serve humanity better with a transformed quality of mind and awareness. All those people who have been able to serve mankind in a greater way had a different mind, personality and experience. They were different people. It is another matter if you just give a few dollars here and there or a chocolate or flowers or a Christmas gift. I don't think that's help.

Today humanity needs inner help. Everybody is unhappy, dissatisfied, scared and sorry, not only in the countries which are prosperous and technologically advanced, but even in those countries where the people live in the most primitive conditions. In the underdeveloped countries it appears that problems are material, but this is not true. Basically, they are spiritual problems.

I'm not talking about the previous ages. I'm talking of our own times. Everyone is suffering from spiritual bankruptcy. Everybody thinks in terms of matter, in terms of desire, passion and selfishness, in terms of religion and hypocrisy. The whole world is one brotherhood they say, and then they kill one another. All of us have one father, one mother. You have one father, and if you disagree with that, you must be executed. This is called religious hypocrisy.

Mankind is suffering from a spiritual illness. Its values, assessments, goals and destinations are guided by a powerful group of selfish people throughout the world, whether they are religious priests or political pundits, business magnates, criminals or even parents. They don't teach us what the truth is and they don't allow us to search for the truth. They want us to get married, rear children, make a home, run a business, do and job, all that is monotonous.

I want to go a different way because I'm searching. I must find out. I want to know why I was born, what my mission or purpose in life is. Am I a biological accident? Am I just a chance product of my parents, grown like a vegetable, or have I come here to fulfil the destiny of nature?

Therefore, if you want to serve mankind, first it will be necessary for you to practise the kriyas and after that, you will have to learn about, discover and realize the energy fields of which you are composed. You will not be able to realize everything totally. For that, you have to be a Christ, Buddha or Krishna, but you can realize something and with the knowledge of the energy fields in your body, in your mind and consciousness, you can help mankind to find the true mission or purpose of existence.

I think that is the greatest service one can do in this age. Even if you go to the primitive, backward countries and open hospitals, orphanages and food stores for them, can you make them happy? Centuries and centuries of history bears evidence that material comfort, even if it is provided in plenty, does not give happiness. A thought or an idea can give you happiness. Happiness is an expression of one's own self and if you can give humanity this happiness, you will be a prophet.

What does it mean when emotions arise strongly in the form of sadness, anger, physical pain in anahata chakra and tingling sensations in the body during meditation?

All kinds of emotions which you experience during kriya yoga and other yogic practices are positive signs of growth and progress. We have lived in a society where fear, agony, depression and sadness are avoided in day-to-day life. Nobody wants to be unhappy or fearful. Whenever the mind is obsessed by sadness or fear, we try to escape. Therefore, when you are practising kriya yoga, meditation or any type of yoga sadhana, all of the emotions which you have avoided and suppressed, which you have not wanted to face will come out. You will have to work out the karma which was holding up your evolution. Everyone must face fear in life; there is no use avoiding it. As much as happiness, comfort, pleasure, love, compassion and charity are wanted, you must accept unhappiness, agony, death, separation, undesirable events, fears, destruction, devastation and so on.

The problem is that man has not trained his mind. He has been wanting the impossible. Everybody wants immortality; nobody wants death. Death causes fear. People can't face it; they can't even think about it. Once I said to my disciples, "I'm sixty. How long will I live? One day I will go away." They said, "Please don't say that."

What is reality? Is happiness reality? Is love, compassion or charity, reality? Then what is reality? Fear is reality. Agony is reality. Disease is reality. You don't want to face it, but it will come out in your practice because you have been accumulating this toxic matter in your mental system for thirty, forty, fifty years. It is only after you have faced it squarely that you will have better experiences. Unless you face this, you can't have the higher experience.

Read the lives of great saints who had illumination. Have you seen the film *Brother Sun and Sister Moon*? What a life Saint Francis faced? You want to be great, you want to be realized, but you don't want suffering, insult and criticism. You don't like scandals about you, but still you want to go further.

There are many barriers between this state of existence and that experience, and what are they? You will have to face your karma, your destiny, your own personality, your own self. You have to cross through the boundary of body, then there are the boundaries of the senses, mind, emotions, intellect and psyche. Checkpoints are there. When you cross the boundary of the body, then there is a startling experience. You are thrown back.

So in kriya yoga, whatever emotions arise, let them come. If you want to cry, do it. If you are afraid, feel it. After fifteen minutes everything will be quiet. Go to the toilet and when you come back, you will be all right again.

Could you comment on the differences between, firstly, a spontaneous awakening of higher awareness as seen in the mystics, secondly, as seen in the life process which tends

to make one more spiritually aware in the second half of life, for instance, and thirdly, as is seen in the awakening of spiritual energy in the kriya practices?

There are some souls who are born like most of us but with higher knowledge and with great awareness because they come from the highest point of life. That is, they descend. They are called incarnations, messengers, avatars or divine beings. They do not belong to the category of those aspirants who are ascending and trying to reach the highest point. This is one quality or category of people.

The second category is those who have practised yoga in their previous incarnations. As a result of those practices and achievements in their previous incarnations, when they are born this time, they are born with that higher awareness and so, at the proper time, suddenly they have the spontaneous awakening. This spontaneous awakening comes to them without any knowledge, practice, aid or guru. They don't even know why this has happened to them.

Then there is the third category of people who strive hard, organize and reorganize the patterns of their mind and consciousness. As a result, they have experiences in kriya yoga, or in ajapa japa or other meditation practices. These are the three categories of people generally known to us.

7

Satsang

Satyananda Ashram, Mangrove Mountain, Australia, 22 November 1983

There is a common belief in the West, perpetrated by certain sects, that a woman has no soul. What do you think and what are the views of yoga regarding this?
In the last quarter of the twentieth century, if you still hold that women have no souls, then you are living in your own world. You are not aware that science, technology and philosophy have made great advancements and they are turning to the same point of truth which tantra has realized long ago. In tantra, the creator is a female. She is known as Devi, Shakti, or the primordial energy.

There have been two currents of thought up to now and they are not philosophical, they are more or less political. One is a patriarchal system and the other is a matriarchal one. European religions have originated from the patriarchal system and according to this system, God the creator is a father, a man, not a mother or a woman. Naturally, if the creator of this world and all the worlds is a father, there is no place for mother. She doesn't exist, and when she doesn't exist she has no soul. That is what they have been telling us for many years.

According to tantric philosophy, *matri shakti* or mother energy is the first creator. In the form of energy, she permeates through all matter. She stands somewhere in between matter and consciousness. In tantra the whole manifestation is seen in three stages. The first stage is consciousness. That is the most subtle or transcendental. We call it the supreme consciousness. The grossest manifestation is matter in the form of existence, in the form of creation, in the form of this great creation of substance, the mass.

In between matter and consciousness is energy, the *shakti*, the creator, but energy or shakti does not create anything; she transforms herself. Energy transforms itself into the form of matter. All the matter you see, the mass, not only in this world but everywhere in the visible and invisible creation is nothing but a state of energy. As such, there is no such process as creation, there is a process of transformation, of manifestation.

When you take a piece of gold and make an ornament out of it, the gold does not create the ornament but the gold is transformed into the form of an ornament. A potter makes pots. The pots are created from a lump of earth. This earth is the instrumental cause. If there is no earth, there can't be a pot. This is exactly the philosophy which many religions have been teaching us. They say that God created the creation like a potter creates a pot. In tantra, the process of creation is described differently. Even as gold is transformed into an ornament, the energy is transformed into matter. Therefore, this whole creation, visible and invisible, is nothing but another form of shakti, the creator.

You haven't seen the creator and I don't think that you will be able to see him, but when you see his creation, you can understand much about the creator. Therefore, in tantra, the creator and the creation are not different. It is the same way in modern science; energy does not create matter, energy transforms itself into matter and matter again is reconverted into a form of energy. When matter is reduced to energy and energy is again withdrawn, then there is supreme consciousness.

This is the case with everything, not only with animals or the vegetable kingdom, but also with men as well as women.

Men and women, animals and minerals, oceans, sun and moon, mountains, pastures and the continents were not created, they were transformed. They are the transformed matter of one kind of fantastic energy. The same energy which is in me is also in my mother, in my sister, in all men and women. This is the concept of tantra and this is the concept of science.

In modern physics we talk about three things: time, space and matter. Time and space represent masculine and feminine energies, and these two energies are to be brought together. They are the opposite poles of energy – male and female. When they are brought together at one particular point, then an explosion takes place. According to physics, this explosion takes place in the nucleus, and this nuclear explosion throws off chain reactions. In physics this chain reaction is responsible for the modern nuclear weapon and for millions and trillions of nebulae which were thrown off into the black space. This is how endless galaxies, solar systems, moons worlds, etc., were created. Therefore, from the cosmic standpoint, masculine and feminine energies have to work together.

If you come to the microcosmic aspect, man and woman, male and female, have to work together because they both have to fulfil the task of creation, the task of transforming energy into matter. As such, it is absolute ignorance to say that women have no souls. If my mother did not have a soul, how did she give birth to me? Because I have a soul. It is better that these beliefs are consigned to the wastepaper basket and are buried forever, so that our children never have to know anything about them. Posterity should remain completely unaware of these, what I would call, politically motivated philosophies.

As a woman, can I benefit from the life of a sannyasin?
In our society, if anybody can benefit to the maximum from sannyasa, it is women. They can enjoy the maximum benefits from sannyasa. After they take sannyasa, they have a status. If they are not married, I don't think they have any status at

all, and for many women marriage is a catastrophe. We do involve ourselves in marriage because we don't know what it's about, but once we know, we will not dare to do it. Our parents are quiet about it. They don't say they know. Even after marriage, what status has a woman got? She is a wife, but not for the whole lifetime. After a few years she may be separated. A woman has no status.

Now, when you take sannyasa, you can utilize your essential nature. Women as a whole are very psychic, highly devoted, intensely aware of the deeper realms of spiritual life. In this world today, I'm not talking particularly about the West, but throughout the world, if there is any spirituality, any virtue, any respect for nobility and dignity, it is because of women. They have maintained it and they have fought for it. Therefore, this natural ability which they have will be properly expressed when they take to sannyasa.

The difficult, rigid and rigorous rules and regulations in the life of a sannyasin are easily maintained by women. They have so much devotion, faith and loyalty that they can easily survive with the guru, and survive with dignity, respect and nobility. I have also seen that in ashram life and in the life of a sannyasin, women have done much better than men. Their minds are more tranquil and one-pointed. Even in the process of awakening the kundalini, women have many more facilities than men. Definitely they have more facilities all around and the awakening of kundalini can be achieved by them long before the men.

In my opinion, those women who are prepared to shoulder the burden of family and children may do so, but those who are not prepared to should take up sannyasa life. After becoming sannyasins and training for a period of time, acquiring inner strength, conviction and knowledge, they can set out to serve humanity. If they want to open yoga ashrams, they can do so; if they want to run charitable hospitals, orphanages, schools and do other acts of service, they can. Or if they want to retire into caves, in total seclusion, and meditate for weeks, months or even years together, they can do that too.

As a sannyasin you are unlimited. You can take up any profession. You can be a gardener, a builder, a cook, an artist, a teacher and you can be a loafer as well. You can even be a meditator, a yogi. You can express your inner talent in any form, in any way you like with dignity, freedom, respect and nobility. The path of sannyasa is the greatest opportunity for those women who do not want to enter into family life.

I do not have any faith in religion, however, I want to attain the highest spiritual experience. Is it possible?
Faith in religion is one thing, practical sadhana is another. I have many disciples in Czechoslovakia, Poland and other Eastern European countries and a few disciples in France who not only do not believe in religion, they don't believe in morality and ethics either, but these disciples, I know, are outstanding. They think very clearly. They behave beautifully and their judgements are accurate. Their inner spiritual experiences are genuine, but they don't believe in God. They don't believe in any kind of religious ethics or morality.

I think religion is based on faith. All that is said in religion has no proof. It can't be proved objectively. You have to believe it, that's all, and when you believe in one doctrine you are more or less hypnotizing yourself. It is a kind of self-imposed indoctrination. It's not only that way with one religion, it's the same with every religion and therefore most people do not understand it.

However, spiritual life is totally independent of your faith, of your creed, because it has something to do with your mind, with your body and with a proper coordination and balance between these two entities called body and mind. After all, when you practise hatha yoga, what has that got to do with religion? Or when you close your eyes and try to maintain balance of mind, when you try to experience inner peace and tranquillity or when you are trying to concentrate on a particular point, what has that got to do with ethics and morality?

It is better, in my opinion, to be an honest atheist than to be a hypocrite. Many times we live like hypocrites. Our faith and our belief and our practical life do not meet anywhere. We profess one thing and we think another and we act yet another. There is a total disunity within ourselves. If you do not believe in religion, it does not mean that you don't believe in God; that is another matter.

There are many people I have come across who do not believe in religion, but they believe in an almighty, omnipresent, omnipotent and omniscient reality. God has nothing to do with an organization. Our religions are organizations, they are institutions. They have the same kind of rules and regulations which the governments have. They tell you how you should dress, how you should stand, how you should pray, how you should keep a straight face, a cast-iron face – don't laugh because before God you must be serious! These are the external rules and these external things do not really matter, even if you don't believe in them. If you don't believe in an institution, in an organization or in all these rules and regulations, it doesn't mean that you are an atheist. A *jnani*, a man of knowledge, can never be an atheist because he has realized the substratum, the source, the nucleus of the total existence.

All religions declare that for higher experience one has to abstain from sex. What does tantra have to say about this?
There are three main views about this question. One is that sex is necessary for procreation and many religions support this view. The second view is that sex is for pleasure, which our modern culture propagates. The third view is that sex can give you spiritual experience; it is the view propagated by tantric philosophers.

This third view is correct because awakening of kundalini and the sexual act are interrelated and interconnected, but this doesn't mean that everybody in the world who is leading this life will have the awakening of kundalini. All those who believe and who think that through sexual interaction awakening of kundalini can take place should remember very well that there are basic yoga practices in hatha yoga which should be practised beforehand.

The sexual act in itself is an animal act. It gives you only momentary bliss which lasts for a few seconds and then gives way to depression and frustration, and that is true for everybody. When you practise those basic practices of hatha yoga which are: kumbhaka, vajroli mudra for men, sahajoli kriya for women, shambhavi mudra, awareness of breath in the form of *Soham* and a few other practices before the sexual interaction, that gives you an abiding experience, which represents the awakening of kundalini.

In the past, religions became puritanical in order to survive in the primitive society, otherwise they would have been destroyed. This was precisely the reason why tantra could not survive. All these revelations of tantra were not accepted by the people. If I spoke about these things in a public meeting of ten thousand people, they would not understand and that is precisely the reason why the tantric science and philosophy became a mysterious cult. It was taught in secret behind closed doors because how can you tell people openly that through sexual interaction you can awaken the kundalini? People would not like it because most of the religions have declared that sex is an unholy act, even though everybody is doing it.

Hardly a few handfuls of people, you can count them on your fingers, may not have the fortune of having the sexual experience, but most people have it. If they do not actually have it, they may have dreamt about it, and even if they did not dream about it, they must have seen animals cohabiting, and still man has deluded himself by saying that this act is unholy. Why has this unholy act survived? What happened to that God? Why did he not destroy it? His creation is perpetuated through an unholy act. Why does he allow it? Why doesn't nature destroy itself? Anyway, this is something for everyone to consider.

In tantra they have dealt with this in very great detail. Many of the tantric texts are not yet translated into English, but a few have been. There is a good book called *Vijnana*

Bhairava Tantra, which has been translated into English. Quite a lot of books have come out and when you read those books, the writers themselves are shy of telling the truth, but in the basic tantric philosophy, the very act of sex is organized. It is said that when you perfect the practice, when you become an adept in hatha yoga, when you have controlled your prana, your mind and your body, then you can also control your ejaculation. When you can control your ejaculation, you can maintain continuity of the orgasmic experience. When you can continue that one experience for about three minutes, an explosion will take place, and that is called the awakening of kundalini.

The ordinary experience which we have for a few seconds is so delightful, so tempting, that we want to have it again and again. If the same momentary experience could be prolonged, say for three minutes or for five minutes with the same intensity, imagine what would happen. My God, you would be lost in transcendence! You would just go into transcendental meditation, transcendental samadhi, and you would never leave your sadhana. This experience of five minutes could be held with total attention in kumbhaka; this is the concept of tantra in which mind and prana are brought together, employing the sexual interaction.

Should children be taught yoga? Are there any such projects being conducted elsewhere?
Yes. Children can and should be taught yoga. I have one disciple in France who is a school teacher. She has been teaching yoga for many years in her school. She started first with minimum cooperation. Later, the education department surveyed the effects of the yogic lessons given to her pupils. They were very positive. Now in France yoga teaching has been accepted in the schools. There was a lot of controversy about it two years ago in the papers. Now there are certificate courses conducted in secondary schools and yoga is being introduced in primary schools. A lot of research has been done into how to teach yoga to children and how it influences their

brain, their faculties, their archetypes, IQ, etc., and their social consciousness, intellectual behaviour and physical growth. You would be very surprised to know what yoga can do for your children so far as their growth in life is concerned.

In India, during the time of the Vedas, there was a tradition that every child at the age of seven was taught three practices: mantra, pranayama and surya namaskara. Then he was sent to the gurukul for further education for a period of twelve years, where he was taught all the sciences by his guru. Nowadays this initiation is merely a ritual in India. The people who perform it don't really understand its practical value. They do it because it is a part of their religion. However, in the last ten or fifteen years I have been talking about yoga in the schools and colleges everywhere and the children have become aware of the reasons why they should practise yoga in their early years.

In the physical body there is an important gland called the pineal. Everybody has it, but in children it is more active than in adults. The pineal gland is the physical location of ajna chakra. It is a master gland which controls the behaviour of the pituitary gland like a stop cork. The pituitary is a wild gland. It produces so many hormones which can create any effect in the body, positive or negative. These hormones which are secreted by the pituitary gland must be properly regulated. If the wild behaviour of the pituitary gland is not controlled, then you will have both physical and emotional problems.

Imagine if the pituitary gland begins to secrete sex hormones at the age of seven, what will happen? So it has to be controlled. These hormones must manifest only at the right moment or time. This is the function of the pineal gland. If the pineal is healthy, the pituitary gland will remain under control. If the pineal is unhealthy, you can expect wild, anarchical behaviour from the pituitary gland, and that's what happens.

An emotional, intellectual and physiological imbalance is not good. I am sixty and I have a certain level of consciousness, of experience and feeling. Supposing some of your children begin to develop my awareness and feeling, they will go crazy because their emotional and intellectual growth must go hand in hand with their physical growth. Children are at their own level and my experience should not develop in them. At the same time, if I become retarded and begin to feel like a child of eight, what will happen to me? Imbalance. When you are twelve physically, you should be twelve mentally, emotionally and intellectually. When you are twenty-one physically, you must be twenty-one mentally, emotionally and intellectually. This is called balance.

This equilibrium can be maintained by ajna chakra, or the pineal gland. If you are physically twenty-one, mentally thirty-four and emotionally fifty-six, you are definitely going to land in the mental hospital. That is called personality imbalance, and this can happen if ajna chakra is not maintained in a healthy order. In order to maintain perfect health of the pineal gland, there are three practices: surya namaskara, pranayama and mantra, and this is the yoga which we should teach all the children.

The fully accomplished sages have stated that the final liberation comes only through self-enquiry whereby one dismisses all thought or maya as unreal and finds that the pure, untainted self is the sole witness. Who is qualified for this practice?

It is said in jnana yoga, it is said in Vedanta philosophy, that you hear the truth from your guru, contemplate on that truth and then realize that truth. This is the basic philosophy of jnana yoga.

You know that there are four major yogas: karma yoga, bhakti yoga, raja yoga and jnana yoga. *Jnana yoga* is the yoga of rationalization, contemplation, introspection. *Raja yoga* is the yoga of concentration, meditation and samadhi. *Bhakti yoga* is the yoga of sublimating and channelling the emotional personality towards your ishta devata, God or guru. *Karma yoga* is the yoga in which you sublimate your energies and the propensities of your mind by detached work. Out of these four yogas, this question pertains to jnana yoga.

If by reflection, by contemplation, or by self-introspection alone, the supreme experience could be achieved, then why is it necessary to practise all these yogas? Just sit down and ask, "Who am I? I am not this body, I am not this mind, I am not these senses." Go on and do it, but the point comes when the question arises: "Can I actually do it? Have I got that intensity of awareness? Will I be able to think about the knowledge of the self without any hindrance, interruption or interception? Can I maintain a constant flow of awareness? Can I?"

If you can maintain an unbroken flow of self-awareness, then you belong to the path of jnana yoga. Don't worry about bhakti yoga, karma yoga, raja yoga, kriya yoga. Just sit down and whatever you have heard from your guru, contemplate on that and maintain an unbroken flow of that awareness. Let no other thought intercept; let no external awareness disturb you.

Who am I? There is a beautiful story. Once a guru invited two of his disciples and they came to him. He instructed them both. "You are the supreme being, supreme experience." The disciples replied, "Yes, we understand that we are the supreme experience.". "Okay," said the guru, "get out." So the two disciples went their separate ways.

One disciple was very happy. He said to himself, "Oh, I am the supreme experience. That means I am God, I am Brahman." And he was twirling his moustache as he went. Then he got thirsty and went to a pond for a drink. While drinking water he saw his reflection. "Good, strong cheeks," he said, "Brahman has nice cheeks. That supreme experience has broad shoulders and big biceps." That was all he had understood from his guru.

When the guru was talking about the supreme experience, the disciple thought that he was relating to the physical body because the disciple could not think of anything beyond the body. When he went back to his people, they asked him, "What did you gain from your guru?" He replied, "Don't worry, I got the supreme experience. All of you should develop it." So all of his followers grew moustaches and beards, and every morning they used to drink buffalo milk and eat cheese and butter in order to develop good muscles.

The other disciple, who also heard the same dictum from his guru, thought differently. He asked himself, "What has the guru said? You are supreme experience. What does he mean: How can this body be the supreme experience? This body decays, becomes sick and dies. Then how can it be? Did guru mean my mind? Is it a supreme experience? No, mind is also subject to happiness and unhappiness, depression and elation, and therefore mind is also changing. A thing which is changing cannot be the supreme experience. Supreme experience has to be constant, infinite, external and always the same. It can't change according to circumstances, situations and modes. So the mind cannot be that." This is how that disciple kept thinking and thinking and thinking, until finally he just entered into deep meditation and then he realized the true thing.

Jnana yoga is the yoga in which you try to discover your inner being by a process of deep thinking, rationalization and contemplation. For this, you must have sufficient control over the influences of the mind. In order to develop control over the mind, you must practise raja yoga. In order to have control, you must have concentration of mind. If you have no concentration, you can't have control of the mind and in order to have concentration, you will have to practise bhakti yoga, kirtan. In order to achieve concentration, your mind must be pure. It should not be soiled like a dirty stomach, passing bad wind or belching all the time. No! Clean stomach, clean mind. How to have a clean mind? Through the practice of karma yoga.

This is the chronological order. Practise karma yoga and clean the mind. Then practise bhakti yoga and achieve concentration. Then practise raja yoga and develop control over the mind, and finally you can practise jnana yoga and contemplate on the truth. These are the graded steps towards jnana yoga, and if you think that jnana yoga alone can give you the ultimate experience without preparing your body and mind, without developing mental control, without concentration and so on, I will not agree.

Since all yogic practices must eventually be seen as modifications of maya, and therefore as unreal, what is the fate of one founded in yoga?

This again is a question based on vedantic philosophy. In Vedanta there is only one truth, called *Brahman*, the supreme being, the absolute. Everything else is called maya. *Maya* means the divine illusion, which does not really exist, but which you see and feel. That is called maya, a non-existent principle of which you have an experience, like dreams. In dreams you see an elephant, but there is no really elephant. In dreams you see a snake crawling over you or even biting you, but actually there is no snake. This is called maya, an experience which really doesn't exist, but which you experience as real.

According to Vedanta, the whole universe is maya. As such, the universe doesn't exist. The sun does not exist, the moon does not exist, the solar systems do not exist, the earth does not exist, you don't exist, I don't exist, because reality is only one; it is absolute. All else that you see and experience through your mind and senses is illusion; it's a dream.

In modern science also, they have been talking more or less on the same lines. They are coming to the conclusion that creation as we see it does not exist. Whatever we see in any way, the sun, moon and stars, you, me, my mother, your mother, it is all time, space and object – hallucination. When time, space and object come together in a particular fashion, an experience takes place. That experience is dependent on the mind, and mind is nothing but a combination of time, space and matter.

If you can extricate time, space and matter from the mind, the mind doesn't exist, just as the golden bangle doesn't exist if you take the gold away from it. No gold – no bangle. In the same way, no time, space and matter – no mind, and if there is no mind, there is no creation. Creation, existence, according to the scientists is an experience. They haven't said it openly as yet, but they are coming to this point and maybe after two, three or four decades, the scientists will be saying, "You see this bit of timber, but it's not there at all; you are just seeing it." This is exactly what they say in Vedanta.

Vedantic philosophy, which is the most ancient philosophy of India, is based on this. There is only one reality: the absolute, and nothing else exists. Whatever you see happening, that is your own dream, your own maya, your own imagination. Vedanta is a very high philosophy.

You see, it is true that everything is fleeting, everything is based on our emotions and on the error of our perception, everything is essentially not true, but then, how to get out of it? If a thorn is sticking into you, you have to use another thorn to take it out and then throw them both away. In the same way, it is through the practices of yoga that a proper vision will be restored and a proper quality of mind will emerge. When you develop that quality of mind, then you can say that this is maya and this is truth, this is reality and this is fiction, but now if you say the whole world is maya, everything in existence is illusion, it's not true. If you get cancer, how much you suffer, how much it affects you! Why can't you say that is also maya?

If the whole existence is maya, it is okay, I agree, then your agonies are maya, your happiness is maya, and your cancer is also maya, blood pressure is also maya, diabetes is also maya. Your wife or husband has divorced you – it's all maya! It's all happening in dream. If you can come to this point of realization, if you can arrive at this experience, where every happening in your life does not affect you, as in a dream, then of course you don't have to practise yoga at all. You should not practise mantra. You should not go after gurus. You should not take sannyasa. You should not come to ashrams, You can just remain wherever you are because you are a jnani.

The man of supreme wisdom is called a jnani. For him, disease and death are both dreams. Prosperity and poverty are both dreams. It doesn't matter what is there and where is there and which is there. Such jnanis are not born every day. They come only once in many thousands of years. To consider the whole of existence as nothing is so difficult, so impossible. A little dream in the night terrifies you so much. Tonight if you dream your house is burning down, tomorrow you will pack and go from there. You will say, "My God, I saw my house burning in a dream!" Even if you know it is a dream, a fantasy created by your subconscious mind, still it has an effect.

When you are affected by the fantasy of the subconscious mind, how can you say that you are beyond maya? You are in maya. You will be in maya. You are in illusion. You are a part of illusion. In order to get out of one illusion, you have to take the help of another illusion. That is yoga.

8

Satsang

Satyananda Ashram, Mangrove Mountain, Australia, 23 November 1983

Last night you mentioned that emotional, mental and physical growth should develop simultaneously in children. I am wondering what happens to children who have deep spiritual awakenings and advanced inner knowledge at an early age?
From time to time there have been children gifted with a spiritual awareness and the general theory of teaching yoga to children does not apply to them. The children who are gifted should be taught more about the spiritual life, inner awareness and the deep-rooted psychic and spiritual forces in them, so that in times to come they can develop in the form of geniuses.

It is said that when Shankaracharya was eight years old, he developed absolute awareness. He became aware of the absolute and then he thought of becoming a sannyasin, but his mother who was a widow would not permit him. Somehow, as the story goes, he secured her permission and went in search of a guru. When he found his guru, he stayed with him for eight years and learned from him the ancient wisdom, theory and practice both.

At the age of sixteen, he set out from the ashram of his guru and travelled the length and breath of India, preaching unqualified monism, *advaita vedanta*, not only the doctrine of one God, but the doctrine of oneness which means everything is just one. At the age of sixteen years, he was able to convince the intellectuals and the masses as well as his opponents. At the age of thirty-two he died. Such people are called gifted children.

When Christ was a child, he was supposed to have lived for some time in an Essene monastery. The monks there found him extraordinary and perhaps they could not cope with his eagerness, intuition and wisdom. So, when he was thirteen, they sent him to India where he lived for a period of twelve years in various parts of the country. He stayed in Kashmir, in Jagannath Puri, in Nepal, in the famous Nalanda University only a hundred miles south of Munger and in many other places. He met a lot of people who had theoretical and practical knowledge both.

Like this, there are many stories of inspired and gifted children and you can read about them in the books. Our children could also become equally intelligent if they were exposed to a spiritual climate. If they are kept in a spiritual environment, they can develop the inner seed of spiritual awareness. As a matter of fact, every child is pure, every child is untainted and innocent. You do not really remember your childhood, but if you did, you would remember that at that time you had the awareness of your self.

You don't have that awareness now. You may be intellectually aware that you have a self. Books tell you that you have a self, *atma*, soul, spirit, and you accept it, but you don't really experience it. You experience all emotions, fears, love, agony and depression; you experience sleep, hunger and pain but you don't experience the self.

When you were children, you did experience the self, you were aware of the self, but gradually, when the worldly maya enveloped you in the form of desires and ambitions, the notion or the idea of the self was completely lost. That is why it is said in the Bible, "Be like a child." It means be thoughtless, desireless and free of everything. Whether it is frustration or depression, death or birth, profit or loss, victory or conquest, it is all a drama, all a game. It is not reality. With a free mind you can maintain that childlike awareness all the time.

Therefore, expose your children to spiritual and yogic activities. Out of such children, those who have come down with the spiritual potential will be known at once and you must let them search for their own path. To those who are not spiritually evolved, you should give yoga, pranayama, mantra, surya namaskara, etc., for their spiritual growth, for their spiritual initiation. Those who have come down with the spiritual potential from their previous life must be given the opportunity to find their own way. They will discover a path for themselves and they will also discover the sadhana which they have to do for their spiritual illumination.

What should I do when I finish this kriya yoga course and leave the ashram? Can I teach?

You have come here to learn kriya yoga and then you will go back home and continue to practise. If you have come here to learn kriya yoga and then go back and teach, that's a different matter. Please don't do it. Before you begin to teach kriya yoga, it is necessary to learn how to handle the experiences of your pupils, if at any time they should arise. Out of dozens and dozens of pupils which we get, someone might develop certain experiences which you, as a new or raw teacher, may not be able to handle or pacify.

You have come here to learn kriya yoga in order to find a way to develop your spiritual awareness. I hope you will understand that you have not come here to learn kriya yoga and then teach it to others. You can teach later, when you have practised by yourself for at least several years. Kriya yoga is the most powerful practice, beneficial for all people who are involved in day to day life, It may not be a great practice for those who have renounced everything, but for those who are involved, it is the most powerful practice.

If you can practise all the kriyas which you are taught here, well and good, but if you don't have that much time and you want to practise only for a short period, say half an hour a day, then take up three practices daily or even two. Do three practices one day, three practices the next day and three more practices the third day and then repeat it. It is not necessary to practise all the kriyas at once. Out of all the kriyas, maha mudra, maha bheda mudra and vipareeta karani mudra are the most important and they take altogether about fifteen minutes to perform.

In kriya yoga you have a lot of pranayama. So, if you are practising all the kriyas, then you do not need to practise pranayama as well because it will be too much. But if you are only practising a few kriyas, say two or three, you can practise your asanas and pranayama separately.

I have experienced a short period of profound bliss through the practice of continuous deep breathing or hyperventilation. How do you regard such a practice?
In pranayama practice, it is said when you do rigorous breathing or deep breathing for a long time, then you feel lightness of the body. That is precisely the reason why many teachers nowadays teach bhastrika pranayama. They do vigorous bhastrika. Sometimes it is more than vigorous, wild bhastrika I call it.

When you practise the wild bhastrika, then the coordination between the sympathetic and parasympathetic nervous systems changes. As a result of that, you feel relaxation, delight, light-mindedness. Of course, it is perfectly all right, you can do it, but momentary delight, momentary relaxation, are not cures for the ills of human life. In order to face and to understand life, in order to be unaffected by life, you will have to change the structure and the quality of your mind. Then only will the delight remain perennial.

If you practise deep breathing or vigorous breathing or even wild breathing for half an hour and then lie down on the floor, you will feel very light, you will feel very great bliss for half an hour, maybe one hour, maybe half a day. But the moment you face any mental problem, all that you have gained, all that you have experienced by that wild breathing will be finished because the changes that it produced were only in the coordination or mutual reaction of the nervous system.

The change did not take place in your consciousness, in your philosophy, in your capacity to understand the events of life. Therefore, side by side with bhastrika, with deep breathing, with vigorous or even with wild breathing, please continue your spiritual practices. We call it restructuring of the mind.

Is it possible to stop thinking? How can one achieve that state?

One can stop the thinking, but this process is not free from dangers. In advanced stages, when you have sufficient control over the mind and awareness, then you can practise stopping the mind. But in the beginning, if you try to stop the mind, then you will develop inner tensions and these tensions will reflect in your personality and behaviour.

There are practices that can create a momentary void or *shoonyata*, but this momentary and fleeting void, in my opinion, is not good for a beginner. In fact, in the higher stages of yoga, when you have achieved total concentration of mind and when you are able to visualize the object of your concentration for a long time without being disturbed, without any interception, then you should try to stop the mind. Then stopping the mind will be very easy for you, just as you start your car; put on the brake and the car stops, but do not practise it now.

There is currently a lot of interest in psychic healing. What are the spiritual implications for the people involved in such practices?

There are certain types of people who have the gift of psychic healing and at some time in their lives, they become aware of this quality in themselves. As a matter of fact, this quality is present in almost everybody. The body is not just flesh, bone, blood and marrow. It is a field of energy. In yoga we call it *shakti* and this shakti is twofold: mental and pranic.

Now, when the pranic force becomes predominant, and you can develop this through the practices of pranayama, etc., then this magnetism flows out of the body. Just as fire emanates heat, the magnet has a field, electromagnetic forces have a field, radioactive forces have a field, so the prana shakti has a field. You cannot see it, but it is there in everybody, except in one who is about to die, because at the time of death the prana shakti is completely withdrawn.

Recently they have conducted research into Kirlian photography. This photographic system has photographed the radiations around an object and it has been seen that each and every object has a field; you call it an aura, halo, or *prana shakti*. Sometimes this field shrinks and sometimes it expands; sometimes it is smooth and even, and sometimes jagged and uneven. This field represents the energy which is emanating from a particular matter or substance. Even a leaf, a coin, a piece of paper has prana. If you take a leaf from a tree, cut it into two and photograph it, then again pluck another leaf and photograph it without cutting it, you will find that the two leaves have different radiations, different areas of prana.

So this pranic or magnetic force which the scientists have been talking about is the same force which is expressed in a psychic healer. A healer is able to transfer his or her prana shakti through those radiations, and those radiations are absorbed by you. Also, please remember, it has been said by many people in yoga that the diseases which we suffer from are due to a lack of prana shakti. When the healer is supplying you with extra prana shakti, then you get better.

In this scheme, the healer should be able to replenish the lost pranic energy in himself. There are dangers in spiritual healing. One is that your prana shakti is lost unless you replenish it. You must have some source. It's a matter of commonsense. Secondly, many times the healer suffers from sickness on account of transference of the disease. So he must know how to get rid of it. I have come across many healers myself who were benign and compassionate, but they used to suffer from time to time.

Therefore, anyone who has this natural gift should also learn how to maintain contact with the eternal source of prana, number one, and how to combat the sickness of the patient which is transferred to you, number two.

How do you feel about rebirthing?
Let me tell you the story of Buddha, otherwise this rebirthing will become a very dull subject. Buddha was a prince. He renounced his kingdom at a very young age and went into an ashram where he practised Samkhya, yoga, etc. The place where he practised his austerities and sadhana was about sixty miles south of Munger.

After living in that ashram for twelve years, practising and learning, he went to a place very close by and became independent. He decided that he was going to realize the truth or else he was going to leave the body. He stopped eating, stopped bathing, sat down in the lotus posture and meditated and meditated and meditated, but nothing happened to him.

One morning he went down to the pond just to wash his face and when he reached the edge of the water, he fainted there because he had not eaten for many days. Exactly at that time, the daughter of the village chief nearby was coming past with a bowl of milk rice which she intended to offer to a holy tree. That is a custom which some Indians practise. They consider a tree as a living divinity, the abode of the divine forces.

So when the girl came to offer the milk rice to that tree god, she found a sannyasin, a swami, a fakir, lying unconscious on the side of the pond. After offering the milk rice to the tree god and consecrating it, she returned and gave it to Buddha to eat. He ate the milk rice and after some time he felt better. He got up and went to sit down under a nearby tree.

That was the full moon night in the month of April. Gradually, everything began to become clear to him. He went back to his childhood, he saw all that had happened to him in the past – his kingdom, his father, his wife, his child, his experiences of innocence, his experiences with his mother when he was in her womb, when he was in her lap, when he was being fondled. He saw his experiences in previous lives and then he realized that he had been born as an enlightened person in many incarnations, and there he became aware of the life of *bodhisattva*, the essence of truth, the essence of knowledge and the essence of enlightenment.

Now, this is the process which is known to many yogis. I'm only making a reference to the life of Buddha, but for those who have come far in spiritual life, this process, which you may call rebirthing or simply remembering your past, becomes just as spontaneous.

I have been in the habit of resisting physical and emotional pain for most of my life. I fear if I release all this negative energy I will be a complete emotional wreck. Am I doing the wrong thing by resisting?

Pain, agony and grief must be experienced. They increase the depths of your consciousness. Comfort and luxury are not good for spiritual development. Please excuse me if I say this; you must experience pain and you should not be scared of it at all. Pain is another form of bliss and it makes your consciousness active, alert, sensitive, analytical and introspective. If you are trying to suppress pain by the usual escape routes, then you are suppressing your own spiritual evolution.

Mankind has found various methods of escaping pain. Whenever you have pain, you take a pain killer. Whatever pain you have, there are escape routes. That is why it is said, if you want spiritual awareness, if you want to purify yourself, if you want to transcend the mundane experiences, if you want to be truly enlightened, you must undergo some sort of rigours, austerities and penances.

Austerity and penance are also painful, but when you accept that pain willingly, then it's called austerity. When you do not want it because you are scared of it, then it is called pain and it becomes painful. However, if you are able to welcome pain and know that it is very good for your spiritual enlightenment, then it won't become painful, it will become pleasant.

Many great saints are examples of that. Was St Francis enjoying the spiritual pleasures or was he facing unbearable pain? Well, for all of us it would be painful. For ordinary people it is really painful to walk barefooted in the snow, to be insulted, to endure hunger and cold, and he had to walk from one end of the country to the other. He built a small church which burnt down. All this should have been painful for him but it was not, because for him it was a process of purification, what you call purging – shankhaprakshalana.

Pain is not something undesirable, please understand it. It is through pain that your inner vision is opened. Those who face pain throughout life have very deep, substantial and true awareness of the higher being. Those who live in comfort and luxury with total security about the future, about money, house, employment, wife and children, do not have a fundamental and substantial knowledge about God. Their God is a capitalist.

Therefore, all the great saints, including Buddha, Christ, Mahavir, Mohammed, Zarathustra – what life did they choose for themselves? Can you think about that choice? Can you understand it? Their choice was poverty, not prosperity, and that is what they taught to their disciples. When Buddha initiated his disciples, he would tell them, "Go on moving around the world, eat just once a day, don't eat twice, sleep only once, just have one cloth, don't keep money."

That is called self-imposed poverty and this is exactly what is taught in the basic Christian philosophy. I would say the philosophy of Christ is that of self-imposed poverty. Christ was not a rich man; Buddha was not a rich man. Buddha was born a king, but he left his kingdom and became a beggar, so he was not a rich man. Similarly, all the great saints whom you have heard about and whom you worship today in the most beautiful temples with marble floors and decorated alters, they were very poor and humble people just like the mendicants you sometimes find wandering in the streets of India. Gurus also are never rich; gurus do not choose riches.

Therefore, pain should be the choice of every spiritual seeker, and remember, we are not talking only about external pain. There is another pain which you begin to experience at a higher level of consciousness and that pain is emanating from the depths of your consciousness. It has no form, no reason, no cause, but it is there, you feel painful. With that pain, you begin to see the reality of your attachments. Unless that inner pain, that deep-rooted pain is experienced by you in the higher realm of consciousness, your attachment to these mundane matters will not go. The gravitational force of maya, of attachment, is very powerful.

Therefore, I say to everyone, "Do not avoid pain!" When it comes, face it squarely, feel it, understand it. Do not suppress it, let it come out, experience it for a day, for two days. Maybe that is the awakening of kundalini. Often the awakening of kundalini is not followed by bliss and delight and exhilaration, but by the experience of pain. Even the pain which you are experiencing for some reason or other, the death of a son, the loss of a business, etc., may be the awakening of kundalini, and you are trying to suppress it.

That is why I tell people that pain is something which you should always accept. You may have luxury and comfort as long as you are weak, but once you become strong, it is better to leave the luxury and comfort and just lead a life which is a living experience of pain.

9

Satsang

Satyananda Ashram, Mangrove Mountain, Australia, 26 November 1983

Can you advise me about sadhana?
You will have to decide on one sadhana for yourself, one practice which you will do at any cost, with absolute regularity, even if it is just for ten minutes daily. Of course, you can do other practices too, like asana, pranayama, mudra, bandha, kriya, meditation, japa, etc. Even if you do not practise any or all of these, at some time you should adopt one practice according to your temperament and inclination.

In the scheme of spiritual life, yogic life, the amount of practice is not as important as the regularity. It is better to practise sadhana for just ten minutes daily throughout the year than to practise for one hour a day, let us say, for six months and then give it up. This ten minutes of daily practice is far more conductive to spiritual progress than one hour of sadhana for six months.

Therefore, you have to decide for yourself what you are going to do at any cost, whether it be asana, pranayama, meditation or mantra. You should not think which practice is more important or which is superior or more effective. You should only think which practice you can do, which practice you can stick to and carry through. Whether kriya yoga is more powerful or asanas are more effective, that is not the consideration. The important thing is whether you will be able to continue with the practice at any cost. When you have selected a suitable sadhana for yourself, you must practise it every day and at the same time become a participant in the scheme of life.

How can we discern what is real and what is not real in life? How can we know that what we are doing with our lives is right for us – or whether we just under some sort of illusion of following a fashion?

When the mind becomes quiet and peaceful, when there are less conflicts in the mind, then you can clearly see into the affairs of life. The problem comes when you try to settle matters through the intellect. The intellect is a confusing reality. With this confused intellect, you are trying to clear up the confusions. So, first attain peace of mind, one-pointedness and balance with yourself, then try to settle matters.

On the spiritual path are there certain awakenings and experiences which are common to everybody, or does an aspirant experience according to the individual personality and karmas?

In the beginning of the practices, the experiences are different according to one's temperament, qualities and nature, according to the tattwas, nadis and swaras also. As you go on practising, after some time the experiences of many aspirants are more of less the same. There is not much difference.

I feel that the present educational system is detrimental to my child's mind. How can this problem be overcome?

Modern education is necessary, but it does not fulfil the requirements of human life. It makes you ready for serving a nation or a community and earning your own livelihood, but it is not able to give you the knowledge of yourself. Therefore, we should have some educational institutions where our children can get secular as well as yogic education.

I have heard it takes many years for a highly evolved being to obtain the right birth. If so, how will I find you, my guru, in my next incarnation?

Why do you worry about the next incarnation? We are always worried about the future. If you remain devoted, dedicated and united with your guru in this life, the same will happen in the next incarnation also.

Is guru God? Is guru's grace from God or guru?

For a disciple, guru can be God. But a disciple must be very careful that he doesn't ask everybody else to consider his guru to be God. My guru is my God, but I don't have to tell you. The relationship between guru and disciple is absolutely personal. I can consider him as my husband, as my father, as my God, as the first and last thing in my life, but that is only for me. When you transcend this border and tell everybody that your guru is God, then the confusion begins.

As God and guru are not different on the inner plane, internal guru and external guru are also the same. External guru is the macrocosmos and internal guru is the microcosmos. Therefore, if I consider my guru as God, that is perfectly okay because that is my reality, but that does not apply to everybody.

I am of the opinion that it is also wrong to tell anybody to worship the God that you worship. My God is Sri Krishna and you may not like him. So you have to discover a God for yourself. I have to discover a God for myself and I have done it. I don't want to copy your God. You discover the form of your reality. You discover the name for yourself. You discover your own truth, because that is what is in you. My truth is in me, your truth is in you.

Guru is something very wonderful. It is something like a detonator. You know how to detonate a bomb? You put a bomb there – but you detonate it from here! There are different types of detonators. Now, the guru is within you, but to realize that you will have to have an external guru. Because in the beginning, if you look inside, you can't find anything.

You can say, "My guru is inside me," and that is perfectly true, but can you see him? Can you feel him? No. What do you feel inside? You feel your mind. You feel contact with the senses. You feel passion. You don't feel your guru. When you feel your guru, you experience tranquillity and harmony, but you don't experience that. This means that you are not in a position to forge a link between yourself and your real guru. So this problem will have to be solved.

Guru is in you. Although you can't hear him, you can't see him, you can't feel him, you don't understand him, you know he is in you. This is the problem. To solve this problem, you will have to go out in search of 'a guru', not 'the guru' which is inside. I call it 'the guru' meaning inside and 'a guru' meaning outside.

You go in search of a guru, and when you find one you will see that this man is nice. He is a wonderful man. He is knowledge incarnate, love incarnate, goodness incarnate. So you accept him as your guru and you express yourself, you give yourself, you surrender your ego, you give your feeling and devotion. Then suddenly a change takes place in you and in your mind.

Your mind becomes one-pointed, and the moment the mind becomes one-pointed, you begin to hear the inner guru. You don't hear the conflicts, you don't hear the passions, you don't hear this or that, but you begin to hear the guru. Here, the external guru, that one, and the internal guru, this one, both become one. This is the secret, that's all.

You briefly mentioned the science of swara yoga. I am interested to know more about it.
Swara yoga is a science which is related to tantra. It is a yoga in which you maintain constant awareness of the breath flowing through both the nostrils and thereby control the influences of the breath on the body, mind and external life. Not much about this science is known to people nowadays, but I have published a book on it which is called *Swara Yoga*.

According to yoga, the left nostril is associated with *ida nadi*, the mental energy flow, and the right nostril is associated with *pingala nadi*, the vital energy flow. These two nadis are connected with the nervous system in the spine. They are also related to the left and right hemispheres of the brain.

Although breathing is just an ordinary affair for most of us, in yoga it is considered to be very important. It is a language by itself. When you breathe through the right nostril while sleeping at night, it means you are going to have a lot of bad dreams. When the left nostril is flowing after lunch, it means you are going to have digestive upsets. If both nostrils are flowing, it means you are ready for meditation.

This is very important for yoga practitioners, because if you practise meditation when pingala nadi is flowing or when ida nadi is flowing, the effects and the experiences will be different. When both ida and pingala nadis are equalized, when both nostrils are flowing equally, at that time you should meditate. Then the experiences are very good and they are genuine.

So try to study the science of swara yoga, but if you are really interested in learning the practice, it will take you one lifetime to perfect it. Swara yoga is very interesting. You can practise it for twenty-four hours. You watch your breath every fifteen minutes. After about a year or so, if you are observing well, you can tell exactly what is going to happen, both internally and externally, because this individual breath is connected with the cosmic breath, the cosmic prana. By watching the behaviour of the breath in relation to the tattwas, in relation to the nadis, in relation to the events around you, you can come to a conclusion more or less on all events of life.

That is why many people in India practise swara yoga as a profession. When you have any problem, you can go to them. You don't even have to tell them what your problem is. You just say, "Sir, I have a problem." They will check their breath and say, "Yes, in three days you will get your donkey back," or anything like that. By checking his own breath, the swara yogi can tell whether a male child or a female child will be born.

When we were studying at school, we used to go to this *swara shastri*, expert in swara yoga. He would tell us many things and they were always exactly right. Anyway, by studying one's own breath in relation to the events, the tattwas, the stars and the day, you can make correct judgements.

10

Introduction to Advanced Kriya Course

Satyananda Ashram, Mangrove Mountain, Australia, 28 November 1983

Existence is not merely a manifestation of matter, and matter is not ultimate. There is a threefold process of evolution going on side by side and these threefold processes relate to life, energy and consciousness. Life is matter, consciousness is the ultimate form of matter, and energy comes in between. If the life force or matter has to evolve to the realm of consciousness, it is important that it has to be exposed to the realm of energy.

This energy which is known by various names is particularly the subject matter of yoga, tantra and all other spiritual sciences. Energy is *shakti* and it is the transforming quality. Even as you place a piece of timber in the fire and it changes the form of the timber, completely transforms it, in the same way, you have to expose your life force, this matter, to the forces of energy. Energy is responsible for converting this gross material force into consciousness, and this is what you have to understand.

Therefore, in the various practices of yoga, tantra and other spiritual sciences, the body, the senses, the elements composing the body, the life force, *prana*, and the mind, *manas*, are all subjected to energy. Energy is that manifestation by which the whole of matter is purified. When this matter is totally and completely purified, then it becomes consciousness. It is for this purpose that this advanced kriya yoga session has been organized, and it is for this that the rishis and saints evolved the practices of kriya yoga.

Quarrelling with unrealities

You will not get anywhere by fighting with your mind, by suppressing your mind, by criticizing and abusing your mind, by torturing and tormenting it by any method, whether yogic or religious. You can be sure about it! That is why millions and millions of people following various paths which teach suppression of mind have not come to any point of evolution.

Evolution is not suppression; it is transformation. Have you seen a flowering plant? It evolves from the seed state and then it gives birth to a beautiful flower. That is called transformation. In the same way, the process of evolution in man should go on unhindered and, in fact, the mind has nothing to do with it. When you consign matter into energy, you are consigning your mind as well and when energy purifies the physical elements, it will purify the mind also.

If you think you can purify the mind through the mind, you are thinking of cleaning dirt with dirt. You can't clean dirt with dirt. You have to clean dirt with clean water. In the same way, many people I know and you know have been fighting with their mind. They want to check their thoughts, passions, ambitions and dissipations. They are quarrelling with unrealities.

I remember a story which relates to this. There was a man whose name was Mulla Nasruddin. Many of you must be acquainted with him. He was a character. One day, when he was sitting in his drawing room sipping coffee and smoking a cigarette, his friend came to see him and said, "Mulla Nasruddin, I have something very confidential to tell you. Please bolt all the doors."

The Mulla replied, "It doesn't matter as there is no one here to listen." However, his friend was insistent, so the Mulla bolted all the doors. Then his friend said, "Look here, I have come to know from a very reliable source that your wife is having an affair with a personal friend. Every night at twelve o'clock she goes out to meet him in your garden and they have a nice time underneath the mango tree."

Mulla Nasruddin was so enraged. He shouted, "Damn her!" Immediately his mind went out of order. By the evening he had cleaned his rifle and checked the bullets about half a dozen times. Every now and then he would come back and check it again. By six o'clock he was already waiting in the garden, behind the mango tree, with his gun ready, so that the moment they arrived – click.

Ten o'clock, eleven o'clock, twelve o'clock came, but nobody turned up. Mulla Nasruddin said to himself, "What is the matter? Do they know that I am waiting here?" Then he began to think and think. Finally he remembered that he was not married at all and the poor man went back inside, unloaded his rifle and slept.

Deprogramming the mind
This is exactly what we have to do; unload our rifles which we have pointed at our mind. Because what we have been thinking about the mind is just a myth. There is no such thing as the mind. We live in a society and we have been taught to think in a particular way according to the social and family training and the education which we have received. Our thoughts, our areas of thinking, our passions, ambitions and desires do not relate to the mind at all.

Nowadays people have cars, so we desire a car. We don't desire an elephant because people no longer have elephants, but a hundred years ago we would have wanted an elephant. Of course, to have an elephant in those days was elegant; people would say, "What a great man. He has an elephant!" Now we don't even consider owning an elephant, but if everybody owns a helicopter, we will no longer want a car. Isn't it so?

Our desires are all fashioned and put into us. We are not free thinkers. Human beings are a brainwashed product of society. We are all brainwashed. Parents, teachers, society, advertisements, television, newspapers, everything brainwashes us. We are being indoctrinated all the time. Therefore, we come to the ashram in order to deprogram ourselves. Whatever has been put into the mind has to be cleared out. So the practitioners of kriya yoga should not worry at all about their mental behaviour. They should disregard the mind and go on with the practices.

Tuition and transmission
In the ashram there are two levels of teaching which go on simultaneously. One is tuition and the other is transmission. The teacher will be teaching you the techniques of kriya yoga externally, while internally guru and disciple will be transmitting and receiving. The practices of kriya yoga which your teacher will be teaching you will raise you to such frequencies where you will be able to receive the transmission of energy coming from the guru.

Therefore, there is a difference between the definition of guru and teacher. The teacher is not a guru. A guru only transfers and transmits the energy, the shakti, the inspiration, and the necessary experiences. The practitioner, with the help of his teacher, improves and adjusts his mental frequencies so that he is in direct contact with his guru.

So, in the ashram, *vidya*, knowledge or a faculty, is given by tuition as well as by transmission. Initiation is not a ritual. Initiation is transmission and transference of the inner forces between the guru and disciple, and that is always how this relationship between guru and disciple has existed. This is precisely the relationship between those who learn kriya yoga and myself.

An ancient tradition
Kriya yoga is one of the most important and powerful techniques that has been handed down to us from one generation to another. From time to time, it was taught in various lands by great and enlightened gurus. Not only

today but far back into the past, kriya yoga was taught and learned. There is a passage in the Bible which describes a ladder that ascends from earth to heaven. You climb the ladder half way with your eyes open and half way with your eyes closed. The rungs of the ladder represent the various practices of kriya yoga.

In India, kriya yoga was considered to be an important part of the tantric tradition. Much before the advent of Christianity, the tantric tradition had already travelled to every nook and corner of the world, but the people in various lands could not retain the purity, the greatness and the sublimity of tantra on account of the limitations and imperfections of their own culture. As a result of this, the tantric traditions in the far east, west, north and south received a setback in different times, but in India the enlightened people maintained this tradition with proper understanding. They began to teach this to aspirants, sincere householders, sannyasins and other people. Out of all the tantric practices, kriya yoga is considered to be supreme.

I do not say that I am the founder of kriya yoga, nor do I accept that anybody is the founder. We do not really know who the founder of kriya yoga is. Just as in the scientific tradition, there have been generations of scientists improving upon the scientific formulas, experiments, etc., in the same way, from ancient times there has been a tradition of experienced people who attained inner illumination and who transformed their entire material life into higher consciousness. It is these people who maintained an unbroken continuity of this tradition of kriya yoga, which has come down to us today.

Therefore, in the ancient texts, we find very clear references to kriya yoga. Of course, it is for the first time that I have brought the practices of kriya yoga together into one book, but otherwise, from ancient times up to today, various practices of kriya yoga could be found in the different texts. These practices found in the various texts and traditions may differ a little here and there, but this difference is on account of the quality of the aspirant.

Nowadays, for example, we teach maha mudra in utthanpadasana to modern people. You stretch your legs out in front of you and grasp your toes. This practice is also given in some of the texts, but actually maha mudra is to be practised in siddhasana. However, not everybody can do it. If you tell people to practise maha mudra and maha bheda mudra in siddhasana, they find it extremely difficult. utthanpadasana, therefore, being the easiest form is practised first, then it is taught in siddhasana.

Do not worry about the mind
So before you begin the advanced practices of kriya yoga, I am going to give you a very important hint. Do not worry about the mind! Practise your kriyas and if you have a mind, let it practise its own kriyas. Let it dissipate, let it wander, let it jump like a monkey or let it sleep – it doesn't matter.

Do your kriyas according to the instructions given to you by your teacher. Don't try to be very yogic. Keep your eyes open. You may not even be steady. You may go on looking at different things, whatever you can. The eyes need not be stilled; the body need not be stilled; the mind need not be stilled. Only the kriyas should be practised, and these will have an effect on your energy fields.

I am always talking about energy fields. I never speak abut mental field because it is like Nasruddin's wife, who doesn't exist at all. The energy field is a reality and it is operating in different spheres: vegetable, mineral, animal and human kingdoms, prana, body and mind. All these are manifestations of energy.

When energy is manifesting itself in the gross form, then it is known as matter, and when matter becomes free from its gross classification and gross limitations, then it is energy. Therefore, matter is nothing but energy. What is matter? The whole universe is matter. This body, this prana, are matter. The mental forces, the thoughts, the emotions are all matter. Don't call them spiritual. They are matter, and this matter has to be transformed.

This transformation of matter into energy cannot take place through the help of the mind. If you follow the paths in which the mind is supposed to effect the transformation, then you will wind up like Nasruddin, waiting with your rifle. That's why I say, please don't worry about the mind. Please don't worry about the senses. Just do your practices and you will find as you go on that you begin to experience the things which are beyond the senses.

When you go on practising kriya yoga, what will happen? The evolutionary energy, that means kundalini shakti, will enter into the path of sushumna and unite with the upper pole of energy. During that period or thereafter, experiences will come to you. These experiences are not only psychic visions, they are glimpses of energy operating on various realms of your existence. At this time, it is not possible for you to understand exactly what energy is and how it operates in various realms of human life and existence, but you can understand that this experience comes when you are not with the mind.

All intimate experiences are born from higher consciousness as a result of the awakening of energy. The experiences which are born of the mind you know very well: frustration, fear, anxiety, restlessness, depression, worry, passion, ambition, hatred. There are hundreds of thousands of experiences born of the mind. However, higher knowledge, higher consciousness, higher experiences are not born of the mind. Intuitive knowledge has nothing to do with the mind, no trace of the mind.

Therefore, as practitioners of kriya yoga, you must learn to live spontaneously, whether you are sannyasins or householders. If you have problems, if you have mental agonies, alright. What is the harm? If you have fears, passions, ambitions, alright. Do not waste your life fighting with these things. You will never be able to find a solution. There is no solution which you can find through the path of the mind.

The problems of the mind are the problems of Mulla Nasruddin. He has to realize that he need not shoot his wife, because she doesn't exist. In the same way, we have too much mental obsession. We are neurotic about our mental functions, "Oh, I am depressed. I am very violent. I am angry." Why do we think that way about ourselves? Why not plunge into the various paths of yoga instead?

Karma yoga will balance your mental problems, not jnana yoga, because those people who are very conscious of their problems will become more neurotic if they practise jnana yoga. Jnana yoga improves the quality of introspection, analysis, contemplation. So if it increases the capacity of contemplation, then you will contemplate more on your problems. By the practice of karma yoga, this extra obsession about your mental problems can be properly balanced. This is a hint I give to each and everybody who goes onto the path of kriya yoga.

The dawning of experience
When awakening takes place, everything known as mental experience disappears. There is absolute tranquillity. Here is a small parable about it. A guru and a disciple were travelling by night. They came to a cave and wanted to spend the night there. The disciple was a very timid fellow. Every now and then he used to say, "Guruji, it is so dark. I'm scared." So the guru would take a match and light it. "Ah, now I feel all right," the disciple would say. Then the light would go out and after some time the disciple would say, "Guruji I'm scared of the darkness."

So all night long the guru went on lighting matches. Finally, in the morning, the sun rose and the disciple wasn't scared any more. In the same way, when the experience dawns, then these problems of the mind will be nowhere. Then you don't have to continuously light matchsticks because they aren't going to help any more. You have been doing that for the last so many years. Stop it now.

Your teacher will tell you about ida, pingala and sushumna nadis; the various chakras and concentration on the chakra sound; how to awaken the shakti, the energy. As a result of awakening the energy, you will feel wonderfully tranquil and elevated. So I wish you all good experiences during your practice of kriya yoga. I may come to meet you again during satsang or I may not, that is not important. We shall try to maintain a link with each other on a different frequency which is higher than the mind.

11

Satsang

Satyananda Ashram, Mangrove Mountain, Australia, 2 December 1983

I have been searching a long time for my true path and have looked at many philosophies and religions. I cannot commit myself to any one. What can I do to find faith in myself?

The path is within yourself. When you are able to withdraw your mind from external experience, and the inner awareness blooms in some form or other, that is the path. The way is one and the destination is one, although the definitions may be many. Religions are many but the way is one.

When you look towards the outside world, it is the world of the senses and the mind through which you can experience the gross manifestation of divinity, creation, the external objects of cognition; this is what you do all the time. But when you try to cognize a thought, a feeling, an emotion or passion, you can't do it. You can feel its impact, but you can't cognize it.

That is your first limitation. You should go through this and then, in the same manner, the patterns of thought should be seen. What are the yantras and mandalas? What are the paintings that you have seen by some talented artist? What is abstract art? It is the form of feeling, emotion, fear, jealousy, love, compassion – that you should be able to see within yourself. That is the doorway which leads you to the inner path. When you are able to perceive your mental feeling, emotional feeling, in concrete form as you see a picture outside, then you have withdrawn yourself from external to internal. This is the meaning.

Until then, you are a gross man. You are just external, roving over the instinctive plane of animals, and you are not beyond that. That is the symptom or indication. When you see a ghost in a graveyard, what is it? It is your absolute and total fear personified. That is its form. In the same way, love and compassion also have forms. You can see these forms and, as I said, these yantras and mandalas are forms of the higher realities.

After this, you go in further, and as you go in the object of your concentration begins to shine within you. First of all, it shines only for a short while like a glow worm. Then you begin to retain it, and finally it becomes stabilized and remains there. The form will shine and illumine itself in the dark areas of your consciousness. That is the path.

Whether you concentrate on guru or on a particular symbol, it makes no difference. The path is only one. I may concentrate on the shivalingam; you may concentrate on Sri Krishna, the cross, a flame of fire; it is all the same. You see the difference because of your sectarian way of thinking, but the path is one. I like the shivalingam, that's all. You like the candle flame, Krishna or a yantra. That doesn't make the paths different. The goal is one and the paths are one. There are no different paths.

Therefore, what you should try to do is to withdraw and awaken the consciousness simultaneously, not one after the other, not one before the other. If awakening takes place before withdrawal, you will be schizophrenic and if withdrawal takes place without awakening, then it will be hypnosis. You will be in meditation for three hours without any experience and you will come out with nothing, because you had only withdrawn from the external world of perception, from the world of the senses.

Withdrawal is not final. If you want to withdraw, you can take LSD, hashish or any other drug, but that is not enough. You have to withdraw, about turn, number one, but simultaneously, you have to awaken that tiny flame of your consciousness which you have chosen to meditate upon, say in the form of a candle flame.

That tiny flame of the candle is the replica of your consciousness. Blue lotus, red lotus, shivalingam, cross, symbol of Om, they are all replicas or symbols of consciousness and this replica of consciousness must be maintained unbroken. Unbroken awakening of the consciousness and systematic withdrawal of the external awareness – that is the path.

I am a medical student. How can I best combine medicine and yoga to help myself and others?
Medical science is a very important science but it has limitations. It may or may not treat disease, but it cannot treat the patient. It has no science for the treatment of man's personality. Therefore, along with your medical practice, you should go deeper into the scientific aspects of yoga and side by side encourage your patients to practise yoga.

It is not only disease which one has to treat, it is the patient who has to be treated. There are many diseases which are born from the deeper mind. They are not merely viral, bacterial or infectious – that is a later stage. Anxiety, depression, passion, frustration, fears, insecurities and all these shades or qualities of your personality create disease.

Intellectually we know that disease is due to anxiety, depression, fear or passion, but knowledge of the cause of disease is not enough. You have to be able to awaken that area of your mind which can really influence the entire process of disease, how it came from anxiety and penetrated into the body.

Therefore, those who are practising medical science must have a deeper understanding of yoga science, yoga technology, hatha yoga postures and their effects on the human mechanism, raja yoga, *dhyana*, meditation, and *samadhi*, supreme equanimity, and how these relate to various dimensions of human consciousness. That is how you can integrate these two important sciences.

If one is participating in the world with inner detachment, is it possible to arouse hostility and resentment in others because they sense this inner detachment? How can one behave so that this doesn't happen?

Inner detachment is a philosophy; it is not an external show. You don't have to express it in your day-to-day action. When you are operating in the family, shop or office, you must work like a normal person. Don't say, "I am so detached." Don't even show that. If you make it an external show, then definitely everybody will become hostile towards you. They will say, "A crazy man has come."

What is the connection between childhood suffering and karma?

During our childhood, we undergo a lot of experiences about which we have no knowledge. Even in the womb, we receive *samskaras*, impressions. When we are born, when we are one year, six months or even three months old, we don't understand what is happening around us, but the inner spirit, the inner man is exposed to everything clearly.

These impressions or samskaras which are imprinted on you during childhood or even in the mother's womb are experienced by you later in life. What you are experiencing today as grown-up people, you have already experienced from when you were a child. Parents are careless; they think that a baby is ignorant and so their expressions and their behaviour are not proper.

With each and every action, they are exposing the child to a certain karma or samskara. This seed which forms in the personality during childhood grows and later that becomes your personality. Therefore, through the practice of antar mouna, you must try to go back to your childhood and realize what mistakes your parents have committed.

What kind of people are the kriyas most suited for?

Kriya yoga is a sadhana of the tantric system and, therefore, those people who want to awaken their energy without coming into conflict with the mind will be very suited to kriya yoga. Kriya is for those people who have already fought with their mind for many years and have not achieved anything. For the people of this age, whose minds are restless all the time and who cannot concentrate, kriya yoga is very suitable.

My sadhana includes japa. If I practise kriyas at home, should this be in addition to or instead of japa?
Mantra is an independent practice. Whether you practise kriya yoga or any other type of sadhana, the repetition of mantra should be done at any cost because the awakening of the mantra potential is very important for any kind of higher experience.

I came to do the kriya yoga course in order to control my excessive energy. However I have been told that the kriya practices increase energy. What should I do?
You must meditate and in meditation you should continue to see the inner form, the symbol. At the same time, you must devote some time to selfless service, karma yoga.

Can you explain to me the two paths to self-realization: one, by bringing energy to consciousness, two, by bringing consciousness to energy?
Yoga is the path of bringing consciousness to energy and tantra is the path of bringing energy to consciousness. These are two concepts. Yoga is directing the mind towards the centre of energy, *shakti*, but in tantra, before dealing with the mind, you awaken the energy or shakti through various means like kriya yoga. When this energy awakens it transforms the whole consciousness.

How can we reach samadhi when we have to struggle to get there by various methods, even if those methods are yogic?
To achieve samadhi or anything in life, you have to make an effort. Sometimes you try this way and sometimes the other way. You are not sure about it, but if you live with the guru,

he will tell you which way you have to take. Attainment of samadhi is not a struggle but a peaceful journey, a peaceful pilgrimage.

How does creative or artistic thought and action relate to the yogic path? Should it be expressed or, like siddhis, be merely witnessed and not indulged in?

Yoga practitioners at some time or another do become creative. They should understand that they should use these faculties as well, but they must ask their guru how to use them. Displays of clairvoyance, clairaudience, telepathy, telekinesis, etc., should not be practised just because you have attained them. You must have knowledge of the laws of nature. It is very important to have this knowledge.

Nature brings man into difficulties. Suppose a person abuses himself and suffers from tuberculosis. A yogi comes along and with the help of his siddhis he just cures him – but he is interfering with the laws of nature because nature meant to correct this man. Therefore, a siddha should know more about the utilization of these siddhis, and this is why one has to live with the guru for a long time.

It is said that ashram life accelerates spiritual progress. Would this apply to most people?

There are two types of knowledge or *vidya*. One is empirical and the other is spiritual. Empirical knowledge is what you call secular knowledge: history, geography, mathematics, etc. The other form of knowledge is spiritual knowledge, by which you realize your own self. It was for this that the ashram system was established many thousands of years ago.

An *ashram* is not a monastery or organization, but a place where you are taught how to realize your spiritual self. That is the purpose of and ashram and therefore everyone who is a seeker on the spiritual path must expose himself to ashram life. Of course, it is a very different life and it should be different.

A few years ago when this ashram was being established, some of the friends who were associated with this movement were not satisfied with it. They wanted separate rooms, central heating, tables and chairs and other things. I did not agree with them. Of course, I did not tell them that if these things were introduced it would not be at all necessary for one to come and live in the ashram.

In India, people go on pilgrimages to purify the *tattwas*, the elements, of the body and mind. They go to an ashram in order to work hard for their mental and spiritual liberation. In the olden days the ashrams were very different. The householders used to go and live with the guru, practise all their spiritual things and, at the same time, participate in the activities of the ashram totally.

I can tell you one story. It is a very famous story in India. It is said that Sri Krishna, who is the author of the *Bhagavad Gita*, who is venerated as an incarnation of divinity by millions and millions of Hindus and who has inspired the Hindu philosophy to such a great extent – he lived with his guru in the ashram for twelve years.

One day he went into the forest with his class mate Sudama. Sudama was a very poor Brahmin's son who hardly had anything to eat. Sri Krishna was the son of a king, but both of them lived in the ashram and worked for the guru. Krishna felt hungry while he was collecting the firewood and asked Sudama, "Hey, have you brought anything to eat?" Sudama said, "Yes, I have a handful of rice." He gave it to Krishna who ate it with great relish.

When Sri Krishna and Sudama returned home after completing their education with their guru, Sudama reverted to the state of a poor Brahmin, while Sri Krishna became the leader of a kingdom of thousands of people. One day Sudama's wife suddenly remembered, "Hey, we are living such a life of poverty and penury, and your friend Krishna is an emperor. Why don't you go and get a little from him so that we can become free of poverty?"

Sudama didn't want to go, but his wife insisted. So, finally, remembering the day he spent with Sri Krishna in the forest, he took a handful of rice and went to meet his friend. When he arrived at the gates of the palace, Sri Krishna came to welcome him and brought him inside. He made him take a bath and gave him fresh garments to put on. When they were both seated together, the first question Sri Krishna asked Sudama was, "Have you got a handful of that rice for me? I am feeling so hungry."

You know, if you were to visit the house of a very rich man and give him a handful of rice as a present, you would feel so bad about it. Usually people give some beautiful things on a gold or silver plate, and he had only this handful of rice to offer to an emperor. So he was hesitant, but Sri Krishna took the rice and consumed it with great gusto, remembering his ashram days and the simple life he had shared with his friend Sudama.

This is the type of ashram we should have here, where the richest and poorest, most virtuous and most vicious, most peaceful and most restless people, all live and work together in harmony. Because in the ashram we do not only exchange associations with each other, nor do we just meet each other physically. We are exchanging energies with each other. We are sharing, partaking, vibrating within the same energy fields.

Because we have become gross and materialistic, we can only understand matter. We don't know that the body is not the only dimension of our existence. We are not just this body; we are beyond the body. When we go to the ashram, we find those positive, spiritual energies flow there, which our mind can't understand and which we can't see or smell, but our inner being understands them very well.

Therefore, in order to maintain the nobility, the serenity and the greatness of those vibrations, it is important that ashrams should be simple, simpler, simplest – nothing artificial. An ashram is not an expression of man's desire; it is a place which gives you what you need – not what you want. The moment desire comes in, the place is polluted, whether it is an ashram, temple, sanctum sanctorum, church or paradise. Even God's house can be polluted if desire comes in there.

Simplicity is another name for divine vibration. For the acceleration of your spiritual nature and experience, expose yourself more and more to the ashram life. When ashrams become an expression of man's desire, then they lose their greatness. Swami Sivananda, my guru, used to say, "Ashrams are born, are created, on account of the pure, mental ray of a yogic sankalpa, not on account of desire."

When you go to the ashram, you must participate in all its activities so that you can contribute to the ashram's progress and growth. If selfless workers work in the ashram for its development, they will also get the reward. The growth of the ashram and your spiritual growth will increase simultaneously.

12

Mantra Yoga

Satyananda Ashram, Mangrove Mountain, Australia, 4 December 1983

Sound is the primordial form of energy, the original substance and basis of the whole universe. This universe with its solar systems, its invisible fields of energy, is an expansion of sound energy. This sound is known as *shabda* in yoga, 'the word' in the Bible, the *mantra* in the tantric system. You must understand that mantra is neither religious nor sectarian. It is not Christian, Hindu, Islamic or Jewish. Mantra is a form of sound.

Sound has different stages of manifestation. Every type of energy, from the primordial to the manifest state, undergoes transformations, changes frequency, velocity, etc. When we talk about mantra, we are definitely talking about one of the manifestations of this primordial energy. Each letter and syllable of the mantra penetrates deep down into various levels of your consciousness.

Man is limited – mind is not

Modern psychology says that mind has three dimensions: conscious, subconscious and unconscious. Thousands of years ago, Indian tantric philosophers said that there are three levels of consciousness: gross, subtle and causal. These three classifications of mind are very broad and general. This mind which you do not know has millions of layers and during your lifetime, during one day of your life, you are functioning on more than one level of awareness. This you must understand.

During the twenty-four hours of the day, whether you are happy or unhappy, your consciousness is functioning or you are living in different realms or layers of this consciousness. You are not existing on just one layer. Not only you but even animals and vegetables are not functioning on one layer of consciousness. By practice and training you can develop your awareness so that you are able to function on thousands and millions of layers of consciousness during your lifetime.

Objective awareness, subjective awareness and transcendental awareness are the broad classifications of awareness. You find it difficult to function on all levels at the same time because you have limitations. Human beings have limitations. You are able to function only within your limited range of awareness and not beyond that. Through the practice of yoga, you will have to overcome these limitations so that you are able to function on unlimited layers of mind and consciousness, but how do we break the boundary? How can we break the confines of evolution? It is possible by sound.

Sound is an explosive force. Even the gross form of sound can completely destroy big rocks. Mantra represents this science. Because of religious training, when a mantra is given to you, you feel that it is something akin to religion and in order to practise it you must be very pious and virtuous, but mantra is more than that. As sound attains higher frequency, the mind also attains a higher frequency. With the evolution of sound, the mind also evolves. Therefore, the mantra which you receive from your guru is a very important force, an important element in the process of your spiritual experience. Remember, constant repetition of mantra has something to do with your consciousness.

Process of disassociation

While repeating the mantra it is not necessary that you should try to concentrate the mind. I have always been telling everyone throughout the world that it is not important to fight with the mind – you must ignore it because there is no such thing as mind. As you go on repeating the mantra, as you are aware of the mantra, you will find that everything is setting into a capsule of experience, and this experience is born of mantra. This experience is not a quality of mind.

The hallucinations and imaginations which you have are the qualities of the mind. An experience of kundalini or of psychic upliftment is not a product of mind. Therefore, the philosophy that the mind should be transformed, pulverized, purified is not a sound philosophy. It is religious philosophy, not a tantric philosophy. The religious philosophies say, "Purify your mind." How can you purify the mind? On the one hand you say that the mind is nothing but a bundle of evil thoughts, and on the other hand you are asking about purifying the mind. You are trying to clean charcoal with Surf.

You will have to ignore the idiosyncrasies of your mind. It has passions, ambitions, jealousy, fears, insecurities and depressions – let them be! Do not worry at all about the mind. That can be done only by the mantra. By continual practice of the mantra you are gradually becoming disassociated from the mental neurosis. I call it psychoneurosis. All of you are neurotics. You are totally neurotic because you say, "I am getting angry, my God! I am feeling jealous; it is bad! No. Why is my mind always thinking and thinking?" This is neurosis. We are all neurotics, obsessed by the mind.

Throughout the world, if you meet people, if you read a lot of books, you will find that everything is directed towards the mind. Modern conditioning has made you so aware of the mind that you are totally affected by it – therefore, you cannot handle it. Do you think that you can handle the mind by analyzing or by intellectualizing? No! You can never handle it that way. You are only suppressing it. When you maintain constant awareness of the mantra, then gradually you learn to be disassociated.

This may take you many years, not just a few days or one week. You may feel better in one week because the more you are away from this idiot mind, the better you will feel, but one week is nothing. It takes time, as disassociation of yourself from the mind is a slow process. You become less and less acquainted; the distance grows. That is the meaning of mantra. The word *mantra* literally means 'by the repetition of which you are freed, you are disassociated'. Mantra does not mean the name of a god or goddess. It means this, 'by the contemplation of which you become free'. Therefore, mantra should be understood in this light.

Methods of practice

When you practise mantra in the beginning, there are certain methods which you have to adopt for some time – practising mantra with the mala, with the breath in various chakras, in the path of sushumna, sometimes pronouncing it audibly, increasing the speed or decreasing the speed, and sometimes pronouncing it mentally. There are so many ways of practising mantra.

The best way is to chant it audibly, then practise it whispering, then mentally. Finally, practise it with your natural breath, deep breath and deeper breath. These are the four main ways of practising mantra. The audible repetition of mantra has greater velocity and less frequency. When you practise mantra with your natural breath, it has greater frequency and less velocity. The greater the frequency, the greater the strength, willpower and vision it gives to your consciousness.

The kundalini energy

Mantra will also become a very important and effective tool for the awakening of that energy which is in constant motion and which, in the process of evolution, is called *kundalini*. You must remember that when we talk about mantra, yoga and tantra, we are also concerned with kundalini, which has been trying to manifest itself in various forms. It has expressed itself in the past when the spirit passed through various incarnations, mineral, vegetable, animal and subhuman. They were manifestations of energy, and now this energy which relates to your further evolution is called kundalini energy.

So far this energy has brought changes, transformation, metamorphosis on the material plane. Thus you evolved from mineral to vegetable, from vegetable to animal and from animal to human forms. This is how evolution took place for millions of years and finally the manifestation is now in the form of this mind, body and other planes that are within us. This is called human evolution and to this extent we have evolved.

However, this is not the last point in evolution. Materially and physically this is the last point in evolution, but with the birth of a human being, the whole process of evolution has taken a new turn from gross to subtle. I am sure that hereafter, in human beings, inner evolution will take place and not outer evolution; not evolution on the level of matter but in the matter of the inner being.

When I say inner being, I mean mind, spirit consciousness, experience, vision, knowledge, but this evolution is not an intellectual substance. You can think about it, but you can't always have it. You can only get it by virtue of experience, and this experience relates to the motion of kundalini energy.

The spiritual experience
A child of four or five has emotional, mental and intellectual limitations. When he becomes twelve, those limitations are gone and he has a different type of emotional, mental and social awareness. Again when he becomes twenty-five, it changes. In exactly the same way, the manifestation of kundalini, the spiritual awareness, will begin to unfold itself.

What is that spiritual experience? Is it an experience of something external, of gods or goddesses or something in a temple or church, or is it the experience of the whole of the cosmos? Is it an experience of the solar system or the vibrant energy in creation? What exactly is that experience and is it exclusive of that experience which we are having now? Is this experience which you are having now a part of that total experience or excluded from it?

Many people say that when you go high, then you don't have this experience. It does happen. There is a level or point of awareness where you have an experience which is not the experience you are having now and this external experience is completely dead to you. You don't know names and forms, you don't know yourself, you don't know this substance, you don't know this time and space and creation. No, you don't know anything at that time. However this is not the ultimate experience, because the ultimate experience is not exclusive, it is homogeneous.

Homogeneous experience is that experience which is made up of one part. This body is not homogeneous. It is a combination of different components. Your mind is not homogeneous. It is also made of components; it is divisible. But this experience is homogeneous, that is, all experiences are experienced at the same time and although you stay separate, you begin to realize and understand that you and the whole macrocosmos are one. This is the nature of total experience and that experience begins with the awakening of kundalini.

How to handle it
To awaken the kundalini, mantra is the easiest, safest, cheapest and best aid, although it is not the quickest way of all. It is necessary that you should not go after the quickest paths because you may not be able to handle the experiences arising out of them. It is important to have the experience, but it is more important to have the capacity to handle that experience. Therefore, when you go on this path, you must first experience a little and adjust yourself, then have a deeper and deeper experience, and go on adjusting yourself.

Having an experience, adjusting yourself and then progressing, you can go very far safely, but if you begin to have the deepest experience now, you may not be able to handle it. You may not be able to drive your motor car or do anything. Therefore, the evolution of spirit must take place progressively. With the progressive method of japa or mantra yoga, you will be able to have a very rich, abiding and perennial experience.

13

Satsang

Satyananda Ashram, Mangrove Mountain, Australia, 7 December 1983

Do mantra and symbol complement the practices of kriya? Can we practise both together?
Kriya yoga is practised independently. However, you can integrate your own mantra into the fifth practice if you wish. Supposing your mantra is *Shreem*, you can replace *Soham* by *Shreem*, or if you like, you can continue with *Soham*. It is not important. In kriya yoga there is a different system of meditation at the end. These practices should not be replaced by your personal yantra, symbol or mandala.

However, you can practise your own mantra and meditation on that mantra quite independently of kriya yoga. Mantra yoga and kriya yoga are two different forms of yoga. You can practise both of them or you can practise one of them. It is not important that mantra and symbol should be integrated with kriya yoga.

Is it possible to experience sahaja samadhi in one lifetime?
Sahaja samadhi is the term which had been used here. *Sahaja* means 'spontaneous, without any effort'. *Samadhi* is a state in which the gross mind drops away completely. There is no empirical, objective awareness in samadhi. Maybe in the initial stages there is a slight awareness of the experience and the

process of experience, but finally, in the state of samadhi, the personal mind, depending on the ego, on the individuality, drops away completely. This means that in samadhi there is no egocentric, individual awareness.

However, in samadhi, the inner experience is slightly different. Those who go exclusively through the path of bhakti yoga have the experience called trance. Trance is a kind of samadhi in which the merging of the individual mind takes place through a practice of growing emotion and devotion. In raja yoga, you are controlling the mind, the patterns of the mind. You control every *vritti* or formation of thought, and by suppressing, by blocking and stopping the manifestations of the mind, you come to a state of *shoonyata* or void.

Here the process is by suppression, by blocking each and every *vritti* or pattern of mind. That is raja yoga, whereas in bhakti yoga there is no suppression. You awaken your emotion, ecstatic feeling or bhava. *Bhava* means ecstatic feeling based on devotion. Devotion is emotion directed towards divinity. Just as passion is emotion directed towards empirical things, devotion is the same emotion directed towards divinity. This devotion and emotion has to be expressed and when you awaken it, you enter into a state of trance. That is called *bhava samadhi*, by which you awaken the emotion through devotion.

Raja yoga talks about savikalpa samadhi and nirvikalpa samadhi. Savikalpa samadhi means samadhi by controlling the fluctuations of this mind. When all the fluctuations are controlled, that is called *nirvikalpa samadhi*. When most of the fluctuations are controlled but something remains somewhere, that is called *savikalpa samadhi*. This is raja yoga.

When you practise karma yoga, where you are expressing your body and mind, where you are not creating tension and fighting with your conflicts, you grow side by side with passions, with desire, with instincts in short, but at the same time internal purification is taking place. The result of internal purification is mental balance.

Here you must remember that mental balance is of two kinds. One kind of mental balance is the psychological process in which you are trying to maintain balance of mind because you think that it is necessary to have good health, good relationships, a good home and a good society, although inside everything is totally unbalanced. Inside everything is in turmoil, but externally you are maintaining a compulsory mental balance because you know that it is good. I am not talking of that balance. When the purification of mind takes place by a constant, relentless and prolonged process of elimination of karma, that purification results in real mental balance.

When you have a bad stomach, it is very uncomfortable. You pass very bad wind and have very bad dreams. Then it affects your liver and other parts of your body. Somebody tells you to practise shankhaprakshalana and it cleans your stomach completely. Even as you clean your stomach through the practice of shankhaprakshalana, in the same way, you have to clean your mind.

The mind cannot be cleaned without undergoing a process of purging. What is this purging? You have a lot of pains in your mind – that's purging. You have bad dreams in the night – that's purging. You get angry many times – that's purging. Like this, nature has created many ways of purging. We do not like them all because we think they are unethical and immoral. We think that it is barbaric to get angry, that it is savage. Passions, desires, anger, frustration, disappointment, greed, jealousy, fears, all these are outlets created by nature for all human beings to practise shankhaprakshalana. They are nature's way of cleansing.

How can you clean the mind? In bhakti yoga there is no such provision. Here God is fine, his glory is fine, his creation is fine, his devotees are fine, the sanctum sanctorum is fine, the flowers and the priest are fine. Everything is so nice there. In raja yoga everything is wonderful and clean: truth, non-violence, celibacy, contentment, non-greed, non-aggrandization, physical and mental purity. You understand how nice these systems are, but you are not facing life there. You are not facing yourself because everything is so nice.

However, in karma yoga you face everything. "This swami talks like a big boss. Oh, what is he talking about? He eats so much, like a glutton, and when I go for food, he says the vegetable is finished. I am working just as hard as he is and when I eat twenty chapatis, he looks at me. I am working on the building and he is going away and talking to that girl. He doesn't work. I'm working so much while he is having a nice time with her." This you can only face in karma yoga, when you are concerned with the affairs of life, when your body is in demand, when your emotions are in demand and when you are relating yourself to every Tom, Dick and Harry.

At that time, you can make a clear classification of the sattwic, rajasic and tamasic nature of individuals. Go closely with yourself. Observe everybody's behaviour impartially without judging anyone, and just see on which level your mind is floating. Sometimes you are full of remorse and guilt. Sometimes you are arrogant and sometimes you are as idiotic as a pig. Sometimes you are as angry as a demon and sometimes you are a gentleman. Sometimes you are a saint. The process of the threefold universal nature of man can be realized by you only in karma yoga. If you do not know yourself in the external life, how can you purify?

Gradually, through the practice of karma yoga, the mind obtains absolute tranquillity within and without. You are at peace with yourself and with everybody else. At this time, when you sit for meditation with your eyes closed or open, after practising kriya yoga or without practising kriya yoga, the mind begins to drop away without any effort and you don't know what is happening to you.

Even as sleep comes to a person who is tired after his day's labour, in the same way, to a person who has practised karma yoga in right earnest, without the sense of ego, with total detachment and dedication, who has yoked his body, mind, emotions, passions, violence, his demonical and animal nature completely to work, spontaneous samadhi comes. This spontaneous samadhi is called sahaja samadhi and it can be had by one in this very life if he understands the role of karma yoga.

Why is it that I have the limited concept of seeing myself as an individual?

Not only you, but everybody in this world is controlled by ego and this ego separates us from others. We are all one and the same energy, one and the same matter, one and the same consciousness. The stuff is one. We are not thousands, millions or billions; we are just one, but we have this individual ego, *ahamkara*, and because of this we operate as separate individuals.

One electrical energy comes into this hall, but you see dozens of lights; they appear to be different to an ignorant person because, if you turn off one switch, only one light will go off, not all the others. If you switch off two, only two lights will go off, not the rest. Thereby, it logically appears that each and every light is different because each has an individual switch. If there were no individual switches, but only one switch to control all the lights, then by putting off one switch all the lights would be switched off.

In the same way, during the process of evolution, the individual has developed this ego in himself and this ego is the remnant of his animal incarnation. Now that we have become human beings, we are trying to realize this ego and by realizing it we are trying to understand that it is through this ego that the separation is experienced. Therefore, in order to rise above individuality and become one with the universality of existence, every field of existence, you have to practise various yogas in order to transcend this ahamkara or individuality.

Is evolution of life on earth in harmony with life in the rest of the universe?

I am no authority on the universe. It is too much for me to claim to know what are the laws of the universe and what is the universe. As we experience this universe now, it is so vast that we can only understand that there is something beyond the sun and something beyond that and something beyond that again. The scientists have been telling us that there are endless creations, hundreds and thousands of suns and solar systems, and this universe as matter is expanding.

In each and every scriptural text, we read about the endless universes and endless creations, their distances from each other and how many suns, moons, solar systems and endless galaxies there are. This is just man's concept of the universe, which is perceived with this gross and limited mind. This is very important. In physics also we have learned about it. The relativity of creation, the relativity of the universe, everything has to be understood in its absolute form.

The relative universe and the absolute universe are not the same. The relative universe is the experience of your relative mind and senses. If monkeys, elephants and donkeys had a philosophy, what would their concept of the universe be? If these animals were endowed with the philosophical capacity of mind as we are in the environment in which they live, what would their philosophy of the universe be?

They would be talking about the laws of universal nature. Thousands and thousands of donkeys gathered together would all be satsangis. They would have satsang. One donkey who is the guru of the group would sit down and another donkey would ask him, "Guruji, please tell us about the nature of the universe." The donkey guru would tell him, "The nature of the universe is to grow more grass."

You see, what can we say about the laws of the universe? We have a relative mind which is composed of time, space and matter, and that is the ultimate boundary, the ultimate confinement of this mind. It is true that the mind cannot go, cannot think or operate beyond these three. Try to think about anything, even about God, paradise or samadhi. You are thinking within the limits of time, space and matter, nothing beyond that, although God is beyond, paradise is beyond and samadhi is also beyond.

We know about the laws of nature related to this body and the world around us. However, Einstein, the great scientist, used to speak about relativity and absolutism. This was a part of his scientific philosophy. The Upanishads, written many thousands of years ago, talk about three forms of existence: relative, absolute and illusory.

One type of experience you have through your senses, through your mind, by coming in contact with the object. This is relative experience. It is dependent on the quality of your mind and senses, and on the nature of the matter with which your mind and senses come in touch.

When you dream, the experiences which you have are nothing to do with your senses or with your environment. They are a product of the archetypes which are stored in your unconscious mind. They are illusory. When you take drugs like ganja, hashish, LSD, etc., the experiences which you have at that time are not relative and they are by no means absolute. They are illusory.

The third type is absolute experience and I don't know how I am going to explain that to you. In relative experience there is no homogeneity. Everything is a compound, a combination of many things. But in absolute experience, there is total homogeneity. It is not made up of components.

Now, the law of nature here is relative. As long as we are operating through our mind and senses, all our experiences are relative. Therefore, our knowledge about nature is also relative. This nature is of two types. One is the lower, empirical nature and the other is cosmic nature. We are not talking about cosmic nature at the moment. We are talking about the lower, empirical nature.

This empirical nature is composed of eight elements: earth, water, fire, air, ether, mind, intelligence and ego. Please do not mistake this nature for the forest, rivers, valleys, hills, dales, rivulets, pastures, gardens, sky, clouds, sun and moon. That is not nature in this sense; that is a product of nature.

In India, nature is known as *prakriti*. Prakriti is the philosophical term for nature. Prakriti is twofold as I told you: empirical and cosmic. About cosmic prakriti I prefer to remain silent, but about empirical prakriti I told you that it is composed of eight elements. This nature is permanently present in each and every substance. Human beings are no exception and in no way superior. The earth, minerals, vegetables, animals, humans, all visible and invisible beings; each and every thing is composed of this eightfold prakriti.

Throughout creation, this eightfold prakriti is in constant motion; it is never static. However, when the whole cosmos is disintegrated, when there is no life anymore, no substance, no matter, no object anywhere; when time, space and matter contract into one nucleus and there is no creation, as it was in the beginning, prakriti is static. There is no motion. When there is motion in prakriti, then there is creation, existence, growth, death, birth and rebirth.

Each and everything is growing from one form into another, and as prakriti takes a forward leap, thousands and thousands of human beings begin to experience the awakening of kundalini. This prakriti which I am speaking about is something very fundamental and basic, something of which we are all composed.

You must remember that there are two eternal realities, although the monistic schools of philosophy and religion don't agree with this. They believe in non-duality. For example, *advaita vedanta* says there is only one reality – consciousness – and nature is produced from that reality. This is the monistic philosophy – one God, everything else, no. But this is not totally logical or scientific.

According to Samkhya philosophy and to yoga and tantra, there are two eternal realities cohabiting with each other, interrelating with each other, moving with each other, interspersed with each other. They are known as purusha and prakriti. *Purusha* means consciousness – no name, no form, no house, no address, no identity, nothing! Consciousness is here, there, everywhere. It is in you, in me, in everyone. It is far yet near – consciousness, soul, spirit, *atma*.

The other aspect of reality is prakriti. Prakriti is primordial nature and out of this prakriti two things can be seen. One is called matter and the other is called energy. This is what you study in physics. Matter and energy are both produced by nature. Nature is the creatrix of matter and energy. Whether prakriti created matter first and then energy or the other way around is not important at the moment. Matter and energy are one aspect of reality and consciousness is another.

In tantra, through various paths of yoga we are moving from material, gross, sensorial consciousness to the field of energy, kundalini shakti. When we have arrived at and realized this energy, then we have to make the leap, we have to go beyond this, because awakening of kundalini and realizing this energy is not the ultimate experience. It is not even the ultimate destiny. The ultimate destiny of everyone is to realize this consciousness which is beyond prakriti. Therefore, the law of this world, the law of this empirical nature starts with prakriti and brings us closer to consciousness or purusha.

Do vivid and powerful dreams signify that one's consciousness is evolving and should one act upon these dreams?

Dreams come from you, even as thoughts and feelings emanate from you. They come from various depths of your mind, from the subconscious as well as the unconscious. There are three divisions of awareness: gross awareness, astral awareness and causal awareness. This is according to Samkhya philosophy. They call it: gross body, astral body and causal body. These three are further subdivided into five fields: physiological field, pranic field, mental field, psychic field and unconscious blissful field. In philosophy they are known as the five *koshas*: annamaya kosha, pranamaya kosha, manomaya kosha, vijnanamaya kosha and anandamaya kosha.

Now, when we dream, these dreams emerge from *vijnanamaya kosha*, the psychic field. They are related to the quality of our mind, the quality of our experience and the nature of love, hatred, frustration, etc., that have been embedded in the subconscious mind in the course of our interactions with life. These dreams do not really mean anything because they only disclose the quality of karma or samskara, the quality of the stock of our mind.

When you practise yoga and are able to go beyond vijnanamaya kosha, or the psychic field, into *anandamaya kosha*, the unconscious field, vivid dreams, reality dreams, living dreams, are experienced by you. Such dreams indicate that you are operating in a different field of consciousness. Of course, most of the time they will not relate to realities at all. They are symbolic. They are just the awareness of what is already there.

I must also tell you that these fields are related to your karma, to your life and to your experience. The karmas are threefold: predestined karmas, which must be experienced at some later time; current karmas, which you are experiencing now; and accumulated karmas, which you have already experienced and which are stored within you.

These accumulated experiences or karmas can remain in the subconscious mind and in the unconscious as well. Some of the experiences are so deep and tangible that they go from the conscious mind to the subconscious mind and then straight into the unconscious. These are called archetypes. The force of this unconscious karma sometimes makes us mad because we have no control over it.

When the force of the subconscious karma influences your mind, you can face it by discrimination, by analysis – but when the unconscious mind explodes it can bring any thought, it can develop, expose and explode any kind of archetype. Therefore, when you are having vivid and clear dreams, you need not interpret them. They are not necessarily prophesies or predictions. They can just be the expression of the archetypes, but it definitely means that you have entered into the fifth body or the fifth realm or your mind.

14

Satsang

Satyananda Ashram, Mangrove Mountain, Australia, 10 December 1983

How can I receive your guidance and maintain a relationship with you without knowing you personally.
The attitude of a disciple should not be like this. The distance is only physical. In fact, guru and disciple are inseparable entities. They are joined together by an invisible link. It is not important that we live to together physically, but guru and disciple should be together in spirit. They should be together in inner consciousness and thereby spiritual upliftment takes place rapidly.

Could you please talk about the tantric disciple?
A tantric disciple is an evolved soul. He has already accomplished a lot of spiritual things in his previous incarnations. He is not raw material but almost a finished product. He becomes a disciple in order to be the link, the medium for the energy of his guru. Just as electrical energy is conducted through the wires and poles and switchboards, etc., in the same way, the guru's energy and knowledge is conducted to various corners of the world by such disciples known as tantric disciples.

What is the relationship between the symbol given to us and our personality?

There is, in fact, no direct relationship between the symbol and your personality. The personality is one thing and the symbol is entirely different. The purpose of the symbol is to awaken the inner spirit, the inner awareness, so that the external mind will be fused and united in that. After that your present personality undergoes a change. Mantra has a lot to do with your personality, name has a lot to do with your personality, but yantra, the symbol on which you meditate, can change your personality and transform it totally.

Can you tell us if by regular practice and devotion, everybody will be able to awaken kundalini?

The path of devotion is the path of bhakti yoga, but bhakti should not be understood in the religious sense. Religion and bhakti are not the same and when you practise a religion, you don't necessarily practise bhakti.

Bhakti is intense awareness of the object you love. This love and attachment is not intellectual, not merely ritualistic, not just an expression of a particular cult. It is a part of your being. You don't have to learn how to love, how to practise attachment. They are already in you. You have brought the essential elements of attachment from your animal incarnations. Attachment is the remnant of instinct. Therefore, this attachment that is in you can be sublimated.

The practice of bhakti is mind-consuming. It is such a powerful path! Once you can handle it, awakening is just a joke, but if you understand bhakti as prayer, rituals, reading of scriptures or just talking about God, then you have missed the point. Those people who have practised bhakti yoga in utmost sincerity have lived a life of total madness. They have not cared for anything substantial, significant or important in this life. For them, love, devotion, bhakti to that ultimate substance has been the sole purpose. They did not care if they were executed or killed, criticized of kicked or even annihilated completely.

Bhakti completely releases the mind from material attachments, from material associations. You can only imagine it. When you love someone in this world intensely, maybe your child, maybe your boyfriend or girlfriend, what happens to you? You overcome many things and many ideas. Even by loving these mortal things, the child or friend, you are able to overcome, to transcend. If you have any idea about how to love the eternal self, transcendence will be a matter of joking.

I will tell a true story from history. There was a princess living in the sixteenth century. She was the daughter of a powerful king in the western part of India. When she was six years old a sannyasin visited the royal palace and gave her a small idol of Sri Krishna. It was very beautiful and this little girl began to think that Sri Krishna would be her husband. When she grew up she was married to another powerful king in western India near Udaipur.

She lived with her husband, but she always thought that Sri Krishna was her husband. She used to say, "Krishna alone is my husband and nobody else." Finally she renounced the kingdom and came to Vrindavan, where Sri Krishna was born and lived there for the rest of her life. At the end she turned her body into light particles and completely disappeared. Her name was Mirabai and she is considered to be the example of supreme devotion.

Ramakrishna, the mad saint of India in the last century, used to say, "If you can turn your attachment from your parents, if you can transform your attachment to your male or female friend, if you can transform and turn your attachment from your property, wealth and all things, and direct it to the one self, the one being, you can find Him here and now. That is what he used to say, "Here and now!"

Once some people wanted Ramakrishna to tell them how to have that supreme experience. Ramakrishna said that he would tell them later at the proper time. One day in Calcutta they were travelling by boat on the Ganga and the same man who had put the question was there. Ramakrishna threw him into the river and he began to howl and cry and scream. When he was brought back, Ramakrishna asked him, "How did you feel when you were out in the river?" He replied, "Oh, I was praying for my life." Ramakrishna said, "Now do that for Him!"

When you talk about devotion, when you talk about bhakti for God, for guru, for anyone, do you have the same intensity of feeling as you have when you are being drowned? No! Our bhakti is lukewarm. With lukewarm devotion nothing happens. We are neither satisfied nor does the experience take place – but there is always a 'but'. What will happen to my car if that supreme devotion takes place? What will happen to my television? Who will pay my bills? You see this 'but' is there and because of this 'but' there is a stopper.

For a true bhakta, awakening of kundalini is just a joke. You can awaken your kundalini through pranayama, karma yoga, bhakti yoga, kirtan, raja yoga, kriya yoga, right hand tantra and left hand tantra. There are many ways, but which is most suitable for you?

If you are a fellow with attachment, then how can you practise bhakti yoga? In bhakti yoga you will have to withdraw all your attachments and direct them towards some being – all, not just fifty percent, sixty percent or ninety percent of your attachment. Not even ninety-nine percent. One hundred percent of the attachment which you have for anyone has to be withdrawn and directed towards one being. That is called bhakti!

Can you tell us about Kali and her relevance to modern conditions, like the relationships between men and women in the modern world?

In India, Kali is a very important and divine entity. Although terrible to behold, she is considered to be a benign, compassionate protector, patron and helper. They call her Kali Ma. *Kali* means 'black' and *Ma* means 'mother'. She is worshipped and venerated by all. Nobody minds what she looks like.

When songs are sung in her praise, if you were to read the translation, you would think they are being sung to a beautiful maiden; but she is absolutely black, very fat and horrible to look at. Her tongue is projecting out and bloody. Her eyes are wide open as if she has just taken whisky, and she wears a garland of skulls, not a tulsi mala which is for sattwic people. She wears snake amulets, bracelets and garlands of snakes. She has six arms and very large breasts.

Kali stands on the body of Shiva who is supposed to be her male counterpart. According to Hindu mythology, every human being is a combination of male and female. The right side is the male aspect and the left side is the female aspect. The right side is known as Shiva and the left as Shakti. This is precisely the concept of the sympathetic and parasympathetic nervous divisions. Kali stands with one foot on the body of Shiva who is lying completely helpless beneath her, while she is dancing over him.

Kali is a part of the trinity. You understand what the trinity is. In India, we also have the trinity. There is a male trinity and there is also a female trinity. The female trinity is made up of Kali, Lakshmi and Saraswati. These three deities represent the three levels related to the awakening of *shakti* or the female power in man.

The female power in man is known as kundalini, and the awakening of kundalini is experienced in three different stages. The first is Kali. When Kali consciousness awakens with the awakening of kundalini, individuality is suppressed and that is indicated by Kali dancing on the body of Shiva. *Shiva* represents consciousness and when the awakening of kundalini takes place, the consciousness is suppressed and awakening of kundalini is dominant.

That is the first expression of kundalini called Kali. Of course, this is very symbolic and one has to understand it correctly. The second manifestation of kundalini is Lakshmi, representing beauty, wealth, prosperity and health. Then the third is Saraswati, who represents learning, accomplishment, art and creativity. This is a subject which you will have to study more about later.

What is ekagrata?

Ekagrata is the Sanskrit for 'one-pointedness.' According to the laws of evolution, the mind has five stages. They are the five evolutionary stages of the mind. The lowest stage is called the inert mind, as you find in the lower kingdom. The next stage is the scattered or dissipated mind, which you find in most animals. Still higher than that is the oscillating mind, which is like a pendulum and which you find in most human beings. Higher again is the one-pointed mind, which you find in yogis. The last stage is mindlessness or the controlled mind. This is the highest state of mind.

These are the five stages of evolution of mental consciousness in all beings in the entire existence – we are not the only beings who have a mind. Just because we can think, feel and remember; that is not mind; that is an expression of mind! A light is not electricity; it is an expression of electrical energy. Electrical energy can manifest itself in many forms as you know, and light is one form.

In the same way, mind can and does manifest itself in many forms, in the form of knowledge, feeling, remembering, understanding, analyzing, anger, jealousy, passion, compassion, greed, ambition and frustration. These are the tendencies or manifestations of the mind; they are not the mind. Just as light is there because there is electricity, in the same way, we have a mind and therefore we are happy, we know, remember, understand, reflect and analyze.

Mind is a deeper substance than we can or do understand and this mind is present in every speck of creation. Stones have a mind, although you may not believe it. The single-celled amoeba has a mind and we too have a mind. But by the time matter has evolved to the point of human incarnation, the mind has also evolved. Therefore, ekagrata is the fourth stage of mental evolution and in ekagrata the mind is only thinking of one object.

There is an ancient story about it. Two disciples were learning the science of archery from their teacher. The teacher taught them the science for a few years and at the end he wanted to examine them. So he called them both and told the first one, "Look, there is a bird in that tree and you have to shoot it between the eyes." The disciple replied, "Yes master, I see it." The master asked, "What do you see?" The disciple replied, "I see the tree and the bird."

Then the master called the other disciple and said, "Look, you have to shoot the bird between the eyes." He replied, "I understand." The master said, "Now, look at it and tell me what you see." The second disciple replied, "I see the beak and the eyes." Then the master said, "look properly and tell me what you see." When he looked again he exclaimed, "Oh now I see only the eyes."

That is called one-pointedness. When everything except the point upon which you are supposed to concentrate dissolves, that is the state of mind preceding *samadhi*, total awareness. When you are able to merge your mind totally with one external point, then you are able to feel the transcendental self inside and not before that. You may talk a lot about the self, the supreme self, the supreme consciousness. You may even explain it, that's another matter, but you can't experience the inner self with this mind. When the water is muddy, you can see nothing. You can't even see your own reflection, but when it is crystal clear, then you can see it.

Ekagrata or total concentration of mind on one object is the master key, the secret. It is not the outside object which is important. You may concentrate on a cross, Christ or Sri Krishna, a flower, a yantra or a mantra. The important thing is the concentration itself. There is a higher awareness behind the existence of everybody. This body is not our total existence; it is a reflection, like the reflection in a mirror, on water, or a shadow of an object against the sun. You are that reflection; you are not reality.

Reality is somewhere else and in order to arrive at that, you have to go through your experience and not through your knowledge. You can read hundreds of books which say the self is immortal, the self is transcendental, but that is intellectual knowledge. You can talk about chocolate, but you can't experience it unless you eat it. Experience is intimate knowledge in which you know exactly what is happening, and that point comes when the mind loses touch with everything else except one point.

Eka means one, not two. When you are concentrating on one object, then there are thoughts, counter-thoughts, under-thoughts, an invisible current of thought. They keep on interrupting that flow of awareness. There is interception and intervention. Draw a straight line on a blackboard and intercept it with other lines. The intercepting lines are other thoughts and the line which is going straight is the current of the flow of consciousness. Whether it is on a yellow flower, a blue lotus, a black dot, red dot or inverted triangle, it doesn't matter.

Please explain the significance of shivalingam.
In India they have a very popular concept called shivalingam. It is very much misunderstood because lingam is a Sanskrit word with two meanings. *Lingam* means 'symbol' and also 'male organ'. So shivalingam is interpreted as Shiva's organ. Actually it does not mean that. *Shivalingam* means 'the supreme consciousness in its causal form'. Everything has three forms: gross, astral and causal. *Lingam* means the causal body, that is, the causal form of Shiva. What is that?

In this physical body there are twelve centres which are considered to be important points of concentration for the improvement and awakening of your consciousness. Of these twelve points, three are most important. One is mooladhara chakra at the base of the spine; the second is ajna chakra at the top of the spine, behind the mid-eyebrow centre; the third is sahasrara chakra, the cosmic brain at the crown of the head. These three points are considered to be the most important forms of Shiva.

The form of Shiva in mooladhara chakra is that of a smoky grey, oval-shaped stone, which has no illumination. The second place of the shivalingam is in ajna chakra and it is black in colour. The third is in sahasrara chakra at the top of the brain, which is said to be the illumined shivalingam. This concept of Shiva has inspired Hindus for thousands and thousands of years to follow the path from gross to subtle, subtle to causal, causal to transcendental, because Shiva represents the yogic process in human life, not the process of matter.

Matter also has a process of evolution, but Shiva represents the spiritual evolution in man. Those of you who have come across this philosophy of Shiva will understand very well that it is at once a concept which relates, not only to your body or mind, but to the highest consciousness in you which is trying to manifest. Therefore, in every temple the Hindus have an oval shaped stone, which is black in colour, never white. This stone is concentrated upon in order to awaken the twelve centres in your body. That is this very important philosophy in short.

In India, Kashmir is considered to be the historical scene of Shiva worship. Then one-third of South India is also considered to be the second important seat of Shiva worship. In Tibet there is a very big, snow-capped mountain called Mount Kailash, which is also in the shape of a shivalingam. Before China took over Tibet, the Hindus used to go to Mount Kailash at least once in their lifetime.

At the bottom of Mount Kailash there is a great lake called Manasarovar and I have been there twice. It is such an inspiring spot! There is no temple there, no priest, no idol and no habitation. It is all wild. On the northern side of the lake, Mount Kailash rises thousands of metres above the snow-capped ranges and when you go there you can feel that there is someone looking at you. You can't see anything, but you have a clear feeling that there is an invisible presence there, and that is absolute.

It is from this particular place that the yoga of Shiva has emanated. The sixty-four scriptures on tantra are dialogues between Shiva and Parvati. Shiva is considered to be a derelict, a sannyasin living in the wilderness, having no home, no place, always remaining in the lotus posture in samadhi.

Are there any karmic connections or karmic debts with people in this life from a past life situation? Do we choose our own parents?

The doctrine of karma is an absolute truth. Nobody should have any doubt about it. It is based on the law of cause and effect. When there is a cause there has got to be an effect, and if there is an effect, there has to be a cause. This life is an effect, it is not a cause. It is the effect of some cause and therefore there is an endless chain of cause and effect which controls not only human beings but the entire creation. Not only visible creation, invisible fields of energy are also controlled by the laws of cause and effect.

Those who have studied science, physics and the deeper sciences know that there is the law of cause and effect. This law is the sound philosophy of karma, migration, transmigration, reincarnation and metamorphosis, where matter is not totally obliterated but transformed. Even after the death of this physical body, the karmas remain and are transferred to another body where you are obliged to undergo all the necessary experiences of the effects of the previous life.

So far as choosing parents is concerned, only a few people can choose their parents. They are the people with higher consciousness. At the time of death there are two types of people. One type becomes totally unconscious. Their mind, senses and awareness become dormant as if they were sleeping, and then they leave their body.

When the spirit leaves the body, it is in a dormant potential state. It is like a seed which is being tossed hither and thither. It has no choice of its own and no awareness of itself. According to the gravity and the quality of karma, nature moves the seed from the old body and, at the proper time, it puts it into the mother's womb. Here you have no choice. According to karma you have to be born into the womb of a mother you may like or you may not like. It is not up to you.

There is another kind of soul who, at the time of death, maintains inner awareness. They are the yogis and you can be like that. They maintain awareness and with this full awareness they just leave the body. They are not sorry. They do not lament or cry. They don't feel sad about the things they are leaving behind: mansions, cottages, horse, bullock cart, motor cycle, television – nothing! They just leave with total awareness.

Since these people are aware, they can decide where to go. Nature does compel them to a certain extent, but since they are aware, they have control over the laws of nature also. These souls have a choice. They choose their parents, which womb they will fertilize, which family they will be born in and for what reason. These are the two types of souls.

15

Satsang

Satyananda Ashram, Mangrove Mountain, Australia, 17 December 1983

How can I overcome negative obsessions, particularly in my life as a disciple?

Obsession is not a negative quality. It is a stepping stone to the attainment of one-pointedness. You do not have to get rid of these obsessions, because they are created by other samskaras, qualities and instincts. You have to replace them and when you are able to replace those negative qualities, then obsession becomes a tool for constant inner awareness. You have to replace them by the practice of mantra, by satsang and by *swadhyaya*, the study of spiritual books and the lives of spiritual personalities. This is important.

When you have a patch of uncultivated land where no vegetable or fruit trees are growing, you find weeds and wild bushes growing there. How do you get rid of the jungle, the grass, the bushes that are growing over that patch of land? You say, "Alright, we will cut down the bushes and pull out the weeds." When you come back after three months, again you will have weeds and bushes there. You can't get rid of them that way. You have to remove the jungle, then plough the soil and grow vegetables, wheat, barley, fruits, etc. Then you will find that there will not be any jungle there; there won't be any unnecessary growth.

The unnecessary growth in the human mind is due to improper utilization and it is due to negligence and carelessness. We are not utilizing our mental faculties at all. In the home we cook, we eat, we sleep, we procreate, we rear children and we have a nice nest house. That is what everybody is doing. Animals are also doing that. They make nests according to their capacity and we are also making our nests according to our capacity. We are not using our mental faculties.

The way we are behaving in the world is more or less like animals because we are all sleeping. According to yoga texts, according to the *Bhagavad Gita*, we are all asleep. Only the *jnani*, who has experienced wisdom, is awake. Therefore, we have to define the state of wakefulness and the state of sleep. We are not aware of our inner self. A jnani, a man who has experienced wisdom, is aware of himself. Since he is aware of his inner self, he is awake. We have no awareness of ourself, the inner self, so we are asleep. Since we are sleeping, we are not using our mental capacities at all.

That patch of land is not taken care of, so unnecessary grass and bushes are growing there, as you have here in Australia. The garden has grown, but you have not chosen what to grow there. In the same way, you haven't chosen the thoughts that come into your mind. They are coming in as a creation of your previous incarnations born of instinct, ignorance, *avidya*. You have not made any effort to use the mind. I'm not talking about improving the quality of the mind. I'm just talking about using the mind.

How to use the mind? You must have a plan, a blue print, a program. Just as you send your children to school and they receive intellectual training, they learn to do mathematics, to read books, they study geography, history, etc., in the same way, you will have to train the mind to think this way or that way. The first training is mantra. First, you practise your mantra at certain times in the morning or at night. Later on, you will practise your mantra from time to time throughout the day or night and finally you should be able to maintain unbroken awareness of the mantra. At that point, the practice becomes spontaneous. You do not have to repeat it. You simply have to become aware of the mantra which is going on all the time by itself.

After this, you will find that your obsessions, whether they are negative or positive, are all gone. This is the way you should deal with the mind. Obsession is never negative. All the great achievements of mankind were accomplished through obsession. All the time, an artist, a musician, a warrior, a conqueror, and even a saint, a yogi, a *bhakta*, or devotee, is thinking about just one thing. This quality of obsession can be transformed into the quality of total concentration and one-pointedness.

Therefore, you should not fight with your obsessions. You should not be sorry about them, nor should you feel bad. If there are obsessions, let them be there. Utilize your mind and have a spiritual program. After attending to your family, your office, your business, whatever time you have left, try to adopt a program by which you can train your mind. I have given you a three point program – mantra, satsang and swadhyaya.

In taking sannyasa, how can I cope with the separation from my family to whom I am very attached?
Attachment is not bad. You must not kill your attachment; you must widen the scope. Why have attachment only for your family? You must have attachment, you must try to practise attachment for everybody. Everybody belongs to you. A sannyasin need not hate his family, his wife and children, but he should include within the fold of his love an attachment to everybody he comes across. Why do you want to love only a few people? You would be very fortunate, very rich and very happy, if you were to love everybody you know and come across.

Therefore, a sannyasin must include everybody within the fold of his love and attachment. If you love someone who is sick, you will feel for him as you feel for your wife and children. It is also not necessary for a sannyasin to think that he has attachment. I tell you again, that attachment is very important. Try to cultivate it, try to improve the quality of attachment and gradually you will find that this attachment is turning into the form of love, compassion and understanding.

Can you speak to us about surrender and what its importance in our life is?
It is really very difficult to intellectualize the subject matter of surrender because it is not something which we can talk about. It is an experience and this experience is the experience of surrendering one's crude ego. This ego is the basis of our individuality. If you go to religious places, the temple or church, you pray and you also speak a few lines of surrender, "I am Thine, all is Thine, Thy will be done." This is verbal surrender.

Real surrender takes place when you can withdraw your ego, which is standing between you and your divinity, between you and your guru, or between yourself and your Self. In order to learn this surrender, you must first have a guru. Practise primary lessons in surrender with the guru, then you can practise surrender to your divinity. When you surrender yourself to your divinity, then life becomes happy and glorious. Happiness or unhappiness, joy or sorrow, whether your wishes are fulfilled or not, you will not care, because you have surrendered yourself to the will of the divine and whatever He brings into your life – that's welcome.

Everybody wants life to be nice, everybody wants happiness, everybody wants good health. Nobody wants to be unhappy, nobody wants to be sick, nobody wants a bad life. But why not? Why should you only want to have your own choice? Why should you choose? Let Him choose. There is a greater reality, a higher reality, a greater law – the universal law. This universal law is responsible for all events, for every experience in your life – your body, your existence, your birth and your creation.

Everything is an expression of that universal law and that universal law is a mighty law. It is an intelligent law, an omniscient law that controls each and every aspect of your life. That realization must dawn. We have seen that from time to time, nations, races and tribes have experienced this. There are people who have surrendered themselves, but here I am talking about the people who are devoted to spiritual life, who are related to a guru and are trying to establish the union with their inner self. It is for those people that the act of surrender at every level is very important.

If one has an ishta devata to whom one is devoted, does one have to find a guru to whom one is equally devoted and must the feeling towards both correspond, or can the guru simply be seen as a guide towards further union with the ishta devata?

Ishta devata is an important factor in your spiritual practice. You have to realize him within you. But guru is more important, because it is through guru that the inner awareness of ishta devata becomes effulgent. In the final analysis, guru and ishta devata are one and the same. In the beginning the guru is the inner awakener and the ishta devata is the form which shines in the depth of meditation. Therefore, you must have them both.

In the book 'Light on the Guru-Disciple Relationship', you say that your philosophical tradition is Vedanta. What does Vedanta mean?

Indian philosophy has six systems. These six systems are graduated according to intellectual evolution and to the nature of experience. The first philosophy is atheism. An atheist is also a philosopher because he gives his own definitions. He says that there is no God, there is no rebirth, there is no karma and there is no continuity of cause and effect. He gives his own philosophy as to how the world evolved, how human beings and animals are born, how the actions take place, etc. That is the first branch of Indian philosophy, which is known as Charvaka philosophy. Greek Epicurianism and Hedonism are also branches of that philosophy.

The second branch of Indian philosophy is Jainism, the philosophy of the Jains. They also do not believe in any God or supreme being. This philosophy states that man is matter and through certain practices and rituals he can evolve, he can transform himself into a greater being, an enlightened one. The third branch is Buddhism, the philosophy of Buddha. Here also there is no God, but there is rebirth. There is emphasis on ethics and morality and a little bit of spiritual life.

The fourth system of Indian philosophy is called Samkhya. Samkhya is a philosophical system which presupposes eternal duality, not monism. Samkhya philosophy declares that *purusha*, consciousness, and *prakriti*, matter, are both eternal. They interact with each other and by that interaction, everything is born in the universe. Purusha and prakriti, matter and consciousness, are constantly interacting at different levels, physical, mental, emotional and spiritual. At all levels they are interacting, at the microcosmic level and at the macrocosmic level.

Now, out of this Samkhya philosophical system, yoga and tantra are drawn. Therefore, the philosophical system of yoga and tantra is also dualistic in nature. The presupposition, the main hypothesis is that consciousness is untainted. It is the non-doer; it is just a witness. It does not involve itself in anything. It appears that the consciousness is being affected, but it is not affected. The rays of the sun passing through blue, green, yellow or red glass appear to be of different colours, but in fact they are not. In the same way, consciousness is untainted.

Prakriti converts itself into two forms, one is matter and the other is energy. In essence, matter and energy are both the same. They are different manifestations, that is all. Energy can be converted into matter and matter can be converted into energy. This is Samkhya philosophy, the fourth system of Indian philosophy, which is considered to be the basis of yoga and tantra, the fifth system.

However, the final and ultimate philosophy, the sixth philosophy in India, is Vedanta. In Vedanta philosophy, they declare that there is only one substance and not two. This one substance alone is creating and recreating everything within itself, and that is the doctrine of Brahman. In modern science you have two theories, the theory of relativity and the absolute. In Vedanta, you have three, the theory of the absolute, the theory of relativity and the theory of illusion.

Every experience which we have is both relative and illusory, no experience is absolute, no manifestation and no event is absolute. The whole of creation, the entire universe about which we think a lot of the time is non-existent from the point of view of the absolute – that is Vedantic philosophy. From the point of view of the absolute, it is non-existent. As long as it is related to mind, object and experience, to time and space, it appears to be real. You are you and I am I. Every object seems to be existing, but that existence which seems to be real is totally illusory.

So, Vedanta talks of three types of existence. The first is illusory, the second is relative and the third is absolute. This is the philosophy into which I was initiated and which I represent. As far as I am concerned, I am a vedantin. I teach yoga and tantra. I talk about hatha yoga, bhakti yoga and karma yoga, I initiate people into mantra, but my personal philosophy is Vedanta. In my personal life, my personal experience, everything is guided by Vedanta and not by yoga or tantra. I am a teacher of yoga, a teacher of tantra, but I'm not a yogi or a tantric. I am a vedantin.

For me, the whole of life is an appearance. Everything that I have gone through is related to time and space, to experience and events. Therefore, they do not really exist in me and my life is like a big dream that I am experiencing, a long dream, not a few hours of dream but sixty years of dream. In this dream, many have come and many have gone. I see people loving, hating, kicking, doing so many things. In my quietude, sometimes I realize that we are all stupid people. What are we doing?

This vedantic philosophy is my personal creed, but I do not teach it. If I teach Vedanta, people will become lazy. They will say, "I am supreme, I am." Because in Vedanta, realization and enlightenment do not come from outside. Enlightenment is not a matter of time; it is here and now; it is in you. You are always realized.

The vedantic philosophy does not believe that you have to realize anything. Gold is gold, whether you realize it as gold or whether you realize it as another stuff. A diamond is always a diamond; whether you realize it as a diamond or a piece of shining stone it makes no difference. You may not know that you are enlightened, but you are enlightened. Now, if I say that you are enlightened, then what are you going to do all day? Vedanta says, "What are you doing, where are you going? All is illusion." There is a story about this.

Once a tiger cub got lost and it was found by a shepherd. The shepherd had many sheep and this baby tiger was growing up amongst them. In the course of time, the tiger cub began to eat grass and to bleat like a sheep. Later on, it happened that while the sheep were grazing on the side of a mountain, a tiger was roaming up on top. When he looked down and saw one who looked like himself grazing amongst the sheep, he was amazed. So he came up closer and asked the tiger cub, "Who are you?"

The little tiger replied, "I am a sheep." The big tiger said, "No, you are not a sheep. You are a tiger like me." The baby tiger said, "Hey, don't try to deceive me. I know I am a sheep and these are my relatives. He's my uncle, she's my aunt, she's my mother and she is my sister." The big tiger said, "Look here, your teeth and my teeth are the same. The colour of your body and my body is the same. We are identical." The little tiger still could not believe it and said, "No, I know that you have some ulterior motive in your mind. You want to cheat me. I belong to this flock."

At last, the big tiger became exasperated and he began to roar. When he roared, all the sheep ran away because they knew the roar of a tiger. Only the little tiger remained. Then the big tiger said, "See, if you were a sheep, you would have run away too, but you weren't afraid of my roar." In order to convince the little tiger, he let out another great roar and the little tiger roared too.

So, this is the illusion of identity which applies to each and everyone. Do we belong to the flock of sheep or do we belong to the line of tigers? Vedanta has always proclaimed that everyone is essentially divine and pure. We are basically the thing in itself. The light, the experience and the knowledge which we are running after is within us. It is just here and now.

However, this vedantic philosophy makes aspirants lazy. They do not want to do japa, to practise yoga or any kind of mental training because they think that they are already realized, they don't have to bring the realization in. So, my personal creed or philosophy is Vedanta, but I teach yoga and tantra because by the practice of yoga and tantra, our body, mind and soul will be purified. Then self-realization will be obtained by us.

Can you tell us about your life in the ashram at Rishikesh with your guru?

I went to the ashram of my guru in 1943. By that time I had done a lot of yoga myself and I had experiences also, but I was stuck at one point. I couldn't go any further, so I went in search of a guru. I did go to many people and finally I came to Rishikesh where I lived with my guru for a period of twelve years. It was not a very comfortable life, on the contrary, it was very difficult for me. Half the time I was sick with hepatitis, stomatitis, gastritis, TB and many other things. Diarrhoea and dysentery were almost a weekly affair.

At the same time, however, I knew that physical sufferings were necessary for one's inner growth. Many times, while practising yoga, kundalini yoga or higher forms of hatha yoga, you become sick. So you give up the practices, thinking that you are falling ill because of them. It is true, the physical body is affected by spiritual awakening. So you begin to feel pain and that pain is terrible. This has been stated by many yogis, including the yogis who were born in the West, the Christian mystics. Along with realization, the experience of pain is there, sickness is there.

Whenever I fell ill in the ashram, I used to feel that with the awakening of spiritual experience, my karmas were being forced out. The purging of karma was going on. When karmas are being eliminated, when the process of the exhaustion of karma takes place, at that time one experiences pain, one expects illness and one feels very bad. Before the experience of *anandam*, of perennial, enduring and undying bliss, one has to go through these experiences. For twelve years my health was very poor. Mentally, I was non-existent because, as far as I can remember, I did not have time to think about myself.

As soon as I joined the ashram, I became a very responsible person there because of my previous experiences, not only spiritual experiences, but other experiences as well. I knew how to manage money, that was part of my early training. I knew how to construct buildings, how to publish books, how to run a big kitchen. I knew how to control the flock, how to manage twenty or thirty people in the ashram. I had experience in management, administration and accounting.

So, in the ashram I was entrusted with the responsibility of many departments. There was a time when I used to carry a big bunch of keys, weighing almost a kilogram! Several times during the course of the day I had to go from one end of the ashram to the other, and I became so lean and thin I weighed only thirty kilos and you could easily count my ribs.

In 1947, my guru initiated me into sannyasa and not only that, he announced that Swami Satyananda had been initiated into the order of paramahamsa, which is higher than sannyasin. So, many of his disciples and devotees came to see me from all over the country and they found that this paramahamsa was so unimpressive, so unshaped. "He has no muscles, no fat, no belly, his cheeks are sunken." They were all expecting to find a fat man with long, flowing beard and matted locks, sitting with his eyes closed like a pontiff.

For twelve years, I lived in the ashram like a servant. You can develop any relationship with guru which is best suited for your evolution. You can consider him as your mother, your son, your friend, your respected God, or as your darling, your beloved, your lover. That way you can develop your relationship with him. I considered guru as my master and myself as a servant because that was very easy for me.

When you look upon yourself as a servant, you have nothing to lose, because a servant has no choice. Whatever guru tells you to do, you will do; I never thought that my guru could be wrong. Fortunately, he was a very good person, but even if he was not, even if he was a murderer I would have followed him. It did not matter to me who he was; I did not care. For twelve years I lived like a servant. I worked with the cows, with the bullock carts, in the garden. I worked in the kitchen, fetching the logs of wood. I never thought about why I was doing it, for what or for whom.

Of course, this was very different to what I was used to. The family from which I came was well-to-do, I would not say rich. Our property extended over stretches of forest, rivers and villages. It was like a small state, an estate. We owned about twenty to thirty ponies, a few thousand sheep, goats and so many cows. Every day from my childhood I was looking after the family estate. In the olden days my family had been warriors, so we had a stock of armour and swords which I also had to look after. It was a large and powerful family system where I had hundreds of people at my beck and call. I would just call someone and tell him, "Hey, go and count the sheep," and at once it would be done. Here, in the ashram, I was living as a servant and I felt that when you live with guru as a servant, your surrender is automatically complete.

Many times my guru used to call me to his kutir and offer me coffee. He never took coffee himself, but he used to keep a tin of Nescafe and from time to time, without bringing it to the notice of the other disciples, he would call me and give me a cup of coffee. It was so delicious! And whenever his dhotis wore out, he used to reserve them for me to wear, even though they were so big. He was a very tall man and his dhotis covered me from shoulder to toes.

After twelve years of hard work, physically, mentally and intellectually, looking after a large institution, I did not want to live in the ashram anymore because I was tired. In 1956, the daily income of the ashram use to be thirty thousand rupees minimum, something like four thousand dollars a day. People used to come and just throw money at my guru's feet. He was so charitable, so compassionate, even at night if somebody wanted milk or anything, he would ask me to go and fetch it.

Once a gentleman arrived from Delhi in the evening after satsang about ten o'clock or so. Rishikesh is very cold sometimes and that man did not have a blanket. So Swamiji called me and said to provide him with a blanket. At that time of night, I couldn't get a blanket, so he said, "Go to Rishikesh and purchase one." Rishikesh was three and a half miles from where we lived and there was no transport. I had to go into town on foot, wake up the shopkeeper and by one o'clock I brought the blanket. Whether there was food or no food, anybody who came there had to be fed. Swami Sivananda was a very generous man and so people used to repay him in a very generous way. He was charitable, so his disciples were also charitable.

After twelve years of service, I was really tired of hard work and I thought, "Now, I am going away. I'm not going to have any ashram, I'm not going to have any disciples and I'm not going to work anymore. I will just wander. I don't even want a room because I would have to clean it." I had worked myself to the extent that I was completely fed up with karma and with desires. I just wanted to be free – no thinking, sleeping by the side of the footpath and begging a little food to eat from the shop or from anybody. And that's how I lived for about eight years.

From 1956 to 1963 I lived like a beggar. I slept anywhere, with anybody, in any place. Every place was my place. But I came to realize that, even if you don't want to work, even if you have no desires of your own, even if you have no wishes of your own, there is a universal law which controls men's destinies. Now with so many ashrams in Australia, in Europe, in America, in South America, in India, you might feel that I want them.

No! I link myself with them because I have realized that my choice and my choicelessness have no meaning at all.

How many times did I try to withdraw myself from institutional association, how many times did I try to get away from this difficult and unwanted position of guruship? I don't want to be guru; I want to remain by myself. And if Swami Akhandananda would not ask me to come to satsang, I would never think of it. He knows it, so he comes to my room and asks, "Do you need a change? I'll take you to Sydney today. I'll take you to Farmsberry Falls. Or, would you like to go to satsang?" I say, "Okay, I can go."

The truth is that even if you become desireless, even if you renounce your karma, your family, your desires, even if you sincerely don't want anything, then the wish of that universal self operates through you. You become the instrument, the medium and that universal self or mind, or the universal stuff, becomes the actor. So I am the medium, not the actor, and for this I lived in the ashram of my guru until I arrived at the breaking point where I detested desire, schemes, plans, ambitions, passions, accomplishment, acquisition, honour, status, everything. I worked for him to that extent and that is precisely the reason why I tell everyone today – work hard and become a true karma yogi.

Those who live in the ashram as sannyasins or as inmates must remember that it is necessary to work hard, with minimum food, with sickness and illness. They should not try to work just a little, otherwise they will have a lot of problems. Why are there so many problems in the Western countries? Because they have no work. If you want to go to the toilet, just open the door, the bathroom is there. If you want to speak to someone, just dial the telephone and talk to him. If you want to cook food, turn on the microwave oven. In one minute everything is done. Therefore, this mind is running wild.

In the olden days, in order to go marketing you had to walk three miles. In order to go to the toilet you had to go to the bushes. In order to fetch water you had to walk half a kilometre. You had to work physically in those days just to live.

Even today, those people who work physically, who exhaust themselves, who tire their body have a much better mental and spiritual life. They have fewer sexual problems.

When I came to the West for the first time, I couldn't even reply to people's questions. Somebody asked me about lesbianism and I replied, "I don't know what it is." Someone else asked me about homosexuality. Of course, nowadays they say that these things are due to hormonal imbalances, but I say that you have a wild mind and your perverse sexual life is its workshop.

You have not used up the energy in your physical body and so the physiological chemicals are out of order. These problems are not merely psychological, they are physiological. I am thankful that I got the opportunity to live with my guru in Rishikesh and give every bit of sweat, every bit of my energy, every part of my mind, all of my emotions, passions and ambitions, that I could work for him day and night like a donkey, like a madman.

I know that, whether my ashrams flourish or die, it's nothing for me. It's like a film which I am seeing and which one day will be destroyed. After all, everything is vanity in the end. One day everybody has to depart from the arena of life, leaving nothing behind.

16

Awakening the Inner Experience

Manly Ashram, Sydney, Australia, 18 December 1983

Beyond the body, mind and intellect, in each and every one of us, there is a being, there is a power and there is a light, but we are not able to comprehend it. We are not able to experience it. The purpose of yoga is to know our centre.

The body, mind, intellect and emotions, as far as we know them, are our peripheral entity. They are not the real self and since we are far from the vision of that inner being, we are incomplete. Therefore, in that incompleteness we experience pain and agony, frustration, fear, meaninglessness and a sense of futility. All the problems we experience in everyday life related to our job, family, business and friends are on account of that incompleteness. If you are able to get to the source of yourself, then you will experience completeness. That completeness is bliss or *anandam*. That completeness is an eternal and perennial joy which no problem of your life can destroy.

The science of yoga is one of the most outstanding paths for attaining this purpose. There are many paths, but I have discovered for myself and also for the people of my generation that the path of yoga is the most suitable one, because the science of yoga originates from tantra. Tantra is a science which says that in order to reach the inner source of your being, you do not have to make any external change in your life. You do not have to be religious, you do not have to be a puritan, a monk, a celibate or a priest.

Even a rank materialist, an atheist, an agnostic, a publican or a hedonist can experience his inner being. This is the primary philosophy of tantra. You have to expand your mind and expansion of mind is possible through the practices of yoga. These practices are contained in hatha yoga, raja yoga, bhakti yoga and karma yoga. A combination, synthesis or graduated practice of all these yoga will bring you closer to the experience of that reality.

Expansion of mind
Expansion of mind is something which is very important and which everybody should understand. Through the expansion of mind you can go beyond the barriers of time and space, and that is the reason why we cannot understand beyond a certain frontier.

The process of knowledge through the mind and senses is limited. If there is a flower before you, you can see it, otherwise you cannot because your senses are limited to the objective category of experience. To experience a sound, a form, a touch, a taste or a smell, you need to have coordination between the mind and senses. If there is no coordination between the object, the senses and the mind, then there is no experience at all. That is called limitation of mind and we are limited in that way.

In order to experience beyond the object, beyond the senses and beyond the mind, it is necessary for an expansion of mind to take place. Supposing your eyes are open and there is no flower there before you, but still you smell one. That is called an expanded state of mind. When the mind can experience without the aid of the senses and without the presence of an object, that is called expansion of mind.

This expansion of mind is responsible for the release or liberation of a certain quantum of energy in your system. This is very important, for if expansion of mind does not take place, if you are not able to experience without the help of the senses, in the absence of an object, then the release or liberation of energy within you is not possible.

Therefore, in yoga there are two processes. One is a group of practices which leads you to the expansion of the mind. As a result of these practices your mind can function beyond time, space and object. You can jump beyond the mind. There is no object yet you can see; no sound yet you can hear; no flower yet you can smell. This is called expansion of mind.

Three areas of awakening

The practices of yoga like asanas, pranayama and concentration of mind develop an expanded state of consciousness in you. How do they bring about that state? In the spinal column there are three important components of yogic philosophy:
1. the psychic centres or *chakras*,
2. the *nadis* or energy flows and
3. the *kundalini* or evolutionary energy.

The chakras are situated at six different junctions in the spine. If you can awaken and energize these psychic centres, then you can have certain experiences, not fantastic or explosive experiences, but mild experiences. These experiences are very pleasant and not frightening. They can give you a lot of bliss and joy, and maybe a type of hypnosis. Awakening of these chakras is possible through the practice of yoga postures. The asanas are not just physical exercise; they have a direct bearing, a direct impression on the chakras.

When you have these mild, pleasant and blissful experiences, they are the first series of experiences related to expansion of mind. It is not necessary for you to take LSD, marijuana or any other type of drug. Of course, I am not criticizing the use of drugs, but if you want to jump beyond your present state of mind, if you want to transcend time and space and object barriers even for a short while, then yoga postures come as the primary practice.

However, after the awakening of the chakras you have to deal with the flow of energy in the body. As you know, within the framework of the spine there are three important flows of energy. To the left side is the mental energy flow called *ida nadi*. To the right side is the pranic energy flow called *pingala nadi*, and in the centre is the spiritual energy flow called *sushumna nadi*. We call these nadis the conductors of energy. Mental energy is responsible for mental functions, pranic energy is responsible for life and activity, and the spiritual energy flow is responsible for spiritual experience.

In order to awaken the central nadi, sushumna, the practice of pranayama is considered to be the best. Pranayama is not just breathing exercises; it is much more than that. If you study pranayama, you will find that the practice of breathing through alternate nostrils, retention of breath and controlling the bandhas at the neck, abdomen and perineum create a stir in sushumna nadi.

With the awakening of this nadi, you begin to have fantastic experiences. These experiences indicate that you have already jumped over your mind and have transcended the time and space categories of the mind. They are much more powerful and impressive than the mild experiences and they have an effect on the *kundalini shakti*, the dormant, potential energy residing at the bottom of the spine.

Behind the mind is energy

The prime purpose of yoga practices is to expand your mind, and as your mind is expanded liberation of energy takes place. What is liberation of energy? It is not liberation in the religious sense. Just as you liberate butter from milk by releasing the essence, even as you liberate nuclear energy from uranium, in the same way, this energy is released.

The mind is matter, a thought is matter, an experience is matter and vibration is matter, although you may not see it as such. This matter has to be exploded. A scientist explodes energy by a process of disintegration, of fission and fusion. In the same way, a yogi considers every thought as matter and the substratum of every thought as energy. The substratum of attachment, passion, love and hatred is energy.

What are love, hatred, compassion, fear and memory? They are not psychological processes; they are substantial and potential vibrations. Imagination is not nothing; it is something. Imagination is a quality of vibration. Fear, anger, jealousy, greed, passion and many more things are vibrations coming from you, me and everybody. They have frequency and velocity.

Forget what you have studied in the psychology books. I am not contradicting or criticizing psychology, I am only trying to point out its limitations. How can you say that a thought is psychological stuff? A thought is a vibration, physiological stuff. It has weight, colour, frequency, velocity and archetypal formation. Every thought, every sound and every movement has a form.

I am existing at millions of places in the world. You also exist at millions of places. You are not just this much. You know nothing about the mind. Mind is like an iceberg. You can only see a small part of it, the rest is not visible to the eye. The way in which the mind has been defined by scientists today in the twentieth century is nothing compared to the definition which was evolved thousands of years ago by the yogis and rishis. Scientists do not know anything about the mind. This centre of energy has to be exploded.

Splitting the mind

Matter is a gross form of energy and energy is the subtle form of matter. Matter and energy are the same thing. In the realm of manifestation they appear to be different. Therefore, thought is matter. Every thought is like a bubble that comes up from the bottom. Where do thoughts come from? They do not come from outside. They are manifestations or expressions of a certain type of energy.

Energy has a certain quantum. Sometimes it is 'leftist' and some time it is 'rightist'. I am not a politician, but these terms were used long ago in tantra. *Vama marga* is the leftist or the left hand path and *dakshina marga* is the rightist or right hand path. *Madhya marga* is the middle path. So, this energy moves sometimes to the left side, sometimes to the right side and sometimes in the middle. It has to be fixed. This thought, this bubble, has to be analyzed, dissected and disintegrated. It has to be separated.

Matter is not homogeneous. Anything that has no component is homogeneous, anything that has a component is not. No matter is homogeneous. There is only one thing that is homogeneous and that is consciousness, *atma*, self, *purusha*. That is homogeneous because it is not composed of any secondary matter. It is one and that is all. But all matter, even a thought, is a composition. Anger is a composition, love is a composition, memory is a composition and experience in concentration is a composition.

What is a thought composed of? Just as this body is composed of bones, marrow, blood cells and tissues, a thought is composed of twenty-six elements. According to Samkhya philosophy or Indian logic, the mind is matter and a thought pattern, whatever it may be, is also matter. They call it *padartha*, which means matter. This matter is composed of twenty-six elements. You have to break the mind as you break energy, as you break uranium, as you break or separate the nucleus.

I am using the word break or split in a scientific sense. Do not use a hammer tomorrow morning and break your head into twenty-six pieces! Those who have studied physics can understand what I mean when I say thought can be split into twenty-six components. How can you split a thought? You can split a thought by the practices of concentration. You can see the different components of your thought in the different stages of distraction, dissipation, oscillation and hallucination.

You do not like all these stages that you are supposed to go through in the practices of concentration. The guru gives you a mantra and you want concentration and samadhi within a week or ten days. You think that you must forget the mind, you must forget yourself and everything, and that is samadhi. Yes, that is samadhi, but do not talk about it! First of all, you will have to split the mind, and splitting the mind or the thought can be experienced only when you face the mind absolutely naked.

You practise your mantra *Om Namah Shivaya* and suddenly you find that your mind has drifted away. You bring it back to *Om Namah Shivaya* and it goes away again. It brings all the components of a thought from inside. So, this is how a thought as matter has to be split. After splitting a thought you will discover energy, and what is that energy? It is experience. When you have inner experience, what you call psychic experience, it is the substratum or the nucleus of matter.

Therefore, behind your anger, passions, fears, jealousy, attachment, behind all kinds of mental and psychological idiosyncrasies, there is energy and you have to separate that energy from each and every thought. As such, those of you who are practising concentration and meditation should remember very well that control of thought is not important. Control of mind is not important. Let the thoughts come out!

The practices which you choose for yourself should make you express your thoughts rather than suppress them. If you take a mantra from your guru and get total concentration of mind within a week or so, then be sure that suppression has taken place, because expression of mind is the basis of all the yogic and tantric practices.

A great awakening

After awakening the chakras and sushumna, the awakening of kundalini takes place. The awakening of kundalini is the greatest event in man's life. It is the destiny of everyone. You have to awaken your kundalini and if you don't do it, nature will do it for you. The awakening of kundalini marks the climax of man's spiritual evolution. A superhuman or supramental race will be the outcome of this awakening.

Man has completed his physio-biological evolution. Natural evolution is now complete in us. The only difference it is going to make is that maybe we will be shorter or taller, heavier or lighter. Maybe we will lose our nose as we lost our tail, but we are not going to have any more tails; it is not going to happen. Physical, natural evolution is complete and now spiritual evolution is beginning.

For this purpose the science of yoga and tantra has come about. Throughout the world there is a very great awakening. In every part of the world, wherever I go, people want to realize and experience the man behind the man, the existence behind this existence. People are very anxious about it and they know very well that this can be done through the practices of yoga and tantra.

A free philosophy
We are told that we have to be good, pure and divine in order to realize the self. I always thought that if I had to become good, pure and divine, then what was the necessity of realizing it? It is only a sick person who needs the doctor. It is an ignorant person who needs light. It is an incomplete person who needs this divine experience. If you have to be great in order to become great, it is a funny joke!

If I have to be religious in order to realize my real nature, I am not going to go after it, because I know that by trying to be pure and good, I am suppressing myself. By trying to be good, pure, noble and nice, I am killing myself, I am trampling over and kicking myself. It is the greatest injustice a man can do to himself. This injustice which you do to yourself has been the main cause of your not being able to realize your real true nature. You have not been able to let yourself be free.

Freedom is my right! I do not mean natural freedom or social freedom. I am not talking about political freedom. I am talking about freedom of mind, of thinking, of feeling, of experiencing, and the freedom of every kind that is related to myself. If a thought comes into my mind, why should I kill it? Why should I denounce it?

Therefore, I thought for many years about how I could find that experience which is beyond time and space. I went to many teachers and everybody gave me very monotonous advice, "Purify yourself!" I thought, "If I have to purify myself before experiencing it, then I am not prepared to do it." Because first of all, I did not believe in so-called purity. In those days I was in the prime of my youth. They told me that I was a Hindu, so I should not eat meat, drink, associate with girls, etc.

Every country, society, culture and religion has its own taboos. You too may have them. What I am telling you now has nothing to do with your tribal, racial and national taboos. You may have them or not; it is up to you. Whatever you are, wherever you are, you do not have to make the least change in the master plan of your life, but one thing you have to do, step by step, is to develop your inner experiences.

First go for the pleasant experiences, then go for the fantastic experiences and finally you must be prepared to face and handle the explosive experiences. These explosive experiences are related to the awakening of kundalini. The fantastic experiences are related to the awakening of sushumna and pleasant experiences are related to the awakening of the various chakras in your body.

Pleasure and pain
I have only spoken about six chakras situated in the spine, but apart from those there are many hundreds of psychic centres everywhere in the physical body. These psychic centres which are in different parts of your body can give mild, pleasant and blissful experiences, and they do give them to you, but you do not know it because you have been so crude in your way of thinking.

Whenever you feel happy, what is that? Whenever you are joyful, what is that? It is an experience. Happiness is an experience. Where has that experience come from? From your wife who has just returned, or from your child who has just come back from boarding school, or from the nice income which you have got in your business? Where have the experiences come from? These experiences emanate from many minor chakras and psychic centres in the body.

Not only happiness but even unhappiness is an experience. Pain is an experience, sorrow is an experience

– and unhappiness is an experience superior to happiness. Remember it! Pain is a superior experience to pleasure, disappointment is a superior experience to contentment, because unhappiness, pain, agony, disappointment, fear and passion come from the minor chakras in the body. I am not talking about the six major chakras, but the other ones.

There are minor and major chakras. Happiness emanates from the minor chakras. Joy, contentment and satisfaction emanate from the minor chakras and still you want to experience these. Nobody tells you that you should experience pain, but I tell you – experience pain and suffering. Suffering, sickness, poverty, injury, insult, thy name is experience! Who wants to have these? Nobody. Christ had them and therefore we worship him. Would you like to be crucified? Saint Teresa suffered throughout her life with pain, sickness and depression.

What is the definition of inner happiness? What is the definition of inner joy and inner bliss? You have your own definition and we have ours. So when these major and minor chakras wake up in your body through the practices of hatha yoga, they give you good health and nice feelings. These hatha yoga practices like neti, kunjal, shankhaprakshalana, uddiyana bandha and many more which you can learn from your yoga teacher are not merely physical, purifactory processes.

They do purify your physical body, it is true, but they also purify the major and minor chakras which are related to negative and positive energy, ida and pingala. In acupuncture they call them yin and yang. In the science of acupuncture, these chakras are related to the meridian points. With acupuncture you can cause pain, suppress pain, kill pain or experience pain, but that is physical pain. I am talking about psychic pain, spiritual pain, pain which you can only experience but you cannot pinpoint.

Go in search of yourself

Now, remember that mind, body and spirit are three in manifestation. However, basically, fundamentally and substantially they are one. Milk, curd and butter – are they three or are they one? They are one and the same. Milk transforms itself into curd and curd into butter. In the same way, when the body transcends its gross form, it becomes spirit. Therefore, this physical body is the gross manifestation of that inner being.

So, the practices of hatha yoga, kriya yoga, raja yoga and meditation, etc., should be combined and you must learn them gradually. Perfect padmasana or siddhasana. Learn how to practise pranayama. Outside of the town is the ideal place for pranayama and yoga. If you have forests, go there. Go to an ashram for one month and just practise pranayama for half an hour a day, then one hour, one and a half hours. If you practise pranayama, you will have experience.

What you are searching for is very close to you. You just have to get out of the intellect. Get out of the mind. Go in search of yourself.

17

The Inner Christmas

Satyananda Ashram, Mangrove Mountain, Australia, 25 December 1983

Every year we celebrate Christmas through our body, mind and emotions. I don't think that our inner spirit can celebrate it. So, there are two types of Christmas celebrations. One we know and the other is when the baby is born within. Now, we are all barren. like barren women who don't conceive. We are childless; the child is not yet conceived.

In order to conceive the child, there has to be union. Without union, there is nothing. That union does not need to be physical; it has to be immaculate. The two forces within you must unite, but at present they are not together. When these two forces unite, then an event takes place. That event is the birth of a divine baby from an immaculate mother. Do you understand?

You can celebrate that Christmas any time in your life, not necessarily on the 25th of December at midnight. The best time to conceive that baby, to give birth to that baby is when you are practising yoga, not while you are cooking in the kitchen, driving a car or operating a computer in the bank. For that purpose you have to set apart some time every day of your life.

The second coming of Christ

This divine baby is the Christ who comes into this mortal plane of consciousness in order to save and redeem us, and in order to destroy the tamasic and demonic forces in and around us. I believe, you may or may not, that this is the second coming of Christ.

Very often it is announced from the pulpit that Christ is coming again, but if he comes in the same way as he came the last time, 1983 years ago, it is going to be a disaster for all of you and maybe for him also, just as it was before. When Christ came, he destroyed *avidya*, ignorance. He denounced the institutionalized forces which were surviving and thriving as the so-called religion. Did he not? And is the situation any different today? Is he going to accept anything that is going on in the name of religion?

Therefore, the second coming of the Christ is going to be nothing short of a disaster on the external plane for those who are waiting for him. I do not know when he will come or if he will come. May he not come! How many establishments is he going to kick? How many beliefs in his name, in my name, in anyone's name is he going to throw out? How many dominations, sects and paths is he going to destroy? It would be a calamity – and ultimately the people would have to think about how to put him into the electric chair. That is sure too!

So, I'm not waiting for him. I do not want to see such a man, who speaks the truth, go to the electric chair. A man who speaks the truth, nothing but the truth, the ultimate truth, should be crucified, should be electrocuted – tick, tick, tick dead in three seconds? No. Then history is going to repeat itself. Another crusade might begin because his disciples will still be there. Our generation and those that come after us will have to pay the penalty. Therefore, I am not praying, I am not waiting for the second arrival.

Knowledge and experience

However, I definitely know one thing. If that higher consciousness, which is called Christ consciousness, Buddha consciousness or Krishna consciousness, is awakened in you at any time in your life, it is not going to bring disaster, nor is it going to put you into the electric chair. It will be the beginning of knowledge, experience, bliss and the feeling of unity with every living being. It is only for this that yoga and tantra are being taught and practised.

Beyond the existence of body consciousness, beyond the borders of the mind and emotions, beyond this local intellect and the deep-rooted egoism or individuality, there is something more in you, in me and in everybody. You have heard about it, but you haven't experienced it because it is beyond the reach of your physical senses, of your physical self.

The intellectual concept of that reality is known to you all. You have heard about it time and again in every scripture, in every book on philosophy and religion, through every guru, through every master, but that is only knowledge. It gives you nothing but information. The real thing is experience, and that experience need not be prolonged to one minute or even to one second. It is a momentary experience, taking much less time than a flash of lightning.

That experience, which can come to anybody within a split second, is the birth of a baby. It is for this purpose that we have to work. When that experience takes place at any time in your life, then you will have to celebrate another Christmas. Then you will dance in ecstasy and joy, as many of the saints have done in their lifetime.

There is an area of joy and ecstasy which is intellectual, mental, emotional, psychological. There you want to be ecstatic, joyful, blissful; you want to dance. That is the empirical side of joy. However, there is another area of joy where you don't know and you dance, where you don't know and you sing, where you don't know but you are compelled to feel the joy and bliss and dance in ecstasy. Then that experience gets out of hand. You don't know how it happens but it happens.

Unless you lose yourself, you can't gain yourself. In losing yourself lies the secret of total acceptance, total achievement.

You do not want to lose yourself because you think, "If my ego dies, what will happen to me?" Nothing will happen. Five bottles of champagne and whisky still bring you back; marijuana day after day, year after year, for ages together still brings you back to the lower, mundane plane.

Every joy, every hypnotic substance, every psychedelic drug takes you somewhere, but ultimately brings you back to the same point of pain and duality. You cannot transcend it in that way. However, there comes a moment in life when your eyes are turned inward and you begin to see the twinkling, the trickling of an experience. Sometimes it appears as a musical note, sometimes as a voice, sometimes a streak of light, a fragrance, a shadow.

That experience has thousands and millions of forms by which it can manifest itself in you, not just one form. If that experience comes to you just once at any time in your life, then you are thrice blessed and after that, even if you commit suicide, I don't mind. The purpose of your life, of your incarnation in the human body, on the mortal plane is justified after that experience and not before that.

Christian or churchian

You may be a great scholar, industrialist, musician, orator, writer, painter or guru, but these are all worldly achievements and they don't go with you. You haven't come here for that. Because of maya, desires, passion, ignorance and so on, you want to have all that. But why have you really come? What is the purpose of your incarnation in this body? Every wise man has said it is for that glimpse.

Of course, that experience is the inner Christmas. Then that light is born and that is called the birth of the baby. You will have to nurture and protect that baby. If he grows and becomes greater within you, then he is the real Christ and you are a Christian. Unless that happens, you are not a Christian, you are a churchian.

Now, this baby is within you but it is beyond you. You will have to cross barrier after barrier in order to reach it and all these barriers are situated within the fold of your personality. They are not external. Your wife is not a barrier, your children, family and friends are not barriers. The barriers are all within you.

These barriers are psychological. In reality they do not exist, but you are experiencing them. In order to remove these painful experiences or barriers yoga has to be practised, because by the practise of yoga and tantra you awaken the consciousness. With that special consciousness you can visualize the inner spirit. With these eyes you cannot.

The birth of a great experience
So, on the occasion of this day, I wish you a promising Christmas at any time in your life. You may not expect to hear Merry Christmas and so forth from me, but I am trying to bring home to you who the Christ is, who Mother Mary is and who that immaculate son is. If you can realize that, if you can understand that, then anyone of you can become the mother. I'm not talking to the ladies only. Anyone can become the mother, because to give birth to a great experience you don't have to be a female.

The birth takes place with the union between ida and pingala, between spirit and consciousness, between Shiva and Shakti, and that union takes place at ajna chakra. With that union, a great experience is born and that experience takes you away, very far away from this earth, from this sky, from this name and form. Sometimes it takes you so far away, to the point where time stands still. You don't feel the time, the space, the object; you don't feel anything! That experience is called transcendental.

Who is the Christ
In India, we celebrate the birth of the divine baby on various occasions, on 25th December with the birth of Christ, in August with the birth of Sri Krishna and in April with the birth of Rama. We think of Rama, Krishna and Christ as representatives of the omnipresent, omniscient and omnipotent spirit in each

and everybody. Of course, those who celebrate these birthdays usually do not understand their significance.

A great poet has written in one of his poems, "Who is this Rama? Is he the son of a worldly father? Or is he that Rama who is seated in each and every heart? Or is he the Rama who has created the cosmos, the universe? Or is he the Rama who transcends creation, who transcends physical birth and who transcends everything?" The answer he has written, my dear ones, is all four.

The same thing can be said about Christ. Which Christ do you mean? Is he the Christ who was born of a worldly father? Is he that Christ who is the indwelling entity in every heart? Is he the Christ who creates the vision of the whole universe within and without? Or do you mean that Christ who transcends everything? The answer apparently, my dear ones, is that he is all four.

Christ came down in the physical body. He was not a myth, not a metaphor, not an allegory, not a symbol, not a replica. He was a man in flesh and blood as you are. Yes! But he means much more to us than that. Even though he did not live in this physical body, he lives in our hearts. Wherever and whenever you can awaken yourself, he is there in your heart. When you think about him, he's not imagination or hallucination. He is there, but you don't know it.

A vision of transcendental reality

Of all the universe you can think about, he is the master, he is the guru, and yet he is a transcendental reality. When he is a transcendental reality, then you also must become transcendental. How to become transcendental? By transcendental meditation. As you transcend the body when you sleep at night, in the same way you have to transcend the body idea, the name idea, the form idea, the idea of 'I', the idea of male and female, the idea of past, present and future; you have to transcend all these put together.

You have to transcend through the smooth passage of consciousness. When you practise pranayama and then mantra, you learn how to transcend. Therefore, yoga teaches many ways for transcending yourself. After all, if you have been able to transcend yourself, to jump over your mind and your existence, then what happens? It is very unpleasant. Duality is withdrawn, dissolved. Once you have a vision of transcendental reality, that's all!

A river uniting with the ocean becomes ocean. A drop of rain uniting with the river becomes river. The individual soul meeting and uniting with the universal consciousness becomes universal consciousness. The local 'I', which has been cleansed all around, is dissolved completely. I am no more! The extinction of this 'I' must take place, and then this inner Christmas will be celebrated by you.

In every age it has been destined that some such person will come who will awaken his inner consciousness and after that he will show the true path to humanity. Let us hope this happens.

18

My Early Life

Satyananda Ashram, Mangrove Mountain, Australia, 31 December 1983

When I was six years old, I had a frightening experience. Of course I could not analyze that experience, and it came to me quite a few times. I could see my body, but I did not feel it, almost in the same way that I see your body, but I don't feel it. Now I see my body and I feel it because the body, the matter and the consciousness, are both interacting with each other. There is an interlink between the matter and the consciousness and, therefore, whenever we see our body we can feel it simultaneously. But sometimes when matter and consciousness are separated, it happens that you can perceive the body but you do not cognize it.

It was 1929 when that experience first happened to me. Fortunately, we did not have many doctors in India at that time, but a few were definitely consulted. However, they could not find anything wrong with me. I was quite intelligent and I did not appear to be a case of schizophrenia or nervous breakdown.

I was also taken to the local healers. The psychic healers in India are of different types. Some of them are spirit healers. They attributed my symptom to a spirit and declared that some spirit had taken possession of me and was playing with my body, my life and my destiny. Therefore, what they proposed to do was throw out this spirit. So they did a lot of rituals, but I don't think that it worked because that experience came back to me again and again.

My quest begins
I come from a place in UP called Almora. It is very close to the Himalayas on the western borders of Nepal and on the south-eastern borders of Kashmir. It is very beautiful and pure there, no smoke, no diesel, no sound, no noise, and Mount Kailash is very close, just over the Tibetan border. Mount Kailash is a very holy place for Hindus. It is supposed to be the residence of Lord Shiva and almost all the mythological stories and legends are connected to it. Although we do not hold it politically, it is in our minds spiritually all the time. At the base of Mount Kailash is Manasarovar, a very large lake, pure and crystal clear.

So this is considered to be a very important pilgrimage place and many swamis, holy men and sages of eminence used to pass through my town on their way to these higher reaches. My father took me to one of those swamis and asked him about the strange experience that was happening to me. The swami said, "Your son is undergoing a spiritual experience which he does not understand and which you also do not know. His consciousness is undergoing a state of transformation. According to the laws of evolution, when you pass from one mental state to another, you have different experiences related to the body, to the objects outside, to your own thoughts and to external things. The sun and the moon, the nature and the objects around you, the people, what has happened in your life and what is happening, appear somewhat different and sometimes totally different. It depends on how great a leap you have taken in the range of experience."

That was what the swami explained and with that my quest for spiritual life began. I began to understand what spiritual life really is.

Who am I?

We were Hindus, and Hindus have always been the most religious people in the whole world, but religion is one thing and spirituality is another. Sometimes they go hand in hand, but mostly they do not. Religion begins and ends with rites, rituals, beliefs, canons and scriptures. Spirituality, the quest for spiritual life, begins where religion ends.

A person with spiritual aims is not following the spiritual path because he wants some worldly things or because he is afraid of some higher entity. No. He is trying to understand his real nature and the events that are responsible for his existence. When he begins to realize that the body is not the ultimate matter, then what next? When he begins to realize that the mind is also not the ultimate, what next? It is like the analytical research of a scientist into matter.

Once upon a time the scientists did believe that matter was ultimate, but then they came to realize later that matter was a state of manifestation and it was not ultimate. So they began to investigate and discover what was behind matter. They split it and came to realize that there are so many elements which comprise matter, and then they came to nuclear energy and so many different types of energy. In the same way, spiritual life is a process of understanding the whole of yourself from matter to spirit, from gross to causal, from visible to invisible, from manifest to unmanifest, and all the elements that you are.

Religion is not a part of this process. Religion is propitiating an invisible entity out of fear, out of guilt, out of ignorance, out of infirmity, out of incompetence, out of your limitations. You are afraid there is a God. You must worship Him. You must pray. Just as it is your duty to pay tax, so it is your duty to pray. If you do not pray, something terrible is going to happen. You must believe in God, otherwise you are condemned. That is the religious ultimatum. So spiritual life is one thing and religion is something else.

I was Hindu and I was brought up to be religious. I had to be religious. I had no choice, no option, because when we are born in a family, in a society, in a culture, we are consciously or unconsciously brainwashed, indoctrinated with certain beliefs. We cannot get out of it. We are not allowed to develop our own personality; we are not free to be ourselves. We are packed with the rotten stuff of our parents and our environment and we cannot avoid it.

So we were religious people, but even at a young age I began to think beyond these temples and sanctum sanctorums. Beyond these there has to be something else, and I began to enquire what exactly and who exactly I am, and what is happening to me. Is there only the body and is the mind an offshoot of the body? Or is mind different from body, is consciousness different from body? All these questions began to come to my mind from the age of ten to seventeen, so much so that I became an outright atheist.

During this period I studied many books written by scholars, saints and sages. I read the *Koran, Bible, Bhagavad Gita, Upanishads, Zend-Avesta, The Imitation of Christ* and so on. I couldn't accept any of them because I thought there are thousands of millions of people the whole world over who are very good, very virtuous, but they don't know who they are, they don't understand themselves. Therefore, I came to the conclusion that even an idiot can become good and virtuous, but morality and religion are one thing, and discovering the true components of your nature is yet another.

What is matter made up of? Let me give you an example. Whatever the matter is, it is not homogeneous. It is not made up of a single element or item. It is a composition of so many elements. Similarly, this 'I' is not homogeneous, it is also a composition of the body, the senses, the mental forces, the prana and the spirit. All these combined together make up myself. That was my analysis, but analysis itself will not do.

You have to experience the body, the senses, the mind, the prana, the buddhi, the ego and the spirit all at different levels. So, I did do a lot of practices, but I could not really experience anything. Maybe you also have tried to do the same, but experience is one thing and knowledge is another. There is a definite difference between knowledge and experience. Experience is intimate knowledge.

My first tantric initiation

When I was eighteen, a tantric yogini came to live in our family. She was an expert in tantra and she initiated me into the actual tantric practices. I was eighteen and she was thirty-five. I was educated and she was illiterate. But she knew the art. She stayed with us for six months and during that time she trained me in every tantric practice. There was nothing which I did not learn from her.

At that time I again began to have the same type of experience which I had at the age of six. This had continued to come up to the age of twelve, but after that I did not have that experience at all. I tried my best to recapture it. I wanted to have that experience again and again, but I didn't have it although I practised many things. With her I had that experience again, but in my opinion it was not ultimate. Every time I was with her I would have that experience, but then nothing beyond that.

In search of a guru

So finally, with the advice of a swami, I left my people and my home and went on an adventure in search of a guru. At that time I did not really know what a guru was. For me it was enough to search for a guru. I did not analyze what a guru really means. I first went to Udaipur in the western part of India. Quite close to that place there was a venerable holy man who was maybe eighty or ninety at that time. I lived with him for six to eight months. He was an expert in the tantric system, but he only knew the theory.

I learned a lot from him about the classical texts of tantra which I did not learn from this lady, but ultimately that venerable sage came to realize that I knew more than he did. He was a master of the science, but so far as practice was concerned he knew nothing. When I used to tell him about the practices, he was surprised, and one day he asked me where

I had learned that from. So I told him that I learned it from a yogini and I went on telling him about all the practices.

Then he told me, "Look here, my boy, this place is not for you. You may go. I cannot teach you all this. I only thought that you are such a promising young man with so much knowledge, maybe I would make you my successor." I told him, "I don't want to be anyone's successor. I didn't want to be my father's successor. How could I become your successor? If at all I had to succeed someone, it would be my father whose property, whose wealth belonged to me."

So I left that place, but I don't remember anything about the journey from that point onwards. It is completely buried in my unconscious. I don't know how many days it took, by which train I went, where I got the money, who fed me along the way, what I ate and what I drank. I only remember coming to a little place near Rishikesh on the train.

I was in the interclass compartment and in front of me there was another swami with great matted locks. He was smoking a cigarette. I felt very tempted, so I asked him, "Can I have a cigarette?" He replied very rudely, "What! Such a young man and you want to smoke cigarettes! You will die of TB." I said, "But you are smoking." He replied, "Yes, I have already lived the life and you have hardly begun."

Then he asked me where I was headed. I said, "I am in search of a guru." He laughed at me and said, "In search of a guru. Well, where are the gurus? Do you have a market for guru?" Anyway, he took me to Rishikesh town and deposited me in one of the temples. Before leaving he said to the priest, "Look after this boy, he is searching for a guru." That was all and I never saw him again in my life. I never knew who he was or where he came from.

Meeting with the guru

The next morning the manager of the institution came to see me. He happened to be from the same town as I came from, and he said to me, "Look here, I will give you a very good job in this institution. You can live here and you will get food free, plus money." I told him, "I have not come here for that. I have come here in search of a guru and I think Rishikesh is the place where I'll find one."

So he directed me to one of the swamis nearby. The next morning I visited that swami. He was a scholar in Sanskrit and the head of a monastery there. I went and spoke to him. He was very glad to see me and he said that he would allow me to live in his ashram, but he would not give me sannyasa diksha because that was not his tradition. I told him, "I don't want to stay here. I want to live with a guru. I don't want to live in an institution. If I have to live in an institution, then I would have been better off at my home." So he directed me to my guru, Swami Sivananda.

Living with the guru

I arrived in the ashram on 19th March 1943. I met Swami Sivananda in the morning and when I saw him all my doubts, my questions, everything subsided. I became calm, quiet and tranquil. From that time, my life with him began with devotion, surrender and dedication, not philosophically, not intellectually, but actually.

For the period of time I lived with the guru I worked hard day and night. For me, a day did not consist of twenty-four hours; forty-eight hours made one day for me. Sometimes I only slept once or twice in a week. I used to keep awake at night by taking the minimum possible food. You can't imagine, and you wouldn't believe, that anyone could ever survive like that – every now and then falling ill with diarrhoea, dysentery, dyspepsia, mouth ulcer and stomach-ache, hepatitis, paratyphoid, influenza, oh my God!

I experienced sickness as a blessing, not a curse. Sickness appears to be painful, to be unpleasant. It brings the thought of death to your mind. After all, what harm is there if I remain sick for six months or one year? Nobody wants to remain sick for that period, but I realized that sickness was a form of blessing. It makes the mind tranquil and free from passion.

When I was living in the ashram I used to do every type of work: physical, mental and spiritual. Not because I wanted to be something or to learn something. The idea of having that experience once again had completely left my mind. I didn't even remember that. I didn't know what I was working for.

If you work in an ashram, in an institution or in any kind of organization, you are bound to have some expectation; of course it may not be totally selfish. Either you work for peace of mind or to create an outlet for your energy, but I was working there without any motive, total dissolution of the salt. I worked as a labourer, as a cart driver, as a typist, as a translator, as an editor. I did everything.

My mind wavers

In 1947 I had a mental attack. From 1943 up to the first part of '47, I was very calm and comfortable. I was a conqueror, but in '47 I began to lose the battle. The mind began to cheat me, to deceive me. It said, "What are you doing here? For whom are you working? Your guru – he's exploiting you! He will have a big ashram and you will have nothing. He's extracting free labour from you. You are an idiot. You are a Sanskrit scholar. You know Vedas, Upanishads, classical sciences. You can speak, you can write, you can edit, even type. You can construct buildings, you know civil engineering, you know architecture. Why are you here? Go ahead, go, go!"

I began to lose the battle. I said, "Yes, I think it is right." So I wrote a letter to a friend in Delhi. Back came the rely that I was appointed as a subeditor of a leading newspaper in Delhi and then came the appointment letter. I wrote to my friend again saying, "But I have no clothes. I can't come in this dress." So he sent me four hundred rupees. I went to Rishikesh to have the clothing made and it was ready with my little suitcase.

On the 8th September 1947 it was the sixtieth birthday of my guru, the Diamond Jubilee, so I thought I'd better attend that. Many devotees and disciples from all over the world had come to celebrate this occasion. I was there on the 8th, 9th and

10th. I decided to leave on the 12th. I did not tell anyone my plans. Nobody knew. Quietly I made my suitcase ready.

On 12th morning I took my suitcase down to the kitchen side and went to see Swamiji. I went and just greeted him. He looked and said, "Yes?" He was a very softly spoken person. He spoke briefly. He did not talk, talk, talk like a parrot. He said, "What's that?" pointing to my suitcase. I said, "I am going." He asked, "Where?" I said, "Back to Delhi."

"Why?" he asked. "I want to be a karma sannyasin," I replied. "But you already are a karma sannyasin," he said. "No," I said, "I want to practise the truth of the Gita. I want to be like Arjuna and fight in the battle of life, yet be above the senses, the mind and the passions." He just looked at me with an air of finality and said, "No, you are not going."

I am reborn

I said, "But I have received the appointment letter, I have made the clothes and my suitcase is ready." He said, "You are taking sannyasa. That is your destiny. If you insist on going, you can go, but the train will not move. If you go by bus, the bus will not move and if you go by horse cart, the horse will not move. Because you are meant to be a sannyasin; that is your destiny."

Then he called a swami with a razor and gestured him to snip off my tuft. "Finished off," he said, "the last link with life is cut. Now throw away your sacred thread. From this day you do not belong to any society, clan or religion."

Then he asked me to go down to the Ganga and take three dips: one dip for the physical attachments, one dip for the mental attachments and one dip for the attachments which are there but are not known. I took three dips and then he gave me the name which you know. Then he said, "From today you have no father, no mother, no relatives, no social obligations, no social commitments. You are reborn!"

"You are born once from the womb of your mother. That is the birth of a physical baby. That is you, that is me. Then you are born from the womb of knowledge, jnana, where guru becomes the tool, the vehicle. And today you are born as a sannyasin. When a sannyasin is born, he is born from the guru. That is his spiritual birth and then he has nothing to do with his previous births."

That was what he told me. It was the 12th September 1947. The day I was supposed to leave Rishikesh, I left my body.

New Year's resolve

So 1983 is dying and 1984 is being born, still in the womb. Before that new year is born you must sing the glory, you must sing kirtan, and when it is born then you have a new year to live and a new year to follow and a new year to experience.

Unhappiness, depression, passion, frustration, happiness, prosperity, good health, friendship and love come to everybody in succession. Life is a mixture of both sides of experience. A man who is constantly happy from birth to death is the most unhappy man. There has to be a combination of experiences and that is what nature has provided.

Sometimes you are sick of these changing experiences, these changing seasons of life. You want everything to be pleasant – but please do not. That is one thing you have to learn for this new year. Everything is love? No. Love is not everything. Hatred is also part of life. Likes and dislikes, happiness and unhappiness, love and hatred are two sides of the same coin. When your wife, children or husband love you very much you like it, but when they don't love you, you dislike it. This liking and disliking should stop and it must stop. At least this should be your resolve, your philosophy for the new year.

All my life I have lived with the good things – pleasant speech, nice friends, agreeable food, beautiful home, lovely wife and children or loyal husband. This year, whatever there is, that is nice. If I have learned to live with happiness, now I shall learn to live with unhappiness also. Here lies the strength of a hero.

The weak man is one who wishes only for happiness and does not want unhappiness, who wants comfort and does not want trying situations, who wants health and does not want sickness, who wants love and does not want hatred, who wants friends and does not want enemies. No. You have to be a hero. That is what the West has to learn.

This is the basic philosophy which has not been taught to you from the beginning. You have been pampered, you have been spoilt. When there is no pampering, then you become strong, and if this philosophy is integrated into the daily life, in your family and in your society, you will find in a few years time the number of mental cases in your country will automatically come down. Because then you will know how to face both sides of life.

Now you only know how to face one situation; you can't face the other. You are able to face, you are taught to face, you are living to face, just the pleasant situations. But when the situation changes, when the tables are turned and everything is loaded against you, then you don't know how to manage it. That is the reason why the mental hospitals are full to overflowing and mental diseases are rampant.

19

Interviews

Satyananda Ashram, Mangrove Mountain, Australia, 22 December 1983–1 January 1984

I am practising kriya yoga but I also want to learn pranayama. Can I practise pranayama as well as the kriyas?

Go on practising the kriyas; you do not have to do additional pranayama. However, you can practise kriya yoga and learn pranayamas one by one – not all together. Learning is not a problem. When you learn pranayama, it does not interfere with your kriya practices, but if you have learnt all the pranayamas and practise them as well as the kriyas, then that is too much.

What does shruti mean?

Shruti means revelation. Suppose I am talking to you. You hear with your ears. This is called words or sound. Now suppose you go to your room and suddenly you begin to hear the same words which I have told you without my being there. That experience is called shruti, revelation. So shruti means the sound which you hear that is not produced by an external object.

Shruti is a very great name. It means you should be able to hear the sound within you in deep meditation, the sound of the guru, the word of the divine, just as if I am talking to you. When I talk to you it is not divine, I am just giving you some kind of admonition, but when you are in your room and your mind drops and you feel that I am talking to you, that is called shruti.

Do you have to do anything to be initiated?
You have only to prepare your mind. There has to be acceptance of that initiation and that relationship, nothing external! It has to be taken from within. I think you should get initiated. It will help you gradually in your day-to-day life, your mental life and also in your spiritual life later.

For some reason I feel very nervous. I don't know why. I am just sitting here with you. What is it that makes me feel like that?
Oh, the relationship between guru and disciple is like this. When butter approaches fire it begins to melt. You don't have to ask why. The emotions, the feelings of a disciple are very tender and when he approaches his guru he begins to submit himself – he becomes all tender.

Recently I have had a lot of aggression towards me from others. How can I avoid this?
It could be your own idea. You should try to be sweet and agreeable to each and everyone all the time. You see, every human being has a weakness and this weakness is that he likes to be accepted. If you don't accept me, I don't like it, or if I don't accept you, you don't like it. This is human nature. So you must always have an agreeable attitude towards others, an attitude of total acceptance – no rejection!

I have felt extremely divided, although I have a strong inclination towards unification. At the same time, I wonder how much perception, learning and knowledge one derives through suffering and pain and whether happiness can in some way blunt the senses. How does yoga fit in with all this?
Yoga will help you to develop your inner awareness, to know more about the role of inner feelings in your life and the

feelings you have described. You want to work for unification and to learn from suffering and pain. When you have developed awareness, you can understand them much better. Your concept, your understanding is very distinct after you have practised yoga.

With that awareness you experience the existence of pain, but you don't feel it; pain does not disturb you. You can see it as a witness, as if you are separate from it. You can separate yourself from pain and therefore there is no suffering, there is only understanding of that suffering. You have to live through pain, but you can always experience pain as a witness.

Is yoga only connected with mystical awareness?
No. Yoga is related with each and every item of your personality. It is related to your body and its laws – that is one aspect of yoga. The second aspect is related to your feelings and behaviour, mind and thinking. Later it is related to your emotion, then to your concept and philosophy. Finally it is related to your mystical consciousness also. You cannot say that yoga is connected with mystical consciousness only. That is one form of yoga, but there are other forms whereby you can influence the body, the nervous system, hormones, etc.

Sometimes I feel very unsure about life out in the world. I feel I need reassurance that something really does exist which is worth living for. Maybe I don't have much faith, but sometimes I feel very lost.
These symptoms are universal. Only a few people are free from them. Everybody is unsure about life, especially here in the West. People are very insecure because their social and family tradition is flimsy and weak and their training is also very incomplete. You get school training: fifth, sixth, seventh, eighth, ninth, tenth class, history, geography, maths, so on and so forth, but you are not taught anything about life because your parents don't know anything, nor have they time to teach you.

They give you the best of things: toys, picnics, jam, chocolates, but not a training for your life. They tell you how to behave if you a girl or if you are a boy. When you grow to fourteen, sixteen, eighteen, what changes will take place in your mind? Up to the age of thirteen or fourteen you didn't know anything, but now you are grown up and suddenly you find you are in the wide world, the wild world! You don't know what to do. If you love a man, he will take you off some day, but if you don't love someone, then what to be, and with whom?

You see, these insecurities and uncertainties and many more which I can't even tell you about now have spread in the West like an epidemic. Everyone has what you are talking about. You are not the first person. Now, in this particular situation, there are a few elements which you will have to bring into your life. First, a steady mind is necessary, whether you are going to marry or not going to marry, if you are going to have child or not going to have a child, if you are going to take sannyasa or if you are not going to take sannyasa, still you must be steady. Find a job to do, a place to live and dedicate your time to spiritual knowledge and practice.

First practise yoga, meditation and relaxation, then higher yoga, and gradually go further. Side by side, if you want to live and enjoy the ordinary life of a householder, then go ahead with that. It can't be one after the other, it must be side by side. If you are living the worldly life, live the spiritual life side by side. Then these uncertainties, insecurities and fears will gradually drop away, although they will always be there with you because they are the qualities of your mind and not the nature of your surroundings. Even if you have the best of surroundings, still you can be insecure.

I have had so much sadness in my life. However, I have learned how to handle myself a lot better now, but I still feel as if life is very difficult. I wish I could find something to dispel this sadness. I have some very good children, a

wonderful career, I'm happily divorced. I study but I'm not very disciplined about my meditation practice.
Everything which is lying within you, which is embedded within the mind, should be brought out and should be seen by you in the form of images and then in the form of feelings. Thereby you will be exhausting and eliminating your samskaras, your karmas, the disturbing part of your personality, and side by side you will also begin to experience inner happiness. Then your sadness or loneliness, or whatever you might call it, will go away.

You will have to practise concentration, any kind of concentration. You can concentrate on a candle flame, a black dot, your own symbol, your mantra, breath, chakras, or on your forehead or nosetip. There are many methods. When you begin to concentrate, after some time the images start coming to you. You can call them psychic images. They are transformations of the awareness of many things which are accumulated in you.

All the feelings or archetypes which are accumulated in you sometimes come out in the form of sadness, unhappiness, outbursts of emotion. Sometimes they don't come because you suppress them. You have to live in society, to visit people and behave in the proper way, so you have to suppress, but at times all these things have to come out.

There is repression, suppression and expression. I am talking about expression. These expressions come in the form of dreams, but you have no control over dreams. However, when you are doing concentration, you are seeing images, and therefore you have control over them and by having control over them, you will have control over your dreams. Every person who wants to have control over the mind must have control over his dreams, but you can't have direct control. You must go through the indirect method. After mastering the images which come in concentration for a fairly long time, then you can control your dreams. This is an inner process. I think you should take that path and the best thing to begin concentration with is mantra.

Sometimes I feel I can't cope with the world that is in flux. I want something that is constant. At other times I feel the richness and variety of that world in flux and move a lot between the two. What is the yogic approach? Do you take the world in all its disparate forms?

We see the world as we see things happening on the television screen. We see things happening – a mother's love, hatred, fighting, quarrels, union, separation. We understand that. At the one time we are able to feel that, but we are able to detach ourselves. The world is in motion, there is inconsistency and influx. We see every form of this manifestation and we try to remain a viewer.

You do become a participant from time to time and when you become a participant, then you have to participate in the suffering and in happiness as well. But when you are able to detach yourself and see things happening in your own life and in the lives of other people, then it gives you some sort of happiness and joy. It is contentment, it is not elation, it is not jumping, it is not gaiety. It is just a feeling of completeness, a sort of fulfilment.

I am a household swami who wants to find God in this lifetime. I have to work outside the ashram. Can you direct me in my function in this life? What can I do to find God?

Whoever you are and whatever you are, it makes practically no difference, if you just close yourself away every day for at least one hour and withdraw your mind from every external awareness. Practise just one thing – mantra, either loudly or mentally, with the breath or on a chakra point, it doesn't matter. Do it for one hour, no more. That resolve you have to make for yourself.

As a karma sannyasin you may do any work, it doesn't matter. You see, you are working in order to live, that's all. In any case, you must devote one hour and gradually in one year or so, you will build up a base. Then you will be able to go ahead with very good speed and for that you can live in an ashram or outside. You can be anywhere; it makes no difference.

I have had a lot of darkness and problems in the past nine years of my life. I am looking for a path, a method to help me. I feel the futility no matter what I do, nothing can get me out. Sometimes I do yoga and meditation, but I have to use my will to get any sense of peace out of it. When I was six I was very cruel to animals. I don't know what made me do it. I wouldn't think of doing it now. I have strong images of knives coming into my mouth. I'm looking for some light. It seems the harder I try, the more I get stuck.

This is due to the dross created by the previous life and through meditation you have to experience these things without fear. You must face them, and when you can go on facing and experiencing them, they will go away. For the time being you will feel very bad, but finally you feel that it has been purged out and you will be okay.

You have to follow that purging process, and when you practise meditation and see these things, just witness them. Don't be afraid of them and don't become a part of them. Be a witness; see what is happening. You don't have to be afraid at all because these things are just latent impressions which have been embedded in your personality for a long, long time. You don't know for how long a time, but they are there. By gradual meditation, they have to come out. They happen in everyone's life and to all the great souls, prophets and sages.

I wanted to see you in the hope that you can help me resolve some of my hostility towards you. Our daughter left our home of love and came to you six years ago. It is a wound in our family that doesn't ease because I see her so happy and at peace with herself. It's worse with her father. I don't know her. She won't come home and it's as though I had given her away as a baby. Why can she not come and see us?

She is at liberty; she can always go if she wants. Nobody is holding her. I don't hold anybody as mine.

Her commitment is holding her.
Well, I don't even talk to her; I hardly see her.

I thought if I met you, I would see why your hold on her is so strong.
No, it is not my hold on her, but her personal experience of the life which she is living. It is so peaceful and so fulfilling in contrast to the life that she must have been living in her family before. So naturally, when we have been living in a very hot country for some years and then we come to a very pleasant climate, we don't want to leave it.

Yes, but she was child, she had no experiences of her own.
A child can always resist her experiences from the age of one and two. Even a child of seven or eight can resist. By the age of twelve, thirteen and fourteen, she can check and examine all those experiences in relation to the present one. This is what the psychoanalysts talk about. So to examine the circumstances one need not be an adult, rather adults are weaker in this respect. They are not able to examine the circumstances by contrast.

There is so much conflict with her father, brother, friends, relatives, uncles, aunts and cousins.
This is, I believe, because many people are working against that fundamental right of a human being. Every human being is independent and you are independent. If you are independent, why am I not independent? We live in a free world where children above a certain age have a right to decide.

Of course, but not with hurt to so many others. It seems to be a denial of what is good in my society that one should satisfy oneself at the expense of the whole.
That 'society' is a very relative substance. What is considered good for society today was not considered good centuries ago.

When I say society, I mean our family, that small part.
That family and society have to change their views according to the changing circumstances of society. The whole of society is changing. In America and Europe it has changed; in developing countries it is changing. We live in a modern society, but the primitive philosophy does not fit in with this. This is a primitive way of thinking, not a modern way of thinking.

What you are speaking about is a very old way of thinking, five hundred years ago people used to think like that. Now man makes his own destiny, whether he goes to nightclubs, to drugs, to the army or on an adventure. Every individual has to be free to choose his or her life and if they want to change the structure of their life, they should be free to do it. We old people who are above fifty or sixty are unable to restructure our minds.

I don't think I agree with you. I really believe I have a responsibility to you, to my daughter, to my husband, to all people and I may say this is not a one way street. They also have a responsibility to me. Surely, if I deny that responsibility for my own equanimity, I'm being selfish.
Responsibility and a sincere desire to help others is always a good thing, but why do we stand in the way of another's happiness? Why am I so selfish? You are happy, then that's okay, but I want to be happy at the cost of your happiness, that should not be there.

Once a person becomes unhappy, then he needs help and it is your responsibility. Suppose I am a mother. As long as you are happy, I have no responsibility and I have no duty, but once you are unhappy, then it is my responsibility, it is my duty, but not until then.

Can you give me some advice about my spiritual development? I haven't been practising yoga recently, but I have started doing aikido and seem to be getting a quicker result.
In order to make progress in spiritual life, you should come to any of the ashrams from time to time and have some lessons on meditation, pranayama and meditation techniques.

Spiritual progress depends upon the quality of consciousness, not the quality of feeling. If you do something now and if you feel better, it doesn't mean that you have made spiritual progress.

Spiritual progress depends upon the quality of your spirit or your consciousness and therefore the basic personality must be transformed by powerful techniques. For that you can go to whichever ashram is closest to your place from time to time and practise some lessons, but whichever practices you do should be able to transform your spirit gradually. You should be able to sit in meditation for half an hour or one hour and have greater control over the patterns of your mind.

Could you explain to me the form of meditation I should do?
Concentration on sound – mantra. That is how you begin. This is the easiest method. Other forms of concentration are there, but they develop experiences that you may not be able to handle. You see, the important thing in every system is adaptation. You don't have to plunge into the depths immediately before you are able to handle the inner experiences.

Mantra, the sound, is most suitable because it develops only mild and pleasant experiences which you can handle and which you can like. After you have been practising mantra for some time, then you can go into the deeper practices of concentration little by little and learn to handle those experiences step by step.

I left the ashram quite some time ago. Still I am the same, but I have had quite a few experiences. I know that what I am involved in is not actually real. So what do I do now? There is no real problem, just life is not that fulfilling for me.
For those who are superior in mind, who are intelligent, life is never fulfilling. If it was fulfilling, I would not have renounced. I would have become a professor, lecturer or landlord, but I renounced. You see, life is not fulfilling and this notion will always remain with you until you are able to realise.

When I realize, what do I do? Do I come and live in an ashram?

No, when you practise you are able to withdraw your consciousness from outside. Then you begin to feel things within you, not on the mental plane, not on the emotional plane, but the initial experience. Gradually you will be in *shoonya*, void, total void, no thinking, and from that state you will come back every time. You stay one hour in the void and then come out, go back and come out, go back and come out.

In the course of time, you become a different person. You don't think in terms of fulfilment. You think just one thing – you are the medium and your guru is now working through you. When the awareness of mediumship comes, then you may start an ashram, a school, a hospital or you may do anything, it's not important.

I know it's not important, but still I have to fill in the days.

As long as you are in realm of the mind, you have to fill in the days, doing something to keep yourself occupied so that your mind doesn't play mischief with you, but once you have gone beyond a certain point, you don't need to fill the day. You can just sleep the whole day, sleep the whole night and then go out the whole day or go out the whole night. You can do anything then, not now.

Now you have to keep yourself occupied, plan your days properly, read books, practise yoga, do your job, come to the ashram. Live life in order to keep the mind properly occupied so that it doesn't trouble you. As you go higher in spiritual practices, you transcend certain barriers. After that you don't have to do anything. You are an instrument. If you are my medium, I will work through you – that's all!

Often when I get over an obstacle I would like to thank you. Is that presumptuous? I think of it as your grace, but I don't really know what it is. I haven't really done anything to deserve it.

The relation between guru and disciple can be used for the wellbeing, spiritual progress and peace of mind of the disciple. The relationship between guru and disciple is a relationship of grace, compassion, help and consolation. One need not think about it at all.

When one is facing certain obstacles in mental life, material or spiritual life, one must try to overcome those obstacles by wisdom and willpower as far as possible, but that doesn't happen with everybody all the time. Many times one becomes weak and at that time one can invoke the help of guru.

In the life of a disciple, the only factor that is important should be guru, and it is the same with guru also. For the guru, the disciples are most important. Obstacles are everywhere. In everyone's life there are obstacles. In material life, mental and spiritual life, there are many obstacles. Sometimes you feel them and sometimes you don't. This relationship is based on absolute grounds of faith.

What should I do, take sannyasa or not?
Well, as far as I can tell you, the best possible advice I can give to anybody is to take sannyasa. However, there are many 'ifs' and 'buts' between my own choice and your possibilities. For me, sannyasa is a most important point in one's life. It is not just this dress.

It is change of dress, change of heart and change of so many things within. Often we take sannyasa and later we waver a little bit from time to time. *Maya*, delusion, assails us, the mind deceives us and sometimes says, "Go again." Many things can happen, but with all that, I think sannyasa is the best choice a man who is heading towards spiritual evolution can make. However, the choice is your!

What sort of yoga should I practise?
The best yoga is karma yoga. The next best is mantra. So, you can have a combination of karma yoga and mantra, then practise hatha yoga.

Could you suggest anything I could do to help me overcome fear?

The best thing to overcome fear is to face it – let it come! Bring it to the forefront of your mind; do not suppress it and do not withdraw yourself. Facing it is the best. You can face it on two planes, the mental and the psychic. On the mental plane let it come spontaneously into your mind for as long as you can handle and face it. Then, when you can't handle it, suppress it. On the psychic plane, when you are practising yoga or mantra and the frightening visions come, let them come. So you must not fight with fear on the psychic and mental plane.

Side by side, you must practise pranayama very regularly. Many times fear has something to do with imbalance or low energy in the nervous system. Of course the seed of fear is in everyone, and when your nervous system is strong you don't feel it, but when it is weak you feel it. So you should practise pranayama with bandhas and you'll be better.

Fear always follows man. Only a person who has realized his own self is absolutely fearless, otherwise everybody has some sort of fear in him always. What I'm telling you is that you might as well be at home with fear – that's all! You can't get rid of it; it goes with man.

How can I extricate myself from myself? Antar mouna was a suggested practice, but since I started this practice I have noticed thoughts come much more.

Let them come! It will be like that for a few weeks or a few months, then everything will be different. First there will be more problems, then there will be confusion. Then there will be a crowd of thoughts and you won't be able to separate or distinguish between them. Then gradually they come in the form of pictures and images. You must go on doing this and gradually you will know how to extricate yourself, how to separate yourself as a seer of thoughts.

How can the relationship with you become closer when you are so far away?

Physical distance is not of any significance. Maybe, sometimes a disciple who is not living with his guru is closer than a disciple living with him. That certainly makes no difference. But there should be certain moments, some time every day, when you should practice, in total seclusion, the feeling of guru's presence as a mother feels her baby's presence, as a lover feels the beloved's presence, and as you feel the presence of a strong emotion.

In the same way, you should try to feel the presence of guru, just for a short time – five to ten minutes. In the course of time this practice, if done every day, will make you feel closer to your guru. Then a sort of communication can be established between yourself and the guru on a subtle plane, and the guidance of guru can flow into you and give you spiritual direction.

I would like to stay and take sannyasa to concentrate on reaching my goal – samadhi. I want the quickest way, not only what is best for me but the best way in life as a whole. Do you want me to take sannyasa?
You see, when you want to look at your face, you must have a mirror. First you must clean the mirror and then you can look into it and see your face. These are the two processes involved in spiritual life. That relates to everyone, not only to you, because the mirror is not clean. We have to put our personalities together; they are in titbits, as you can see from your dreams and from your thinking process.

There is a thought process going on here; it breaks. Then there is another process; it breaks somewhere. There is no continuity. So, it is a good idea to take sannyasa. Live that life, gradually improving on it, because the day you take sannyasa you don't really become a sannyasin, but you are stepping towards it and gradually you bring your personality into integration. That is the way to inner and spiritual awareness.

There is no such thing as the quickest way in my opinion, but there is a way with fewer difficulties and greater speed.

Either you go through the city or you go through the bypass, where you have fewer obstacles, fewer red and green lights. With sannyasa, the spiritual process is accelerated.

The experience you are trying to achieve is always there in you, but there is a big barrier between you and the experience. That has to be broken. That thing is just beyond this wall. You don't have to develop it as you raise a child or a garden. It is there in its perfect form and this experience is eternal and in everyone. It is a state of experiencing. What each and everyone is supposed to do is to experience that.

All the barriers which are between myself and the experience are to be removed. For that purpose, sannyasa is a facility, it helps. The mind is made free from extra burdens and you can be spontaneous.

I had an experience while I was walking along chanting. It was like a big bird was going to hit me on the back of the head and it made me spin around. I went on chanting and I felt something coming up behind me. It came very close and walked into me. When I walked, it felt like two people were walking on the same foot. For a long time it worried me. Every now and again it comes up.

The first thing about this is that there is nothing to fear. This experience that you had is an indication of a development of psychic awareness – nothing has come from outside. There is not an external agency in you, but the development of a higher frequency or higher consciousness in you which you have experienced in the form of a second body, a bird and other experiences.

Now, when such experiences come to you again, you should not obstruct them or be scared. You should just observe them as if you are witnessing quietly what is happening. What will happen? Why will it happen? When will it happen? No, none of these questions! Whatever is happening, just be impartial, an unaffected witness.

Sometimes it makes me want to sing.
Okay, sing. But you should not be affected by it in the sense of, "What is happening; why is it happening; is it good; is it bad; what will happen?" No! Just sing. Don't give any opinion; don't come to any conclusion. Just witness – nothing else, just as you witness a dream, an aeroplane, a forest or a garden.

We are from Northern Germany and we have a strong desire to go back and teach yoga.
It is a very good idea to go to Germany and teach yoga, but in Europe there is one problem. All over Europe, the teaching of yoga is organized into federations – Swiss Yoga Federation, German Yoga Federation, Belgian Yoga Federation, French Yoga Federation, British School of Yoga, Dutch Yoga Federation, even Polish Yoga Federation. These federations are nation-wide and you have to become a member of that federation in order to teach, otherwise you won't be recognized.

It is not difficult to become a member. You just have to take a teachers training course and pass an examination. Then you can get a certificate and you can teach, but your activities are limited. You have to go according to the federation regulations and there is great competition in Western countries because teachers are like flies there. In one city there may be five hundred teachers.

Everyone is criticizing each other and trying to kidnap each other's students. Here, in Australia, this doesn't happen. You can go to any yoga school or ashram on your own, but there they send their people and kidnap the students. If you have fifty students, somebody will come to your class and kidnap them one by one. You will have a lot difficulties.

There are two ways of surviving in the West, particularly in Germany. The first is knowing the language and second is being part of a foreign institution, then it will work. You see, when you go there and start a school of your own, it is a German school, but if an overseas institution, say for example, Satyananda Ashram Australia, starts a branch in Germany like it has done in New Zealand, then it is called a foreign institution.

Then you will be given great respect. People will come to you because you are foreign. You see, this is human psychology, human nature. So keep these two things in mind. If you want to go and teach there, if you can help people there, well and good, but one suggestion which I will make – don't involve yourself with those competitive organizations. They are very tight, so many rules and regulations, such high fees, and you are caught up.

We are thinking to return there to live with our friends like before and try to give our form of yoga. Whoever wants to know about it can come, not in the sense of competition for students or anything like that.

That is a very good, idealistic approach, but in this world of reality, idealism does not succeed all the time. Of course idealism is good, I know, but the world is a world of reality and when you begin to teach in Europe they will ask you, "What are you teaching?" "Yoga." "Oh, are you competent to teach yoga?" "Yes." "Where are your certificates?"

That is Europe, you see. It's very organized and not very free. You have to show authentic backing. You can't go without it, no matter how qualified or how much of a genius you are. That applies everywhere, not only with yoga. You may have a shop and the goods from England and France and America sell better than the German goods. German goods sell well outside Germany.

When people speak about being aware of physical vibrations or anything from another person, what is that experience like? Am I blocked that I don't experience this?

No. You have gone above that; you have transcended that state. That is not a very high achievement but a primary achievement in spiritual life. When people are psychic to the vibrations of other people, the environment, so on and so forth, it is an early achievement, not a later one. So don't think you are blocked. It is not a disqualification. You just don't belong to that psychic state.

What about intuition, is it something that will come?
That is a high achievement, not everyone is intuitive, at least not very intuitive, although sometimes intuition does come to people on the spur of the moment.

Is there always a mental experience when initiation takes place? I did not experience anything during initiation that I can recall.
Yes, you did have the external experience if your intellect or mind could distinguish it. It is like a seed that has gone into the womb and will sprout and germinate in time. When you put a seed in you don't see it, but the activity is happening within. Sometimes you have an external physical experience and you feel exhilarated, ecstatic and all that.

As I told you, you don't belong to the physical, psychic category. Whatever has happened to you, whatever influence has gone in, you don't need to bring in the body. Like the seed within the soil, in the course of time, it will develop into a genuine spiritual experience.

More often than not I like to be alone. Sometimes I feel lonely in that aloneness, but often I feel quite comfortable. I tend to shut myself off from other people or force myself into relating to other people who I feel I want to be away from.
At various stages of spiritual life, one has to act differently. In the beginning of spiritual life, one must try to avoid undesirable associations and deal only with desirable and compulsory associations. When you are practising and experiencing something within yourself like peace of mind, oneness, concentration, then you should associate yourself with activities, actions and karmas.

It can be any work, like cooking your vegetables, gardening or housework where your mind is extroverted. Here you are not actually associating with anyone but are associating with the external activities. A spiritual aspirant who is developing in spiritual life and doing well must compulsorily associate himself with such activities where for some time the mind and senses are extroverted.

He does not have to associate with the people, but with the action, the work. Eventually there comes a time in the case of a very rare sort of person, when one has to close oneself completely off from people, from work, and remain in absolute solitude, do one's own sadhana and experience, but that's not for long. Then there again comes a time when you have to relate with every event, with everybody, desirable or undesirable, it doesn't matter.

This is not the same for everybody; it depends upon the state of your evolution. At the moment, in my opinion, you should relate more with the work and a limited amount with people. You may clean this room, wash your clothes, work in the garden, or help someone in sickness. You are not concerned with people here, you are concerned with the work. This is not complete solitude, but it is as good as that.

My son is going through a stage of being very negative and seems to be stuck in that state. He lives with his mother and came here with his sisters about two weeks ago. He quarrels a lot with his sisters and his mother and doesn't do his school work.

It is better that he should be left to himself – no interference, no admonitions, no advice! Give your children food, give them games, talk nicely and sweetly on matters other than study and behaviour. Don't give them any suggestions. Just change yourself and his mother should change herself too. If he fights, quarrels, disobeys, misses study, don't say anything. That is the only way to make him self-conscious, to make him aware, otherwise he will not develop that awareness himself because you are doing it for him. You stop doing it and he will develop his awareness.

Can he go to yoga classes?

If he wants, let him go. If he doesn't, let him not. If he wants to come here, let him come. If he doesn't want to come here, let him not. If he wants to stay here for a few days more, let him. If he doesn't, let him go back. Studies are not important; nothing in life is important. It is the man who is important. As long the man is healthy, he will pick up the race at any time. This is what I feel.

I was given the symbol of a flame. What does it mean and how should I use it?
Every day at some time, either in the morning or at night, you must meditate on the flame; try to see it inside. Just sit down quietly, make your body still, keep your eyes closed and then concentrate on that flame – the fire and the flame is coming up. It is meant for that purpose.

Would you please explain the philosophy of karma sannyasa and how it is possible to become a sannyasin while living in the world?
Karma sannyasa means living life fully, working hard and relating to everything and everybody, doing your best in your work, in your studies, in your relationships. However, at the same time you must try to develop a keener awareness of the inner voice so that the external life does not affect you – just as a lotus leaf is born of water, lives in water and grows up through water but is not tainted or affected by water.

If you notice, a lotus leaf is always dry. Have you seen it? In the same way, even though you are living in the world, doing all your work and duties, relating to everybody, accordingly you must keep your mind unaffected like a lotus leaf. You must experience life, joy, happiness, sorrow, pain, pleasure, success, failure, everything, but you should not be affected by it. That should not touch your soul.

This is the philosophy of a karma sannyasin. You must live in the world like a lotus leaf. Interact with life. Do everything. Fulfil your duties, responsibilities, commitments, obligations, but disidentify yourself.

How does initiation into karma sannyasa change our lives?

You know that this initiation into karma sannyasa enables you to function in life as an ordinary person, but at the same time the change has to be felt internally, not in relation to the obligations and work, but in relation to the effect on the mind. Everything in life, whatever you do and whoever you meet, leaves behind some karma in the mind, whether it is happy or unhappy, pleasant or unpleasant. Even the things happening within, positive and negative thinking, feeling and sentiment, all leave some seed behind, some impression.

That impression or seed later influences your whole personality structure. You will have to wipe out this residue from time to time by maintaining a sound philosophy and sound thinking. That is the main practice of a karma sannyasin. Happiness comes and goes, pleasures come and go, people come and go, but what they leave behind in your mind, that must be changed. That should not be able to affect your personality and behaviour.

Come what may, you must do some yoga practices every day. Of course, when time permits, it is good to practise a number of things – asana, pranayama, meditation, japa, etc., but it not always possible to practise them all due to preoccupations. However, you have to practise something every day, very regularly. You may like to do asanas because they make you feel good, or you may prefer to do only mantra because that is easy.

You have to decide for yourself which of the sadhanas you will practise at any cost, which is most suitable for you, whether yoga postures, pranayama, kriya, meditation or mantra. So that sadhana becomes your central axis, the central basis of your life. The practice may only be five minutes or ten minutes once a day, either in the morning or at night or at any time of the day, but it must be regular.

20

Shivalingam

Satyananda Ashram, Mangrove Mountain, Australia, 10 January 1984

Before I go on to explain about shivalingam, I would like to clear up a few misunderstandings about it. Unfortunately the word *lingam* as it is given in the Sanskrit dictionary means phallus, the male organ. In the past, when the researchers first began to explain and write their thesis on shivalingam, they did not know much about Sanskrit, its history and grammar. They just took the dictionary meaning literally, which gave lingam as the male organ; shivalingam, the male organ of Shiva. That is how the whole misunderstanding occurred. Then when other research scholars wanted to do research on *Shaivism*, the cult of Shiva and shivalingam, they also made the same mistakes.

Symbol of cosmic consciousness
According to Sanskrit grammar and the philosophy connected to that, the term *lingam* means a state of existence which is invisible, which is unseen, but which is there nonetheless. Most artists, poets and thinkers can understand this very well. Can you see your emotions, frustrations, happiness and joy? No. If they are in you, you can feel them, but if they are not in you, you can't feel them, although they may exist in the other person. That

means the ordinary emotions in human beings have a form, although it is invisible.

In the same way, consciousness is abstract. I'm not talking about human consciousness. When I say consciousness, I mean the cosmic or total consciousness. You may use any word for it you like, even God. The consciousness is invisible, abstract and infinite. It cannot be comprehended. The ultimate reality is incomprehensible to anyone, even to a saint or a yogi, much less a paramahamsa. If you want to comprehend that ultimate reality, there is only one way – you have to become that. It is not possible otherwise.

Therefore, that consciousness which cannot be comprehended by any means, by anyone, should be comprehended by its symbol, and that symbol in Sanskrit is known as *lingam*. It is not the phallic symbol; it is called shivalingam, *Shiva* means absolute ultimate total consciousness, cosmic consciousness or universal consciousness. These are all just names. *Shivalingam* is just the representative, the symbol of that cosmic consciousness. That is the first important point which must be understood by everyone.

A universal tradition

Today it is only in India that the shivalingam is worshipped, venerated and meditated upon by the majority of Hindus, not by all Hindus and not by any other religion, Christianity, Islam, Buddhist or Judaism. Nobody else worships the shivalingam nowadays. But if you go back into history and study about the ancient civilizations which flourished in the middle ages and even much before that in the dark ages, you will find substantial evidence to prove that, in ancient times, the worship of shivalingam was prevalent throughout the world.

In South America, symbols have been found dating back to the ancient pre-Columbian civilization, which prove that worship of Shiva was very prevalent in the cultural philosophy of the Aztecs, Incas and other indigenous tribes of Red Indians, even in Mexico. Early in this century and during the last century, when some of the oldest churches in England were excavated after damage, they found shivalingams at the bottom.

How shivalingam was preserved
I do not want to go into greater details of this here, I just want to tell you that although Shiva's worship is practised by the majority of Hindus in India and is accepted by all Hindus, it is not particularly Hindu. The only reason that the shivalingam can still be found here today is because the Hindus have very carefully preserved it. The Hindus form a very tight community. Anything they get, they will keep. They don't want to destroy any form of language, art, culture, religion, customs, dress, food, etc. That is the kind of people they are.

This applies not only to their religion, but also to their political ideology. Communism will die and nobody will even know about it, but in some remote corners of India you will find it still being practised. Hindus are a museum in this way. That is why you can find anything in India. You can find jumbo jets and bullock carts, the most modern fitted toilets and open latrine buckets. You can be sure, even in the twenty-first, twenty-second and twenty-third centuries, somewhere you will be able to find them still.

Throughout the world, on every continent, there have been massacres, wars and political destruction from time to time. This happens in every country and nobody can stop it. As long as there is religion, there is going to be massacre. Religion protects, patronizes and feeds political ideology. What happened from 1939–43? What happened in Cambodia? What happened during the Chinese revolution, the Russian revolution, the Iranian revolution?

It has happened throughout the world in this way. In North and South America, the Indians were destroyed; in Europe, the Celts; in Russia, the Slavics, Mongols and Huns. Even in India there have been periods of mass destruction when whole philosophies and systems were destroyed, philosophers and priests were killed and sanctum sanctorums were brought down also. You know about that and if you don't know, please read about it. It is important to know where humanity has made a mistake and where it will make a mistake again and again.

In India, however, there is a particular class of people which has been moving along very calmly and quietly. I'm using the word India, but actually I'm speaking for the Hindus. The Hindu culture is a cryptograph of civilization. A cryptograph is a microscopic account of all the achievements and blinders, successes and failures, wars, treaties, creativity and destruction of man in cipher form hidden underneath the ground. Many civilizations in the world have left cryptographs on rocks, on tablets and on paper in the form of poetry, imagery and traditional forms.

In India, however, they created a section of people that are known today as swamis, sannyasins, renunciates, hermits. They have had various names from time to time and the Hindus told them, "Look here, you live apart and have nothing to do with politics, with sensuality, with social administration, with upkeep of the family. Here is a house, money and food. You learn, study and teach the science of consciousness'– just do that much. The science of the consciousness, of the spirit, of your own nucleus – that's all you study, that's all you learn, that's all you experience and that's all you teach. Don't teach social things."

That is why a swami will never tell you how you should marry, whether you should marry or not. No. If you ask me, I would say, "Do whatever you like," because that is not my subject. Therefore, the Hindus were able to preserve the science of shivalingam. I'm not using the word religion here; I am using the word science.

The establishment of Shiva temples

Why did they preserve the science of shivalingam? Why is Shiva worshipped throughout India in the form of an oval shaped stone? What is the tradition about it which people do not know? This oval shaped stone is not carved or man-made.

It is found exactly in that shape, ranging anywhere from a few inches to about fifteen feet in height. It is brought from the banks of a river called the Narmada, which originates in central India and flows towards the west, ultimately merging in the Arabian sea. That is one important thing which you should know.

Secondly, all the Shiva temples in India are not established just because somebody has the money to do it. Some fellow gets a dream in the night and he's told, "Go to that place and dig fifteen feet down." So he goes and digs and finds a shivalingam there. Or he is told in a dream, "You establish a shivalingam from that part of the Narmada. Go to the river, bring it back and establish it." It is mostly the innocent people, the very simple folk, who get such dreams and have the shivalingams established. The villagers and the people from the town, rich and poor, donate enough money to raise the temple.

This is how the temples of Shiva are built in India. It's not because you have the money and you decide that at Mangrove Mountain there should be a church and so you build it there. No, that is man's effort, intellect or whim. It is not due to your wish that you should create a house of God. God should make his own house. Who are you to think of making a house for him? This house must be built to represent him, to symbolize him. That is called a temple, sanctum sanctorum, church, mosque, or house of God.

Therefore, there has to be an intuitive flash in meditation or in dream. The consciousness must be illumined. When that consciousness is illumined, then these things should happen. Then the temple has to be built. Many people ask me, "Why don't you build a temple in Munger?" I say to them, "But I didn't get the order. If I get an order, I will build it. I will do what I'm ordered." This is the second point.

Trigger of consciousness
The third important point is that shivalingam is not a god. It has nothing to do with ritualistic worship. It is a very ancient

replica of an event which triggered man's consciousness and brought him from the state of ape man to human. In the depth of human consciousness, in the centre of the brain, there is an unseen force, an invisible power or substance, without which you are not a man. You know that you are. You know that you know you are. You know that you know that you know you are. A dog does not know it. A peacock does not know it. The little birds do not know it. A kangaroo does not know it. You know it, right?

Millions of years ago, however, you existed but you did not know it. Your forefathers lived in caves like any animal. What happened to him that, unlike any of the other animals, he just jumped over the fence and began to feel what happened yesterday, what is going to happen tomorrow and what relation the present has with the past and with the future? How did he jump over the fence? The scientists say it is all due to the process of natural evolution. No. Up to the human body, everything is moving within the domain of natural evolution, but awareness is not the subject matter of natural evolution.

The sphatik lingam

In Shaivism they say that the real shivalingam is crystal, but this crystal shivalingam is not available to anybody. In India we have the crystal shivalingam. In Sanskrit it is called sphatik lingam. This *sphatik* or crystal lingam is only found in a few places and then it is not moved, but a temple is built around it. We were fortunate to keep the sphatik lingams in India. When the invaders came to India, they took away everything of value, but they did not remove the shivalingam because they thought it was a dirty Hindu god. They took away the jewelled crown, they took away the peacock and it flew to Iran, but they did not take the crystal lingam and it was the most precious thing.

Why is crystal precious? It has been scientifically proven that crystal has many effects on matter, on substance, and on the brain. It is not just a simple stone. Of course, all stones and minerals have different properties. Crystal grasps all the sound vibrations. Any sound vibration passing through the sound matrix, through the dimension of sound, will hit the crystal objects. It may be a small crystal ball, a crystal mala, crystal beads or a crystal lingam.

When you expose yourself before a sphatik lingam, then something begins to happen in your brain and consciousness. This is exactly what happened millions and millions of years ago. When our ancestors confronted the large rock of crystal, their consciousness began to explode. That great explosion or awakening which took place in them happened on account of the psychic images that they began to see within themselves.

Many people who take LSD see these images. With open eyes you can see them sometimes, with eyes closed you can see them, in meditation you can see them, in dreams you can see them and when you are under the sway of a drug you can see them. Those images which you see relate to the movement of an inner consciousness. They don't relate to your brain. Dreams definitely do not relate to your day-to-day life. Dreams do not come through the experience which you have gained. Dreams come from some other source. Please remember it.

Of course, many times when you dream, you see almost the same things which happen during the day. I'm not talking about these dreams. The source of the dream is something which you have not experienced. It is somewhere you have never been. The source is in your unconscious. It is beyond the conscious and the subconscious mind. It is in the unconscious, *anandamaya kosha*, the causal body, as it is called.

In Samkhya philosophy and in Vedanta, the causal body is known as *linga sharira*, the linga body, the subtle body, which is there but you can't see it. When you see the sphatik lingam, it explodes the images from the causal body or the unconscious, which is in you and which was in your ancestors also. That is how, when your ancestors somewhere in the north or south pole, or in America, Africa or India, confronted the crystal shivalingam, they jumped over the fence.

With that leap the human evolution started. With that leap, you began to know that you are existing. That is why concentration and meditation on the shivalingam are considered very important, because it can explode the inner source of awareness where infinite knowledge is hidden and where the possibility of the great evolution of man is stored.

Man is not at the final stage of evolution. What man is experiencing today is not the beginning of the end. It is not the end of the beginning, but the beginning of the beginning. You have started. You have now begun, and gradually the consciousness will evolve to a point where every man will become a superman. So in short, this is the philosophy of shivalingam.

The twelve jyotir lingams
In India there are thousands and thousands of temples where this oval shaped shivalingam is worshipped, but of all these only twelve are considered as jyotir lingams. *Jyoti* means light. *Jyotir lingam* means illumined lingam. These are not Narmada lingams, they are crystal lingams. Eleven of these are situated at different places in India and the twelfth is in Nepal.

Every shivalingam has a special name. The name of the shivalingam in Nepal is Pashupatinath, which means 'lord of the beast'. The names of the others are Somnatheshwar, Mallikarjuna, Mahakaleshwar, Omkareshwar, Kedareshwar, Bheemashankar, Vishveshwar, Trayambakeshwar, Vaidyanatheshwar, Nageshwar, Gushmeshwar and Rameshwar.

Each year hundreds and thousands of people go on pilgrimages to these places. In the month of March there is an important day, the fourteenth day of the dark fortnight. It is called *Shivaratri*, or the night of Shiva. This is an undeclared holiday in India. Nobody goes to the office. The whole day everybody is fasting; they don't even take a drop of water or a drink of tea. They only practise the mantra *Om Namah Shivaya*.

In the evening they do not stay at home and sleep, they go to the temple and all night there is worship. The people sit close to the lingam. There are many priests and brahmins and throughout the night they go on repeating the thousand names of Shiva, one after another. At the top of the lingam there is a copper vessel with tiny holes from which water continuously drips onto the shivalingam. All night long it drips and drips and the people meditate.

The philosophy of shivalingam

Now, the most important thing that we have to learn from this is that the external shivalingam is responsible for awakening your inner shivalingam. In tantra, in the kundalini science, it is stated that in this physical body there are also twelve places where this shivalingam is situated. There also it has the same shape. Out of these twelve places, three are considered very important. The first is at mooladhara chakra, the second is at ajna chakra and the third is at sahasrara chakra. It is said that in sahasrara the finest consciousness resides in the form of an illumined shivalingam.

Maybe after some time, scientists will discover that man's evolution, man's nature and its transformation, man's consciousness and its awakening are not influenced by the external things of society, religion, politics, ethics and morality, but they are manifested from somewhere within you. That is the Shiva in you and it was there even when your ancestors were alive millions of years ago. That is the finest matter in this physical body.

That fine matter was also present in the ape man, but he did not have substantial exposure to his awareness. He only knew fruits, he only knew grass, he only knew the little insects. He only knew that he could be killed by tigers and leopards. He only knew that another ape woman had given birth to a baby, that was all. He did not know that he was her husband; she did not know she was his wife.

The knowledge of relationships, the knowledge of perpetuation of emotion was not present in him. There was just action controlled by nature, not by consciousness. If I love you, it's controlled by my mind. If I hate you, it's controlled by my consciousness, but the apes did not have that consciousness. They killed each other. They did feel hungry, they did feel passionate, but nothing beyond that.

Up to that point, the ape man was under the domain of nature, *prakriti*, the natural forces, the Darwinian law – right? And if nothing had happened to the finest atom, the finest particle within him, the ape man would have remained an ape man up to this day. Similarly, if nothing happens to your finest particles, you are going to remain exactly what you are today. You will bear children, there will be generations after generations. The language might change, political ideology might change, construction of buildings might change, administration might change, but you will remain exactly the same, having the same type of consciousness, maybe even lower, but not higher.

What happened to those people who called themselves civilized two or three thousand years ago? What happened to the Romans, to the Greeks, to the Babylonians, to the Egyptians? Why were all these ancient civilizations destroyed? Because they could not evolve within the realm of consciousness. They evolved within the realm of matter. Instead of travelling by bullock cart, they travelled by plane or train. But the consciousness remained the same, static.

How does this consciousness move? Movement in the finer particles of consciousness takes place when the images blow. That blowing of consciousness comes in the form of experience, in the form of colours, in the form of sounds, in the form of music, in the form of unseen fear, in the form of many, many things. That is not empirical, not material, not concrete; it is more than that.

Therefore, I often think that those madcaps who see many more things than we do are more evolved. Maybe they are at the threshold of higher experiences, so we cannot see what they are experiencing. We just say they are mad because they are not able to adjust with the level of our consciousness, but maybe we are mad because we are not experiencing what they are experiencing.

You see, the most important thing you have to remember is that if you want to get out of this level of consciousness in which you are, then you have to use some such means which will have a direct effect on the inner force, and that inner force is called Shiva. This is the philosophy about shivalingam.

Bodies within bodies

Please understand that lingam in this context means causal body. Broadly speaking, you have three bodies, which can again be subclassified into ten bodies. This is not only said in Hindu philosophy, the Rosicrucians and Freemasons also said the same thing. If you read the old Celtic traditions in Europe before Christianity came, you will find it there as well.

In fact, in all of the ancient philosophies you will find this idea embedded. Man is not made of one body alone – there are three bodies called the gross or material body, the subtle or astral body and the causal or Shiva body. These three are again categorized into ten. So, around this body there is one halo, another halo, a third halo and like that you have ten halos representing ten different bodies.

Now, you can separate these ten bodies, or you can lead the consciousness from one body to another, from the first to the second, to the third, fourth, fifth, sixth, seventh, eighth, ninth and tenth. It is beyond the tenth that there is the bodiless itself. The *atma*, the self, the absolute, the *Brahman*, the God is beyond these ten.

If you have to arrive at that point, if you have to experience that which is beyond the three and beyond the ten, then it is important that you have to jump and jump and jump and jump – nine times over the fence. Now what are you doing? You are trying to jump. Do you know from which fence you are trying to jump? The first.

21

Meditation: A Tool for Man's Higher Evolution

Kuranda Ashram, Australia, 21 January 1984.

One of the most important aspects of yoga is meditation and it is definitely a very difficult one, For thousands of years, wise men have formulated various practices leading to an experience in meditation. These ways are known as the path of *dhyana yoga* or meditation. The elementary or preliminary practices of yoga are intended to develop a climate or atmosphere in the physical body in which meditation happens automatically. I must tell you here that if one can meditate properly, one is one's own master.

Now, from this, you can understand that meditation is a science which intends to make you a master of yourself, of your physical, mental, emotional, intellectual and also spiritual evolution. Man is a combination of various forces and every force has its own laws of evolution. All these forces assembled together are what you are. When you start practising meditation, you are initiating or accelerating the process of evolution in every realm of your existence and every dimension of your personality.

Scientific conclusions

In recent years, scientists have done a lot of research on the effects of meditation on the physical body, the mental and emotional behaviour and also on the psychic fields. They have come to the definite conclusion that when you meditate, changes do take place in the physical body, in the nervous system, in the endocrine system, in the blood pressure and so on. Numerous articles have been written by these scientists who are trying to tell us that during the practice of meditation, when your body is completely quietly and tranquil, the greatest changes, the greatest transformation is taking place from head to toe. These changes can be registered and seen on the most sophisticated machines today.

In addition to this, some scientists have also proved that while you are meditating, you are not only involving yourself in so-called psychological or subjective practices, but you are creating within yourself a field of energy like the electromagnetic field. There is a kind of energy wave which is transmitted by a person in meditation and this wave of energy, this field of energy, can be transmitted to people at a great distance. Experiments have shown that two persons stationed sixteen hundred miles apart were able to transmit and receive this energy which is generated during meditation.

This is a very important aspect related to your psychic being, not just to your physical being, mental personality or emotions. There is a kind of energy which you are generating during the practice of meditation and this energy can be transmitted, number one, and experienced by yourself, number two. This energy can also descend to the mental, emotional and physical levels, thereby changing the quality of the body, the mind and the emotions. This is a very important point. It has also been found that regular practice of meditation can improve the quality of intelligence, which is so important for children.

Unification of awareness

The practice of meditation is not a physical exercise. It is a method of producing complete and total tranquillity and absolute steadiness of the body. At the same time, there is something within you which is working very dynamically. You can use any word for it you like. That awareness, that attention, that mind, that consciousness must be unified. At this moment it is diversified, running in all directions to each and every object.

The consciousness in an individual flows through the sense organs: eyes, nose, tongue, skin, ears. This energy of the mind flows outward, receives stimuli and thereby experiences sense objects. This area of sensory experience should be withdrawn. That is the first practice in meditation. You have to disconnect your awareness from the sense objects through the sense organs.

If you have to put off the lights, what do you do? You have to disconnect the lines of the main switch, then there will be no light. In the same way, the light of the senses through which you cognize external objects such as forms, names, sounds, touch, taste, smell, has to be disconnected for the time being in order to practise meditation.

The practices which you know are the tools, the methods through which the sense organs have to be detached from awareness. One of the most important and most effective tools to establish this is mantra. There are other ways also. Some people practise concentration on a candle flame with eyes open, others sing kirtan. There are many methods, but the easiest and most powerful is the practice of mantra with the rhythm of the breath.

Creating an explosion

Mantra is a syllable which represents a sound. This sound can completely control the mental fluctuations. As the sound has waves, it has frequencies, it has velocity. When you practise mantra and the sound is ingrained in your mind, then the consciousness undergoes a great transformation. Therefore, those people who want to practise meditation must first of all find a mantra for themselves.

Mantra is a special science. When mantras are repeated mentally or even verbally, they create a certain sound vibration and you know that sound is a form of energy. It's not just A, B, C, D. every sound has its own wavelength, its own frequency.

I am producing a sound now. It has its own frequency. The same sound, when it is thought within the mind, increases in frequency. The higher the frequency, the more powerful is the sound. At a particular level, this sound explodes and the explosion of sound creates an experience.

Now, coming to an important point, meditation is not just a mental exercise. If you first close your eyes and try to concentrate by force, to withdraw your mind by force, again and again, that will not give you meditation. Before meditation comes, you have to accomplish one stage, bring about one experience, and when that experience takes place, you get into meditation. Therefore, meditation is not an effort. When you are practising mantra, you are creating a certain frequency in the mind and at a particular point, you are creating an explosion. When that explosion takes place, an experience happens.

What is that experience?
Experience is an inner knowledge. You begin to float out of this external plane and you begin to see with your eyes closed. You begin to experience, to visualize things which are not actually there. Some people see lights, flowers, colours, oceans, mountains, beings, etc.; that is called experience. It is a kind of inner perception which takes place on a different dimension.

It is very clear that when this experience takes place you have raised the level of your awareness, you have actually gone up from the ground floor to the first floor or maybe from the first floor to the second floor or the second floor to the third floor. If experience does not take place, then in spite of working hard on concentration, you are not going to change the level of your awareness. With every shift of awareness, an experience takes place.

In yoga it is said that there are seven levels of awareness. The first level is where we are now. It is called the sensorial level, the level related to the experiences connected to the senses. In this particular level of awareness, all your knowledge is related to the object through the senses. The mind is experiencing a flower, a sound, an object through the senses. The mind is experiencing because of the proximity of the object. If the object is not there, or if the senses are not functioning properly, the mind cannot experience it.

This is the first level of consciousness and there are said to be seven levels. As you shift from one level to another an experience must take place. There is no going from one level of awareness to another without experiencing something. That experience is so important and in order to develop that experience, in yoga and in meditation they have various tools or methods. One of the methods is *pranayama*, breathing. Another is *bandha*, contracting the anus, abdomen and throat. Another, as I have said, is mantra and like this there are many.

The purpose of meditation
Everything depends upon which level of awareness you are at. We are all here in one place, but we do not belong to one level of awareness. Our consciousness has already evolved differently. Physically we may look the same, talk the same language, discuss the same topics, but there is something in you and in me called spirit, the self, the man behind the man, and that spirit or self undergoes systematic transformation through the practices of meditation.

How does this occur? Take a lantern which has been burning throughout the night, and now the flue has become black so the lantern is not giving off proper light. What do you do? You clean the glass. As you clean the glass, the light shines through in its resplendence. In the same way, in each and every being there is a higher quality of spirit. An experience of that light is important now. You do not have to bring the light inside; it is already there. If you can remove the veils, if you can transcend layer after layer, then you will find that luminous spirit is already there.

Therefore, the purpose of meditation is to be able to experience that light. By the light, we mean that which can illumine the darkness which has enveloped our consciousness, which can illumine the whole fund of knowledge and can give us an understanding, an experience of ourself. Therefore, everyone must understand that meditation is not an occult practice alone. It is not only for the purpose of improving the quality of the body, but it is a systematic course by which one can come close to one's own inner self.

In terms of hatha yoga

Now, I will explain this in another way. Many of you know about hatha yoga, in which there are three important energy channels situated in the spinal cord. In physiology these three channels correspond to the parasympathetic, sympathetic and autonomic nervous system. In hatha yoga, they call them ida, pingala and sushumna, or moon, sun and the self.

These energy channels flow within the framework of the spine. To the left is *ida*, which carries the mental energy. To the right is *pingala*, which carries the *pranic* or vital energy. These two flows originate from the bottom of the spine and cross each other at four junctions in the spinal cord. One junction is at the sacral point, another is at the solar plexus, the third is at the cardiac plexus and the fourth is at the cervical plexus. Finally these two energies meet at the medulla oblongata near the pineal gland at the top of the spine.

Apart from these two energies, the mental energy and the pranic energy, there is a third energy which originates from the bottom of the spine and goes straight up the centre to the top. However, this third channel of energy is not operating in most people today. It is silent. In yogis who practise asana, pranayama and concentration, this energy becomes active, but not in everybody.

The energy which flows on the left side controls all of your mental functions. It is the conscious force by which you think, feel and know. The energy which flows on the right side controls all your physical movements. That is the life force by which you walk, eat, digest, evacuate and perform all actions. These two energies are intended to help us carry on with this life which is given to us by nature. If there is any imbalance in these twofold energies, then there is disease, either psychosomatic or somopsychic. Therefore, in order to promote health and wellbeing, balance of the mental and vital forces must be maintained. That is hatha yoga.

More than this, however, the energy known as sushumna, which is existing in the centre of the spine, must be awakened. *Sushumna* is the important spiritual energy which is referred to in many scriptures, but now it is inactive, sleeping. How to awaken this force? They say that you can awaken it through meditation, when the mind and objective experiences are withdrawn and the physical body is forgotten.

At this time you do not know where you are. Time, space and object are annihilated. Only the light shines in front of you. It is at this time that the awakening takes place and then you begin to experience many things. These experiences are so profound that they can transform your whole life, your philosophy and your values, and bring you closer to your real nature.

Therefore, I say that the purpose of hatha yoga is to prepare you to meditate. Sometimes there is some sort of misunderstanding regarding this. People think that they can meditate even when they are lying on their back. No! There are certain yoga postures which are meant for meditation and these should be studied and learned from your teacher.

During meditation the spine must be erect, upright and straight. This is the first important principle. Secondly, when you assume the correct posture for meditation, then you can control your physical body during deep meditation. Otherwise, if you meditate as you are sitting now, as you withdraw the mind, as you transcend the consciousness, you may fall down because there is no support for the body. Therefore, the classical meditation postures, siddhasana, padmasana and vajrasana, are very important. Those of you who want to take to the path of meditation seriously must accomplish these postures well beforehand.

Transcending materialism

Finally, meditation is related to the evolution of human consciousness. You know about the laws of natural evolution, how the physical body grew, how it evolved, how it was transformed. With the advent of man, the birth of man, the physical evolution has terminated and the spiritual evolution has begun. Therefore, we are now in the first chapter of spiritual life and in this human incarnation, the sole objective for us should be to evolve spiritually. To evolve spiritually means to be able to understand what lies within us – beyond the body, beyond the senses, beyond the mind and beyond the ordinary understanding.

This consciousness, knowledge, understanding and cognition, which you are aware of now, is not the ultimate. There is something more than this. Beyond name and form, beyond subject and object, and beyond the senses with which you are capable of understanding, seeing and recognizing, there is something more. You don't merely exist for the external life.

This external existence and this external experience are not the ultimate. There is something beyond it. Do you think that seeing, hearing, touching, smelling, tasting are the only forms of knowledge? Is there nothing beyond this? Those who think that there is nothing beyond this external life are known as materialists. When man's experience, knowledge and understanding are confined to objective matter, that is called materialism.

Where there is no object, there is no experience – that view is called materialism. But there is something beyond matter. Even if there is no object, there can be an experience. Then you have transcended materialism, you have transcended the philosophy of matter and with this the quest for spiritual knowledge begins in man.

It has been said by many great people that man's limited experience is not the ultimate. There are layers and layers of experiences and you can experience almost every level of your existence through the process of meditation. The science of meditation is the ultimate object of yoga and a tool in man's hand for his higher evolution in order to channelize and polarize the energies of the whole universe and of the whole of mankind.

I have come to the conclusion that man must practise meditation every day. If you cannot do it in the morning, please do it at night, when your stomach is empty or half-loaded. Sit with your body upright and straight. Your eyes can be closed and fixed either on the nosetip or in between the two eyebrows. Concentrating on the breath or on your mantra, try to get the first experience, then the second, then the third, fourth, fifth, sixth and seventh experience. Nobody knows what that is because in the seventh experience, experience and experiencer are one and the same.

22

The Practices of Yoga

Kuranda Ashram, Australia, 22 January 1984.

Yoga is a very ancient and a universal science as well. If you have studied the history of the ancient tribes either in India or in South America or even in Africa, you can easily draw the conclusion that those tribes understood and believed that mind can control matter. Of course, in the last few decades, the intellectuals and scientists have been trying to understand the mysterious rituals of those tribes, which are still existing in some parts of the world today. They have come to the conclusion that these rituals are just external, but more important are the forces of the mind, of the spirit or of the psyche, which are behind them.

Thousands of years ago when the continents of the world were different than they are today, those civilizations did realize, did discover that in everybody there is something very mysterious. They did not call that mysterious substance mind or body. They did not call it the universal God as the Muslims, Hindu and Christians do today. They called that mysterious substance psychic power or inner power and they learned different ways to manifest it. Then they maintained and perpetuated that tradition. They knew very well that even as your body is able to handle matter or substance, in the same way, or even much more efficiently than that, the inner spirit, the inner being or the inner force can control matter.

That is the one important thing which these civilizations discovered.

Yoga is a continuity of that realization and that understanding. Of course, in our times, yoga does come from India, not from China, Russia or any other part of the world. Historically speaking, yoga does come only from India, and it comes from the most northern part called the middle Himalayas where many great masters, gurus, saints, sages and spiritual personalities have lived for hundreds of years.

All these places are situated on the banks of the Ganga river, starting from Rishikesh and Haridwar up to the mountain peak of Badrinath. So when I say that in our times yoga comes from India, I don't mean Madras, Bombay, Trivandrum, Udaipur or even Delhi or Calcutta. No. It comes from those parts of India where the Ganga flows from the Himalayan peak down to Rishikesh and Haridwar.

It is to these places that I came in 1943, forty years ago. I was quite young then and I was trying to understand what the force within man is. There I lived for many years and met great people, illumined people. I tried to understand more about this force from them.

A practical system
When you are trying to understand this inner force through the mind, through logic and through books, it is called intellectual understanding. This intellectual understanding at most can give you an idea that this force is existing, but it doesn't make you a master of it. In order to handle this force, what is important is to live the yogic life and to practise yoga.

Just by reading a few books on football and trying to understand all about it, you don't become an expert player. In the same way, yoga is also a perfect system, but it is very practical. You may listen to me for one century or even more, but you won't get anywhere. You will just be satisfied, "Oh yes, now I understand what this inner force is." But knowledge of the inner spirit or inner force is not the ultimate purpose of yoga. The main purpose is to put you in touch with the inner experience and that is certainly different from knowledge.

The physiological aspect of yoga

The science, philosophy and practices of yoga are universal. They are not bound by any culture, tradition or religion. These practices are concerned with everybody's existence. They are not concerned with prayers, devotion or religious beliefs. The practices of yoga are concerned with what you are, a combination of physical, mental, emotional, psychic and mysterious forces. Therefore, the result which yoga produces is intimately related to your body, your mind and your emotions.

Now, it is up to us how we accept yoga and why we choose yoga. It is up to us to choose a purpose. If we have an unhealthy body, with imbalance in the nervous system, blood pressure shooting up and down, inefficient elimination of toxins, or imbalance in the glandular system, then it is the physiological aspect of yoga which we should choose and practise.

In the last four or five decades, research scientists in America, France, Poland, Germany, India and Japan too have found that the practices of yoga do control the activities of the body: nervous system, respiratory system, digestive and excretory systems, endocrine system. Not only this, in the last twenty years, some scientists have also come to the conclusion that through the practices of *pranayama*, what you call breathing practices, you do not merely create oxygenation in the body, but you also control the fluctuations of the two hemispheres of the brain.

It is not only that when you practise pranayama, you inhale oxygen and the blood is purified, the lungs are purified, the nervous system becomes balanced. Of course that is quite true, but pranayama is much more than that. They have found that when you breathe through the left nostril, the activities are accelerated in the right hemisphere of the brain, and when you breathe through the right nostril, the left hemisphere of the brain undergoes extra acceleration.

A scientist has written a book, *A Storm Every Hour* – a storm in the brain, because the breath has its own cycle. It does not flow erratically. On the first, second and third days of the dark fortnight, at the time of sunrise, the left nostril begins to flow for one hour and twenty minutes or round about. After that it changes to the right nostril for one hour or one hour and twenty minutes. Every hour or so it changes; one hour right, one hour left, one hour right, one hour left. During this period it has been found that the brain hemispheres undergo changes in acceleration. This is just a bird's eye view I am trying to give.

The psychological aspect
If you want to improve the physiological condition of the body and brain, if you want to train this grey matter, if you want to put this grey matter under control, then you have to choose for yourself those practices of yoga which relate to the body. If you are undergoing stress and strain, if you are suffering from anxiety, neurosis, nervous depression, fears, psychosis and personality errors, then in that case you will have to choose for yourself those practices of yoga which control, which relate to the psychological behaviour of man.

We live in a family, in a society, in an environment, where we have to suppress ourselves. Mankind as a whole is not free to act as it chooses, because man is not disciplined. If people throughout the world were more disciplined, we would have evolved what we call a free society. We would be free to do what we like, go wherever we want, but we can't do it because humanity today consists of anarchists, undisciplined people. If you tell everybody, "Think as you like, do as you like," you know what can happen.

Therefore, in this undisciplined society you have to suppress yourself. You suppress your emotions, thoughts, passions, anger, hatred, worries and love. You suppress your understanding too. This suppression overloads the mind. It is as if you have accumulated a lot of garbage and there is no place to throw it out. Then what are you going to do with the garbage? You have to keep it inside your house. For one day, two days, one month, two months, one year, two years, ten years, you pile the garbage up there, and finally what will happen? There will be a foul smell, stinking, looking bad, sneezing, coughing, feeling very bad, nausea. You understand? This is going to happen.

Now, how are you going to deal with that garbage which you have piled up in your house for the last twenty, thirty, forty, fifty, sixty, seventy years? Let it remain there and suffer, or throw it out the back gate in such a way that you don't wash your linen in another's courtyard? Throw it away you must, but how? You must choose those practices of yoga related to the psychological behaviour such as *yoga nidra*, psychic sleep, or *antar mouna*, inner silence. These will help you.

Awakening the inner force

In recent years they have found that mental problems can be successfully contained by certain yoga practices. But if you want to awaken your inner force, if you want to realize and experience the mind behind the mind, if you want to have contact with the man behind this man, if you want to realize that substance in you which has no form but which is a force, if you want to handle that something in you which has no name but which has speed and frequency, then you will have to choose for yourself those aspects of yoga. I am talking about kundalini yoga, kriya yoga, tantra and those practices which enable you to awaken that inner force.

Of course, I understand that everybody would like to awaken this inner force, whether one is qualified or not. Therefore, in the practices of yoga there are stages. First you must practise hatha yoga in order to improve the physical processes of the body as a whole so that you can go ahead. If your body is full of toxins and the inner organs are not functioning properly, if you have constipation or pain in the joints, weak heart, respiratory problems, nervous imbalance and your brain is unable to resist the force, how can you go ahead with the awakening of the self?

If you pour boiling water into an ordinary glass tumbler, it will crack. For that you must have a special glass tumbler, so you can pour boiling water and it will not crack. In the same way, when awakening takes place, it does relate to the body. The body comes under its influence, although that inner force has nothing to do with the body. Remember that the inner force is completely different from the body, but at the same time, when awakening of energy takes place, the body does come under its influence. The nerves, lungs, heart, digestive organs, muscles, bones, capillaries, brain cells, everything come under its influence.

The energy flows in the body
In hatha yoga, therefore, the asanas, pranayamas, mudras, bandhas and systems of purification are considered to be most important prerequisites to spiritual awakening and nobody should say that these exercises are just physical in nature. This is not the correct way to explain hatha yoga.

Last year I was in Japan and I met a great research scholar, Dr Hiroshi Motoyama. He has been working on the science of acupuncture for many years. Later he started working on the effects of yoga on the energy points or meridians. He found that the first chapter of my book *Asana Pranayama Mudra Bandha* gives an important asana series known as *pawanmuktasana*. It is a very simple series and nobody can believe that these practices have so much to do with the energy flows, energy points or meridians in the body, which are hundreds and hundreds in number.

These energy flows are connected to the sympathetic and parasympathetic nervous systems, not only in the spine but throughout the body. Who can believe it? If you teach people these exercises they say, "What are you teaching?" I say, "We are teaching yoga. These are not just finger exercises, wrist exercises, elbow exercises, shoulder exercises." If you are translating the practices in this way, you are doing a great disservice to the scientific aspect of yoga.

Dr Hiroshi Motoyama has exposed these practices to his researches. In his research he has improvised what he calls a chakra machine. *Chakra* means plexus. Plexus is a place where the nerves, the energy channels, join together in a junction. First they come in and then they go out, just like the trains come into the junction and go out, come in and go out. These energy junctions are called chakras.

There are six important major chakras in the body. In the books on kundalini yoga they talk about six chakras, *shat* chakras. Please remember that these six chakras are the major chakras; they are not the only chakras. There are thousands of other junctions in the physical body and from those minor chakras, minor plexuses, the energy flows in and goes out. These are the acupuncture points.

So, Dr Motoyama exposed this pawanmuktasana series and he wrote a commentary on it. It is available in Japanese, not in English. I have asked him to translate it into English now. In Japan it became so famous that people now have two ways of doing acupuncture. One way is putting the needle in and blocking or channelling the energy, and the other way is pawanmuktasana. So you can say that acupuncture is a method of pawanmuktasana and pawanmuktasana is a practice of acupuncture.

The purpose of yoga postures

These yoga practices which we call *yogasanas* are not just exercises; they are postures. Please remember that and don't misunderstand me. I don't want to criticize anybody's viewpoint. The very word *asana* means posture or position: *matsyasana*, fish posture not fish exercise; *mayurasana*, peacock posture not peacock exercise; *shalabhasana*, locust posture not locust exercise; *yogasana*, yogic posture not yogic exercise.

Asanas do look like exercises because you are making certain movements, but these movements are not so much related to the muscles or the joints, the biceps or triceps. They are related to the points in the body from where the energy is distributed to all the different parts. Therefore, yoga postures are intended to release the energy which is blocked at these points. Whenever the energy is blocked or suppressed, the practice of yoga releases it.

Now, when people come to the yoga classes, they are told, "Oh, you practise yoga and you will feel better." So they go and practise yoga and they do feel better. Why do they feel better? Because by the practice of these yoga postures, the energy which was blocked somewhere has been released. These are the important aspects of yoga which one has to understand first.

An integrated practice

Now, coming to a very important point. When you have to choose for yourself a certain type of yoga, you must remember you are choosing it for yourself, not for your pupils. I am particularly telling the yoga teachers your personal practice and your system of instruction cannot be the same. I may practise kundalini yoga but I don't teach it. You will have to teach your pupils the yoga which is necessary for their physical and mental health, and for this, you will have to understand the effect, the impact of every yoga practice.

We talk about karma yoga, bhakti yoga, jnana yoga, raja yoga, mantra yoga, hatha yoga and a few more yogas. These yoga practices must be combined for greater results. Only one type of yoga doesn't produce great results. If we emphasize only hatha yoga and reject other forms of yoga, then the development in the personality will be lopsided and not integral. You are not just the body, the emotions, the intellect or the psyche. A combination of all these makes up your personality. Therefore, when we talk about personality, we are talking about all four aspects.

In order to develop your personality you should practise karma yoga, raja yoga, bhakti yoga and jnana yoga side by side. There are people who only talk about jnana yoga because it is very comfortable. You only have to think, to contemplate, that's all. You don't have to practise pranayama. You don't have to get up in the early morning. You don't have to keep any discipline regarding the body and the mind, etc. So what happens? You do develop rationally but it is one-sided development.

As I told you, man is a combination of dynamism, emotion, psyche and intellect. Simultaneous development of all these four aspects will help you in developing an integrated personality, and an integrated personality is what is important in man's life. An integrated personality has fewer mental problems, fewer emotional breakdowns. The chances of nervous breakdown are rare.

The main problem that we are suffering from in our time, both in the East and the West, is that we have overemphasized, overfed, one aspect of our being and the other aspects are starving. If we go on taking protein and no carbohydrates, what will happen? It is one-sided development of the body. Or if you go on taking just carbohydrate and no protein, again one-sided development will take place.

Even as various vitamins and nutrients are necessary for the all-round development of the body, its tissues, chemicals, secretions, etc., in the same way, your personality also needs certain nutrition and vitamins. So for the balanced development of the personality, you have to have an integrated yoga practice.

The correct proportion
When I talk about yoga I talk about integral yoga, a yoga of synthesis. I do not overemphasize just one aspect of yoga, because I do not think it is right. One thing is certain. If you are cooking two kilos of vegetables, you don't put in two kilos of salt or two kilos of butter. There is a correct proportion. In the same way, in the practice of yoga there is also a correct proportion and that is indicated in my books because I have practised it.

There must be seventy percent karma yoga, twenty percent raja yoga, hatha yoga, kundalini yoga, etc., five percent jnana yoga and five percent bhakti yoga. If you try to practise seventy percent dhyana yoga, kundalini yoga, kriya yoga, tantra yoga, you will go to the mental hospital. Or if you practise seventy percent jnana yoga, then you become an intellectual giant, but you remain a pygmy in other areas of your personality. Or if you practise seventy percent bhakti yoga, you will be saying, "Oh God, Oh God, this mike is working because of God's grace. This flower is red because of God's grace. Oh, today it is not raining because of God's grace." You bring God everywhere, even into the toilet. Too much bhakti is not good; it brings about an imbalance. Too much raja yoga also causes an imbalance and too much jnana yoga creates imbalance too. Because you are gross, so you need a greater proportion of karma yoga.

23

Satsang

Kuranda Ashram, Australia, 22 January 1984

How can a Sanskrit mantra whose meaning I do not know help me in meditation?
Mantra, when received from your guru, is intended for daily practice. Either once or if possible twice, you should set apart at least ten minutes every day and practise the mantra with absolute regularity. It is not necessary to practise it for one or two hours daily, but it is of the utmost importance that you practise it every day.

When you practise mantra, you should fix your mind at one particular centre, for example at the tip of the nose or between the two eyebrows. You can also fix your mind either at the tip of your tongue or at the root of your tongue, or in the nostrils through which the breath flows in and out. These are just examples. You can use any centre – the heart centre, navel centre, throat centre, crown centre.

It is necessary to fix the mind at one centre in order to achieve a certain amount of stability, because when you are practising mantra, your heart and lungs are both involved and your nervous system, sometimes sympathetic and sometimes parasympathetic, is also influenced. I am telling you this on the basis of scientific experiments that have been conducted in many countries. Therefore, if you concentrate, if you fix your mind on one point in the body or outside on some point during the practice of mantra, then you can attain greater steadiness in the fluctuations which are natural to your nervous system.

When you close your eyes, you will observe that the eye movements are always there. These eyeball movements become very rapid when your mind is unsteady and restless. Rapid eyeball movement should be stabilized. As little eyeball movement as possible is best. How can you check these eyeball movements? In order to check them, you have to keep your mind at one point. Therefore, an inner centre or external centre is of great importance.

Now, if you fix your mind at the nosetip while repeating your mantra, all the time your inner gaze is centred and you will find that the rapid eyeball movement is minimized to a great extent. The eyeball movements have a direct impact on the retina and on the brain. If you can stop your eyeball movements for about a minute or two, the impact can be realized on the brain as well as on the nervous system.

In yoga, therefore, there is another practice known as *trataka*, in which you keep a steady object or point in front of you, say an unwavering candle flame or a black dot or a shivalingam. When you gaze steadily at that point for a minute or two or even three, without winking or blinking, you give indirect training to your eyeballs. Steadying the eyeballs is an indirect way to create relaxation in the mind.

The mantra can be practised in very many ways. Some mantras are short, others are longer and some are very long. Gayatri mantra is a very long mantra; it is a combination of twenty-four syllables. Some mantras are monosyllabic, just one syllable like *Om*, *Kleem* or *Hreem*. The shorter the mantra, the easier it is to practise it with the natural breath. You synchronize your mantra with the incoming and outgoing breath and feel it each time you breath, like *Soham, Soham*. This is one way.

Another way of practising the mantra is to rotate the mala and with each bead you chant the mantra mentally. The third way of practising the mantra is to concentrate at the eyebrow centre, creating a focal point. If you are not able to create a focal point, then take a very small coin and fix it at the eyebrow centre for some time, so you can feel the central point and you can feel the rhythm, the beat there. You can practise your mantra with the beat. It is a natural rhythm. This is another way.

You can also concentrate on the chakras, which are six in number. You can concentrate on one of them or on all six, one by one: one day mooladhara, second day swadhisthana, third day manipura, etc. Fix your mind on the chakra and then repeat the mantra mentally. Or you can concentrate on the tip of the tongue and you will feel the pulsing rhythm and with that you can practise the mantra. So there are many ways of practising, repeating, chanting and thinking of the mantra.

However, for those of us who are educated or literate, one form of mantra repetition is very difficult. Maybe some of you can do it. Say your mantra is *Om Namah Shivaya*. Naturally when you are repeating it, you are simultaneously aware of the written form of the syllables. That is a limiting adjunct. *O-m N-a-m-a-h S-h-i-v-a-y-a* is not the form of the mantra. That may be how you understand it, but that is a limitation.

What is mantra? *Mantra* is sound and when you are practising mantra, you should try to become aware of the sound wave rather the form. *Om* is spelled *O-m* in English; in Sanskrit it is written like this: ॐ. So when you think of *Om Namah Shivaya* according to written language, according to the characters that you have studied, that is limiting. You should make the mantra devoid of the external form which you have given it according to your language and according to your understanding and limitation.

Sound is a pure form and when you do not understand the sound, then you give it a form according to its written characters a, b, c, d. That is the supposed form of the sound which you have created for your convenience. As you write the letter 'a', you are not aware of the form of the sound 'a'. Then what is the form of the sound 'a', what is the form of the sound 'b'? That form is called the sound form and that sound form is very easily accessible to people who have not studied anything.

This realization came to me many years ago when I initiated one illiterate aspirant into the mantra *Om Namah Shivaya* and I told him to concentrate on it. I did not know myself what a powerful thing I was telling him. After a few days he came to me with fantastic experiences. I said, "What were you concentrating on?" He replied, "On the form of *Om Namah Shivaya*." Then I asked him, "What is the form of *Om Namah Shivaya*?" And he narrated something I myself did not know. I'm educated, so for me *O-m N-a-m-a-h S-h-i-v-a-y-a* is the form, but he was a step beyond this. He had made the mantra completely devoid of its external manifestation and formation.

So, what is the real form of your mantra which your guru has given you? It is something which you have to arrive at, and you have to arrive at it by going through this unnecessary, external, superfluous form which is given to you: *O-m N-a-m-a-h S-h-i-v-a-y-a*. You have to climb using this step, but you have to get above it.

Then with the mantra comes the symbol and this symbol is intimately related to the mantra. Sound has a form. Many experiments have been done on this. Years ago, when I was in France, I happened to see a book written by a very celebrated artist. He said that when you produce a sound such as *Ooommmmm* or such as the sound I am producing while I am talking to you, you produce waves in the *akasha*, in the mind space. These waves are then formed into a certain structure of their own. Sometimes these sounds which you produce take the shape of a flower, bird, animal, deva or rakshasa. Sound and form are interrelated. What you see around you, trees, animals, creatures, are the forms of an invisible sound.

He had a theory and that theory is very close to kundalini yoga and tantra. He stated that these forms, which are known as symbols, *yantras* or *mandalas*, are nothing but the mantra personified. If you write ॐ: one curve, two curves, three curves, crescent moon and star, that is the mantra personified, sound personified. So, for every sound, for every mantra, there is an object of personification. What is your symbol? Your symbol is fire. What is my symbol? My symbol is a shining star. That symbol is the personification of the mantra which your guru has given to you.

So when you want to practise mantra, have a mala. At an appointed time, sit down, fix your posture. Don't start the mantra immediately. First chant *Om* loudly, *Oommmmmm* . . . three times or more. Then do some pranayama for one or two minutes. Then take your mala and begin the practice.

Don't worry about the mind. Don't worry about distractions. It is very good if your mind wanders in the beginning of the practice. This is a positive sign. If you practise your mantra very strictly without allowing a single thought to come to the area of the mind, you will have problems later on when you go a step further. It is something like wanting to travel to New Zealand or Fiji and going to Sydney Airport and realizing you have not brought your passport. You have to go back to Cairns, you see!

So it's important that the mental fluctuations and wanderings of the mind, restlessness of the mind, the little insignificant or even significant thoughts, must be allowed to come out. Let them come in mobs, let them come singly, let them come and assault you. Let them come in the beginning, if you want a peaceful and tranquil meditation later. Do not try to bypass the quality or the quantum and the nature of your personality. That is what you are.

So when you are practising mantra, if the mind is wandering, start repeating a little bit loudly, *Om Namah Shivaya*, *Om Namah Shivaya*. Automatically the mind is going somewhere and you are here practising *Om Namah Shivaya*, *Om Namah Shivaya*. Suddenly you realize you have gone away and you come back, *Om Namah Shivaya*, one time, two times, third time, again the mind slips. This is how the sadhana should be practised, with great patience, so you have a greater understanding of yourself.

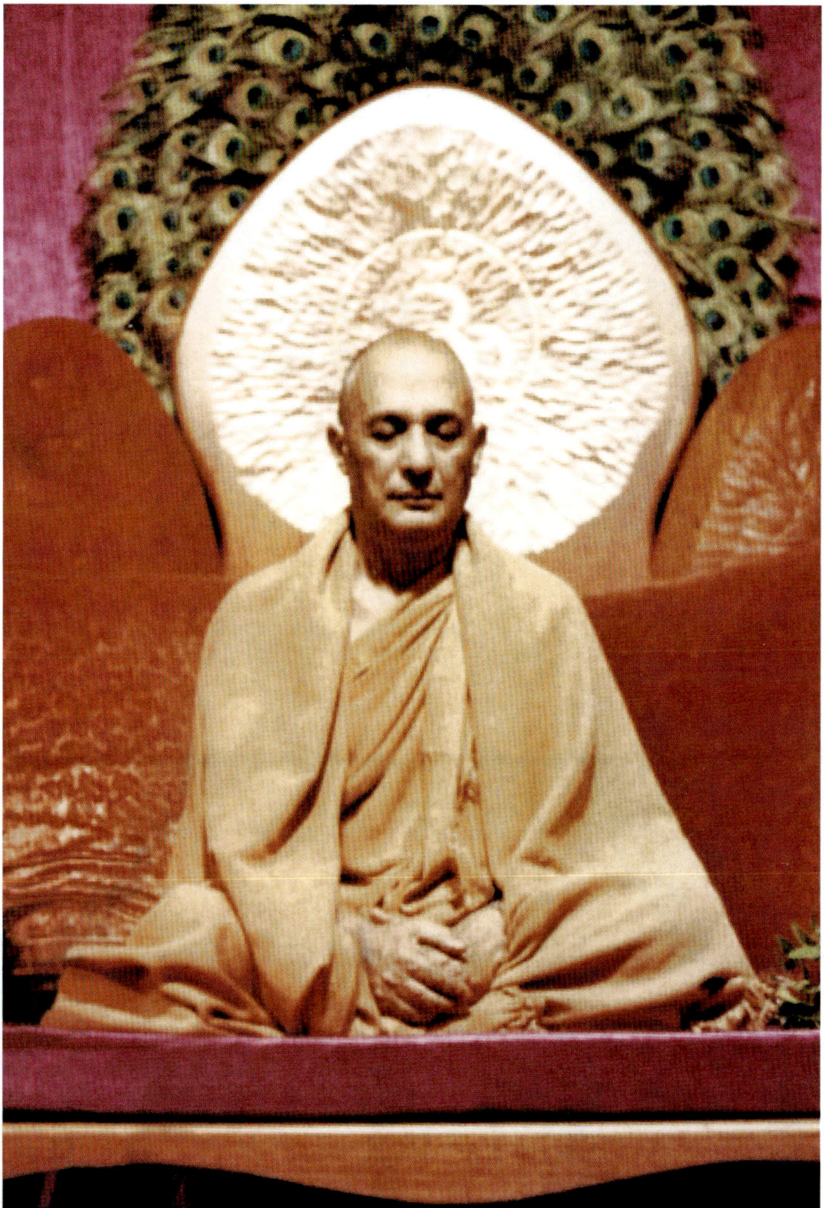

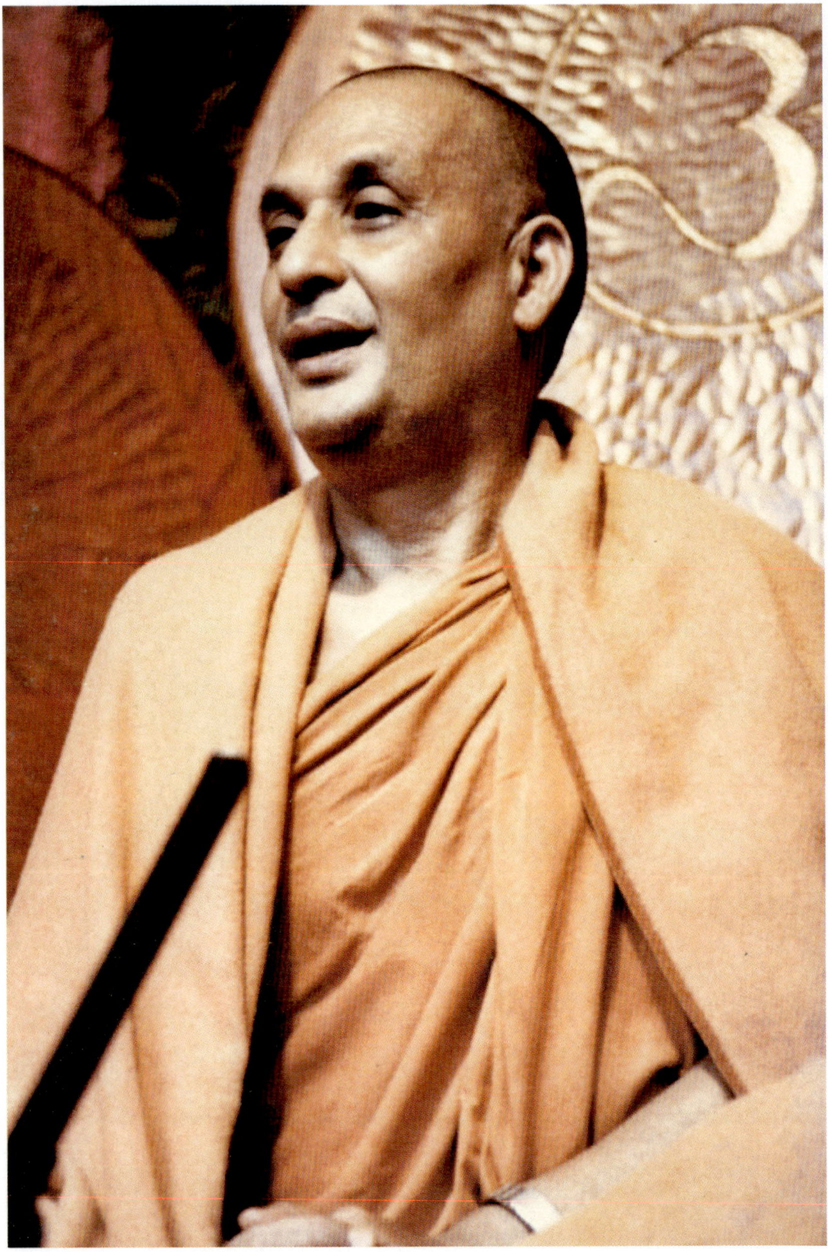

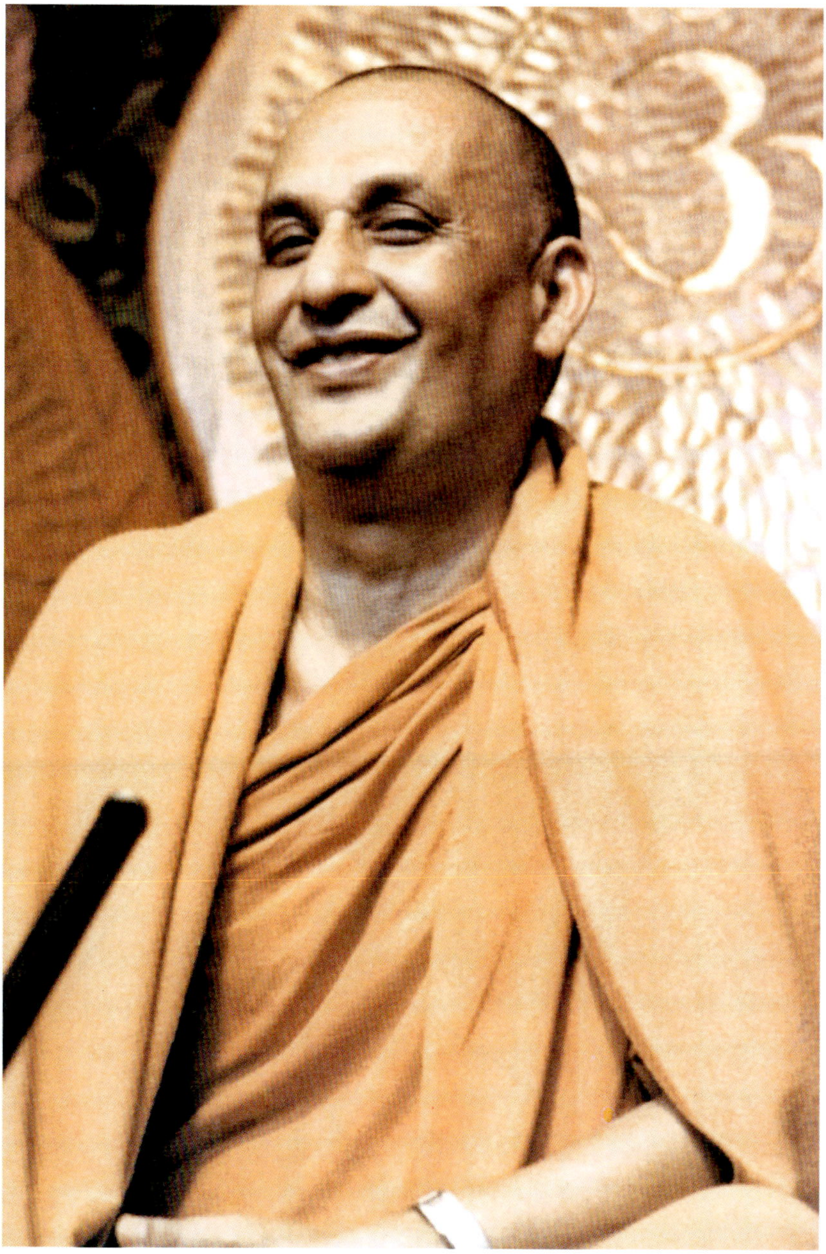

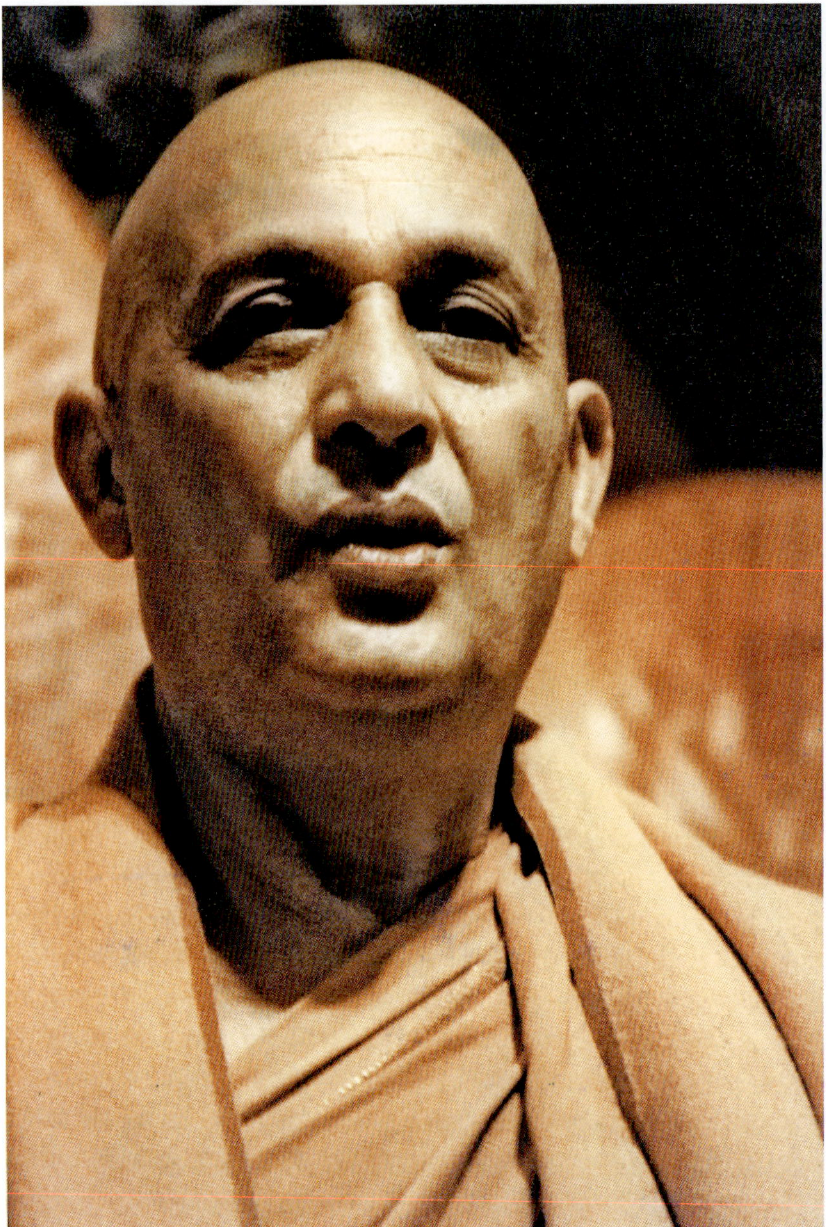

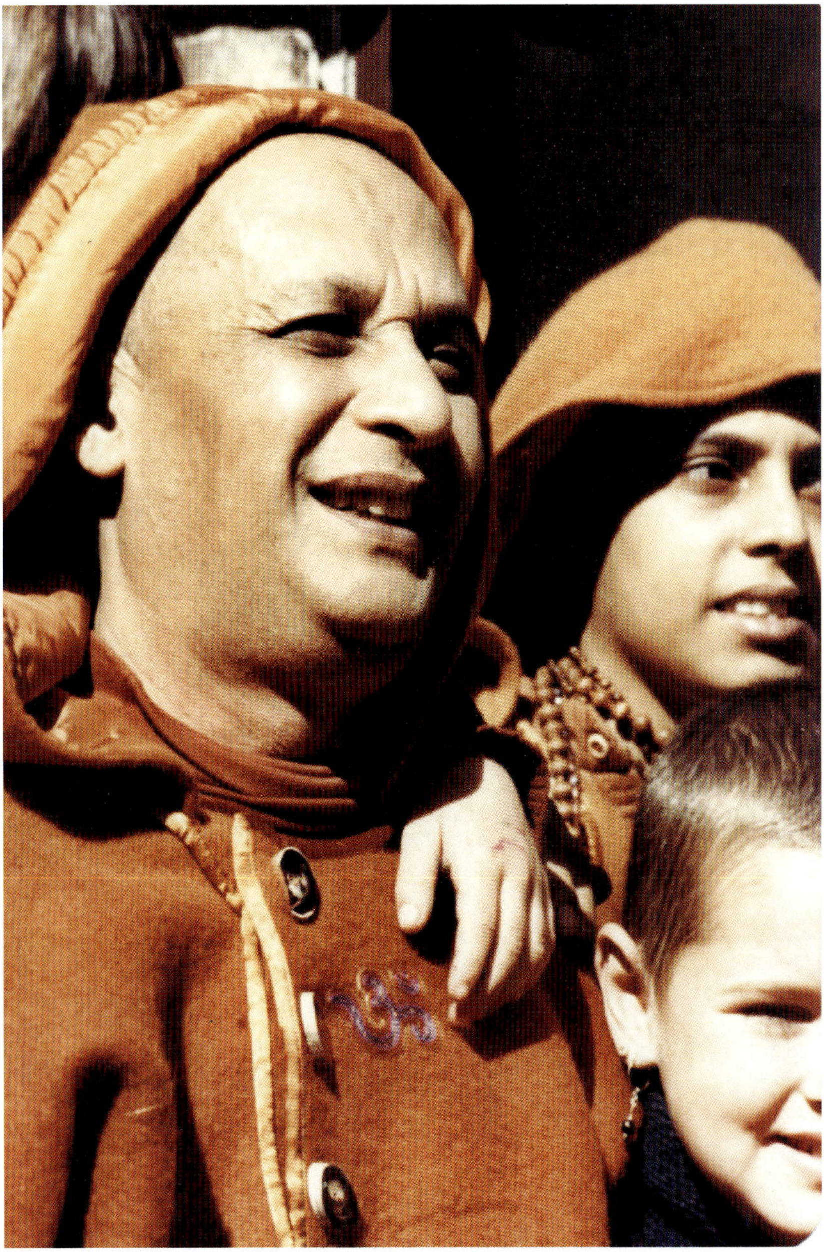

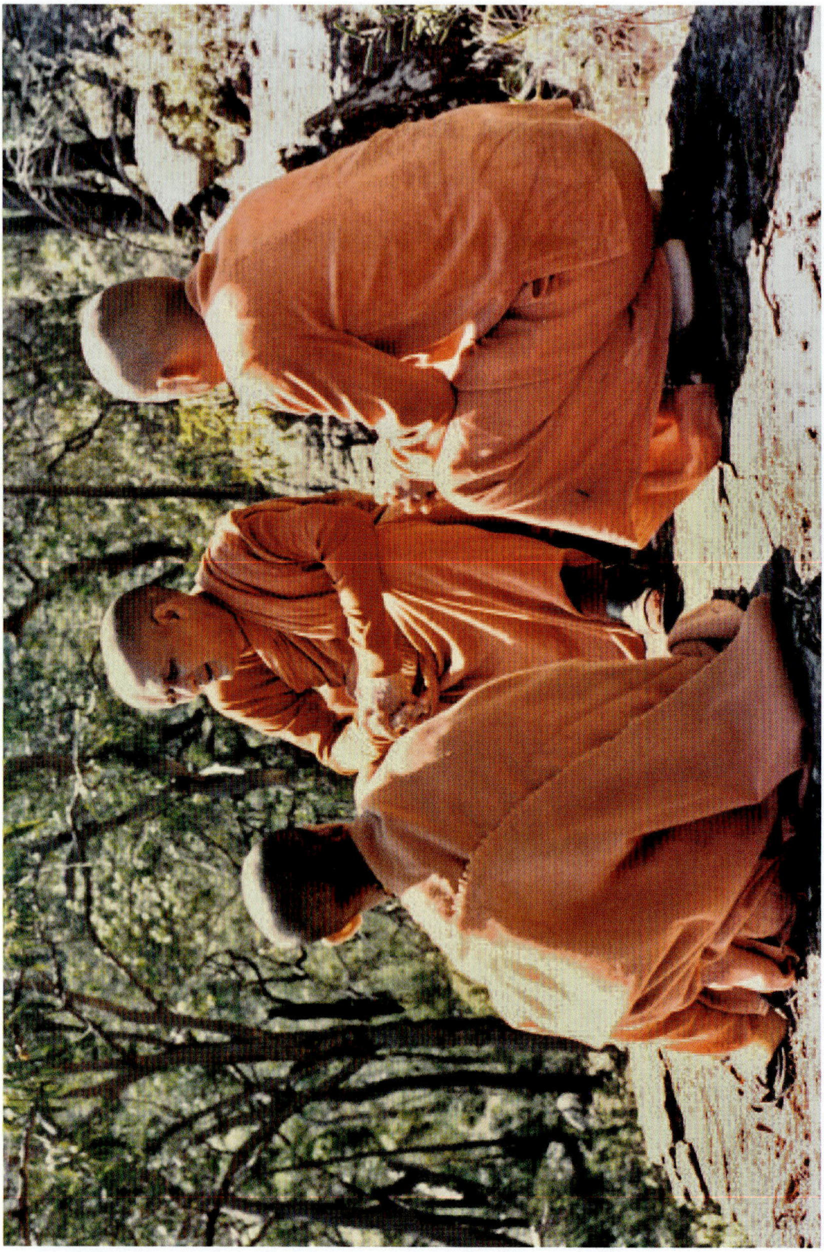

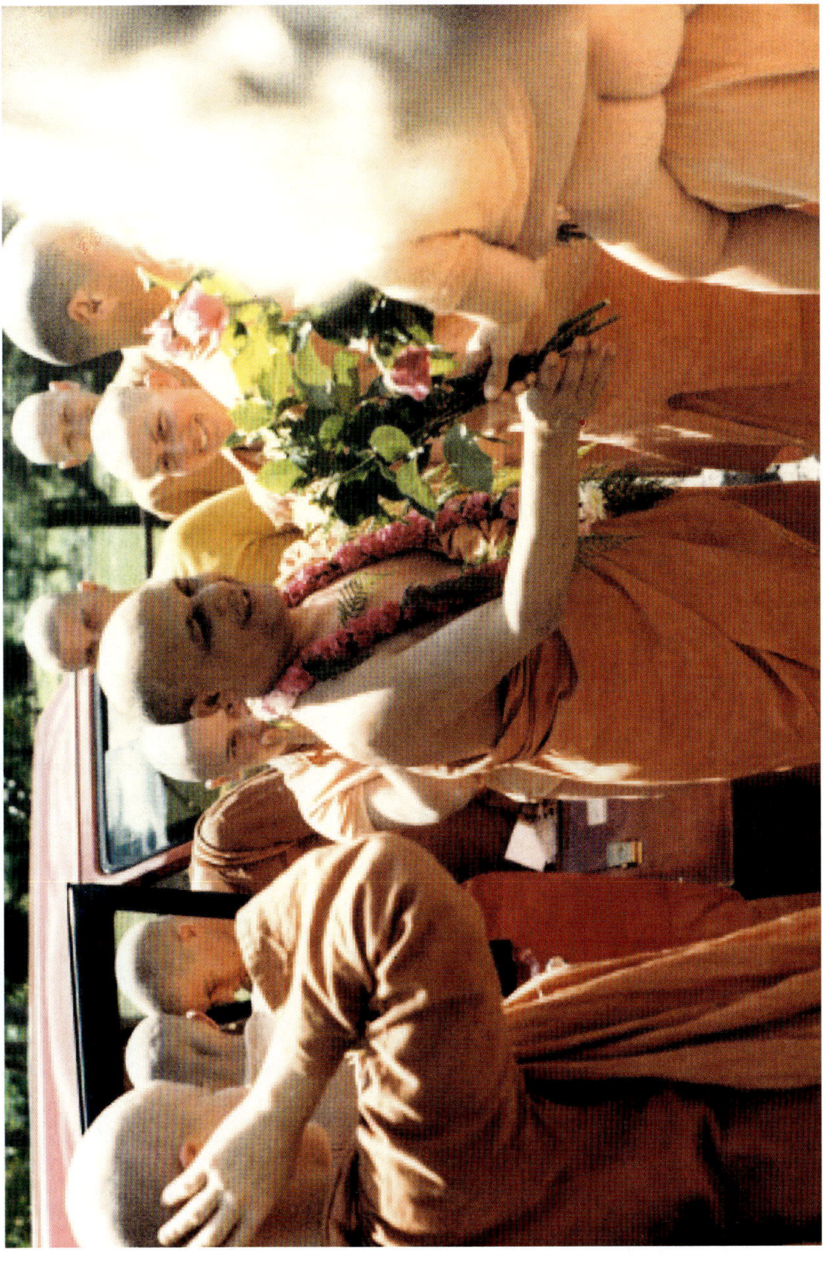

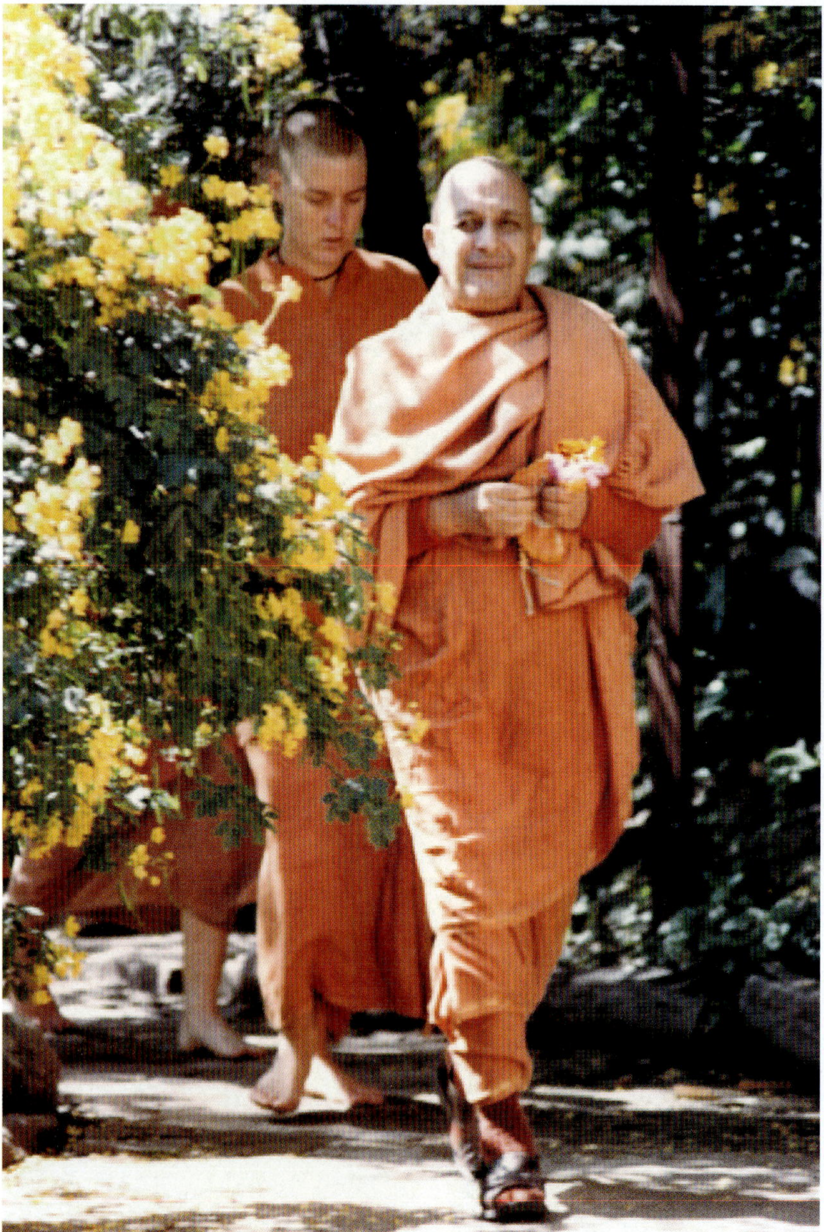

I am married with a family. Can I take karma sannyasa? What are its obligations?

The life of a householder is not the life of a sinner. It is a stepping stone towards spiritual life. There are thirty boys in a class, fifth class or sixth class. Some are industrious and work hard; they get first class marks. Some are average; they get second class, third class marks. Some are hopeless; they are in the class but don't study. There are some who want to study but cannot, who want to understand but cannot, and they fail. In the same way, there are householders who are serious, sincere and alert, who understand that this stage in life is given to them as a stepping stone towards spiritual enlightenment. They realize that they should make the best use of this opportunity but they don't know how to do it. It is these people who can be initiated into karma sannyasa.

Karma sannyasa means renunciation of the consequences of karma, or detachment from the egotistical involvement with the affairs of life. It does not mean that one has to renounce karma. It does not mean that one has to renounce one's association with life. One can have children, wife, husband, family, it is all right, but then there is another aspect of it and that is an internal, deep-rooted, neurotic attachment which is not at all necessary. There is a certain element of attachment which is necessary to keep everything linked together, to keep family members, job, profession and so on together. It is necessary, but when you think about it, there are certain elements of attachment in your nature without which you can definitely get on very well in life. I'm talking about the unnecessary involvement with ego in the day-to-day events and occurrences of life, but that detachment comes only by practice.

What are those affairs of life with which you have to maintain a link, and what are those affairs and attitudes of life where you have to detach yourself? This is the sadhana of a karma sannyasin. It is not that easy to explain this to everyone because we have always been hearing, "Work without attachment, live with detachment." But this is a very incomplete expression. If I ask you to live with detachment, what does it mean? How far and how much should you be committed and where do you have to disassociate yourself?

That dividing line has to be known by karma sannyasins. The initiation into karma sannyasa does not at all prohibit you from anything that is related to life. Whether it is family, marriage, progeny, work, wealth, property, accomplishments, ambitions, passions, happiness, unhappiness, tragedy, right behaviour, wrong behaviour, positive habits or negative habits, all that goes side by side with life.

There is an area where your life is producing an effect. With everything you do, everything you think, everything that happens to you or which you create, an effect is produced. It is that effect which again rebounds – that gives you happiness, that gives you unhappiness, that gives you sorrow. The karma sannyasin learns how he can make himself free from the impulses and effects of the karma.

How does the natural alternation of the breath through the nostrils every hour and twenty minutes fit in with nadi shodhana pranayama?

There is a book available on this subject called *Swara Yoga*, which you can read. This is a very intricate science. The two nostrils relate to two different types of energy. The lunar energy flows through the left nostril and the solar energy flows through the right nostril. Solar energy is hotter and lunar energy is cooler in temperature. These two nadis change over every one hour and twenty minutes, provided there are no imbalances in the body. If there is anything wrong in the physical system, then there is a disturbance, an interruption in the natural rhythm of the breath.

The breath has its own calendar. On the first, second and third days of the dark fortnight, at the time of sunrise, the left nostril flows for one hour and twenty minutes, then changes. On the fourth, fifth and sixth days of the dark fortnight, at the time of sunrise, the right nostril flows for one hour and twenty minutes, then changes. On the first, second and third days of the bright fortnight, at the time of sunrise, not the left but the right nostril flows for one hour and twenty minutes, then changes, and at the time of the changeover, both nostrils flow freely for some time. This is the subject matter related to the science of swara yoga about which you must make some sort of study.

When you are practising *nadi shodhana pranayama*, alternate nostril breathing, at that time, both the nostrils begin to flow equally, not only the right or the left, but both. It does not happen if you just practise a few rounds, but if you practise for five minutes or more, then you will find both nostrils begin to flow freely.

When both nostrils flow freely, it is an indication that your sympathetic and parasympathetic nervous systems are in absolute balance and that the central nervous system is now beginning to function. At this time you will have wonderful meditation. When both nostrils are flowing freely and equally, that is the period of sushumna nadi. The flowing of sushumna indicates the activation of the central nervous system. At this time both hemispheres of the brain are operating equally. There is a balance between the vital forces and the mental forces, and during these moments of balance, meditation takes place. When meditation is over, practise five or ten minutes of pranayama.

Are there any exercises to combat smoking habits?
Smoking is related to nervous depression resulting from tension. When you have tension, there is a tendency towards depression in the nervous system and at that time you feel like smoking.

The parasympathetic and sympathetic nervous systems have an outflow and inflow of a certain amount of energy. Just as electrical energy is flowing here in a certain voltage – 220, 110 or 32 voltage energy – the nervous system carries energy impulses which can be measured through modern instruments. When you practise bhastrika or kapalbhati pranayama, for example, both the sympathetic and parasympathetic nervous systems register accelerated electrical impulses on the chart.

This means that when you are practising kapalbhati or bhastrika, your sympathetic and parasympathetic nervous systems are supplying extra electrical energy to your body. However, when the mind is overloaded with anxiety, overthinking, ambition, building castles in the air, etc., then the nervous system at one point refuses to supply the necessary electrical energy that is required.

For example, this electrical wire can supply 220 volts of electricity, so the mike and the electric lights are working alright. But if you connect a big machine here, then you will find the moment you switch it on, the electric lights will be comparatively dimmer or the fuses will blow. That is also what happens in nervous depression when the nervous system is unable to supply the required energy to the body and brain. So at that time, you need a little bit of smoke, nicotine, to boost up the nervous energy and you feel better.

I feel those who want to smoke should do it and those who do not want to smoke should not. However, if you say, "I don't like to smoke but still I smoke," then that is not good. You assert that it is injurious to health and still you go on smoking. No. If you are going to smoke, then speak like Churchill. Once some people said to Churchill, "Smoking is bad." He said, "There can be no greater nonsense." And he lived a full life as far as we know.

You have to be a strong person with a weak habit, not a victim of a weak habit. If you are a strong person, the weak habit will not create any disaster in your life. If you are a weak person with weak habits, you can have all sorts of problems, constipation, nervous breakdown, cough and cold, lung cancer and this and that. However, if one is very sincere and wants to get out of the habit of smoking, the best thing is to practise pranayama in the morning and a relaxing practice like yoga nidra at night.

Are there any exercises for an ear damaged by the noise of a gun shot?

If there is any organic damage, then it is always better to consult a surgeon, but if it just functional damage, then bhramari pranayama can help you. *Bhramari pranayama* is plugging the ears and then producing the humming sound – *Mmmmmmm*.

Why should we be given a spiritual name? Is there a real need for this name?

Everything must have a name. A man's name is Mr Brickfield, but then the organs of his body have different names; they don't have the same name. Lungs, heart, intestines, capillaries, bones, muscles, do you also call them Mr Brickfield? You have a name which was given to you at the time of birth for the purpose of legal and social identification. However, that name was not chosen according to your karma and qualities. Everybody has a spirit, an inner being of light, which is different from the body. Therefore, a spiritual name is not a physical name.

A spiritual name is your name which relates to your inner self which you should try to be, which you will be, which you will accomplish. I believe a spiritual name also alters the destiny. Before I went to my guru, my name was different and I am sure that when I received my name from him, my destiny completely changed. Then I identified myself with my real being, with my real nature, with the higher processes which controlled me or which would control me.

A spiritual name is also a link between guru and disciple. Guru and disciple are two important aspects of a relationship which mankind is now trying to learn more about. We know about the relationship between husband and wife, between man and woman, between parents and children, brothers and sisters. We also know the emotional patterns which are linking them, but there is another relationship for the fulfilment of man's inner desire and that relationship is the guru and disciple relationship.

It is not a mystical relationship, a religious relationship, a physical relationship, or even an emotional relationship. It is a relationship about which we do not know very much, and when this relationship is formed between guru and disciple, then there has to be a link between both of them, and a spiritual name is definitely a link.

What can we do for our own children and those of other parents to assist their personal and spiritual development?

Children are divinity personified. They are very evolved beings. Therefore, it would be very wrong for parents to think of providing children with spirituality; it's like sending coal back to the coalfield. No. You have to learn from them rather than teach them. The innocence, the simplicity, freedom from inhibition, the sweetest and purest smile, love and tenderness, these are the things which you have to relearn from children. All the great men in history were able to think spontaneously like children. They had childlike qualities. They were not childish, of course; children are never childish. It is grownup people who are childish. We have to become childlike.

I personally think you should not worry about your children on any front, for anything. There is nothing to worry about. If you want to worry about them you can, but before they are procreated, you understand? When you transfer the seed of existence from one body into another body, it is at that time that you have to think what quality of seed is being implanted. Is it a disease-free seed? Is it a quality seed, or is the seed which you are transferring from one body to another an infected seed?

After you have given birth to a child it is too late to think about him. You can definitely make a social animal of him, a Christian or a Hindu, a capitalist or a communist, an Australian or an Indian. You can make him a political animal, nationalist animal, a philosophical animal, but you can't make him a divine being, because you have created him.

The only thing you can do is learn from children. Try to smile like them, to be tender like them, to speak like them and to be worry-free like them. If you can become free from worries like children, you will have no blood pressure problems. If you can play like children, then this world with so much cruelty and brutality, so much shrewdness, cunning and deceit, so much hatred and jealousy, horror and danger will become a world of joy and happiness.

Your family, your home should become like an ashram where your children can play, where they can read and talk to you as if you were friends. Do your children speak the truth to you? Do you allow them to speak the truth? No! In any family where the parents are disciplinarians and puritans, children will not speak the truth; they will always tell lies. I'm talking about the whole world. Children will tell lies because parents do not want them to do certain things.

Many young people from the Middle East go to Europe and there they drink a lot. When they return to their home, their parents ask, "Did you drink there?" They say, "No, Mummy. I don't like to drink." They are telling lies. Religion teaches us to tell lies. Ethics and morality is the breeding ground for dishonesty and hypocrisy. If I want to do something, I do it, and I tell you because you are my mother. You love me so you must tolerate me. If I'm a bad boy all right, if I'm a good boy all right, if I'm a prostitute all right. You are my mother; I am your son or daughter. You love me; I love you. We understand each other.

If you want your children to be true, you must be very relaxed with them. Don't talk of ethics, morality, purity and religion; they are the breeding grounds of total hypocrisy, sad incidents and accidents in history. I have met people who are rank atheists but number one honest; you could always believe them. I have seen priests, Hindu and Christian both, who were very dishonest people. They think one thing, speak something else and do something entirely different. There is absolutely no unanimity, no unity between their thought, word and action.

So please allow your children to be unanimous in thought, word and action. Don't try to breed or bring forth a generation of hypocrites, but a generation which can speak the truth, which declares it with all boldness, even if they are hung on the cross, even if they are burnt on the stake. Each must be one who can proclaim the truth, for whom there is nothing else except truth. You understand truth? Truth means 'as it is'.

You must bring up children who are not a product of religion, ethics and morality. Your children must be products of your love and understanding and the deep-rooted intimate relationship between mother, father and children. The family must become an ashram, a community of friends, where parents and children live together. They have different roles within the family structure such as husband and wife, brother and sister, parents and children, but all are members of the same family.

Are there drugs that can be an aid to enlightenment or spiritual realization?

Yes. People have tried to create experiences very close to enlightenment through various drugs. Not only today but thousands of years ago, the Hindus used to drink soma. They extracted this liquor from a creeper and after taking this soma drink they would chant the Vedas. It is written in many books that they used to experience heavens, blessings, angels, archangels, divine beings, devas, devis, time, space and many things. But suddenly the soma drink disappeared to the point where today, even in India, the ayurvedic doctors who know the entire science of herbs, do not know which is the soma creeper.

In books it is written that if those people who are enlightened or who have developed higher qualities take the soma drink, they will have very good experiences. Those who are tamasic and undisciplined, whose minds are filled with jealousy, greed and negative traits will have very bad experiences and they can go insane. The books have made it very clear that these drugs can induce an hypnotic state. As a result of that some experiences do take place, but these are not related to enlightenment. These experiences are related to the fluctuations in the levels of nervous energy.

When there is a fluctuation in the energy level of your nervous system, at that time the brain also fluctuates.

According to the fluctuation of the brain, various types of experiences do take place, but these experiences are physiological in character, not spiritual. People who have had these experiences in life see no change in the quality of their life. Their life is the same, habits are the same, limitations are the same, so where have they changed?

Whether it is awakening of kundalini or experience through drugs, the most important thing is, has it improved the quality of your life? Are you a master of time, space and object? Have you been able to bring the polarities of energies together? No. You haven't even controlled the weaknesses of your body and mind. How can you say these experiences relate to enlightenment? No. The experiences which relate to enlightenment make you a Buddha, Christ or Mohammed. Gold is gold, a diamond is a diamond. You can always see it. When you become enlightened, you are not just a man, you are a superman.

Later, many other drugs were tried. In South America the Indians used mescaline, mushrooms and peyote. In Africa and in India they tried ganja, cannabis indica and other herbs which are not widely known, but I don't think that there is any history of people who are enlightened through the use of cannabis indica. There has to be a reference to a few people, that this man used it and was enlightened, or she used it and was enlightened. We don't have any such reference, but we do have references of enlightened people like Buddha, who did not use cannabis indica.

In recent years, some other experiments have been made into mind-expanding drugs, especially LSD. This is a drug which invades the nervous system and certain areas of the brain. As a result of that, it gives fantastic, explosive experiences and those experiences are sometimes marvellous. One of my disciples in America took LSD and he used to see beautiful colours. When he came out, he would try to put those colours on the canvas with his brush. Peter Max is his name. He became a very good artist.

When you take drugs, it definitely alters the level of consciousness. I won't say it is bad or good, or you should do it or shouldn't do it, but definitely any drug for that matter does change the level of awareness. As a result of that change the experiences – the colours, the forms, the sensitivity – everything changes, but enlightenment is something more than that or something other than that, and that enlightenment is an entirely spiritual affair. It can come without drugs.

Now, I'll tell you about my own experience. I also used drugs, not that I believed in them, but I wanted to know if they worked. For nine months I lived in the Himalayas, near the place where Ganga originates. It was icy cold. I stayed there in total seclusion and all day long I used to do pranayama and smoke ganja. During those nine months, I did have experiences and those experiences were fantastic. In the same room which was closed and dark, I could see mountains, devas, rishis, saints, sages, hillocks, valleys, everything. It was such a good cinema.

However, as a result of using ganja for a protracted period of time, first of all I lost my physical health. I had an attack of pleurisy. Secondly, I lost a very important faculty which had developed in my early life; I had a fantastic, photographic memory. If you gave a lecture for one hour and I just heard it once, I could type it verbatim, but after smoking ganja for nine months, that memory was completely gone. So it means that smoking ganja damaged a very important part of my brain and if I had continued it for a longer period, I would have lost my entire memory as well.

Therefore, we must be careful about the use of herbs and drugs. We do not want to try just anything for the sake of enlightenment, at the cost of the great faculties of nature like memory, patience and understanding. Enlightenment must go hand in hand with your day-to-day life. If enlightenment does not go hand in hand with your daily life, then it is better not to think about it.

24

Inauguration of an Ashram

Rocklyn Ashram, Australia, 27 January 1984.

I have come here to inaugurate this ashram. When I was here last year the swamis were working and planning to put everything together so that the ashram could be ready by October. It did not happen, but now in this new year, 1984, the ashram has taken shape. It is not complete. The ashram is an external structure. There has to be a spirit in it. A temple without a spirit, a church without a spirit, an ashram without a spirit, a body without a spirit is nonsense, you know.

Kindling the light
Spirit is symbolized by this light because we need it. In the dark of night, when you want to go out you take a torchlight with you. If you don't have a torchlight, you will stumble. You may even fall down and break your head and bones. In the same way, there are various levels of man's existence where he needs light. Everywhere there is darkness. We are not able to see within ourselves. Our minds, thoughts, emotions, ambitions, everything is moving in the realm of darkness.

Therefore, you must understand that the essence of light has to be brought in. In the ashram also there has to be light. The person looking after the ashram has to be a light so that, in the course of time, he can fill the hearts of his students and disciples with inner awareness. Light and inner awareness mean the same thing. When the inner awareness grows in the mind, in the intellect and heart of the disciple, then and only then has he been given the light. When the inner awareness grows, gradually inner happiness increases, understanding changes and things begin to change. That is why we inaugurate an ashram with the kindling of the light.

Money represents ego

Building an ashram is a very difficult task. In 1943 when I went to live with my guru, Swami Sivananda, in Rishikesh, it was left to me to build the ashram. At that time, people would give everything but not money. So I came to the conclusion that flowers represent emotions, love, softness, tenderness, the heart. When people give flowers, they give their hearts because the heart is also as tender as those flowers.

Money represents ego. Nobody likes to submit his ego. One likes to give love, tenderness, emotion and heart, but nobody likes to give the ego. Everybody wants to protect the ego, to keep it safe, because it is through ego that man operates in this world of duality. There are quite a few things in this world which represent ego, and money is definitely one of them.

In 1964 I started building an ashram in Bihar, India, but it was not difficult for me at that time because I had learnt how to handle the ego. If you know how to handle the emotions, you get a bunch of flowers, but I have a trick by which I am able to handle the ego. Therefore, I sometimes get blank cheques. Never in my work in India have I found any difficulty in money matters, not even for a day, not even for one item.

Why we work

For me, the most important thing is to understand what I am doing and why I am doing it. There has to be some relationship between myself and the work that I am doing. Am I doing this work in order to fulfil my own ego, to satisfy my passion, to fulfil my ambitions, so that someone may say or write that Swami

Satyananda has one thousand and eight ashrams? In the same way, why do you work and how do you work?

The definition of a yogi and a sannyasin is very clear about it. You must work with your body, senses, mind, emotions and intellect, employ every possible means that you have on hand for the work. The work is not merely intellectual, emotional or even artistic only. It can be the work of a farmer, trader, painter, taxi driver, truck driver, electrician, plumber, or even a swami, prime minister, chief minister, governor or police commissioner.

The secret is detachment. You have to work with detachment. And for what? For money? Of course, it comes. If you are a plumber, an electrician or a driver, you get so many dollars per hour or per day, but that is different. Why do you work? A yogi or a sannyasin works for the purification of his awareness. There is dross in your mind and you have to clean it. The dross of the mind cannot be cleaned unless you involve yourself in *karma*, in action. Otherwise, it can't be done. Therefore, a yogi or a sannyasin or a highly evolved person works with detachment for the purification of the self.

Detachment is not renunciation
If you leave your job, your wife or husband, and just run away – that is not detachment, that is renunciation. I'm not talking about renouncing anything, leaving anything, abandoning anything. I'm talking about living with the things of life, with the people in your life, without attachment. When I use the word detachment, I don't mean lack of love. You can love with detachment. Love with detachment gives you total, enduring satisfaction without frustrations. Love with attachment can give you happiness sometimes and something else sometimes.

When I use the word detachment, I'm not talking about renunciation. Detachment is a philosophy, a way of thinking and a level of understanding also. When this level of understanding comes to you, then you should build the ashram. Before that, you should not. Otherwise instead of a house, you are building an ashram and you are only replacing the superimposed position of your attachment.

I'll tell you what the trick is. You know I have always been a builder. At the age of ten, I started reorganizing my family property – building, repairing the old houses, keeping an inventory of the livestock, fields, etc. By the age of sixteen, I had completely reorganized my entire property, which was large. When I came to Rishikesh, to my guru, I started building the ashram, purchasing typewriters, papers, carbonpapers, posting letters, everything. Then when I came to Munger, I started building Bihar School of Yoga and later Ganga Darshan.

However, when I leave any place, whether my family place, guru's place or even the ashram that I myself built in Munger, it doesn't stay in my mind. I can't think about it and say, "Why am I not there?" I don't carry with me the past impressions of any place or anything which has happened in my life, and that is the reason why I am able to control the ego of the people.

In order to control the ego of the people, the most important thing is detachment. You can control the whole family if you live with a total sense of detachment, or as a swami you can control the entire ashram.

Developing the ashram
The ashram here in Victoria is situated in a wonderful place. All around you there is nothing but trees and kangaroos. You are completely with nature. I only hope that the government, or anybody else, does not destroy this beautiful forest around your ashram. You must also protect these things because they protect you, they give you life.

All of you here and also many more people should think of developing this ashram so it becomes an ideal centre of knowledge and of light. People from many parts of the state should come here from time to time and give their share of work to create vegetable and flower gardens, plant trees and make this hall a little bigger.

Victoria has the largest number of yoga teachers in Australia. In Melbourne itself there are hundreds of yoga teachers and many more people practise yoga in Victoria than in other states of Australia. Once they begin to come to the ashram there will be hundreds of people, so you will have to hold regular classes on yoga here.

I will come to Victoria again, and remember that in the course of time I will be able to visit different towns and areas in this state. I have been thinking about it for a long time. I have many places in my diary where I should go. The swamis must prepare my tour of Victoria in one or two years, from city to city, town to town and village to village.

We should have seminars and classes on yoga everywhere and we should send yoga teachers to those places. It is such important work in our times, when leaders are thinking about survival and we are thinking about how to attain inner knowledge, inner peace and higher awareness.

The purpose of yoga
It has come to my mind that through the path of meditation, of *dhyana yoga*, we can achieve higher awareness. Yoga must be understood properly. *Yoga* means union and communion. The path of meditation brings you closer to yourself. When you are not meditating, you are far from yourself, you are united with the objects, with the things outside, with the external world, the sensorial world, the empirical world. In meditation, as you transcend the external boundaries, the awareness of name and form, you gradually come closer to your self. Your self is very important. What you know about yourself is not your self. The concept or the idea which you have or the way you understand your self is not the true understanding about your self.

We are in a state of ignorance and therefore whatever we understand about ourselves is not correct. There is something else which represents our reality and that reality is called the self, the *atman*, the consciousness. It is for this that yoga has to be practised. Of course, great sages and saints, whatever they have taught, they taught the wisdom only for this purpose which I'm talking about. Unfortunately, what they taught became a religion and religion cannot teach this. This is why all religions have failed.

The practices of yoga gradually take you from one level of awareness to another: physical, mental, psychological, emotional, psychic and beyond. This experience may not come to you in one single day. It can even take a whole lifetime, but to some it can come overnight. That experience of your real nature is called yoga. Yoga means union and that is communion.

When the lower self, the external mind, the external consciousness, merges with the universal consciousness, nameless consciousness or total consciousness, that is called union, confluence. Just as the river merges with the ocean, when this personality, this man with name and form is lost for some time, then a light shines within yourself. That light guides you to a greater and limitless light. That is the purpose of yoga.

Preparation of body and mind

In order to train the aspirant to achieve this experience, the different paths of yoga have been designed. They are not separate from each other. Karma yoga, bhakti yoga, raja yoga, hatha yoga, mantra yoga, kundalini yoga or other forms of yoga are not superior or inferior to each other. They all have a place; they are complementary to each other.

In order to develop yourself, to improve yourself, to improve the quality of the body, the mind, the emotions and the awareness, these yogas are designed. The experience I am talking about is a very wonderful experience, but that experience is preceded by many experiences which are difficult to handle, which are disturbing, which can influence the body and the mind. Therefore, it is important that the body, the mind, the emotions, the ideas, the philosophy, everything must be prepared. That is what we do in yoga practices.

Of course, that higher experience of union, that transcendental, brahmic experience is a sweet experience; no problem, no disturbance. It is absolutely tranquil, but unless you are well prepared and have trained yourself before that, you can't handle the preceding experiences.

Spontaneous awakening

Experiences of kundalini awakening can come to anybody, even without practising kundalini yoga, and they have come. In the last century and in the beginning of this century, many of the doctors in the West have had to rethink whether all the people in the mental hospitals who were classified as psychotic cases were really mentally ill, or did their problems have something to do with the awakening and evolution of mind and consciousness.

The psychic researchers of London, New York and various other places have been able to consider the question in thousands of cases, where they have found that not all mental imbalances necessarily pertain to madness. The psychic imbalances, mental imbalances, emotional imbalances, bouts of anger, greed, violence, passion, sexual crimes, do not necessarily pertain to madness only. They can be consequences of the awakening of the mind, spontaneous awakening.

This spontaneous awakening does take place in many people who take cannabis indica, ganja, hashish, LSD and other drugs. While singing, dancing, listening to music, this spontaneous awakening can take place. Even by sexual intercourse this awakening can take place. In a fit of anger, this awakening can suddenly take place.

Of course, the phenomenon of spontaneous awakening relates to every human being. Just as physical evolution takes place in animals, in the same way, spiritual evolution is also taking place in you. Even if you do not practise yoga, you will definitely have that experience one day. That is the ultimate destiny of mankind. By the practice of yoga, you are only accelerating that process of evolution, number one. Then by the various forms of yoga, you are training your mind and the body in order to handle the experience.

Importance of siddhasana

That is why we say you must first become an expert in siddhasana. Do you know what *siddhasana* is? Pressing the perineum with one heel and pressing the abdominal viscera with the other heel and then sitting properly with the spine erect. Why do you practise it? Can you not awaken your kundalini sitting in an easy chair? Can you not awaken your consciousness while lying flat on the floor? Why only in this asana?

That is important to know. That is why in yoga they have laid emphasis on this practice. A lot of experiments have been done in America, Japan, India, etc., on the effects of siddhasana. When you sit in siddhasana, what happens? Is it merely a physical position or has it something to do with your nervous system, sympathetic, parasympathetic or central nervous system? Or has it something to do with the brain? Or does it affect your blood pressure? What happens in your body? What happens to your blood pressure, to your heart, to the rate of oxygen consumption when you are sitting in siddhasana?

Of course, scientists today are only working on physical parameters, but even then I think these aspects must also be understood. Do you know what happens when you sit in any asana when you are feeling drowsy? Supposing you are meditating, then suddenly your consciousness drops. You will fall down unless you are already sitting in siddhasana or padmasana with your back upright and straight. In these postures you can remain in that superconscious state for two or three hours without any ill effect or any injury to the body.

Steadiness of posture

It is also important that when you have an experience in meditation you must be able to face it. We cannot face many fearsome things. There is a story which illustrates this. A disciple went to his guru to find a way to attain the superconscious state. His guru told him, "Okay, I will give you a method, but please remember that until you complete this practice, don't leave your asana, don't move your posture. Just remain there for one hour, two hours, three hours."

So the disciple was sitting on the bank of the river Ganga doing his practice. He sat in padmasana on a rock with his deerskin and a piece of cloth beneath him. He transcended his body, he transcended his name and form. Then he saw inside that a cobra was sliding towards him. He wanted to open his eyes, but then he remembered his Guruji's instruction not to move the body. So he continued to sit there and the cobra went away. That means that he was able to handle the experience.

The next time he was sitting again on the bank of the Ganga doing his practice and after some time he found that the level of the water was rising. It came right up to his knees, then up to his navel, then up to his nose. He was about to get up, then he thought, "No. Guruji said don't leave the posture until the practice is finished." So he continued to sit and everything was all right.

The third time when he was practising, he went very deep and in the depth he experienced that he was sitting in his drawing room and a telegram came which read, "Your mother is dead." My God! Immediately he came out of meditation. I am giving you an example of the kind of experience that takes place which can break your meditation again and again.

Many great saints and sages have described the experiences that take place in meditation. You can read about it in the books. Of course, they talk about heaven and hell, etc. For many days and nights they lived in a different dimension, different world, but finally they came through, because those were people who had purified their body and the mind and all the images within.

Yoga is the means
So, when I'm talking to you about yoga, right from the beginning I do talk about hatha yoga, pranayama, shatkarmas,

but kindly remember that is not the ultimate aim of yoga. Hatha yoga is the means, it is not the end. There are people who only need hatha yoga in order to maintain a healthy body. That is all right, but for serious sincere intelligent aspirants, hatha yoga, raja yoga, jnana yoga and all the other forms of yoga are the means to higher evolution.

25

Satsang

Rocklyn Ashram, Australia, 28 January 1984

How important is a guru in one's spiritual life? Is it not possible to achieve the same result without a guru?
This question is a very ancient one. For thousands of years, all throughout history, people have been trying to understand if they can realize themselves without an external aid. Whenever this question has crept into people's minds, it has been precisely due to the presence of a strong ego. Those people who do not possess a strong ego find it very easy to accept a guru.

If you look at this problem from a practical point of view and compare it with everything else in life, then you will surely come to the conclusion that a guru is very important in the life of a person wanting to tread the path of enlightenment. You need a teacher for every science, then why not a teacher for spiritual science too? Why should a question like, "Do I need a guru?" arise in your mind? Did such a question arise in your mind in school and college when you set out to learn mathematics, physics, geography, chemistry, astrology or biology? No! Because there the matter was purely intellectual; your personality was not involved.

It is much easier to surrender intellectually because when we surrender intellectually, we feel that we have nothing to lose. We know that there is nothing to fear in intellectual surrender, because it can be revoked, it can be withdrawn whenever it does not suit us. This is exactly what happens in our marital relationships. Our marital relationships fail because they are based on the intellectual plane and one can withdraw from them whenever the situation becomes difficult.

Our belief in God is also intellectual. I am referring to that belief, that understanding and knowledge which we have learned through our religious preachers. If the concept or belief in God was natural in you, if it had originated in you and was not taught to you by the scriptures, preachers or parents, not even by your environment, then it would not be intellectual.

When you come to the point where you want to decide whether a guru is necessary or not for spiritual life, please be sure that if you want enlightenment, you must proceed through a path. If you want to have higher experiences, you have to follow a path. You don't just jump into the domain of inner experience. It doesn't just come all of a sudden; you have to walk on the path. Before you walk on the path you have to start your journey at some point, and the guru is a very important factor here.

Now, coming to the reality. Guru is within you. Guru is not an external factor, not an external being. He is the inner teacher, the remover of ignorance, but even though the real guru, the *satguru*, is within us, very close to us, we can't hear him. Even if we hear him, we don't understand because the language of the inner guru is not the language that we understand. Therefore, to awaken the inner guru, who will show you the path of enlightenment, an external guru is necessary, who will gradually train you to understand the language of silence, of infinity, of eternity. It is with the external guru that you will be practising the whole circus. This external guru is like a detonator. Just as you detonate a bomb, in the same way, the external guru is the detonator to awaken the inner guru.

The question of guru is a very important question for one who is searching for inner life, for one who is trying to experience something beyond the body and mind and yet does not really know what happens. Many times I have known of people practising meditation on their own because they understand that meditation means emptying the mind. Everybody understands it like this. They read many books written by scholars who have not actually practised meditation.

We are inspired by these books and when we practise meditation, we begin to see light, to experience subtle forces. We begin to go deep within and then, suddenly, we are seized by fright and we stop meditating. If we had had a guru at that time, he would have explained to us that these are the experiences which one has in meditation and they are a part of our personality. These forces are the energy fields which we are beginning to experience. So – we should do this and we should not do that. This is how we should live, this is how we should think and this is how we should act.

Therefore, a guru is necessary for initiation, for teaching and also later when awakening of kundalini takes place. In this context, I suggest you read my book *Light on the Guru and Disciple Relationship*. It is a very important relationship which everyone must understand. The guru-disciple relationship brings about the fulfilment of spiritual aspirations in life. You know that every relationship you experience brings some kind of fulfilment, whether it be paternal, fraternal, marital or any other form of relationship.

When you undergo these relationships, you do have certain fulfilments, certain experiences. In the same way, there is a higher relationship between guru and disciple which brings about a greater fulfilment, a greater experience. But, of course, if you are not sincere, if you are casual in spiritual life, then you don't need a guru, because a guru is essential in your life only when you have become a true seeker.

How can we recognize a guru and how can we establish a closer relationship with him?
When you meet a boy or girl, how do you recognize that he or she loves you? When you meet a guru, you must have

devotion, faith and sincerity. If you are a seeker, you will recognize your guru. If you are not a seeker, you will never search for a guru. Therefore, those who are seekers on the spiritual path and who are faithful in their search will always recognize their spiritual guide.

I didn't have much of a problem, but of course I had to search. After I left my parent's place, I went to Rajasthan. There I lived with a very respectable and wise old man. He taught me the theoretical part of tantra, but he was not my guru nor did he become my guru. Earlier, when I was with my parents, I learned the practical side of tantra from a tantric yogini, but she was also not my guru.

Then I came to Rishikesh. There I met a swami whom I wanted to stay with, but he directed me to my guru, Swami Sivananda. When I went to him, I forgot everything; I was at peace. The surrender was complete, the devotion was total, and the understanding was unclassified. I lived with him from 1943 till 1956 as a part of his being. It never came to my mind to question whether he was my guru or not.

It is a very important relationship in the life of a disciple. When you meet your guru, you begin to experience spiritual life. That experience may not be the experience of kundalini, but definitely it is an experience and that experience makes you go deeper into yourself and brings you closer to your guru. That experience makes you completely stupefied. The intellect is stupefied; you can't think!

I used to think a lot about how to find a guru and who my guru would be, but when I met him I forgot to judge him. Therefore, one should judge one's guru before making him guru. After you select your guru, it is better not to measure him because you can't.

How should I practise mantra?

Mantra is a sound. The purpose of the mantra is to create a foundation for spiritual awareness and to detonate an inner experience. Sound is a form of energy and we can create a transformed state of sound by increasing the frequencies.

When the frequency is increased, then the sound waves can act on the external plane and also on the internal plane. So mantra is not just a holy word, it is sound and sound has frequency, velocity and colour. This is a very important subject and a lot of work has been done on the power of sound. Sooner or later, the energy produced by sound will be used by the scientists, but here I am talking about the effect of sound on the mind.

The mantra should be received from the guru, then you should practise it regularly in a certain way. In order to control the mind, you can use a mala, like a tulsi mala. You can practise the mantra with the rhythm of your breath or by concentrating at the centre of the two eyebrows or on the tip of your tongue. You can also repeat the mantra by concentrating on the palpitation of the heart.

There are other ways of practising mantra. If you have deeper concentration, you can concentrate on one of the *chakras* or psychic centres. There you can practise your mantra for one hundred or two hundred rounds. In this way, every month you can practise your mantra by concentrating on one of the psychic centres from the root of the spine to the top.

You can also practise mantra with pranayama. That is considered to be very powerful. You can adjust the number of repetitions of the mantra with inhalation, retention, exhalation and external retention in the following manner: one unit inhalation, two units retention, two units exhalation, one unit external retention.

When you are practising mantra with pranayama, then you must also practise bandha. *Bandha* means locking or contraction of the three important psychic centres in the body at the throat, abdomen and perineum. The perineum is the area between the excretory and the urinary organs. Contraction of the perineum is known as *moola bandha*, contraction of the abdomen is called *uddiyana bandha* and contraction of the throat is called *jalandhara bandha*. These three bandhas should be practised during retention of the breath. Of course, details must be learned from your teacher.

When you practise mantra, gradually your mind finds a space, it finds a centre, a basis, a substratum. After this, you can start your practices of concentration.

I do not understand detachment. Can you give some examples of how a person with detachment will react in life?

Detachment has nothing to do with renunciation. Detachment is not carelessness or indifference. Therefore, this science of detachment has been explained in detail in the *Bhagavad Gita* and *Yoga Vasishtha*.

In the *Gita*, there is a famous dialogue between a guru and his disciple. The disciple does not want to involve himself in the work and he says, "I want to renounce everything." But the guru replies, "No, you should not renounce." Then the disciple asks, "Without renunciation how can I attain realization?" The guru replies, "Realization can be obtained without renouncing." So the disciple asks, "If I do not renounce, then I will be attached to the things of life. Will that not hinder my spiritual progress?" The guru says, "No, you can live life fully. You can interact with every being, every object, every event in life and experience everything fully, totally, but without attachment."

This is the attitude by which a yogi lives in the world without being affected by it. Due to ignorance, however, most people are attached to relationships, events and experiences. Therefore, on account of your interactions and relationships with people and events in life, you experience joy and sorrow, happiness and unhappiness, satisfaction and frustration. All these things which you experience from day to day in your family, in your society and within you, are an outcome of the interaction between yourself and the events of life.

Therefore, there are two important points to remember. One is called *karma*, the action, and the other is the fruit of karma, the result of the action. When you are concerned with the karma and not with the results, that is called detachment, but when you are not so concerned with the karma as you are with the outcome, then that is called attachment.

Attachment is not related to karma, please understand this. Nor is it related to your interactions with a person, an event or an experience. Attachment is concerned with the fruits, with the outcome of karma, and that is very important to understand, not only for a householder but for everybody. In the course of your life, every day you interact with people through whom you experience love and hate, happiness and unhappiness. When the experience becomes unpleasant or dissatisfying, you do not know what to do. You think if your wife or husband is a cause of unhappiness, then you should leave her or him. So you divorce each other but that does not solve the problem either, because you have renounced; you have not detached yourselves.

Renunciation of an object or a person is one thing and detachment from the fruits of the interaction or the relationship is another. That is the central theme of the *Bhagavad Gita*. Sri Krishna says, "You can operate in this world through the body, mind, senses, intellect, emotions, etc., but you must remember to act with detachment and for the purpose of purification. Then, whatever you do in life becomes yoga."

Now, we come to another important point – how to practise detachment. If you can realize the true purpose of your existence, only then can you practise detachment, not otherwise. When you understand that you are not born just to live and die, to enjoy things and forget them, but for a greater purpose, then you will begin to discover your real nature. This state which you are experiencing now is physical, mental and emotional; it's not spiritual. Therefore, when you realize that you are born in order to grow spiritually, to know your true nature, to experience things beyond time, space and matter, then your life as a householder takes on a different meaning.

When you are born you grow up, you are educated, you marry, you have a family, a job. As long as everything is going smoothly, you remain immersed in total ignorance, but suddenly, you get a knock or a blow, a jolt, a shock. You desert your wife or she deserts you. Your business collapses, your friends betray you or you become sick. Then comes a realization. You look all around and you begin to see what life really is.

This is when discrimination and detachment start to develop. Sometimes you become neurotic, thinking and thinking about one thing for a day or two or three, or maybe even for one month, two months, three months. Finally you get annoyed, you get tired and you say, "How long am I going to think?" At that point what are you trying to do? You are trying to withdraw yourself from that obsessive thought. That is detachment.

It has nothing to do with marriage, investments, trade, business, property, romance, sex and drinking. Either you do it or you don't do it, that's up to you. If you want, have it. If you don't want it, throw it away. But if you think that throwing away an object or a relative is detachment, and enjoying it is attachment, you are absolutely wrong. That is where man has always made mistakes.

In the *Gita*, Sri Krishna was instructing Arjuna about detachment in the middle of the battlefield while the missiles were flying overhead and hundreds of people were dying in the war. Here the battlefield represents our own personal battle in life. This means you should be able to practise detachment even when the scales are heavily loaded against you, when everything is going wrong, when your love has been betrayed, when your confidence has been shattered, when your friends have deserted you, when your philosophy and deep-rooted convictions have fallen through and failed to help you.

What happens at that time? We call it nervous breakdown. In a nervous breakdown, when you stand your body trembles. Your mind is thinking and thinking all the time about something; it is not at all steady at one point. Your palms are perspiring. If you try to hold anything, your hands shake. When you get a little fever, you think it is encephalitis. If there is a little hard lump somewhere, you think it is a tumour or cancer. If you cough, you feel it is TB. If there is a little pimple, maybe it is going to be psoriasis. The mind is always negative.

At the same time you misunderstand your own people, your trusted friends, you don't even have confidence in your own self. Maybe you have millions and millions of dollars in the bank, but you still are afraid. This is called despondency. The first mental disease that man suffers from is despondency, dejection, frustration, nervous breakdown. What can I do? Should I do this, should I do that? There is conflict all the time. That is the first step to yoga.

When you get angry, when you get violent, when you are terribly unhappy, what do you do? Do you surrender or do you fight? You fight, because you are trying to create a balance, you are trying to come out of that situation. When you are frustrated, when you are angry, when you are doing something wrong, you try your level best to get out of that situation. That is called detachment; that is called yoga.

You must understand detachment and dispassion. These are very important philosophies of life. I can give you one simple example. Many years ago in the Munger ashram I had a cook. He was a very good cook, very responsible. He used to work day and night. When anybody was ill in the ashram, he would work overtime and give the best possible service to him. When the swamis got ill, he would serve them with his heart, with his mind and body, but he would never become nervous.

One day he received a letter from his wife that his son was ill. He got nervous. About a month after, he went to his village. I wrote him a letter, "Please come back. A seminar is going to take place. Fifty people are coming from Bombay and there is nobody here to cook." He wrote a letter from there saying, "I will come when my son gets better."

This is an example of attachment and detachment. He served the swamis and inmates of the ashram. He did his cooking job from three in the morning until ten at night, eighteen hours a day, with love, joy, devotion and respect for me and for the others, but with no attachment. He would go to his village once a year; he had interaction with his wife and child once a year, but when he received the news that his son was ill, what happened? He was affected.

So, attachment can be practised, can be experienced, can be formed, even with a person whom you never live with, while detachment can be practised with the people with whom you are interacting throughout the day and throughout your life.

According to many authorities the mind causes most of our problems. Which is the best way to control the mind?
I don't believe in controlling the mind, so I am not going to tell you how to do it. I am going to tell you how to de-control the mind. Of course, I understand that most people feel very troubled by the way they understand their mind. If my mind is thinking a bad thought, let it think it. If my mind is thinking of killing someone, it's all right, let it think it.

The mind is neither good nor evil. No thought is good and no thought is evil. You must understand everything in relation to the cosmic evolution of which you are a part. I am not talking about God. I am talking about the evolution of matter, mind and energy. This evolution relates to the whole universe – earth, sun, galaxies and invisible energy fields about which you are not aware. They are also evolving.

In the course of evolution, you have come to the point now where your mind is thinking this way and you can do nothing about it. Science will never be able to change the thinking of your mind. If you suppress your mind, it will have damaging consequences. The mind undergoes stages of evolution from the animal mind to the saintly mind. Your present state of mind, which you are trying to control, the negative mind, is in one of those stages.

According to yoga and tantra and samkhya philosophy, the whole mind, not only your mind but the mind which is in an animal, an insect, a hippopotamus, a seal or a dolphin, the mind as matter, as a substance, as an energy, is evolving. It has five stages from the lowest to the highest.

The first state of mind is found in animals and creatures. It is the inner mind, but it is not active, not functioning. It is dull, inefficient, dormant, inert. That is the first stage which nature has undergone, which the individual soul has undergone through many incarnations, maybe hundreds of thousands, when you had a mind but did not know it.

The second stage is the scattered, dissipated mind. You have seen a monkey; you give it something and it is soon forgotten. There is a waxing and waning in the behaviour of the mind. Millions of years ago even early man was like that. He was conscious of something for some time and then he forgot it. When he was very hungry, he climbed to the top of a tree in order to pluck an apple and then he forgot about it. He came down and half way he met another fellow with another apple. He took a stone and wanted to throw it at him. Instead he forgot half way and threw the stone aside.

This is called the scattered, dissipated, disintegrated mind. The movement of the mind is there but there is no sequence, no link between one behaviour of the mind and another. There is a total division, a total split. This is the second stage of mind visible in animals and early man, and maybe some people are undergoing that stage even today.

The third stage is called the oscillating mind. Most of us belong to that category. Do you know how a pendulum oscillates? It goes out and then comes back again to the same point. Our mind is moving towards cognition, perception, understanding, and again it comes back to the same point where it had started. That is why when you wake up in the morning after a night's sleep, you remember that you are the same person who slept last night.

There has to be a link between the different states of mind. If there is no link, the next morning I will be thinking, "Who am I?" because I cannot relate to my previous state of experience and knowledge. Now, because of the oscillating tendency, because of the evolution of the mind to this state of oscillation, I am able to relate myself with my immediate and distant past. This is called an oscillating mind, and it is the third state of mental evolution in the realm of nature.

You must understand that mind is basically matter. It is not homogeneous. It is composed of twenty-four elements which undergo permutations and combinations in the course of evolution. Therefore, the mind is not psychological stuff. It is born of matter and all matter has a mind. The rocks, minerals, vegetables, leaves, flowers, wood, everything has a mind, but it is inert; it is in an unmanifested state.

In human beings the mind is now mostly in the oscillating state and the appearance and disappearance of knowledge, the awakening and merging of knowledge, linking one fact of life with another, connecting time, space and object, is the quality of mind which humanity is passing through now. This is the third stage.

Now, the fourth stage in the development of mind is called the one-pointed mind, and that is yet to come. The mind becomes one-pointed at the time of perception, of cognition, of thinking, of awareness. There is just one point, not two; there is no oscillation. That is called the mind of a yogi, one-pointed mind. That is called concentration and with that begins the evolution of the superman, not the superman of television but the superman of Sri Aurobindo, Annie Besant and Aldous Huxley. The birth of that superman takes place when the mind perfects the fourth stage of evolution.

The fifth stage is when the mind is under total control. I am talking about mind as a force, not as a thought. Do you think mind is thought? Do you think it is emotion, passion, anger, jealousy? No, that is not mind! Mind is a force.

Anger is a force, jealousy is a force – what happens when you don't like something? You develop anxiety, which is an expression of the force of the mind. During the process of the evolution of your mind, you will develop anger, passion, negativity, worries, anxiety. They are the symptoms of the growth of the mind, not the decline or degeneration of the mind. This is my view. In my youth I had many problems with my mind. I felt I had to understand the truth and I read many books where they talk about control of the mind, but when I realized that mind is a force, then I began to understand why we should not try to control it.

Therefore, do not ask me about controlling the mind. You should try to accelerate the evolution of the mind by subjecting it to one-pointed concentration. As you meditate, you are subjecting the mind to a different time equation. You know the mind is subjected to time, space and object. These are the three categories of the mind. The time here and the time in meditation are not the same. Twenty years in the other galaxies equals thirty thousand years in this galaxy.

It is therefore necessary to understand the relationship of time, space and object in relation to the mind. When you enter meditation, as you are transcending the external sound, the external knowledge and the awareness of your own self, then you are entering into another time dimension. So, when you talk about controlling the mind, you are talking about a very dangerous subject, because in order to control the mind you have to control time. Unless you control time, you cannot control the mind, because time, space and object are three interrelated aspects of the mind.

In my opinion, householders should live like householders without any guilt or complex about the mind, but they must live like *karma sannyasins*; I mean sannyasins in the home. In ancient days in India there used to be people called *rishis*, they had a wife and children, disciples, obligations and everything, but they were highly realized people. They were very powerful people who understood the deeper nature of reality. If you know about them, you will become very optimistic about your own life.

26

The Philosophy and the Practices of Tantra

Rocklyn Ashram, Australia, 29 January 1984

Tantra is a great science in itself and therefore it will not be possible for me to explain everything about tantra. First of all I will tell you what people have understood or misunderstood about it. Tantra is equated with black magic and many hideous rites and rituals. People think that a tantric has black powers under his control. Therefore, many times in history and in many civilizations, tantrics have been misunderstood and the science of tantra has also been misused.

Right from the beginning man has tried to understand how the mind can be expanded, because he has come to understand that by expansion of mind there is a fountain of energy in him which can be released. Therefore, in tantra the basic substance is shakti. *Shakti* means energy, potential, or a great power. Just as you have a great power behind uranium, in the same way, within the mind or behind the mind, in the final analysis of the mind, there is a great fountain of energy.

In tantra, this energy is known as shakti and this shakti is symbolized by Kali or Durga, who are understood as deities or divinities. The shakti behind the mind and at the base of the mind is a fantastic force, but how to manifest it? How to release that energy from the fold of matter? You know very well that scientists have released nuclear energy from gross matter. Now, in the same way, how to release that shakti from the mind? This is the primary process in tantra.

An expanded mind

In order to release the shakti which is at the base or at the nucleus of the mind, you will have to expand the mind. Expansion of the mind relates to the practices. There are not only a few, but very many practices through which you can expand the mind. What is expansion of the mind? Just as you stretch rubber, in the same way the mind has to be expanded.

The mind has its limitations. If there is a flower, then only can you see it, otherwise not. If there is music being played, then only can you hear it. If someone is standing in front of you, then only you can see him. If there is no flower, then you can't see it, you can only think about it. If there is no music being played, you can't listen to it, you can only think of it. If there is no one standing in front of you, then you can't see anyone, you can just think about him. This is the limitation of the mind. The mind of a man can only experience those objects which are placed before him. When an object of experience is present, only then can the mind experience, otherwise it cannot.

But it is possible that one can see a flower even though it is not there. One can smell a fragrance even though the gross odour is not there. One can hear music even though it is not being played. If the mind is capable of experiencing that, then it is an expanded mind.

In recent years, expansion of consciousness has become one of the most popular phrases in America. One of the leading doctors there wrote a book about LSD. I have met him and he once said to me that by taking LSD you have certain experiences and these experiences are due to an expanded state of consciousness. If the consciousness is not expanded, then it cannot visualize all these things. So, therefore, to release the shakti from the fold of the mind, the mind has to be expanded, which means that you will have to develop the capacity to perceive, to visualize, to smell, to hear, without the aid of an object, in the absence of an object.

Inner visualization

In India there is a term which is often used for this inner perception. They call it *darshan*, which means 'to see face to face'. If you go back to your home and in the night or in your meditation I happen to be present and you can see me very clearly, that is called darshan. Darshan means inner visualization. Therefore, all Hindus believe that the greatest gift is darshan.

If you are meditating on a deity, on a particular form, on your guru, on a particular sound or sensation, then you should be able to materialize that as tangibly and as substantially as in reality; and this can happen. When this happens, a release of energy, a split takes place. That is called materialization and it is a very important aspect in tantra. The aspirant, the disciple of tantra, has one goal before him, to be able to see the object of his choice face to face as tangibly as in reality, but he does not regard this as hallucination or imagination. He considers this to be the release of his inner potential.

This faculty is something very important, something very mysterious about us. There is something inside us which can jump out and that something can assume a second form. It can operate, it can move, it can create things. That is a force which is not subjective. Hallucination is subjective, imagination is subjective, thought is subjective. I see my guru in myself, that's one thing, but I see my guru, my deity, in front of me and I am able to converse with him the same as in reality, that's another matter.

That may seem to be a kind of madness because it does bring some sort of shift in consciousness for a short period. For some time you are a bit unbalanced, but then you have a guru, you have practised and you have understood that the form in front of you is a manifestation of yourself which has been released.

The universal mind

From uranium to thorium, to helium, when you split and split the elements and separate and separate them, what is left ultimately is the nucleus, the centre of an object. Every object, plant, mineral, stone, everything has a nucleus. There is nothing in the universe which has no nucleus and that nucleus has to be exploded. Mind has a nucleus. You may think that mind is a psychological substance, but it is something more than that.

I am talking about the mind, not the brain – and this mind which I have, which you have, is part of the universal mind. Two lights may appear to be different, but they are not. They are separated by the two globes, that's all. So far as the energy is concerned, both function on the same power which is being generated at the powerhouse. In the same way, all minds are integrated parts of a universal mind and they function on the same universal energy.

The universal mind is something like an egg, and the substance of which this universal mind is constituted is a kind of protomatter. In the centre of the egg, there is the bindu. *Bindu* means point, centre, nucleus. Situated at the two ends of the egg are the opposite poles of energy, known as time and space.

Here, time is not measurement, like 1-2-3-4. This is what we can understand, that's all. Time is energy and space is energy, and they represent the positive and negative poles of energy, minus and plus. As long as these two poles are separate, nothing is happening. But during your yoga practice, or during any practice of unification, any practice of concentration which brings about one-pointedness, including LSD (I'm not prescribing it, I'm only giving you an example), these two poles of energy which are opposite to each other travel towards the nucleus.

From each side of the egg, time and space come closer together and finally they meet at one particular point. When they unite with each other, then an explosion takes place and this explosion is known as the awakening or the manifestation of kundalini.

The natural evolution

This kundalini is the source of the primal power, the dormant, eternal power which man has been inheriting for millions and millions of years. According to tantra and yoga, we are not born for the first time, nor shall we die forever. The matter has always been evolving, the consciousness has been evolving, not only from one cell or amoeba, but from the unmanifest state to the manifest state. These are the two broad dimensions they have made. First everything was unmanifest, then it became manifest. When consciousness became manifest, it did not just become a man or a horse, an amoeba or a plant, it first became a field of energy.

So this is how natural evolution has been taking place for millions of years. The universe existed before this earth was born; consciousness was existing before this earth was born. Since the very beginning, this evolution has been going on and right through the course of that evolution, the spectrum of kundalini, the seed of kundalini, the nucleus of that shakti has also been migrating and transmigrating from one kingdom to another, from one species to another, from one incarnation to another, but it has not yet been able to manifest itself.

It was only when man developed awareness of time and space, that the possibility of the awakening of kundalini became imminent. There are thousands and thousands of intelligent animals throughout the world, dolphins, seals, horses, dogs, elephants, but they have not yet developed that consciousness which can conceive of time and space. Awareness of time and space is the special quality of human beings. So, in tantra, expansion of mind has to be achieved through the practices.

The necessity of form

In India we know that God is formless, yet we have created a form because we know that it is important in order to maintain the awareness and to release the potential. If you try to concentrate on a certain thought or idea, you can continue to think about it for some time, but as your consciousness becomes deeper and deeper you will definitely lose touch with that thought or idea, you will forget all about it. But when you keep a statue or a picture before you, you will be able to continue to behold that form, even at the very deep levels of your consciousness.

The picture and the statue each have their own effect on the human mind. A picture has two dimensions, a statue has three. The effect on the mind created by a two-dimensional object is much less than the influence and impression created by a three-dimensional object. The statue, which has three dimensions, fits in with the quality of the mind. Therefore, we know that God is formless, He shall be formless and He was always formless, but at the same time, in order to release your potential energy, it is necessary to keep a form in front of you. Then what happens? You see yourself in that gross form and you can talk to that gross form, maybe not for hours, weeks or months together, but for some time.

A greater force
I'll give you an example of this. It is a true story that happened in my own state. About thirty years ago there was a school inspector who was a very devoted man. A Hindu is supposed to show the highest reverence for the swamis and he was that type of man. To any swami who came to him he gave clothes, shelter and food.

One morning as he set out to inspect a secondary school, he saw three swamis approaching him. He prostrated and invited them to his home. Then he went out and purchased rice, dal, vegetables and made food for them, completely forgetting about the inspection, as he was such a devoted man. After feeding the swamis, he bade them farewell and then proceeded on his inspection tour.

At about four-thirty in the afternoon he arrived at the secondary school, because he had to sign the register. When he entered the gates, the watch keeper of the school was astounded and asked him, "Sir, why have you come all the way back again? Have you forgotten something?" And when the inspector went in he found that his register had already been signed. Afterwards he thought about this for a long time and he realized that there is a greater force behind man's physical existence.

Shortcuts of tantra

If only one can release that force, then one can do many great things in one's life. This is the science of tantra – to expand the mind and release the energy. But how to do it? For that purpose the science of tantra has the practices of yoga. Yoga is the practical side of tantra, but these are the paths that take you very slowly towards this development, like raja yoga, bhakti yoga, karma yoga, jnana yoga, pranayama, kirtan, etc. These paths take a lot of time; they are called the circuitous paths.

However, there are shortcuts in tantra and these are very steep paths. They are known as the powerful path of tantra. I know these practices but I do not teach them. One is to go to the burial ground and practise meditation in the middle of the night. While you are there, you keep a bottle with you, and when you are struck with fear, you take a drink and then sit down again. That is called *shmashan sadhana*, burial ground sadhana.

I did that practice when I was barely fifteen years old. My father belonged to a particular sect called Arya Samaj, which is like the Protestants here. In the West, you have Roman Catholic and Protestant, and in India we have Hindu and Arya Samaj. One is the ancient cult and the other is a reformed cult. My father did not believe in any ritual things.

One of my friends told me about this burial ground sadhana and which mantras you have to use. So, without telling my father I used to go to the burial ground every night under one pretext or another. My father wondered what was happening and where I was going at midnight because fifteen years in India is a very innocent age. He couldn't even imagine that I was going to some girls, because in India fifteen year olds are just children. When he found out that I was going to the burial ground, he was so angry with me that he threatened, "If you go again, I will shoot you."

So I went to see my friend. He consulted his teacher and he said to get some ashes and burnt bones and practise it at home. So I brought it, but I did not take it inside. I kept it on the terrace in a flower pot and in the night I used to go there and do my practice. One night my father woke me up at twelve o'clock. He asked me, "What are those noises on the terrace?" I said, "I don't know."

So he took his rifle, as he thought it might be a thief or something, and went up to the terrace to have a look. He found nothing and went back to sleep. Again he heard someone jumping on the terrace, on top of the house. I began to think it was a spirit in the bone which was jumping. The next morning when he went there, he found the ashes and the half burnt bones that I used for my tantric ritual. He asked me to take it away and throw it somewhere. I said to him, "You please do it." But he would not touch it.

When fear comes – face it
So, this is one of the methods called burial ground sadhana, where you create fear, manifest fear, fake fear, and conquer fear. There the whole of your consciousness, the whole of your mind assumes the form of fear. The mind is completely full of fear and that fear is projected outside and then it is materialized. Therefore, those people who suffer from phobias should not worry about it. Fear is an expression of energy. Don't be afraid of the fear! When fear comes – face it, let it come!

A few years ago, one of my disciples wanted me to teach her this sadhana. I said, "Okay, bring a bone from the burial ground and keep it in your room." She was very happy. She went and brought one or two pieces of bone and kept it in her room. I gave her a nice silver plate, a red cloth, some rice and many other things. I said, "Just keep them and in the night I'll tell you what to do." When the evening came, she could not enter her room, she was so overcome by fear.

I said, "Okay, I'll give you another room." She said, "Oh no, I'm going to come into your room!"

I told her, "Now your fear is manifesting and you have to let it come out. You are a young girl, twenty-five or thirty, you are not going to die of a heart attack. Go in the room. There will be fear. The heart will be throbbing, there will be palpitations, there will be sweating. The ghost is coming, the apparition is coming, the spirit is coming. It may be a skeleton, it may be dressed in white with a beard, it does not matter. You must face it." But she could not.

Then I told her, "I'm not going to teach you this sadhana. A tantric has to be a very strong person, very obstinate. He may have fears, but he must decide to face them. He should not try to bypass the fear or to remove the fear or to suppress the fear. He must decide to explode the fear, explode it completely so that it comes out. Look, there it is, a skeleton. There it is, a white ghost and he's looking at you, he's staring at you and when you look down he doesn't cast a shadow. You know that spirits have no shadow." That is one shortcut.

Exploding the passion

Another shortcut, which again I am not asking you to do, is called *shama sadhana*. A young girl of sixteen years lies down naked, touching a part of your body. You feel passion, passion, passion. You are not going to do anything else, remember. You are only exploding passion and passion and passion. Sometimes it becomes so intense that you just go crazy.

So you understand what *brahmacharya* is – you have nothing to do with her; she is just there, she is your symbol. But she has to be a yogini or else she'll go crazy and you should also be a yogi. She should be an aspirant and you should be an aspirant. She should be strong and you should be strong. She should be able to arouse her passion without succumbing to it and you should be able to awaken your passion to its fullest extent, that's all. This is also a shortcut.

Of course, a karma sannyasin can practise it more easily, and I can tell you, it gives you more joy, more bliss and greater tranquillity. It gives you absolute pleasure, much more than you get by actually expending, exhausting or terminating the passion. You should not terminate the passion – let it come! That is tantra. Fears, passions, all that you call negative, comes out. The whole of your consciousness takes the shape of passion, takes the shape of fear, and stands in front of you.

In the Hindu pantheon of gods, you know, Hindus have a catalogue of gods, there is a deity called Kali. *Kali* means 'black'. She is the slayer of time, the destroyer of time. Time is a concept, a category of the mind. Kali is the killer of time. If you haven't seen her photo, you must try to obtain one. She is the ugliest of the ugly, the fattest of the fat. She is nude and has snakes all over her. She doesn't wear a tulsi mala, but a skull mala and her tongue is protruding out in the lion's pose, all bloody. Her eyes are red as if she has drunk bottles and bottles of wine. Beneath her right foot Lord Shiva is lying. This is the symbology of the awakening of all these forces.

Do not destroy the forces of the mind

Please understand that fear, passion, hatred, jealousy, anxiety, worry, obsession are not negative qualities. They are what is in you. You should not suppress them by ethics, morality, religion or guilt. Please do not kill them, do not injure them. They are an aspect of the uprising forces. At the time of the actual awakening of kundalini, when this great, unprecedented, historical event takes place in your life, you are overpowered by absolute fear. You are overcome by constant, consistent, continuous passion for days and weeks together. You are always thinking about sex, sex, sex, and about having affairs with every man or girl you know.

Can you imagine that this unprecedented event in your life should be accompanied by such an experience, which you call sinful, unethical, immoral and debauched? That is what has happened to everybody in the past and that is what has also happened to me, but I was told beforehand. I knew that all these expressions of consciousness, all these forces belonging to my mind were not something I should try to kill or destroy.

I can tell you that I have experienced jealousy, greed, passion, fear, worries, anxiety, obsessions, neurosis, psychosis within a very short span of my experience, and all of you do undergo these experiences in your lifetime. You are trying to find a solution for this because your society does not want half mad people. If you are ten percent mad, you must go to a doctor; if you are fifty percent mad you must go to a mental hospital.

You must understand that every person who does not behave properly in society and with his family members is not insane. He is undergoing a crisis in consciousness and he does not know it because he has never exposed himself to the spiritual realities of life. He has not understood what the mind is. He has not understood what mental force is. In fact, many of our religions do not go parallel to the theories of evolution; they don't believe in evolution. Therefore, the whole mistake is there.

A worldwide tradition

The path of evolution is the path of tantra and has survived down through the ages. Celtic civilizations used to practise tantra. In South America the older tribes of Incas and Aztecs used to practise tantra. The Jews in Israel, the Sumerians, the Babylonians, the Hellenes used to practise tantra. Even today there are still tribes like the N'um in South Africa which practise tantra, because they have understood that in each and everyone there is a greater force, much greater than the ordinary mind, much greater than the ordinary normal intellect, and that force can control the affairs of life. This, in short, is tantra.

A great scholar of the tantric tradition

There are many great books written by Indian, English, French and German scholars on tantra. There are many ancient texts translated by Sir John Woodroffe – *Shakti and Shakta, The Serpent Power, Garland of Letters, Tantra Sadhana,* etc. How did he come to do this?

Woodrooffe's pen name was Arthur Avalon. During the British period in India, he was the Chief Justice of the Provincial High Court in Calcutta. One day he was dictating a judgement and halfway through he changed his mind. He called his stenographer in the evening and dictated another judgement. Halfway he stopped and changed his mind. He did this half a dozen times. His stenographer was not an Englishman, he was a Bengali. The people from Bengal are known to have inherited the tradition of tantra in India. In Bengal there are many great scholars of the tantric science.

The Bengali said, "Sir, may I tell you something? You have changed your mind half a dozen times. This is not the fault of your intellectual judgement. I believe that the two parties, defendant and appellant, are conducting some tantric rites somewhere. When the tantric rite of the defendant, which is supposed to last for three, five, seven or nine days, is at the point of completion, it will be affecting your mind in one way. And when the tantric rite which the other party is conducting to win his case comes to the point of termination, it will be affecting your mind in another way. That is why, sir, you keep on changing your mind every now and again."

Arthur Avalon was an Englishman and he thought that this was all rubbish, but he could never dictate that judgement. Although he tried his level best, he forced himself to do it, but still he could not. Of course, he was a very important man in Indian society at that time and he used to meet with many of the wealthy and educated people, professors, doctors, lawyers, scholars, and he began to ask them all, "Is it true that certain rites create an energy field which can affect the mind?" Remember, he was living in Bengal where most people from top to bottom believe that one can release energy, and that energy can be transmitted and directed to another person and put him under hypnosis.

So he began to think and think, to read and read. Finally, he entered into the deep, wild woods of tantra. He went to Nepal and there he collected manuscripts from the library of His Royal Majesty of Nepal. He went to Kashmir and various temples and places in the south of India. He met great scholars, pandits, acharyas, sadhus, tantric mendicants, and he himself became a tantric.

In the final years of his life, one could not recognize Sir John Woodroffe as one from intellectual England. He used to live the life of a Hindu brahmin. Hindu brahmins put on a dhoti and wear a sacred thread. They have a tuft of hair at the back of the head and they don't wear anything stitched, only unstitched cloth. They lead very systematic, disciplined and puritan lives. He became a pandit like that.

In India, people have very great respect for this man who has done tremendous work in discovering and revealing this science of tantra, and he has brought this philosophy and this science of tantra to intellectuals throughout the world. Today his books are read by everyone and I believe even in Russia there are translations of his books.

QUESTIONS AND ANSWERS

What are the dangers of meditation?
Of course, there is danger in anything you do the wrong way. If you do not know how to cook, you will burn your fingers. If you suppress yourself and if you are obsessed too much by your mental personality, then your meditation will not succeed.

When you meditate, let your thoughts come out. Do not try to concentrate very hard. In this way, if you go on in the path of meditation scientifically and systematically, there is no danger. Of course there are people who try to practise meditation and give up the practice after some time because they find that the more they meditate, the more they express their negative tendencies.

One of my disciples said that before meditation he was pure and after meditating, his mind was filled with filth, and therefore he preferred not to meditate. I told him, "You were constipated, so you were feeling all right. But last night you took fruit salts and this morning you are purging. So you are complaining that the food was bad because you are purging in the morning. This purging, my dear, was necessary for you. If you had continued with constipation, then you would have developed other ailments, other complaints. Now that you have started purging, please continue, don't stop it."

In the same way, when you sit for meditation, you are closer to your entire self. Then you can listen to the tumult and vagaries of your mind, then you can perceive the behaviour, character and personality of your mind. When you are not in meditation, you are extroverted, you are aware of the sense objects. You are far from yourself and since you are far from yourself, you do not see yourself, you do not know what is inside. That is the reason why when you do not meditate, you do not face yourself, you do not face your personality.

But when you begin to meditate, to do mantra, to look within, then you become more and more aware of the tendencies of your mind. They may be horrible or filthy, they may be anything, but I prefer to say that the closer you come to yourself, the more you begin to witness the movements of consciousness in the realm of evolution.

In the same way as a snake sheds its skin, we also shed our skin, but for that the proper time has to come. We have always lived in a world of glorious idealism because of our skins. The elders of our family wanted us to behave in a particular way because that was necessary to maintain their social or national vanity. They wanted us to live a particular life and for that they created idealism – this is ideal, that is not; this is good, that is bad; this is right, that is wrong. And they kept on changing the values from time to time according to the changes that took place in the cultural or political context.

There was a time when the ladies put something on their head and covered their body. That was considered to be the sign of a cultured society, and today? They had to change it. So they created idealism, but that is not right. You have to be guided by realities, and the reality is within yourself.

There is no danger in meditation. If you can't concentrate, it doesn't matter. You can practise hatha yoga and develop the capacity for sitting in one yogic posture for one hour, two hours, three hours. *Padmasana* or lotus posture, *siddhasana* or adept's posture are the two postures best suited to meditation. In the morning or at night sit down in the corner in your lotus posture, with the hands in either yoni mudra or chin mudra. Close your eyes. Fix the gaze at the nosetip, mid-eyebrow centre, heart centre, navel centre or anywhere. Sit upright and straight.

Practise your mantra or concentrate on the inner sound, *nada yoga*, or concentrate on your breath or sing a song for one hour. Allow the mind to do what it likes. Let it keep on thinking, building castles in the air, exposing fear. If you want to think of a man or a girl, go on. If you want to think about how to earn money, millions, billions, trillions, do it! If you want to become the prime minister of Australia or the secretary of the United Nations, if you want to destroy Russia or America, if you want to make the whole world Protestant or Catholic, or if you want to break into houses or banks and take all the money, go ahead and think about it, no problem. Sit for one hour, try for two hours, and weekly, monthly or periodically try to extend the time so eventually you can sit for three hours.

Then, one fine day all these energies will unite with the central energy and suddenly, like Buddha, like Christ, like any other sage, you will find things are melting and everything is happening by itself. You will not know what to do. You will not be required to know what to do, you won't have to think, "Now what am I to do?" It is as if you have been thrown into the upper portion of Niagara Falls, then you don't know what will happen next. You are just moving along with the flow of consciousness, you can do nothing else, you have to become a part of that event.

Therefore, there is no danger in meditation. Sit down properly – *Om Namah Shivaya* . . . *Om Namah Shivaya* . . . *Om Namah Shivaya* . . . You begin to think about your job . . . *Om Namah Shivaya* . . . Oh my mind is so restless, I'd better do some pranayama. No, I am too tired . . . Okay. My God, Thou art in heaven.

You see, this is what you have been doing all the while, wrestling with yourself, with your mind. Who is controlling whom? You are fighting with yourself. The right hand is pulling the left hand, the left hand is pulling the right. The entire atmosphere of antagonism is self-created. You are creating a split in your own mind. One part of the mind is fighting with another part of the mind. One tendency of the mind is fighting with another tendency of the same mind.

You are slapping yourself, you are kicking yourself, you are suiciding yourself. Therefore, from today, whenever you sit for meditation, say to yourself, "Mind, do what you like, I'm not going to stir for one hour." This is called regularity in meditation. Such a person will not come across any danger, but if you keep on fighting with the mind in meditation, some of you, not all, might have some mental problems.

What is the significance of mantra initiation?
This is a very important initiation in the life of a seeker. Even as a seed is sown in order to have a plant or a tree, the mantra as a source of inner experience is planted on this day of initiation. The heart, the mind, the consciousness of the disciple is like fertile soil. When you aspire to spiritual life, when you are trying for and searching for inner awareness, higher awareness, then you have already made your soil ready. In that fertile soil a seed has to be planted.

The mantra is that seed. In the course of time the seed germinates, sprouts, grows and fructifies. In the same way, this mantra will grow in the form of inner awareness. This is a very wonderful and powerful beginning to spiritual life because the mantra creates inner experiences which bring you closer to your inner self. The mantra transforms the quality of the mind. The gross mind becomes subtle and more and more refined. It gives relaxation, tranquillity and equipoise.

When you receive a personal mantra from the guru, you should try to practise this mantra every day, at least once. It is important to maintain a minimum regularity in your mantra yoga. You can practise the mantra with concentration or without. You can practise it audibly or mentally, with the breath or by singing, or by just maintaining awareness of its vibration. You can practise with your mala, one hundred and eight times. The main thing is that you must practise it every day. How and when you practise it is up to you.

There are many ways of practising the mantra in order to avoid monotony. You can practise by listening to it also. Make a tape recording of your mantra and when you have no time, you can listen to it while you are doing other things. Hearing the mantra, singing the mantra, saying the mantra, whispering the mantra, thinking the mantra, seeing the mantra, writing the mantra, visualizing the manta are all forms of mantra yoga. You can devise other methods for yourself.

The practice of mantra in the beginning should be done at an average speed, but gradually the speed should be made slower. You should never practise the mantra fast. You are not promising that you will complete one round of the mala every day. Your promise is only that you will practise the mantra every day, even if it is for ten minutes, three minutes or one minute.

Regularity is your commitment. Fulfilment of a quota is not your commitment. You have no quota. Sincerity, aspiration, love, devotion, dedication have no quota. As you go on practising your mantra, after weeks or months you should make it slower and slower. As you slow down the speed of the mantra, the mind also becomes slower and slower, and the frequency is increased. Velocity is reduced, but frequency is increased. The frequency of your inner awareness is increased.

You should understand that mantra is a very important beginning in one's inner life and you must practise it every day. For children, of course, it is a good practice. Do it a few times, ten or twelve times. If you can't do it in the morning, do it at night, or even write it, but do it every day

27

Purpose of Ashram Life

Rocklyn Ashram, Australia, January 30, 1984

Yoga has gone around the world. We have ashrams practically everywhere, on every continent, in every country. We have ashrams in South America with headquarters in Colombia, in the USA with headquarters in San Francisco, in the UK with headquarters in London. Then, all over Europe there are very prosperous and progressive ashrams in France, Holland, Belgium, Norway, Sweden, Denmark, Finland, Spain, Italy, Greece, Germany, Switzerland. There are yoga movements in Czechoslovakia, Poland, Rumania, Bulgaria, Hungary and a bit underground in Russia. Yugoslavia has a very progressive yoga movement. You can't imagine the enthusiasm, interest and keenness shown by ordinary workers, scientists and hospitals.

In Asia we have ashrams all over India, Nepal, Singapore, Japan, Hong Kong and Australia. There are more than twenty-six ashrams in Australia alone, which stretch right from the south up to the north. This area also includes Fiji and New Zealand. The Australian ashrams have their headquarters at Mangrove Mountain. The ashrams in India and Nepal are controlled by BSY Munger directly.

Working harder than ever

In this way a network of ashrams has spread all over the globe. Besides these ashrams, we also have yoga schools all over the world where our disciples and devotees teach yoga privately, but the ashrams are different from yoga schools. I use the word ashram because it postulates a very important idea of expression: physical, mental, intellectual and emotional, which we find very hard to do anywhere else.

There is a pattern of life in the ashram which is completely different to the pattern of life you have in your environment or homes. Ashrams have to be different, and they have to provide, to create opportunities and facilities for the aspirants to live there more simply and to work harder, not softer, than they have ever experienced before.

The word ashram is a Sanskrit word. *Shram* means 'effort, labour'. A person who is working hard is doing shram. This is the Sanskrit expression. Now, working hard on the physical plane in the kitchen, in the garden, building construction, cleaning, management, etc., is external or physical hard work. That is also shram and that is one aspect of ashram life.

At the same time, there is another way or dimension of working hard and that is the inner dimension: spiritual labour. You are trying to tread upon the path and you have undertaken an uphill task for yourself. It is not flat, plain ground. You have to pass through mountains, fields, valleys and many difficult terrains. You have to face various areas of your personality and for that you also have to work hard. To concentrate is to do stupendous labour. That is also shram.

Meditation is inner labour. Working in the ashram in the form of kriya yoga is also shram. That is why I have chosen the word ashram rather than yoga association, yoga academy, yoga school or anything else, because I want to make it clear that you have come here and you will be coming here for shram. Yes, for shram, labour, and the harder you work, the better is the quality of relaxation.

If you are a lazy person, the quality of relaxation will be very inferior. If you are labouring hard, physically, mentally and spiritually, if you are a hard worker on the external as well as on the internal plane, then the quality of relaxation will be superior. You must remember this. That is why we have created a network of ashrams all over the world.

A new lease on life
Everyone should understand that they must spend some time every year in an ashram to express their physical, mental and intellectual energies and create things – bring forth vegetables, fruits, houses, roads, rooms. You have to create and that will give you a new idea after some time and that is going to be a discovery.

At this moment, many of you think that because you live with your family, you have to have attachments and you have to face the consequences of attachment and detachment, love and hate. You go through many ups and downs on the emotional plane in relation to your interactions with your family members and friends, and you find it very difficult to change the quality of your experiences. You want to change the quality of your experiences arising from your interactions, but you find it very difficult.

When events in the family and society go against you, you are shocked and unhappy. You don't know how to manage it. You see, living in an ashram, working hard for the ashram, creating things, gives you another glimpse of your experiences with your people and friends, every now and then. After involving yourself with the ashram work mentally and physically, you will discover something. You will find a new idea, a new approach to the problems of relationships in daily life.

The difference between ashram and yoga school
The same events which disturbed you long ago will not disturb you any more. That is why I tell all of you to come to the ashram from time to time, even though you may have already learned various forms of yoga from the swamis. You might say, "I have learned hatha yoga, meditation, yoga nidra and various other forms of yoga. Now I can practise that at home. The ashram will only teach me about the inner

self, higher awareness, etc., nothing else – and I already know all that."

No, that is not the sole purpose of ashram; that is the aim of a yoga school. You can go to a yoga school and learn all the hatha yoga, raja yoga, laya yoga, this yoga and that yoga, theoretical and practical yoga. A yoga school can give you no more than this academic training, but an ashram will give you the training which will influence deeper layers of your personality.

Gathering impressions

The deeper layers of your personality pertain to the unconscious about which you don't know. When you look at a beautiful flower, you know it, you experience it, you understand it. You are aware of the entire process of influence, of impression on your mind. There are many things in your life which are influencing you, but you do not know it.

These influences or impressions do not go through the conscious mind. They go straight away into the unconscious, sometimes through the subconscious, but not through the conscious mind. Of course, every experience which passes through the conscious mind is transferred to the subconscious and finally to the unconscious, and every experience has a form.

Look at a flower, clouds, trees, rain, light, bad things, repulsive things, good things. They are creating vibrations. They are related to your mind, to your understanding and thereby they create an impression. That impression is called *samskara*, that is, seed. The seed of a mango, coriander, wheat or rice is called samskara, impression.

These impressions keep on flowing throughout your life and you are simultaneously absorbing impressions on various planes of your consciousness, not just on one plane. That is why you say that the human mind and human consciousness is too complicated. Inside your mind there is a video camera which is switched on day and night from the time you are conceived by your mother, up to the time you are consigned into the grave. Everything without exception is continuously being recorded there.

Totality of experiences

No influence or impression can be missed. Everything is there, but at various levels. There are certain impressions which are imposed on your mind by circumstances and events. You can erase them by self-analysis, psychoanalysis, intellectual analysis and religious analysis. There are various forms of analysis by which you can just erase them, but there are other impressions which cannot be erased by analysis or even by proper understanding and discrimination.

You can understand them but you can't erase them, because every experience passes through various layers of your mind and finally gets embedded in the unconscious mind, the storehouse of karma. In this storehouse of karma there are billions of these samskaras. They are preserved there with absolute accuracy. They are stored there just as you have a storing system in the computer; you call it a floppy disc.

In the same way, you have a microscopic floppy disc and it is formless. That is the beauty of it. It has no form, no weight, no dimension. It is there and comes out in dream. It comes out during moments of imbalance, during emotional fits and during meditation. It comes out when you are angry, violent, compassionate and tranquil.

These samskaras which are embedded in your consciousness in millions and billions and trillions are formless, but each seed is different and each has a relationship to one of your experiences in life. We experience not just one thing, not just a few dozen or a few hundred, but thousands and thousands of experiences pass through our consciousness every day. Can you imagine it!

From the time we are born, up to this day (thirty, forty or fifty years), whatever we have gone through, lived through and experienced is there; it is not destroyed. It comes out sometimes in the form of recapitulation, memory. Where does it come from? It was there and we are able to bring it forth.

All these samskaras or impressions which you take in throughout the day and night, consciously as well as unconsciously, are the components of your personality. That is what you are. You are not just this body, no! You are not just the habits, but something beyond this. The personality, the composition of the totality of the experiences which the individual has had right from the time of conception to the point of the grave and maybe before and later – how is one going to manage with this totality of experiences?

It is for this purpose that I thought very well for years together and I came to the conclusion that ashram life can help you to manage with the known and unknown areas of your experiences and personality. Therefore, whenever you have the opportunity, you should come to the ashram for a week, three months, six months, one year, three years, or maybe for a lifetime, it depends on you situation.

When you come to the ashram, you can shave your head and don this geru cloth. Then after six months or one year, geru the cloth again. Whenever you want, you can restart your life. You will definitely find a change in your relationships with the people around you.

We are all one

There is a beautiful story, and with this I close. There was a farmer whose wife died. He called the priest and requested him to chant sutra and mantra incantations for her wellbeing in the other world. The priest began to pray. The farmer asked, "Are you praying for my wife?" The priest replied, "I'm praying for her as well as for all the sentient and insentient beings." The farmer exclaimed, "But I asked you to pray for her exclusively. Why are you praying for all?"

So the priest explained, "It is my *dharma*, my duty, to pray for all beings, sentient and insentient, living and dead, for your wife is one of them." The farmer said, "But please make an exception. I do not want you to pray for the man who lives next to me because he is a rascal. If you pray for all beings, living and dead, then you are praying for him also, and I don't want you to do that."

This is how everybody lives life, but we have to be different, because the whole universe is embedded together, united by one thread and that thread is in you, in me and in everyone. It is in order to experience this that we come to stay in the ashram for some time. And when we have caught a glimpse of that totality, then we are able to return to our homes with a new vision of life, which will help to guide us through even the most difficult situations.

QUESTIONS AND ANSWERS

What is the spirit of the ashram?
An ashram is not just an external structure; there has to be a spirit in it. A temple without spirit, a church without spirit, an ashram without spirit or a body without spirit is nonsense. Spirit is symbolized by light, because we need it. In the darkness of night, when you want to go out you take a torch with you, and if you do not have a torch light, you will stumble.

In the same way there are various levels of man's existence where he needs light, and everywhere there is darkness. We are not able to see within our own selves. Our minds, thoughts, emotions, ambitions, everything is moving in the realm of darkness. By chance we sometimes experience happiness, but it has come to us only by mistake; we do not deserve it.

As human beings we are travelling within the spiritual darkness and therefore the essence of light has to be brought in. In the ashram also there has to be light, and the person who is looking after the ashram has to be a light, so that in the course of time he can fill the hearts of his pupils and disciples with inner awareness.

Light and inner awareness mean the same thing. When the inner awareness grows in the mind, intellect and heart of the disciple or pupil, then and only then has he been given the light. When this inner awareness grows within him, gradually inner happiness and understanding increase, and then things begin to change. That is why we inaugurate an ashram with the kindling of a light.

What is the purpose of work both in the family and in the ashram?

You may work with your body, senses, mind, emotions and intellect. You may employ every possible means that you have at hand in the work. It's not merely intellectual or artistic work that I am talking about. It can be the work of a farmer, trader, painter, driver, electrician, plumber, or even a swami, prime minister, governor or police commissioner. The secret is detachment. Of course, money comes, rewards come, power comes and glory comes, but you have to work with detachment.

A yogi or a sannyasin works for the purification of his awareness. There is dross over your mind and you have to clean it, but it cannot be cleaned unless you involve yourself in *karma*, in action. Therefore, a yogi or a sannyasin works with detachment for the purification of the self. Detachment is not renunciation. I'm not talking about renouncing a thing. I'm talking about living with the things of life, with people, without attachment.

When I use the word detachment, I don't mean lack of love. You can love with detachment. Love with detachment gives you total and enduring satisfaction without frustration. Love with attachment can give you happiness sometimes and unhappiness sometimes. I'm not talking about renunciation when I use the word detachment. It is a philosophy, a way of thinking and a level of understanding also.

When this level of understanding comes to you, then you should build the ashram, before that you should not. Otherwise, instead of a house, you are building an ashram and you are only replacing your attachments. That is the trick.

28

Radio Interview

Satyananda Ashram, Mangrove Mountain, Australia, 9 February 1984. Interviewer: Bobby Gladhall

Could you tell us what you are doing in Australia at the moment?
I am touring all the establishments and centres which are dedicated to the teaching of yoga all over this country as well as New Zealand.

Do you think there is a resurgence of interest in yoga at the moment in Australia?
Yoga has always been a way of life in Australia. When I first came here in 1968, I found that yogic awareness in Australia was superb. In the last few years, Australians have been trying to accept yoga not only for physical benefits but for mental development and for the growth of the spiritual personality.

Do you think you could possibly give us a short definition of yoga?
Yoga is a practical science for the transformation of mind and personality as a whole. At the same time, it has got its own positive bearings on the physical health of man. In the yogic science, we think that when the mind is sick and the spirit is under the veil of ignorance, then diseases develop in

the physical body. As such, the science of yoga tries to deliver mankind from physical diseases and mental unhappiness by helping him to discover the innermost area of his own self or personality.

In India, for thousands of years, yogis have experimented, practised and perfected the science of yoga in order to initiate a process of evolution in the total nature of man, which means the physical, mental, emotional and intellectual as well as spiritual levels. These yoga practices are defined or classified, such as the yoga of action, *karma yoga*; yoga of emotion, *bhakti yoga*; yoga of psychic balance, *raja yoga*; yoga of rational analysis and understanding, *jnana yoga*. Similarly, there are various practices of yoga related to different dimensions of man's personality.

You understand, man is not merely intellect, a body or emotions; he is a composition of many factors. These yoga practices which I have just enumerated are intended to develop the different areas of man's personality, like emotion, mind, psyche, body, etc.

So would yoga involve being able to distance yourself from your emotions in some way or to be in control of them so that you won't be led astray by them?
No. In yoga there is no such thing as suppression or renunciation of the emotions. You see, we believe that if one part of our personality is unbalanced or suffering from disharmony, then the other side of the personality becomes predominant. If an emotional crisis appears in our personality, it evidently means that there is imbalance somewhere. So, if you try to harmonize that aspect of the personality, then this emotional crisis can be brought under control. You don't have to reject or renounce it.

How much of your life have you practised yoga?
Well, I have been exposed to the practices of yoga for the last fifty-six years.

What is tantra?

Tantra is a science which includes practices for the expansion of mind, thereby releasing the innermost energy in man. This is the simplest answer I can give. In the ancient tribal cultures of India and throughout the world, there have been many practices peculiar to those tribes, which intended to help the mind to function beyond its given boundaries and confinements.

As you know, mind can function when there is an object, when there is a given knowledge, but can mind function without an object, without a base or without a substratum? That is called expansion of mind. When that expansion of mind takes place, when the mind can function even in the absence of a substratum, without the help of the senses, then a certain amount of energy is released within the human consciousness.

So, *tantra* literally and practically means expansion of mind and liberation or release of energy. As you release the energy from matter, in the same way, either in the mind or in certain areas of this physical body, or even in the spirit, there is an inherent energy potential. That potential has to be released, and this is possible only when you are able to expand the mind.

29

Dhyana Yoga

Gosford Ashram, Australia, 12 February 1984

Yoga is not new to the Western world. In the last few decades it has made an absolute breakthrough and it has been accepted by a large majority of thinking people throughout the world. Yoga is considered to be a science of life, but it is also important to know what yoga really means and what is the primary as well as the absolute purpose of this science. We practise hatha yoga, yoga postures and pranayama, breathing. Most of us understand that this is yoga, but some of us who are exposed to other forms of yoga, like relaxation, concentration and meditation, think they are higher forms of yoga.

In the science of yoga, however, the various yogas are classified according to the temperament of the individual. Each person is a combination of body, mind, emotion and intellect. I'm leaving the spirit for the moment. Progress in all four elements is necessary for an all round growth of one's personality. If your physical growth is satisfactory and your emotional, mental and intellectual growth is not, that is called lop-sided development of the personality.

Most of us are suffering from a lack of harmony and balance in the growth of the personality. We think that if we can grow externally on the mental plane or on the intellectual plane or even on the physical plane, then we are really growing. It is because of this lop-sided growth that there are so many problems within us. The psychological problems, emotional problems, problems of the physical body, problems related to relationships in the family as well as in society, must be traced back to an unbalanced growth in our personality.

Yoga means harmony, harmonious development of body, mind, emotions and intellect, therefore we have karma yoga, bhakti yoga, raja yoga, hatha yoga, jnana yoga, nada yoga, laya yoga, mantra yoga and kriya yoga. Yoga is a science and these are the faculties or the various branches which have to be practised and imbibed in our life in a balanced way. So, the most important thing we have to understand is yoga in relation to our own life and personality.

Unification of the mental forces

One of the forms of yoga which needs thorough explanation and which is very important for the people of our times is *dhyana yoga*, the yoga of meditation, the yoga of absolute awareness or the yoga of total attention to your inner being. It is this particular yoga which will bring about a total transformation not only in your mind and emotions, but throughout your personality.

Dhyana yoga is not concerned in any way with your religion. It is a practice through which you can train your mental forces to unite. Mental force is a concrete force. It is energy like radioactive energy, electromagnetic energy or any other form of energy. It is not an abstract thing. Mental energy is not merely psychological. Mind, mental energy, thought, emotion, these are all forces. Just as you produce energy in the external field and that is again transformed into various forms, in the same way, within us is that energy which we call mental energy.

In the practice of meditation, the mental energies which are distracted and dissipated are united. Take a magnifying glass, for example. When a magnifying glass concentrates the energy of the sun, it can burn a piece of cloth or a piece of paper. The same energy of the sun, which was dissipated, could not do that, but with the help of the magnifying glass, you are able to concentrate the solar energy and thereby make it more powerful. In the same way, our thoughts which are always distracted, dissipated, scattered, broken, inconsistent and full of conflicts must be concentrated.

If the image of our mind were drawn on a blackboard, depicting one line for one process of thought, you would find that you could never draw one line straight. Therefore, through the practices of meditation we try to train this primitive energy and thereby make it more powerful. This is the fundamental principle of meditation.

A therapeutic system

In the last few years, scientists in India, Poland, Japan and America have been working with the most sophisticated instruments, trying to assess the effects of meditation on the physiological and psychological processes. What is the effect of meditation on man's personality? How does he behave? How does he think? How does he make decisions? How does he react? What are his constructive contributions to humanity?

This is a very important breakthrough in the field of science. Not just a few hundred but thousands of researches have been conducted. I myself have been the coordinator in some of these projects. In fact, there is a well-known doctor in Melbourne, Australia, Dr Ainslie Meares, who has experimented with the effects of meditation on the physical body. This means he has been working with the effects of a mental process on the physical process. For example, in people suffering from cancer, which is a deadly disease, it was found that through the practice of meditation, a physical process can be initiated in the body which relieves and in same cases brings about a remission of the disease. This is an important point which you must understand. In meditation you are working with the mind, through the mind, in the mind. The whole process is mental, but the result produced is transferred into the physical body.

The practice of meditation does not merely change the course of thinking, feeling and sensing, it also changes the course and behaviour of the blood pressure. It not only makes you aware of your inner spirit or inner self, but at the same time it can suppress one hormone and express another. This is something which you have to understand and it is on this basis that we have to say meditation is also a therapeutic system.

Disease is not just physical

How does the practice of meditation create these effects on the physical body? How does the practice of meditation reduce the stress which is going on through the cardiovascular system? How does it help to cure the patients suffering from such diseases as multiple sclerosis? What happens when a patient suffering from multiple sclerosis practises meditation under the guidance of a teacher, and how is he cured?

In England we have many ashrams and centres as we have in Australia. There our teachers and swamis work with patients suffering from multiple sclerosis. Through the practices of yoga and meditation, patients who have never left the wheelchair are able to walk. This happens because the mind and body are interconnected; they are interrelated, they are interspersed one within the other.

When the body is affected, that effect is transferred to the mind and it is called somopsychic disease. When the mind is affected, the effect is transferred to the body and it is called psychosomatic disease. A disease is caused in the physical body and a disease can originate in the mind. Your thoughts can be sick, your philosophy may be sick or your emotions may be unhealthy.

Just as you have disease-producing bacteria, viruses and germs outside, in the same way you have disease-producing thoughts, emotions, feelings, philosophy and beliefs within you. How are you going to treat them? You have to believe that your physical diseases, your mental diseases, your family disturbances, your emotional disturbances and disturbances in your life as a whole are not just physical. They are deep-rooted within you. Therefore, the practice of meditation is taught.

Thought power

The scientists who have been researching the effects of meditation have been working very thoroughly. They have even gone to the extent of discovering that when the mind is fully concentrated, it can transmit waves. Therefore, a thought is not merely subjective. When you produce a strong thought, positive or negative, there are moments when that thought can travel from one point of space to another, from one person to another. Sometimes it does not travel; it gets mutilated. If I shout from here, you may be able to hear, but by the time my shouting reaches the road, it will be mutilated.

Therefore, the mind is a force and what we think is transmitted. This has also been scientifically investigated. In Soviet Russia they have been experimenting on the forces of the mind. Two important documents were published. One is *Psychic Discoveries Behind the Iron Curtain* and the other is *Possibility of the Improbable*. I am going to cite one of the experiments concerning the effect of concentration, the effect of a thought produced by a trained mind.

Two individuals were transmitting a particular thought to each other. They started from a short distance, say about one metre and finally this transmission and reception took place at a distance of sixteen hundred miles. Both of them were enclosed in a Faraday's cage, which electromagnetic waves and radio waves cannot penetrate but thought waves could. They succeeded in the transmission and reception of each other's message.

How can such a mind be developed? How can you train your thought currents? This science is known as the science of meditation, dhyana yoga. All the forms of yoga which you learn from your teacher are preparatory to dhyana yoga. Of course, hatha yoga is very good for the physical body, it makes the body supple, energetic and healthy, but that is not the primary purpose; that is a by-product. Yoga therapy is a by-product of yoga. All the forms of yoga are actually preparations for the practice of dhyana yoga.

Pranic healing

Now, what is dhyana yoga? I'm not going to tell you anything abstract or psychological. I know that this physical body is not just blood, flesh, bone, marrow and nerves. There is energy flowing in it. In yoga, they talk about two forms of energy. Just as an electric cable has two forms of energy, positive and negative, symbolized by '+' and '-', in the same way, in this physical body, there are two distinct flows of energy, different in quality, in quantity and in effect.

These twofold energies flow within the framework of the spine and they are distributed to every portion of the body by thousands and thousands of channels. Where a disturbance happens in the distribution of energy, disease takes place. This is called an energy block. These energy blocks which are formed in the physical body are responsible for physical diseases, mental diseases and emotional problems. That is why in China the acupuncturists used to block or release the energy at different points along the meridians or energy channels.

When you practise meditation, this energy which flows throughout the body becomes one-pointed and concentrated. When concentration takes place, then you can direct this energy to whichever part of the body you like. This is called pranic healing.

In India there are thousands of such healers. Every village has one or two. They just touch the body or forehead and you get better, because they are able to concentrate all their forces at one particular point, say in the thumb, and that energy is transferred to you. You may be suffering from a lack of energy in some particular part, and when that energy is transferred to you, you get better.

Three basic formulas

In order to practise meditation, first of all we need a basis or substratum for the mind, because the mind is unqualified, the mind is abstract. We don't really know what the mind is. Is thought mind? Is emotion mind? Is feeling mind? We don't know. We know mind is energy, therefore, we need a base.

In yoga and in tantra, there are three principles upon which the mind finds a base. These are known as mantra, yantra and mandala.

Mantra versus hypnosis

It is very important to know the truth about mantra because there is a lot of misunderstanding about it these days. Many intellectuals say that mantra is a hypnotic substance, which it is not. A lot of research has been done on this subject and it has been found that when a mantra is repeated, the changes that are taking place at that time are not the same as those which take place in hypnosis. If you hypnotize a person and then check his brainwaves, oxygen consumption, skin resistance, heart rate, respiratory rate, you will find that they are entirely different to a person who is practising meditation with mantra.

When you practise meditation on *Om Namah Shivaya* or any other mantra, at that time alpha waves are followed by theta waves, whereas in a hypnotic state, when you are hypnotizing a person he just passes straight through alpha stage to delta. His brainwaves first go into alpha and then they go to delta. A person who is practising mantra will first register beta waves for a short time, then alpha waves, then theta waves. That means in mantra chanting your brain becomes dynamic, whereas in hypnosis your brain becomes neurotic.

It is necessary to understand this point, because many people will say to you, "Hey, you practise meditation, it is auto-hypnosis!" I tell you it is not auto-hypnosis because the results, the scientific conclusions on mantra and on hypnosis are entirely different. Mantra and hypnosis are two different topics and we don't have to confuse them with each other in any way. When the mind and senses are withdrawn, there are two distinct stages which we undergo. One is relaxation and sleep; the other is relaxation and dynamism. The practice of mantra relates to this latter side of life.

The primal sound

Mantra is a sound. Sound is of various types according to frequency and velocity. The sound which I am producing when I speak is gross. It has a velocity, but low frequency. However, if I say within myself that I am speaking to you now, then it will have greater frequency and less velocity. Do you understand the difference between velocity and frequency? Mantra has frequency. Of course, the frequency depends upon the nature of the sound, because every sound is not the same.

In the Vedas, it is written that *Om* is the ultimate seed, the ultimate form, the primal form of all sounds. There has to be an origin, a beginning. A tree is born out of a seed. Various sounds which you produce have to be reduced to certain sounds. There are thousands and thousands of words in the dictionary, but ultimately they are all reduced to twenty-six sounds. We deliver lectures, we talk day and night like parrots, but what is all that? The permutation and combination of twenty-six sounds, and these twenty-six sounds can also be reduced to an ultimate sound called *Om*. So, the sound *Om* is the primal sound, *the* sound, the seed sound or *bija mantra*. It is from this one sound Om that all the other sounds have developed.

In Roman script they say A, B, C, D, E; in Devanagari or Sanskrit they say *ka, kha, ga, gha*. These sounds which we produce are formless. They have no form; they have waves. Of course, the ultimate form may be soundless, waveless, but the sounds which we produce are formless. Again, when they are accelerated, when they are blown up, they have a form. This form is known as colour: red colour, blue colour, yellow colour.

Everything is the form of a sound. What you see with your eyes is the external manifest form of a sound. This sound is the ultimate energy; it's not just a voice which I'm producing when I speak. When the sound is produced as I am producing it, this is one form of sound, but the ultimate form of sound is when you produce one mantra in your mind constantly: *Om . . . Om . . . Om . . .*

So, in order to start meditation you must practise a mantra, and when you practise this mantra for some time, then things begin to take place. The mind begins to move towards unification. Many thoughts, ideas, imaginations and feelings are unified. I will not be able to tell you more about mantra here because this is a very great science.

Yantra explodes the unconscious forces

The second basis for the mind is yantra. Yantras are to be used for stimulating the unconscious. The conscious mind is something which you know, but the unconscious you do not know. In everyone of us there are unconscious forces that shake our entire being like earthquake tremors which are going on underneath the earth. There are many currents going on underneath the earth, but you don't know it. In the same way, there are many thoughts, images, feelings, currents, waves which are going on within you.

These unconscious forces which are embedded in your mind, within your personality, have to be brought up, and for that, meditation on yantra has to take place. There are thousands of yantras and you have to select the one which is particularly suited to you. Concentration on that yantra along with your mantra will bring out the deeper forces of your mind. When these deeper forces come into your conscious mind during meditation, then you begin to see images, colours, lights, visions. These psychic experiences which take place in meditation and sometimes without meditation relate to your unconscious mind.

Mandala: the centre point

Then there is the third basis for the mind called mandala. *Mandala* is a pictorial concept, a pictorial form. A two-dimensional mandala is a photographic picture. A three-dimensional mandala is a statue. It is said that the three-dimensional mandalas are very powerful. Even in modern psychology, Dr Carl Jung has said that when the mind is consumed by the awareness of three-dimensional mandalas, then it can unify itself with itself.

That is precisely the reason why people in India practise idol worship. Every Indian knows very well that God has no form, as every religion believes. God has no name. We even go a little bit further. We believe that God does not do anything, although other religions believe that God does everything, including the work of a magistrate or a policeman. According to this philosophy, God is not an actor; he does not do anything. Nature, *prakriti*, is an actor. God does not act; he is a silent witness to the whole drama that is taking place. We believe that, but at the same time we know that whatever God may be, for the purpose of our evolution, for training and controlling the mind and dispensing with the disturbing emotions, we do need something solid.

Therefore, the concept of the three-dimensional mandala came in the form of a statue or a murti. Actually *murti* doesn't mean statue, it means a symbol. There has to be a symbol. Why? When you sit in meditation, what are you going to concentrate on? There has to be a basis, a centre point, a nucleus. Every object has a nucleus, a central point. You have a nucleus. And by concentration on the mandala, which is the external form or pictorial concept of that nucleus, you are able to arrive at that centre point within yourself, which is also the centre point of the whole universe. This is the aim of meditation.

Where is that nucleus?
Now, unless there is an explosion in the nucleus, there cannot be an awakening. The nucleus is the centre point, the deep seed of the object. The external form is only a wrapper, a cloak. The body is a cloak, the mind is a cloak, an external wrapper. In yoga they say that the nucleus is at the bottom of the spine where the tailbone ends, in between the urinary and excretory organs in the area of the coccyx. In the female body it is situated behind the cervix.

I am talking about a physical thing, not a psychological or immaterial thing. There is a small residual gland, just like a mole, situated at the end of the tailbone, and at that particular point in this physical body is the seat of the nucleus. If an explosion takes place in the nucleus, that is called nuclear energy. Why do you call it nuclear energy? Because an explosion takes place in the nucleus when time and space come together. When two poles of energy join each other at one particular point, then an explosion takes place. That is physics.

This spot in the physical body is known as the seat of kundalini, remember that word. There is no thinker anywhere in history who has understood this important point. Please excuse me for saying so. I am talking about a particular point in the physical body which people consider to be most unholy. You are trying to search for that higher reality, higher than you, fifty feet, seventy feet, ninety feet and beyond, but I am talking about an important point which is located in your physical body, at that particular part of the body which puritans never think about or speak about. I speak about it day in and day out. It is called *kundalini*; it is the primal energy, the energy related to the evolution of man.

You know that Darwin's theory of evolution pertains to the evolution of nature, but in the cosmos, in the universe, evolution has taken place first from the unmanifest to the manifest. That is the first phase of evolution, the first milestone, from invisible to visible. The second was from visible to man. That is the law of natural evolution as propounded by Darwin, which is exactly as propounded in Indian philosophy. The third evolution is from the awakening of kundalini to samadhi. That is the completion of evolution.

The importance of practice

The practice of meditation through mantra, yantra, mandala or any other form of yoga is intended to create one-pointedness of mind. For a moment, time is lost, self is lost, you are lost. There is nothing but that little point for a short period, and that is the point when awakening of kundalini takes place.

People have tried to awaken this kundalini by drugs, by religious practices and by many other methods. Some may have succeeded, but most of them have failed. However, there is an enduring practice which leads to this awakening, handed down to us through many thousands of years, and that is the practice of yoga and meditation. Therefore, if you want to awaken the kundalini, it is necessary to devote at least ten minutes every day to the practice of *dhyana* or meditation. If you find it difficult, then do some preliminary practices first such as asana and pranayama. You must become an adept in the two meditative postures, padmasana and siddhasana. They are not just postures; they are related to the interconnection of the energy forces in the physical body.

Padmasana is intended to create the posture of the lotus. That is important in yoga because when awakening of kundalini takes place, it makes headway to a particular point which is considered to be a thousand-petalled lotus situated in the centre of the brain, exactly at the point where the pituitary gland of our medical science is situated. In kundalini yoga it is called *sahasrara chakra*, the thousand-petalled lotus. The lotus is something which is related to the mystic explosion and manifestation of man's lower energy into higher energy.

So, try to practise meditation every day, if possible, in padmasana, the lotus posture, or in *siddhasana*, the adept's posture. The best time to practise is in the morning when your body has broken down most of the toxic matter. If you can't practise meditation with the help of mantra, yantra or mandala, then start with pranayama. It takes time to perfect it – you have to learn, you have to understand, you have to practise.

Ultimately, meditation is the easiest thing in life. It is easier than sleep. Do you know why it is easy? Because not to think is easier than to think. For thinking you need energy. In not thinking, you don't need any energy. Switch off everything and just sit down. So find out a mantra, find some time, get yourself inspired. Who knows, some illumination might come and then the effect of mantra or the effect of meditation will be felt in your daily life, in your decisions, in your relationships, in your physical health and everywhere.

30

Radio Interviews

Brisbane Ashram, Australia, 17 February 1984. Interviewer: David James on 4ZZZ FM

Swami Satyananda is unique in his scientific approach to the ancient disciplines of tantra and yoga. He insists that yoga was once and is now re-emerging as an international culture free of any sectarian or religious overtones. He states that the process of evolution is not complete in man and can be hastened by the practices designed to activate the dormant brain. Could you tell us something about this ancient science?

Yoga has been with us from the advent of human civilization, for thousands of years. Even early man did experience the physic events related to expanded consciousness. He began to wonder what it was, but he could not define it, he could not explain it, so he attributed those things to spirits, ghosts, demons, gods. This is how he explained it. He did not know that what was happening or what he was experiencing and seeing was an expansion, an extension, of his own consciousness. He thought that a higher hierarchy, a god from heaven, some angels or some ghosts had come and done it.

I won't say that I have readapted or reinterpreted yoga for modern society. In fact, the conditions of modern society are basically the same as they were many thousands of years ago when the ancient culture was at its peak. Every culture has its peak during which many mental and emotional problems come up. At that time, yoga was experimented upon and applied. It was found to be very adequate and so we are applying the same thing today.

Is the yoga that is practised today in the world, basically the same yoga that was applied say, two thousand years ago?
It is basically the same thing. The practices of concentration, relaxation, awakening of the potential energies in man, the hatha yoga postures, the breathing exercises are all the same. The ultimate goal of yoga is to help everybody to discover the nucleus or the centre of his own being, in other words, to experience himself completely and totally, not partially.

Before this ultimate goal is reached, however, everybody has an objective which he wants to fulfil through yoga, like good health, one-pointedness, relaxation, creative intelligence. That is not the goal, that is the primary objective which he wants to obtain, but finally he has to discover the goal for himself.

According to yoga, meditation is a state of complete experience which dawns spontaneously as a fruit of these practical disciplines. In recent research in the field of endocrinology, it has been established that meditation exerts a profound harmonizing influence on the body's endocrine glands and stimulates microsecretions in the brain itself which transform the experience and the awareness of the meditator. Do you think that such practices can help to bring peace and harmony to the world?
In order to create a harmonious situation or a peaceful environment, collective meditation is of great use. So, in the beginning of meditation practice you have to learn along with others, but if you want to generate fantastic energy, to be able to transmit the great energy, then you have to practise meditation on your own.

Talking about a third world war, a nuclear holocaust, do you think there are enough good people, enough good energy in the world to avert or lessen the potential of a nuclear war?
I do not think there will be nuclear war. There will be wars; pocket wars will always take place because the human mind is full of jealousy, anger and greed, but not nuclear war.

Do you see an increase in yoga around the world?
Yes. People have come to understand that concentration of mind is very important for the evolution of mankind, for the evolution of an individual. If you want to change or improve the world, it is necessary that you transform the quality of the mind, because society is an expression of the individual.

How can we establish greater harmony within ourselves?
You must develop a harmonious relationship between your daily work, your emotional patterns, your feelings and your awareness by conscious practise of your daily activities, like karma yoga, your daily work, your relationships with people, and concentration of mind. Most important of all is the practice of mantra.

Whichever mantra you have, you must practise it every day with absolute regularity. This practice of mantra becomes the basis of progress, coordination or integration in the totality of your personality. You see, you are a body, you are a mind, you are a spirit. There has to be harmonious development, and when harmony is lost, then there are problems.

Interviewer: Janine Walker, ABC Radio Network

How does yoga tie in with science? One thinks of yoga as something that is beyond science.
Well, I think the practices of yoga do bring about a change in the complicated and intricate processes of the human body, the nervous system and the brain, thereby accelerating the

pace of evolution in the physical matter and making the brain more efficient, more disciplined and more creative.

We would all like to do this, but how easy is it? You and your followers have obviously spent a lifetime on it.
Of course, it's a very ancient theory. When you are able to handle the practices of concentration, of one-pointedness, the intricate and complex system of the brain undergoes an evolutionary change. Thereby the sleeping centres, the unexplored centres in the brain, begin to express their faculty or their property, which otherwise remains dormant in an average individual.

Well, psychologists tell us that we use only one-tenth of our brain's capacity or power. How can one tap into the other nine-tenths, because each man and woman must surely have more propensity to do things and to achieve things?
The science of yoga concentrates on the awakening, on the evolution of this process in the brain. Besides this, the various practices, the classical practices which are related to physical exercises, breathing, relaxation, concentration, or even the mystical practices of yoga are all directed towards the expression or awakening of this facet of the brain.

How long does it take to learn to use even part of the other facets of the brain which are virtually dormant in most of us?
It is very difficult to say because there are different types of people in the scale of natural evolution. Some people are able to get the result very soon and others take a little more time.

But you are speaking from the aspect of a culture which goes back for thousands and thousands of years. Our culture doesn't go back that far in the western world.
Culture and human beings are two different things. A culture may go back for a few thousands of years, but according to

the law of natural evolution, human beings have been existing for more than a few thousand years.

But surely the culture under which we grow and learn has an effect on us as people.
I think the present culture in the West is a short-lived culture. Earlier in the West and in the East, the psychic cultures promoting the evolution and acceleration of the process of the brain and mind were much more predominant, like the Celtic culture or Atlantis.

So many people from the West are coming to India and turning to masters like you to study what your culture has to offer. Why is this? Why is it that India and people like you hold such a fascination for the West which has mastered the most intricate modern technology?
Well, the West has perfected the science of matter and after having experimented and discovered the science of matter, it has realized that there is something behind matter. They have gone to the point of discovering energy and some of the scientists are even thinking about the consciousness behind matter. This discovery made by the scientists has opened the eyes of the people of modern counties in the West.

Now, they are trying to discover that energy or consciousness which scientists say is behind the mind, because the mind is not just matter. Therefore, people are trying to contact spiritual masters in India because Indians have perfected the philosophy of spirit, consciousness or energy behind the apparent matter.

Do you find that Westerners want quick answers from you or are they prepared to work for what you have to offer?
They do expect very quick answers from us and we can also give quick answers, but one thing is very important, that is, the handling of awareness, of consciousness behind the mind is not an easy affair. It needs a lot of discipline and training.

What sort of training?

It requires training to be able to handle the experience. During meditation, during the awakening the consciousness changes, the mind changes, feelings change and one may not be able to handle that feeling unless one is properly disciplined. That is why when we teach yoga, we want the discipline to be aptly requisite to the practices.

Yes, it's rather frightening to think, as you suggested scientifically, we use only one-tenth of our brain power. If suddenly one were to increase the power, it would be like an increased surge of energy into a machine. If you can bring it down to a low denominator, it's like using a toaster and suddenly finding it's ten times hotter. It would take some kind of control and discipline to be able to handle the energy without burning the toast.

That is why in yoga, all-round discipline related to the physical, psychological, emotional and environmental interactions is required, so that the awakening of the dormant nine-tenths of the brain may be properly handled and used by you. There are many people like artists, musicians, writers and great statesmen who have been using more than one-tenth of the brain even today, but of course everybody does not have the ability.

There are many different forms of yoga and there are different kinds of practitioners with different ideas and different emphases. How does a Westerner seek out the best of whatever there is to learn?

You see, there has to be a proper synthesis for the development of the total personality, whether one is an Easterner or a Westerner. In the synthesis of an integrated approach, the development of the physical body, mind, feelings, consciousness and awareness have to go together. It is on this basis that we have to make a selection of our practices.

What subjects will you be dealing with at your public lecture and seminar?

At the Queensland Cultural Centre, I will be speaking on meditation, one-pointedness – absolute one-pointedness. At the seminar, I will be talking on relaxation and awakening the potential of the evolutionary energy in every individual, which will enable him to master the creative intelligence dormant in him.

31

Dealing with the Mind

Brisbane Ashram, Australia, 18 February 1984

Yoga is a practical science; there is very little theory in it. The practicality of this science is intended to develop an integrated personality. Therefore, the practical techniques of yoga cover the problems of the body and its complex and intricate systems, the mind and its known and unknown realms, and something more than that – the powerful, dormant unconscious in man.

Yoga covers various parts and aspects of our personality. Of course, many people nowadays and also in the past have explained yoga in terms of mysticism and occultism. If you prefer, you can call it magic. There is nothing wrong in this and nothing untrue, because a proper mind controlling the body and its functions, the emotions and the unconscious dimensions of the human personality can work wonders. I would not say that yoga is something divine, because that is how religion explains it and I am not a spokesman of religion. I understand that the practical techniques of yoga are intended for the good of everybody in this day-to-day life.

Why problems, why conflicts?
Today, in this twentieth century, with abundant prosperity, the acquisition of power and technology, we are the unhappiest culture in history. We have so much: a lovely home, secure

job, insurance policies, and yet we commit suicide. There is so much fun and diversion in our lives such as games, sports, TV, but still we go crazy and wind up in mental hospitals.

In a country like India, where there is extreme poverty, no proper medical care, no social guarantee, no economic security, we can understand if people commit suicide and go to mental hospitals. One can say, "Poor boy, he had no job and couldn't handle it, so he committed suicide." But why the mental problems, why the conflicts here in the West, where everything in life is ensured?

The simple answer is that our Western culture has not integrated the practical aspects of mental and physical training imparted by yoga. Here you have a powerful and organized religion, but it has created neurotics and psychotics. It has not been able to handle the problems of the human mind and body. It has not been able to handle the problems of that part of the mind which is not known to you, which blows when you become crazy, which awakens when you are mentally derailed, which expresses itself in dreams.

Therefore, it is so important for everyone, not only here in the West but throughout the world, that yoga should be understood as a science which can train the various aspects of your thinking, feeling, emotion and expression. I would say that yoga is the training, reorientation and education of the whole mind. The various forms of yoga, known as *karma yoga*, the yoga of action, *bhakti yoga*, the yoga of devotion, *raja yoga*, the yoga of the psyche, *jnana yoga*, the yoga of the intellect, and *kundalini yoga*, the yoga of the dormant potential energy in man, should be properly understood and practised.

The physiological basis of the mind

This evening I will try to speak to you on a very important aspect of yoga. It is important because it is devoted to controlling the various energies, currents, fluctuations and modifications of the mind. We have not understood the mind. A thought is not the mind. Emotion is not the mind. Anger, fear, sorrow, compassion, mercy, love, hatred – these are not the mind! They are the *vrittis*, modifications, fluctuations, expressions of the mind. Through logic, intellect or a process of thinking, we are fighting with the expressions of the mind. We are not dealing with the mind.

If you destroy these light bulbs, you do not destroy the electricity. It is still there; you're only destroying the external manifestation of energy. If you control anger and passion, if you suppress ambitions, you are doing nothing to the mind because, according to yoga, the mind is *shakti* or energy. It is related to a particular flow of energy in this physical body. It is not an abstract thing; it has a physiological base.

Tantra and yoga relate the mind to two energy flows in this physical body. The behaviour of these flows can be registered by modern machines. These flows are of two types. One is responsible for all your mental actions, feelings, knowing, remembering, anger, fear and so on. That is called the mental part of your physical existence. I am not talking about psychology, I am not talking about something abstract, I am talking about something which is existing in your body in the physical form, which can be seen, measured, registered, presented and understood in the form of data.

Now there is another flow of energy in this physical body, which is responsible for all the physical actions, motor actions like digestion, secretion, excretion, reproduction, sneezing, coughing and so on. Moving and talking are motor actions. So there are two types of actions in this physical body, motor action and mental action. In yoga they are known as *karmendriyas*, which represent physical action, and *jnanendriyas*, which represent mental action.

Malfunctioning in the energy circuits

These two forms of energy flow within the framework of the spine and are distributed to every part of the body through four main junctions. One is situated at the root of the spine, another at the solar plexus, the third at the cardiac plexus and the fourth at the cervical plexus. These are the four junctions.

The twofold energies are distributed through these four main junctions to various parts of the body by 130,000 *nadis* or energy channels, out of which 72,000 control or manage the cardiovascular system. This, of course, is indicated in the classical texts of hatha yoga, but in the modern researches conducted in India, Poland, Germany, America and Japan, scientists have also confirmed this idea. If you have studied the science of acupuncture and the research done on the flow of energy meridians and energy blocks, then you will understand exactly what I mean and what yoga is trying to explain.

Throughout the body, this energy is flowing and carrying the mental energy and physical energy. When there is a block, there is a problem. You know what I mean when I say energy block, but try to understand it much better. An energy block is something very concrete, something very real and this energy has nothing to do with external nutrition. I am not underrating the value of nutrition. Food has its own nutritional value, but I am talking about the original energy, which is called *prana*. This energy is very important for the proper functioning of the body and mind.

If the pranas are not functioning, if there is a blockage, a repression or a suppression, then you have physical diseases, mental problems, problems regarding behaviour, relationships and so on. Whether you are suffering from diabetes, high blood pressure, schizophrenia, psychosis, neurosis, worry, fear, excessive thinking or loud thinking, that is precisely due to malfunctioning in the energy circuits of your body.

You know this microphone is working, these lights are working, because the energy is flowing. If the voltage drops or the fuse or main switch blows, what is going to happen? That is what happens in this physical body and therefore in yoga we insist on the practice of hatha yoga. When we talk about hatha yoga, it is necessary to tell you that these yoga postures are not only exercises; they have something to do with the balancing and harmonizing of these twofold energies in this physical body.

Dhyana yoga

In Japan and many other countries, they have been doing a lot of research on a very important subject, which has been misunderstood in many Western countries. That is the subject of *dhyana yoga*, the yoga of meditation. I have to use the word meditation because you understand it that way, but actually dhyana is not meditation. The literal meaning of *dhyana* is absolute and total awareness, not partial awareness. Dream, thinking and hypnosis are partial awareness. In dhyana, the practices must lead you to develop a total awareness of the whole mind, not only the inner mind, but the external mind also. As such, this is a special science.

It has been indicated that when the practice of dhyana or meditation is done, changes not only take place in the mind, but in the external, intricate and complex systems of the body as well. The hormones are influenced and in certain practices, even the production or suppression of sperm and ova is also seen. The heart, circulatory and respiratory system and the process of metabolism undergo definite changes. Therefore, we must understand that when we are practising hatha yoga, the physical postures, the effect is taking place inside the mind and when we are practising meditation or dhyana yoga, the effect is taking place in the physical body as well.

However, meditation is very difficult to practise if it is not understood properly. When properly understood, it is the easiest thing that one can do, easier than sleeping or thinking, but we think that to control the mind and fix it on one particular point is meditation and concentration, No! If you study the main text on the mind by Sage Patanjali, the *Raja Yoga Sutras*, he says that you do not have to control the mind, you cannot control the mind and you should not try to control the mind.

Sage Patanjali's system

When you try to block or to stop the faculty of awareness, then you are doing something very damaging. You have to deal with the modifications of the mind, and for this purpose,

Sage Patanjali has suggested two important methods. One method is called *abhyasa*, which means constant practice. The other method is *vairagya*, which is translated as dispassion or disidentification.

When you are thinking, you are identifying with the feelings. When you are frightened, you are identifying with the process of fear, and this identification creates mental problems. Now, there is no harm in feeling angry, passionate, crazy or frightened, but you should disidentify yourself. This process of disidentification is not an intellectual process. You cannot just suggest to yourself, "Oh, I'm going to disidentify myself." You have to experience it. A thought has to be experienced and it has to be seen. It has to pass through the arena of your mind and consciousness, as a motorcycle or a car is passing.

Nowadays, when most people sit for meditation, what they want is that the mind should become completely vacant. That is the problem. That is why modern psychologists have commented that meditation is not good, because they think that making the mind vacant is dhyana. Why? Because there is a term which has come to the West – void or *shoonya*. By shoonya they mean zero, no thought, completely vacant mind.

Sage Patanjali makes it very clear that if you want to have total control over this fantastic energy called the mind, then you must employ two techniques. One is disidentification and the other is the actual practice. The actual practice is related to raja yoga, which is a system of graded practices in eight steps, and the seventh step is known as dhyana yoga.

When you want to practise dhyana or meditation, then you have to create a substratum or base for the mind so that it does not become vacant. For that purpose you have three practices in yoga and tantra. One is called mantra, the second yantra and the third mandala. This is important, for if you want to understand the mind properly and realize the whole mind, then you have to create a substratum, a basis.

Mantra relates to the sound, internal sound and external sound. Every sound is considered to have immense power and potential. When the mind is brooding over a sound for a particular period of time, then certain changes take place in the frequency of the mental energy. The inner waves change. That is one way. The second way which has been worked out lately is by yantra. In the tantric science there are certain geometrical formations which are related to the deeper impressions of the inner mind, not the external mind; these are known as *yantra*.

Purging the mind

How can you experience the totality of the mind, how can you experience deep and peaceful meditation, if you have not fixed up the karmas? Karmas are deposited in you in the form of impressions. Every experience which you have gone through in your life, knowingly or unknowingly, during the innocence of you childhood or maybe now, creates an impression. That impression is something like a seed. It is absolutely invisible but it is there. That is called *karma* or *samskara*. I call it archetype.

Whatever you experience in your day-to-day life is immediately transferred into your consciousness in the form of a symbol. If you undergo dejection, disappointment, frustration, victory, success, happiness or unhappiness, that experience is converted into an archetype or karma. Just as an avocado or mango tree has a seed which does not look like a tree but produces a tree, in the same way every experience has a symbolic impression within you and this remains there for millions and billions of years.

As long as you have consciousness, everything you experience is being photographed and stored. Nothing is missed. That is called the totality of karma and this totality is within you. When you sit for meditation, all these stored up impressions begin to come up into conscious view. Suppose you are trying to meditate on your guru or your symbol, but so many other things come into the mind at the same time. Of course, you don't want to allow these things to come into the mind because they are so unhappy, so undesirable, but you must let them come.

When your stomach is bad, you take a laxative or purgative. You go to the toilet one, two, three, four, five times. You don't like to go so many times, but you must do it because your stomach is bad. How do you know your stomach is bad? Because it is paining or you are passing bad wind or maybe you tongue is coated or you are not feeling hungry or perhaps you are nauseated. These are the symptoms. In the same way, all these undesirable experiences and impressions indicate a sick, overloaded mind and suggest that you must clean it out.

When you sit for meditation and practise your mantra and your yantra, you will find that thoughts keep on coming into your mind all the time. You are trying to concentrate on a point and those thoughts come this way and that way. How are you going to deal with them? Are you going to suppress them? If you suppress them, they will come again. Finally, if you don't allow them to express themselves in the proper way, then they will come in the form of disease, psychosomatic disturbances, personality defects and even in the form of cancer.

Learn to disidentify

Therefore, the karmas should not be suppressed. They should come out. Let them come! However, you must learn how to disidentify before you try to express them. This is an important point and this is where everyone is making a big mistake. You start to meditate without learning to disidentify. You do not know how to practise antar mouna, how to see a thought, a form, a vision, a colour, how to hear a sound or music within the mind. They appear and disappear. You must observe each one with an attitude of detachment – "I'm not that; that is different."

Most of the time, however, you try to combine an experience with feelings – that's the problem! Fear is nothing, but when you combine fear with feeling, then it creates fright. The idea of death is nothing. You can see yourself lying there in the coffin. There is no problem as long as you can just observe it, but when you combine that experience with feeling, then there is fright. So, vairagya or disidentification has to be learned first, then you can practise meditation.

Now, when you are practising concentration on a particular yantra, the mystical experiences begin to take place. You feel that there is a lot of overwhelming thinking and emotional processes, and you begin to see experience after experience. I'm using the word mystical here, but I'm trying to tell you that these mystical experiences are nothing but the symbolic formations of your karma and they also have to come out.

When an experience passes through your consciousness and you have learned how to disidentify, that seed dies. If you take a few seeds of wheat or coriander and sow them, they will germinate, but if you fry them first and then sow them, they will not germinate. A karma, a samskara or an archetype becomes actionless when it is processed through disidentification. Therefore, in the scheme of yoga and meditation and in your life, you must learn how to disidentify, how to separate the seer and the experience. This is important.

You know the secret

Happiness and unhappiness are nothing. Love and hatred are nothing. You have given them a value, a weight, a meaning, but they are only the passing experiences of life. You can identify with them as many times as you like. You can also disidentify with every experience of life. Then where is the mental problem? Where is the nervous breakdown? Where is the conflict?

Conflict is eternal, but as long as you disidentify yourself, you are not affected by it. You know it is there. It is a reality, of course, but you disidentify yourself. Frustration, disappointment, unhappiness, heartbreak, sadness, defeat, greed, every emotion is there. You know it, but you know the secret, the method, the technique of disidentifying yourself. So learn how to disidentify, not intellectually but by practice; and secondly, you should find out the proper practices for yourself.

Some practices may not be suitable for you. Some people cannot practise hatha yoga, some cannot practise voluntary concentration and some cannot even practise mantra. There are various practices of yoga according to the quality and temperament of the individual. Karma yoga is for the dynamic person. There are some people who can't meditate, who can't practise any form of yoga, but they can practise karma yoga through work.

There are people who are predominately emotional by temperament; they must practise bhakti yoga. There are people who are mystic and psychic by nature; they must practise raja yoga. There are people who are intellectual and rational by nature; they must practise jnana yoga. So there are various types of yoga; you must choose the practices which are most appropriate for your individual nature.

32

Satsang

Brisbane Ashram, Australia, 19 February 1984

Are the practices you advocate for raising the kundalini dangerous?
Every time I speak about kundalini, people think that there is some danger in its awakening. Every path of progress is beset with difficulties. Awakening of kundalini pertains to the evolution of human consciousness. When this evolution is undergoing a phase of transition, there is some crisis everywhere. When you are passing through those critical stages in the physical body during puberty and menopause, is it not dangerous? This is related to the process of evolution.

Evolution relates to matter and mind. In the course of evolution, the body evolved from lower stages to higher stages. That is the law of natural evolution. In the human body the law of natural evolution changes and becomes the law of spiritual evolution. Mind is overtaken by supermind, individual ego is overtaken by cosmic ego and empirical intelligence is overtaken by cosmic intelligence. So, awakening of kundalini relates to the law of spiritual evolution.

Even if you feel that awakening is dangerous and that you should not venture to awaken kundalini, you must remember that in the course of evolution, mankind as a whole is gradually going to experience evolution and the explosion of kundalini, if not now, then after a few hundred thousand years, and we must pass through the danger. So, I would like to suggest that the word danger be replaced by the word crisis. Crisis is inevitable when you are passing through a stage of transition from one state or body to another, say from animal to human. From one state of mind to another, from an ordinary mind to a yogic mind.

When awakening of kundalini takes place in mooladhara chakra, it has to be guided through the path of sushumna to sahasrara chakra in the brain. Therefore, awakening of kundalini is not the only thing that we are trying to engender. There is something more beyond the awakening of kundalini. This is the primary event, but then the energy has to be raised to the highest centre, thereby utilizing it to awaken man's highest potentiality.

In the course of human history, thousands of people have been born with awakened kundalinis. They used that creative energy to develop various forms of knowledge. Not only yogis, clairvoyants, prophets, saints and sages, but even some of the great army leaders were born with an awakened kundalini. Some of the most cruel people in history were also born with an awakened kundalini, but not a fully established kundalini.

When kundalini is fully established, it is another matter, but when awakening of kundalini takes place, that energy can be channelled in any direction. You can be an intuitive artist, a writer or poet, or a great statesman like Mahatma Gandhi, or a great musician or composer of music, vocal or instrumental, perceiving the great melody that one realizes in the deepest and highest consciousness, which the ordinary mind cannot conceive and produce. Even a carpenter can utilize that creative energy which one has at the time of awakening kundalini.

When kundalini is being awakened, you do not become religious, pious, virtuous or a so-called puritan. No! You may think about drinking or sex all the time. This is an important point which you must understand. When the awakening of kundalini takes place and man's powerful, capable, expert and efficient consciousness comes into the forefront, it replaces this mind with its limited capacities and takes over the functions of life as a whole. Therefore, a yogi, a statesman, a painter or even a dacoit can function wonderfully with an awakened kundalini.

Now the question is, how can we awaken this kundalini? Classically speaking, life has to be properly organized. In ancient India, the whole lifespan was divided into four *ashramas* or stages. The first was brahmacharya ashrama, the second was grihastha ashrama, the third was vanaprastha ashrama and the fourth was sannyasa ashrama. These four stages of life were intended to produce a condition in which the awakening of kundalini could gradually take place without disturbing man's emotions, desires, passions and the events of life.

In the texts pertaining to yoga and tantra, there are practical methods given for the awakening of kundalini. I can tell you that the awakening of kundalini is not nearly as difficult as handling the awakened kundalini and guiding it to sahasrara chakra. Before awakening the kundalini, you must think about how to handle it and guide it to the highest centre. I can bring a tiger or a leopard to you right now, but can you handle it? You must know how to tame the kundalini. So, there are two important points which have to be considered: one, how to awaken the kundalini and two, how to tame the kundalini.

The taming of kundalini is very difficult. Usually people with an awakened kundalini become very proud. They do not know how to use their higher energies so they practise clairaudience, clairvoyance, telepathy, hypnosis, mesmerism and many other things. This is how they utilize this superior power which is intended for spiritual growth.

The tantras talk about raja yoga, hatha yoga, laya yoga, mantra yoga and kriya yoga. These are most important and powerful practices for awakening the kundalini. These practices must be properly related to the stage of your life. For example, if you are a householder, the method of kriya yoga, which you can find in the tantric tradition and which is being taught by many gurus today, is a very simple but powerful method for the awakening and taming of the kundalini. Kriya yoga is a combination of seventeen practices in which the awakening of kundalini takes place by a systematic method.

Here, you should remember that controlling and suppressing the mind are not necessary in the awakening of kundalini. There are some techniques which should be practised without trying to control and suppress the mind. One of these practices is known as khechari mudra. There are two ways of performing it. One is practised by hatha yogis who cut the root of the tongue and then elongate it. This practice is not suitable for everybody.

Then there is another form of khechari mudra which is used in kriya yoga, together with a practice called ujjayi pranayama. Here, you must fold you tongue back and stick the under surface to the upper palate for as long as possible. In the course of time, say about a year or two, the tongue slips into the upper epiglottis. If you are a vegetarian, it will be easier and quicker. If not, it will take a little more time.

Now, in the inner nasal passage there is a particular nerve ending connected with the cranial passage at the top of the brain, at the place where the Hindus in ancient times used to keep a tuft of hair. That place is called the point of *bindu*, which means 'drop' or 'centre'. It is believed that from that particular centre a tiny amount of serum or secretion is emitted, and that fluid is known as amrit in tantra.

Amrit means nectar or ambrosia. What is that nectar? When khechari mudra is practised, the tongue touches a particular nerve ending. Then the stimulus is transferred to the higher centre in the brain and that fluid begins to flow. When it flows and is absorbed by the body, your state of consciousness changes, just as when you take cannabis, ganja, LSD, peyote, or even alcohol, you undergo a change or an altered state of consciousness.

When this amrit is absorbed by the body during the practice of khechari mudra, then the restless mind becomes quiet and one-pointed. Passions, desires, imaginations, dissipations just drop away; they disappear. We do not know why they are even happening and why they are not happening any longer. This is how the so-called problems of the mind are solved through the practices of kriya yoga.

Now, there is another important aspect of kriya yoga and that is the awakening of the chakras. We have spoken about the awakening of kundalini, but nobody has asked about the awakening of the chakras and sushumna. The process is this. First you must awaken the chakras before you venture to awaken the kundalini. After the awakening of the chakras has taken place, then you must awaken *sushumna nadi*, the central nervous canal. Only then must you venture to awaken kundalini and to tame kundalini. These are the four stages, please remember them.

The awakening of the chakras is very important. When the chakras begin to awaken, you have mild spiritual experiences. You may call them psychic, inner or even divine experiences. When they come to you during the practice, they do not frighten you. They do not alter the state of your mind totally and there is an experience of peacefulness.

When you awaken the chakras like mooladhara, swadhisthana, manipura, anahata and so on, which are located in your body, you have different experiences related to the instinct, intellect, ego and emotions, and to the different chapters of your mental personality. They are like beautiful and colourful dreams which you are experiencing consciously. When the experiences are taking place, you are not only witnessing the experience, but you are also experiencing the experiencer. So with these experiences, you get used to inner experience. That is called awakening of the chakras.

Awakening of the chakras can also be done with the help of hatha yoga postures such as *padmasana*, lotus pose; *sirshasana*, headstand pose; *bhujangasana*, serpent pose; *shalabhasana*, locust pose. These yoga postures are intended for the awakening of the chakras in the body. If the chakras are not awakened, the awakening of the kundalini becomes stagnant.

Besides these practices, there are many other ways of awakening kundalini, such as the path of the *pancha tattwas*, five elements, which most people today know very little about.

What is the devil?

Frankly speaking, I have thought about it for over fifty years and I have come to the conclusion that the devil is not an external entity. The devil is not a person. The devil is the working of one's own mind.

The whole mind, the whole body and the whole of life are in a process of evolution. This evolution is classified into three stages. One is called *tamoguna*, the inert state, the next is *rajoguna*, the dynamic state, and the highest is *sattwa guna*, the balanced state. These are the three stages of total evolution.

In relation to these three stages, the mind has five chapters. Mental evolution can be divided into five parts. The first state of mind is dull, the second scattered, the third oscillating, the fourth one-pointed and the fifth totally controlled. These are the five stages of the mind. When the mind is in its primitive state, it has certain propensities, certain instincts, which are not properly understood by people, and therefore they call it the devil.

In India, we have two great epics. One is the *Ramayana*, the story of Rama, and the other is the *Mahabharata*, the story of two tribes, the Kauravas and the Pandavas. In the *Mahabharata*, there is a very important text called the *Bhagavad Gita*, which is a dialogue between Sri Krishna, the master or guru, and Arjuna, the disciple. This dialogue is in eighteen chapters, each entitled with a different type of yoga.

If you have ever seen the *Bhagavad Gita* in pictures, you will remember a chariot scene with Sri Krishna as the charioteer and Arjuna, the warrior, sitting behind with his bow and arrows. That is an important scene in which we talk about the two cosmic forces, the two eternal forces in the universe and in this individual body and mind.

These two eternal forces are always in friction, trying to pull each other in the opposite direction. In religion these forces are known as the divine force and the demonic force. However, I do not accept this view. I know that evolution is not just a forward movement. When you talk about evolution, about progress, about forward movement, then you must also accept that there is a force pulling back at the same time. If that backward pull is not there, then evolution does not take place.

When a car or an aeroplane moves, when your body moves or when anything moves, there is always a pull which is holding it back. That is why the movement is taking place and this movement is related with a certain force of gravity which is the nature of the object, the nature of the movement.

When you create movement, it is not just one movement; you are creating two opposite movements. When you see, hear, talk, move or act, you are not creating just one movement; you are creating two movements and each is opposing the other. Thus an act is taking place. This is the law of motion, of action, of cognition and perception, and in religion, one of these movements is called devil and the other is called divine.

You see, I was studying in a convent during my childhood. At the age of six I had some spiritual experiences which I did not understand, but by the age of ten I realized that these experiences were related to the consciousness. However, one of the teachers in the convent who knew what happened to me said that these experiences were the work of the devil. I accepted this story for some time, but then I began to work out exactly what it meant.

I thought to myself, "Is there some sort of demon, spirit, ghost, apparition or angel influencing me from outside, or is there some force inside me which is creating that experience?" I tried to work it out for many years. Then when I was eighteen, a yogini came to stay with our family. She initiated me into all the practical aspects of tantra and then I came to know that there is nothing like the devil. There is nothing like impurity. Everything is a dream of consciousness. Everything is an experience in relation to the stage of evolution you are going through. So, in my opinion, either there is no devil or if there is, you are the devil!

What is karma sannyasa and who is eligible to take it?
There are many forms of initiation or *diksha* for the evolution of spiritual life. One form of initiation is *mantra diksha*, initiation into mantra by the guru. When your guru gives you a mantra to practise as a form of sadhana, that is called mantra diksha. Mantra initiation is for every aspirant, for everyone who has even a little inclination or minimum aspiration for spiritual growth. Too much sincerity is not demanded of him. Even a little bit of sincerity or aspiration is enough for one to decide that one should receive a mantra from the guru.

Then there are the people who are determined to live a different kind of life, who have independent beliefs and an independent faith, different from the scriptures, different from the canons, institutions and organizations. They live by their own philosophy and faith. They don't depend on material or emotional relationships. They do not depend on the elements of security. Then they go to a guru and take *sannyasa*, total renunciation. That is only for a few people and I am not going to talk about it here.

Then there is the third type of initiation or diksha for the type of people who have thought well about the purpose of life and the possibilities of spiritual illumination in this life itself, and who have understood that even though they are caught up in maya, even though they are caught up in dreams, still they can have the deeper, greater and abiding spiritual experiences. They can understand, discover and realize their own selves without changing or renouncing the external things of life. For them, there is initiation into karma sannyasa.

Karma sannyasa is intended for regular householders, those who are involved in accomplishments, who have a family, children, emotions, fights, quarrels, everything desirable or undesirable: love, passion, greed, property, a bank balance, cars, sports, but at the same time they are keen on developing the inner experience in their lives. It is for these people that initiation into karma sannyasa is suggested.

In the eighteenth chapter of the *Bhagavad Gita*, the disciple asks his guru, "What is renunciation and what does it mean?" The guru replies, "Some people renounce life itself, others renounce the actions but not life and still others renounce the fruits of the action and not the action. Yet others renounce neither the action nor the fruits."

The last category is the category of karma sannyasa. They do not renounce *karma* (actions) and they do not renounce the fruits coming from the actions. So what do they renounce? They renounce the doership, the actorship. They disidentify the ego, which is the most important principle involved in every sphere, every affair of life. Disidentification of ego, *ahamkara* (*aham*: I-ness), is very important in the life of a householder.

As a householder, we undergo different types of experiences: happiness, unhappiness, failure, success, sorrow, joy, insult, harassment, loss, gain, frustrations, disappointments. We undergo these experiences and every experience disturb us. Sometimes they not only disturb us, but completely put us out of order – accident! We don't know how to function further – nervous breakdown! We make mistakes as a result of which we commit suicide, kill somebody, do all kinds of funny things, or even escape from life.

The experiences arising out of the events of life dislocate our personality. They disintegrate our personality completely, we are thrown into pieces. But if we are able to disidentify, if we are able to separate the ego, then these things will still happen, because life is a mixture of all experiences, but they will not affect us.

Disidentification of ego comes when you are processing your personality through a system or through some of the techniques of yoga as well as through philosophical self-analysis. So, this is the path of *karma sannyasa*, where you are a sannyasin while acting and operating in this sphere of life.

What does Samkhya philosophy say about reincarnation?
We have six systems of philosophy. Out of these six systems, there is only one system which does not postulate reincarnation. I will name them one by one. The first philosophy is the atheistic philosophy and this does not talk about reincarnation. It says there is no reincarnation. When you are cremated, you are put an end to – and there is no survival of consciousness. However, the other philosophies like Jainism, Buddhism, yoga, Samkhya and Vedanta all talk about reincarnation, and this reincarnation relates to the consciousness behind our existence.

Samkhya philosophy propagates the theory of reincarnation. It says that as long as you have desires and karma, the seed is intact and it will be reborn. However, when you have no desires, no passions, then the seed is still there, but it is totally fried and roasted – it will not germinate.

Everything in this universe is born, dies and is reborn out of the same seed. Seed relates to the body, the mind and the consciousness. I was born of my mother and father; that is the physical reincarnation, the continuity of the physical substance from one body to another. That is also the survival of physical matter. However, I am not talking about reincarnation in this context.

In Samkhya, reincarnation belongs to the realm of *purusha*, consciousness, and, therefore the purusha has to fulfil this desire. When desire is fulfilled by following the path of *vairagya*, disidentification, then there is no rebirth any more.

Can you tell me what a mandala is and how and when it is used?
In tantra, a photograph, picture or *murti* (statue) is known as a mandala. In fact, mandala is a Sanskrit term which has often been referred to, particularly by Dr Carl Jung, who has used the term mandala for pictorial concept and who wrote so much on mandalas. After him, many other great thinkers in modern psychology have also given a lot of thought to these mandalas.

Mandala in Sanskrit means 'aura, halo or circle', which you see around the pictures of great and wise men. Mandala is an aura and therefore it should mean the divine effulgence. This divine and spiritual effulgence is also present in great saints, gurus and divine personalities. Therefore, their statues and pictures came to be known as mandalas. That is one explanation.

Secondly, when you project your mind onto something or somebody, then your mind assumes that form, and when your mind assumes that form, that perception and cognition takes place inside. Suppose you are looking at a candle. The perception is taking place within you and not in the candle. The perception is a subjective, not an objective event. However, before this perception of the candle can take place in you, the mind has to transform itself into the form of the candle.

When the transformation of the mental energies has taken place in the form of that candle, or in the form of your child, your guru, a lotus, a rose, a divine personality, or in the form of melodious music, when the mind has transformed itself completely or partially, then the perception takes place there. This is called mandala.

However, the picture, photograph or statue is absolutely insignificant so far as its qualities are concerned. It is simply a picture, a photograph or statue, but when it is assumed by the mind, when the mind has transformed itself and accepted it, then the formation of the mind is important and not the picture or the statue. It is not the guru who is important, but the absorption of the guru, the acceptance of the guru. When the mind has transformed itself into the form of guru, that is called mandala. So *mandala* means inner pictorial concept.

There are two forms of mandala. One is the pictorial mandala or photograph, which has two dimensions: height and breadth. Then there are three-dimensional mandalas, which have height, width and depth. These three-dimensional mandalas are considered to be murtis. Murti doesn't mean idol or statue. *Murti* is a Sanskrit word which literally means 'symbol'. Murti is a symbol because it represents a fact, just as in science you have equations, symbols and theorems in order to explain a scientific fact. You cannot explain a scientific fact in any other form except equations. That is called symbology. This murti represents a fact, a truth and it has to be explained and analyzed.

For example, let me tell you about Kali. In India, particularly in Bengal, there is a goddess called Kali. She is very hideous and dreadful, fat, nude and black. Her bloodstained tongue is sticking out. In one hand she holds a sword, in another a skull, in the third a discus. She has bracelets and amulets of serpents on her arms, and around her waist she wears a skirt made of human arms. Beneath her right foot, Shiva lies asleep on the ground.

She is simply horrible and if she were real, not just a photograph, murti or picture, I think all of us would faint on the spot. Her image is more dreadful than death. It is as if you are at the end of the hangman's rope or sitting in the electric chair – that's her form. It is a murti which symbolizes the awakening of kundalini, the great force in man. When that *shakti* or power is aroused, it wakes up and unless it is tamed it is like Kali.

I will also try to explain the meaning of murti. Murti does not just mean statue or idol, as I have said. Therefore, one who is concentrating on a murti is not an idolator. Consciousness has no name and no form. I am not talking about mortal consciousness; I am talking about spiritual consciousness, *atman*. That consciousness is nameless and formless, but at the same time, if you want to evolve spiritually, then you have to create a symbology of that formlessness.

That formless and nameless consciousness has to be explained in terms of a symbol. That symbol is called murti and it is three-dimensional. When you concentrate on a particular murti, then it is easier for the mind to transcend itself, because the mind has certain special characteristics. The three-dimensional murti can help the mind to concentrate, transform or restructure itself as quickly as possible. Indian philosophy believes that the ultimate principle is formless, nameless and timeless, but at the same time, if you have to restructure and transform your mind, you need a base.

33

Expansion of Mind

Brisbane Ashram, Australia, 19 February 1984

In India they have been experimenting for thousands of years with various techniques in order to express the deeper layers of the mind. Manifestation of the deeper phases of the mind and experiencing one's deeper and greater personality is a very difficult task. We are not able to control our external thinking process. We are not able to control our dream experiences. How then can we experience control of the mind? If you do not know how to drive and you want to run your car properly, you have to find a proper driver. If you are not able to get a driver, you are not able to drive the car at all. If you try, you are going to meet with an accident.

The same thing applies to the mind. Mind is controlled by a greater intelligence. The whole process of thinking, feeling, memory, cognition, dream, sleep, right knowledge, wrong knowledge, in short every cognition and perception, is not controlled by the mind.

Mind is not an autonomous object. There is a controller of the mind called intelligence. In yoga we call it chit. *Chit* means consciousness or awareness. Now, in order to go to the realm of chit or inner consciousness, they have developed various techniques in India. They have used every method, sometimes cultured and sometimes crude, to gain control over the mind.

The sages, saints and wise men of the past realized that if intelligence can be controlled, if chit can be handled, then man can experience the depth of happiness and enduring satisfaction, because that is his goal. Nobody wants to be unhappy; everybody wants to be happy. Through all that we do, we are trying our level best to eliminate the pain, the misery. Whether it is the culture, religion or technology, everything is directed towards the elimination of pain and the acquisition of permanent, enduring, immortal happiness.

Many cultures, nations and religions in the past have come forward and advocated various ways to eliminate man's sufferings, but in the course of time it was found that none of these systems really worked. The same thing happened in India also. The wise men propagated certain systems and when they did not work, then they began to evolve better ones. Out of all these systems created throughout history, tantra has stood the test of time and continued to work wonderfully right up to the present day. Yoga is an offshoot of tantra, which is a practical system based on a particular school of philosophy.

The doctrine of duality

There are six main systems of philosophy in India, and one of the oldest is known as Samkhya. It talks about the two primary forces which exist in every speck of creation, animate, inanimate, visible, invisible, vegetable, mineral, animal, human and even divine. According to Samkhya, everything that exists is a composition or interaction of two primary forces. These two forces are known as *purusha*, consciousness, and *prakriti*, nature. So, interaction between purusha and prakriti, between consciousness and nature, is creation.

In modern science they say that interaction between matter and energy is responsible for creation. In this physical body also there are two primary forces. We are a combination, a result of the interaction between consciousness and nature. Here, nature does not mean the forest, river, ocean and sky, although in the West we talk about natural food and natural environment; in philosophy, nature is the creative force behind everything that exists – *prakriti*.

In Samkhya, nature is of two types, empirical nature and transcendental nature. Empirical nature is composed of the eight elements: earth, water, fire, air, ether, mind, intellect and ego. These eight elements together constitute what we call empirical nature and transformation of these eight is responsible for the visible creation which you have not only on this earth but in all solar systems and galaxies.

When I say creation, you may think I am talking about some religion or some creator. No! It is a process which is inherent in itself. Nature is self-created. There are two realms of nature: one is the creating or creative nature, the second is the transcendental nature, about which I do not know. Therefore, I am not going to talk to you on that matter.

Purusha and prakriti are also known in tantra as *shiva* and *shakti*. Therefore, shiva should not be misunderstood as a male and shakti as a female. In Samkhya, tantra and yoga, and also in modern science, they talk about two opposite poles of energy which are always trying to come together in all matter, in every substance, in everything.

In a stone, in a leaf, in human beings, in the womb of a mother, in sperm and ova, these two poles of energy interact from opposite directions, and they are in us. They can be termed positive and negative energy, but more than that, in modern physics these two poles of energy are also known as time and space. Time and space are two categories which relate to energy systems.

By time I do not mean this time and by space I do not mean the space you know about in geography. Time and space are qualities of the mind. The mind is composed of these categories: time, space and object. Mind cannot exist without time and space. If you have to transcend the mind, you will have to transcend time and space. When you are able to transcend time and space, you are able to transcend the mind. This is also the concept of tantra.

Many people think that tantra is a science which is linked with magic, cemeteries, drinking wine, eating meat and having illicit sexual relations. That is what many books have been published about. However, tantra is a system in which they teach just two things – expansion of the mind and liberation of energy. These two must be understood together. If you want to release, liberate and express the deepest intelligence in yourself, you will have to learn how to expand the mind. If you cannot expand the mind, you cannot liberate your energy.

In modern physics what do they do? They expand matter, split it into elements and then a nuclear explosion takes place. We want to achieve the experience of our inner being or inner self, or arrive at our own nucleus, our own centre, because everything in this universe has a centre. There is nothing in this creation which is without a centre or nucleus. This nucleus is called intelligence, atma or chit. You may use the word bindu. *Bindu* means 'point', 'drop' or 'centre.' This centre has to be explored and experienced at some time or other in life because that is the destiny of man's existence.

How can we experience it?
In tantra they have suggested expansion of mind. Now, this expression came to the West in the mid sixties when the prophets of LSD began their work on altered states of consciousness. People who took LSD began to have some sort of experiences related to time and space. Either time and space became confused or it came together. They began to have fantastic experiences. The psychologists and thinkers in the West called it expansion of the mind, because when the consciousness expands, then you have those experiences.

What is this expansion? You have certain experiences in your day-to-day life related to perception, cognition, audition, touch and taste. These experiences are related to mind, senses and object. If your senses are intact and the object is present, only then can the mind have that experience, otherwise not. There may be a lotus flower, but if you are blind, you cannot see it. You have a mind, there is an object, but there is no sense medium. If I am deaf and you play music, I can't hear it, although it is there and I have a mind.

So, the limited category of experience is dependent on the mind, object and senses. That is the boundary of millions of people. They can see a lotus flower if it is there, otherwise not. They can hear music if it is being played, otherwise not. They can taste sweet and sour only if something is brought in touch with the tongue. This is called the barrier, fence or boundary of man's cognition, perception, knowledge and experience, but is experience limited? Can't we experience beyond this boundary? Do you believe that man's experience is total and that there is no experience beyond it? No.

The philosophy of materialism, which flourished for many thousands of years and became very powerful in the last one hundred and fifty years with man's dependence on material objects, proclaimed that there is no experience beyond these five experiences. You can see an object if there is one there, but if there is no object and still you can see it, they will say you are crazy. If someone is playing music, shouting or singing, and you can hear it, this is fine, but if you are able to hear music when nobody is playing it, they will say, "Send him to the mental hospital!" If there is nobody in this room, yet I am able to see a form or a figure here, say my guru or somebody else, they will say, "He is suffering from schizophrenia, a split personality."

This is on account of the powerful influence of the philosophy of materialism which has existed for many thousands of years, but which has flourished in the last century. We are under the hypnotic spell of that culture and that philosophy. Of course, in the last forty or fifty years many swamis and wise people and many thinkers even in Western countries have came out and declared that experiences are not dependent on object and senses. An experience is a quality of the mind; it is not the quality of the object. An experience does not take place outside but inside.

The Buddhist philosophy had four schools which were very systematic. One of the schools is known as Vijnanavada, the doctrine of *vijnana*, of inner, supreme and intimate intelligence, of special cognition. It says that experience does not depend on an object, but is a quality of the mind and whatever you experience: a form, sound, touch or taste, it is happening within you because your mind is capable of experiencing itself.

Therefore, what do we do in the expansion of the mind? We try to explore the qualities of the mind. You can hear a sound when there is no sound. You can see a form when there is no form. You can have the taste of chocolate or anything, even though it is not in your mouth. In the same way, the experiences related to the mind have to be made free from the objective fencing. That is called expansion of mind and when you are able to create that situation then the liberation of energy takes place.

This energy is within you; it does not come from outside. It is inherent but dormant and secretly hidden in man's physical frame. In your physical frame there is a centre of energy at the bottom of the spine. In men it is at the root of the tailbone in the area of the coccyx and in women it is behind the cervix. It is just a simple physiological and ordinary gland. You can cut it out and throw it away and nothing will happen. That is its physical existence.

However, within the realm of that gland there is an infinite *shakti* or energy. That has to be liberated and that is the meaning of liberation, emancipation, *moksha*, *nirvana* and truth. I do not know anything beyond this; but the easiest way to awaken, to liberate that energy is to practise something which will create expansion of the mind. Then mind will be able to experience things without the presence of an object.

In India there is a tradition of inner experience. They say that the ultimate accomplishment of human beings is to have darshan. *Darshan* means to see. Darshan is inner vision or perception. It is not psychological or emotional; it is actual and real. In darshan you have face to face experience of your inner reality. The experience of intelligence leaps out of you and you can see that intelligence in front of you. This is the very important thing in tantra. Therefore, there are certain practices which they have talked about, known as yoga.

Mantra, the means of inner exploration
Here I will tell you something about mantra because I think it is necessary to understand how important mantra is. Mantra does not relate to a divinity nor is it the name of a religious entity. *Mantra* is a sound principle. Sound is a form of energy. Just as you have electromagnetic, radioactive and other forms of energy, in the same way sound is also energy. This sound is unmanifest. When it manifests, it is known as mantra. With the help of this sound you can create expansion in the area of your consciousness.

Mantra is in the form of a seed. Just as you have the seed of coriander, avocado, passion fruit or wheat, in the same way this sound is in the seed form, in the *bija* or primal form. The frequencies are dormant, there is no velocity, no property, but when you produce the sound on the mental plane you create vibrations by bringing about an interaction between your mind and the sound. Mind and sound are both linked together. The sound is fixed with the mind, then vibrations are created.

By expressing the mantra, thinking the mantra or practising the mantra, repeated vibrations are created. These frequencies have to be properly understood. They are waves. Animals interact with each other through frequencies. They don't say, "Come here", "Go there", "I love you", "I hate you". They have frequencies. Similarly the vegetable kingdom, the trees, plants, leaves, flowers and fruits have frequencies through which they link or communicate.

Then you have radio frequency. If you have a frequency, you have a field, a radioactive field, an electromagnetic field. Because there is a radioactive field, the radio waves are received by you in your transistor. There has to be a field. In the same way, you have a field for these frequencies and that field has to be created by you.

When you are practising your mantra, the mind adapts to the sound. *Om* is one sound. *Hreem* is one sound. *Hraim* is one sound. *Om Namah Shivaya* is a combination of many sounds. Gayatri mantra has twenty-four syllables; it is a combination of twenty-four types of sounds which are adapted by the mind and then certain frequencies are created.

Sound has frequency and velocity. When sound has greater velocity, it has less frequency. However, when it has greater frequency, it has less velocity. Therefore, these sounds which have greater frequency can go deeper into your being. I am using the word 'being'. I am not talking about your body because you are more than your body. Your being is infinite. You can go deep into yourself for miles and miles, for eternity, and you will never come to an end.

That is what Indian philosophy has been talking about for thousands of years. Physically you are finite, one hundred and twenty pounds, five feet and three inches tall. That is talking about the body, but you are beyond the body. When you talk about consciousness, awareness, the self, the chit, you can go far into yourself. So, with the help of the mantra you have to explore your own depth. However, this depth cannot be explored by external means of exploration. The frequencies have to be increased.

The practice of mantra

When the guru gives you a mantra, you have to practise it at a particular time with absolute regularity for at least ten to twenty minutes. The practice of mantra can be done with the help of the natural breath, by concentrating on one of the chakras, with the help of a mala, or by concentrating in between the two eyebrows and feeling the subtle rhythms and pulsation there.

The practice of mantra can also be done with the help of the psychic breath. You can feel that psychic breathing is taking place in the spine, up and down from mooladhara chakra to ajna chakra. Or you can just concentrate on the tip of your tongue by folding it back and sticking it to the upper palate for two, three or four minutes. When the tongue touches a point in the upper palate, then you begin to feel some sort of pulsation – tuk, tuk, tuk. With that rhythm you practise your mantra, *Om* . . . *Om* . . . *Om* . . ., absolutely mentally.

Mantra can also be pronounced, but when you pronounce the mantra, it is not so effective. It is alright for beginners. Suppose the mantra is *Om Namah Shivaya*. You can chant or sing it, but the effect will not be very great. If you want the mantra to be powerful, then it has to be absolutely internal. You have to feel it.

When you practise mantra, please do not worry about the process of mental experience at all. Worries and anxieties, hatred and passion, broodings and anticipation or reflections, whatever is happening in the arena of the mind, let it come. Don't stop it. If the mental experiences, the waverings, oscillations, dissipations or broodings of the mind become too many, then at that time you chant the mantra a little louder.

For that purpose, the mala is very important. If you practise mantra mentally and your mind goes into the wilderness of brooding, you will be lost. Only after fifteen or twenty minutes you will say, "Oh, I have forgotten my mantra!" Sometimes the mind has a very powerful hypnotic influence. You keep on building castles in the air. You go on thinking and don't even know where you are and how you are related to the mantra, but it is equally important that expression of the mind must take place.

You should not suppress or withdraw the mind. You should allow the mind free expression, whether it is violence, greed, jealousy or passion. Whatever it is, let it come, let it express. There is nothing unholy or wrong, and if there is anything unholy, it must come out. Why do you keep it in you? Why should you maintain and protect the unholy and the dirt in the mind when it is trying to come out? When you have bad wind, you should expel it because by retention you are only maintaining the harmful effects.

Purging the mind

Mantra has a very important role to play here. Remember, when you practise mantra you are not going to obtain concentration of mind immediately. If you experience peace and concentration immediately, it means either you are a very evolved person or you have blocked the process of the expression of mind. The first important result of practising the mantra is called purging, and everybody has to experience this.

What is purging? When you have a bad stomach, you take a pill and you purge – once, twice, thrice, four, five, six times. Or if you are suffering from diarrhoea or dysentery, you go once, twice, ten, fifteen times, and you get tired. That is called purging. Even as you purge on the physical plane, in the same way you have to purge on the mental plane, you have to purge out your karmas, your samskaras. You have to let them out, throw them away. It takes some time, maybe six months or one year. So, if you are practising your mantra and your mind is restless, negative propensities loom, you become angry and greedy, mean and petty-minded, it is a good sign. Don't feel guilty about it.

I am telling you the path by which you will be able to contact your intelligence. Most people make a mistake here because they are religious. For years they have been taught not to think bad things, not to think unholy things. Whether you accept a religion or not does not matter, still man is basically religious. Religion inhibits free expression – it means fear, guilt and shame. We think that we are inferior and dirty. We have fear of this and fear of that, because we are religious by nature and not by institution.

Therefore, when a thought comes into your mind, you try to stop it because you think that you are polluting the atmosphere of the mind, whereas it is just the opposite. When a bad thought comes into your mind, your mind is becoming purer. I have experienced it. At the verge of final experience, many saints and sages have said that when awakening of kundalini takes place, when the chit shakti of intelligence is awakening, at that time, all the garbage, all the dirt comes out. All day, all night, you think about nothing but what you call 'unholy'.

So, when a bad thought comes into your mind during the practice of mantra, it is an act of purging and you are getting rid of it. This will happen for some time. You must have patience; you should not expect concentration and equilibrium all at once. It is because of this that people are not making satisfactory progress in spiritual life. When I used to practise mantra, I would hold the mala in my hand. Many times I did not know how the fingers were moving. Only when I came to one hundred and eight where there is a point of termination, I realized, "Oh, one hundred and eight I have missed" because I was not so much aware of the mantra, I was aware of those things which you call unholy.

In the beginning I did behave like a religious man. I thought this was bad and that was bad. Later I thought, "Well, if it is bad, what can I do? I have been practising for three months and it is coming again and again. Okay, let me practise awareness of all the garbage. Let me take it out, the stinking, the foul and the dirty." It gave me a very good experience in the end. Therefore, the practice of mantra is a very important part of yoga.

Awareness of the symbol of form
After the practice of mantra, a symbol must be maintained and that form should not be changed. You should try to formulate, construct or create that form within the realm of you intelligence, imagination and feeling. It is not a thought, not a feeling, but an act of your concentrated, creative intelligence. When the mind assumes concentration, then an image is created. When the mind goes deeper and loses touch with time and space for a short fraction of time, then you can see the image, otherwise not.

People can see colours inside; they do not merely think or feel these colours, but they see them. That is possible only when, for the time being, concentration takes place and time and space are lost. It is necessary that contact with time and space must be lost for at least a fraction of a second, then that image or *murti* or symbol shines before you. That is called inner vision. For that to take place, you must fix a form for yourself.

That form can be anything. It can be a statue, a photograph of a person, a yantra or geometrical shape. Or it can be any symbol according to your temperament, constitution, nature or quality of being. When the practice of mantra has been done for some time, say ten or fifteen minutes, you must practise concentration on the symbol for some period of time, say two, three or four minutes, with your eyes open sometimes and of course your eyes closed also.

You may not succeed every day. You may feel that there is a shadow of that form. You may try to construct that form within the realm of your mind and you may not succeed at all, but there will be moments when time and space get fused and a flash will take place. This experience can come at any time, and when it comes to you, then you have covered a long, long journey in the path of yoga.

34

Awakening the Evolutionary Energy

Gold Coast Ashram, Australia, 20 February 1984

In the last fifty years, scientists, social thinkers and politicians have been facing a very great problem related to the human personality, body and mind. They have been searching for a way to rectify these problems of disease, sickness, mental disturbance, disorientated social structures and stress-born diseases.

All over the world, cultures which are based on materialistic philosophy are not able to cope with these problems, but some of the wise men have discovered the science of yoga. First of all, they thought that yoga was a religion, a mystical science, that it had something to do with black magic or that it was a sect of ascetics. However, the more they went into the details about yoga, the more they found that it was a practical system for the all-round development of the human personality.

What they found so wonderful about yoga was that it was far from intellectual gymnastics, that it was a down to earth practical system which controlled the total human personality. It covered the whole human being, not only the body, mind, feelings and emotions, but also the deeper self. Of course, there have been certain difficulties which some people do experience from time to time, because yoga is related to the ancient Hindu culture and it is a very old science.

Once upon a time yoga was practised by most of the people throughout the world, but political accidents happened in history and people forgot about it. I have been talking about yoga to all kinds of people from every nation and culture and I have found that if yoga is explained to them properly, they can utilize its beneficial effects. It is not for the sake of yoga that I teach, but I think that the problems from which mankind suffers are curable through the practices of yoga.

Yoga is more than exercise

The science of yoga is very great. The branch of *hatha yoga*, physical postures and breathing techniques, is only one part of it, but that in itself is very vast. These physical postures and breathing techniques of yoga work on the body, mind and emotions, and are able to transform the quality of human experience and human consciousness.

I am not talking about exercises. Yoga is not just physical exercise. The physical postures known as *asanas* and the breathing techniques known as *pranayama* have little to do with muscles, but more to do with energy channels or energy cycles in the physical body. It is in this respect that a few scientific observations from all over the world should be studied.

Many years ago in Poland, a team of scientists took it upon themselves to experiment on and study the effects of *sirshasana*, the headstand pose, upon the human mind. This research was carried on for more than six months by a team of approved doctors and scientists. At the end they found that this particular posture was very important not only from the point of view of the physical body, but from its immediate effect on the behaviour of the vital hormones and endocrine secretions in the physical body. They came to the conclusion that this particular physical posture does not merely influence the physical processes in the body, but brings about a change in the mental and emotional behaviour.

It is so important to understand that these yoga postures do not act on the physical body alone, like many other systems of exercise. We have many system of exercises throughout the world, but we cannot and should not compare yoga postures with them. The intricate yoga postures have a direct bearing on the endocrine secretions and some of them have a direct bearing on the hormonal processes which control the physical, mental, emotional and intellectual side of human life. So the headstand pose was the subject of study and it was found that it can help an individual to gain tranquillity.

The interrelation of body and mind

When the mind is restless, when the emotions are disturbed and you experience nervous depression or nervous breakdown, when you are not able to control the influx of the thinking process, not able to resolve the conflicts in the mind, at that time, if you resort to intellectual methods you will fail and you do fail. You cannot rectify the emotional, psychological or intellectual problems with a defective, limping mind.

If the mind is sick and ailing, if it is limping, how can this inefficient mind, this sick mind, treat the emotional problems? It is true that we can put people under hypnosis for the time being, but that does not solve the problem of personality, because personality is our totality. However, if we can change the whole process, the whole permutation and combination of systems in our body, then we can create an effect.

Tranquillity is an effect; sadness is an effect. In the same way, sorrow is an effect and insomnia is an effect. You cannot say that they are just physical, nor can you say they are just psychological. There cannot be a line of demarcation drawn between physical and psychological. There is no absolute division between somatic and psychic.

There is a book which I came across many years ago called *How to Stop Worrying and Start Living*. Everybody read the book and tried to put it into practice, but they could not stop worrying because that worry was generated by a defective combination of forces in the physical body. Is fear just psychological? Are greed and violence just psychological? No. Is a thought a psychological thing or is it a product of various forces in this physical body?

This is what hatha yoga talks about. If there is an imbalance in the adrenal secretions, you will have fear. If there is an imbalance in the relationship between the pineal and pituitary glands, there will be excessive passions. The suppressed state of one hormone, of one chemical structure of this physical body and the predominance of another factor creates a particular problem.

A personal experience

About forty years ago I had a confrontation with my guru, Swami Sivananda. He was a very calm, quiet, forgiving, forbearing, enduring and compassionate swami, but somehow I got very angry. I was young in those days, twenty-one. I threw the bunch of keys at his feet and said, "Look after your own ashram!" Then I went to my room and closed the door. I was so angry I did not know what to do. For two days I did not come out of my room and I did not eat anything.

On the third day, he called me and said, "You are very angry." I said, "Yes." He said, "Don't be sorry about it; find a way." I said, "But I have been thinking about it so much. Every morning I make a resolve that I will not get angry, I will not lose my temper, but later I forget it." He said, "Your energies are in disarray." So he taught me one yoga posture called shashankasana and told me to practise it for as long as I could.

I practised that asana first for ten minutes at one stretch, then later I used to practise it for three hours, because for me there was no other problem during my youth except anger. I had so much anger that I could have killed anybody. I couldn't control it. So I thought, "If I can control anger, I can control anything in life." Of course, everybody has his own problem. My problem was anger; your problem may be something else. I practised shashankasana and it did help me.

Earlier than that, I practised many different systems. I studied in a convent school with Christian sisters who used to teach me that when you get angry, you should not do this and you should do that, but nothing worked. The swamis or priests in India used to tell me, "When you get angry, drink water." Everybody suggested every possible method. You know, once I got so angry with my father because he told me not to go out in the evening, I just took a rifle and threatened to shoot him. This was the type of anger I had, but just by the practice of shashankasana it was finished. How?

This anger was not a psychological process. It was just a process related to the glandular balance. In *shashankasana*, what do you do? You bend forward and there is tension or stimulus created in the adrenal glands and they secrete a little more or a little less adrenaline according to the requirement of the system. When the adrenaline is injected and absorbed by the system, then the chemistry in the body changes and the behaviour of the sympathetic and parasympathetic nervous system also changes.

When there is balance between sympathetic and parasympathetic nervous systems, there is calmness and tranquillity. So, in the science of hatha yoga, the body, mind, emotions, intellect and feelings are all interrelated. They are not considered as different from each other. Your mental problems, conflicts, psychosis, schizophrenia, anger, excessive passions, lack of memory, absence of coordination, exhaustion, guilt, or even lack of passion may be due to a faulty system in the body.

The philosophy of shakti
If you analyze this physical body, it is a combination of material and non-material components. If you analyze the physical body from the yogic point of view, it is more than just bones, blood, secretions, oxygen, ribs, ligaments and cells. If you analyze a racing car moving at top speed, then you know that it is not merely the steel body but also the power of the engine. In the same way, you must understand that from the yogic point of view, in this physical body there is a system of energy, a system of *shakti*.

This energy which I am talking about is not abstract, mystical or magical. I am talking about concrete energy which you can see and understand. This energy is the basic philosophy of yoga. If you want to understand yoga, you will have to understand the basic philosophy of shakti, of prana, of force or forces within the body. Even if you have force in the external field, in the same way, you will have to accept the existence of a force or forces in this physical body.

Then you have to talk about how the practices of yoga such as asanas, pranayama, mantra and meditation create an effect. Many times we see people suffering from anxiety and melancholia. They go through different systems of treatment, but they do not get any better. Finally they hear from someone about yoga and as a last resort they try it. Within a few days, just due to those yoga practices, without any intellectual or analytical process involved, they get better. How do they get better?

If you want to understand how, then you have to stop misinterpreting yoga as just a physical science. All the practices of yoga: hatha yoga, bhakti yoga, karma yoga, raja yoga, kriya yoga, laya yoga and many other forms of yoga are related to the law or the force of shakti in the physical body. You will have to tackle the forces in this physical body, not only in connection with diseases and mental problems, but even if you want to meditate or concentrate or develop the power of your will and tap the inner source of energy.

What are these forces?

The forces in the physical body are known by two names. *Pingala* is the solar force and *ida* is the lunar force. These two forces are granted by nature and it is through them that all the physical and mental actions are taking place. When these two forces are disturbed, imbalanced or in disarray, then problems arise in your body, mind, emotions and everywhere.

Many times, on account of your lifestyle, food, thinking and habits, there is an energy block in your system and this is responsible for various types of problems. If you can unblock, if you can create a balance, if you can harmonize these two forces in your physical body, not by analysis, intellect, feeling, hypnosis or suggestion but just by simple mechanical practices, you can obtain the desired results.

This is a very simple philosophy. You are now sitting in this room. There are quite a few lights on and the microphone is working. If one of the fuses in the main switch blows, what will happen? There will be darkness. If there is a short circuit, the fuse will blow and there will be darkness. To remove that darkness, you will have to correct the short circuit. You have to change the fuse and then the force will flow here again.

So, the yoga practices relate to the two forces in this physical body. What are these forces? Are they abstract or are they physical in nature? Scientists have been working on this and they have found that these forces in the physical body can be registered by the most sophisticated instruments, and they have done it. Not on the basis of what they have done, but on the basis of the ancient yogic texts, let me tell you that there are two forces that originate at the bottom of the spine and flow upwards to the top of the spine.

These two forces in the spine are responsible for the physical and mental actions everywhere in the body. You feel, touch and taste. You move your body, digest, secrete, sneeze, cough and wink. All these actions and feelings are controlled by the two forces. All the systems of yoga are connected with these two forces. *Yoga* means 'connection' or 'union'. When the two forces are brought together in a state of harmony, that is called yoga.

Meditation and the mind

There are various forms of yoga and all of them have something to do with one or more aspects of your personality. For example, *bhakti yoga* deals with the emotions. Emotions are very powerful; you should not underestimate them. They can make you commit suicide, kill someone, become a martyr, a patriot or a saint. They can make you do anything! This emotional personality in man is very important and it has to be properly understood. For that purpose, we have the practices of bhakti yoga.

There are other types of people who have very restless minds. Their mind doesn't rest all the twenty-four hours.

It works even during dream and sleep. Even when the brainwaves are changing from beta to theta, theta to alpha and alpha to delta, the mind is moving in some way or another. Those who want to control the mental influxes, the mental functions and channel the energies of the mind for a better purpose should practise raja yoga.

Raja yoga is a combination of the practices in which the relationship between the brain, the senses and the external objects is decided. This is important because most of the problems in our day-to-day lives are on account of our distorted mental behaviour. We may think that we have a normal mind, but we don't. We don't know anything about the mind and this is the tragedy.

What do we know? Anger, greed, passion, sorrow, happiness, joy, anxiety, worry, compassion and mercy; this is not the mind, but its modifications and expressions. These are the bubbles of the mind but not the mind itself. In order to gain mastery over the mind, we will have to know the mind and then it can be controlled. It is influenced by so many factors which are within us.

So, in raja yoga they have a system of meditation or *dhyana*. It is such an important subject. Everybody knows about it and wants to meditate every day with their eyes closed – to stop thinking, to see something inside, to experience psychic things, inner things. Dhyana yoga or the yoga of meditation is the highest form of yoga.

Though the practices of meditation are concerned with the mind, they also have a direct influence on the physical body. When you are meditating, you are not only dealing with the mind, you are dealing with the whole of yourself: the body, mind, intellect, emotions, feelings, psyche and so on. Various forms of yoga like karma yoga, bhakti yoga and raja yoga are preparations or preliminaries. They prepare you for meditation because meditation is something more than what we have understood. Not only in Western countries but throughout the world, meditation is explained as a practice of self-hypnosis. There is a clear difference between meditation and self-hypnosis. Dhyana yoga is a process in which you try to understand the whole of your mind. First you awaken the energy, then you go in and try to understand the total mind.

The evolutionary energy

There are various techniques of meditation and one of these is known as mantra. *Mantra* is a sound. After practising this for some time every day, the mind becomes calm, quiet and one-pointed. Then an experience takes place and this experience is important because it relates to the awakening of kundalini.

Kundalini is the evolutionary force which resides within you, and the awakening of that force has to take place through the practice of yoga. Meditation is the key by which you can awaken the kundalini shakti, This kundalini shakti is considered to be the awakening of the greater and higher consciousness in man. It controls the mind, body, experiences and the whole of our existence. Therefore, the purpose of meditation is to awaken the kundalini.

What is that kundalini according to yoga? Let me explain. At the bottom of the spine there is the tailbone and at the end of the tailbone is a tiny gland. This gland is considered to be the reservoir of that dormant energy. When meditation takes place and one-pointedness begins to arise, an experience is exploded. When that inner experience takes place, activities start in that particular gland or centre of the body.

When awakening begins, then you have a series of spiritual experiences, because the energy which is dormant in that particular centre relates to the higher consciousness, not to the normal, empirical, physical or objective consciousness. It is a deeper consciousness. Then the experiences begin and these are known as yogic experiences.

Throughout history there have been many people who have experienced the awakening of kundalini, but few could understand it. They thought it was some spirit, ghost or external force which was obsessing them, haunting them and possessing them. However, this was the external manifestation of an internal happening. When this evolutionary energy begins to unfold, it takes over the whole consciousness. So, the practices of meditation, mantra, bhakti yoga, hatha yoga, ultimately lead us to mastery over a greater force which is inherent in us. They are all designed to awaken this evolutionary energy.

Pranayama and kundalini

I have been working on some experiments and I have found that during the practice of pranayama, many changes occur in the physical body; so many things are happening. You are not merely inhaling oxygen and exhaling carbon dioxide. Pranayama is much more than that.

For example, in *nadi shodhana pranayama* you practise inhalation through the left nostril, retention of the breath, exhalation through the right nostril, then retention of the breath – this is the breathing technique. When you retain the breath after inhalation, then you contract your perineum and throat; after exhalation, then you contract your perineum, abdomen and throat. These areas have to be contracted when you are retaining the breath.

At that time, two different things are happening simultaneously at two different points in the physical body – one in the brain and the other in the perineum. The perineum is situated at the area between the urinary and excretory organs. In yoga it is known as *mooladhara chakra*, the coccygeal plexus, which is at the end of the tailbone. That is the seat of kundalini, the primal energy, the evolutionary energy, the non-material force. In pranayama, the events take place at the upper and lower centres at the same time.

The science of brain breathing

It has been found that when the left nostril is flowing freely, the right hemisphere of the brain is undergoing activity and when the right nostril is flowing freely, the left hemisphere of the brain is undergoing activity. When both nostrils are flowing freely, then the whole brain is active. I have written a book called *Swara Yoga* on this subject and you can read that in order to understand more about it.

The left and right nostrils have something to do with the lungs, but more to do with the brain. The left nostril is related to ida, the moon, and the right nostril to pingala, the sun. The left nostril is considered to be cold energy and the right nostril to be warm or hot energy. These two breaths control the two forces in the physical body. The left nostril controls the mental functions throughout the body via the brain, and the right nostril controls the physical actions.

It has been seen by scientists and thinkers that both nostrils do not flow together freely for any length of time. But if they do, then one can experience spontaneous meditation without wrestling with the mind. This is because when both nostrils flow together, the spiritual channel opens. At that time the mind drops, thoughts disappear, time and space are lost, ego, name and form are withdrawn, and gradually the mind loses touch with the external reality.

That period without time and space is called the flow of *sushumna*. At that time when ida, pingala and sushumna are in confluence, the whole brain is active, and when sushumna flows freely for one, two or three hours together at a stretch, then there is a storm in the brain. When that storm occurs in the brain, immediately there is an explosion in mooladhara chakra or the seat of kundalini.

In the science of swara yoga there is a natural cycle or rhythm of the breath. The right and left nostril do not flow erratically. On the first, second and third day of the bright fortnight, at the time of sunrise, the left nostril will flow for one hour and twenty minutes. After that, the right nostril will flow for one hour and twenty minutes. Then left, then right will flow alternately for three days. Every fourth day there is a change of shift in the order of the breathing rhythm. This is one cycle.

Biorhythms

This system has been studied by many scientists in America, Japan and even behind the Iron Curtain. I myself have subjected many of the swamis in Munger to watch their breath for six months and note everything in a diary. They checked their breath every hour and wrote it down. When they were suffering from cough, cold, diarrhoea, dysentery, anger, hatred, worry, depression, laziness, etc., they recorded any change taking place in the breath cycle.

There is an ancient text called *Shiva Swarodaya* written in Sanskrit and I read that book many years ago. In those days I did not know much about pranayama. I thought it meant breathe in more oxygen, breathe out more carbon dioxide. Then I read a small paper on biorhythms, the rhythms of the breath, prana and the mind, combined together. I thought, "Yes, this is important."

You can control the mind through the breath. You can control the thoughts, emotions, physical diseases, experiences and not only that, you can also awaken the shakti within you by the knowledge of the rhythms of the breath, the biorhythmic knowledge. Then I started working on myself. When my sushumna, both nostrils, used to flow freely for about half a minute or one minute, I found at that time I could make very accurate decisions, one hundred percent accurate. You can try it yourself.

In between the ida cycle and the pingala cycle, there is a short span of say a minute or even less when both nostrils flow freely. At that time, the mind becomes very clear in everybody, not only in me. However, it is only for a very short period. During the time when pingala, the right nostril, is flowing, we have seen an increase in digestive secretions like saliva, hydrochloric acid, bile, enzymes, etc. When the left nostril is flowing, the digestive secretions are suppressed, their flow is decreased.

All these factors have to be studied in relation to the breath. From this we can also conclude that the practice of pranayama is related to the awakening of the forces, to the awakening of an experience, and it can control the body, mind and emotions at the same time. But please remember that merely breathing in and out is not pranayama. Those of you who know pranayama may practise it, but those who do not should learn from a competent yoga teacher.

Purificatory practices

According to the science of yoga, before the practice of pranayama, the practices of hatha yoga must be undertaken. What are the practices of hatha yoga? Nowadays people think that postures are hatha yoga, but actually hatha yoga is a very systematic practice in which purification of the physical body is taught. There are six practices through which the physical body is purified. After purification of the physical body, then the practice of yoga postures and pranayama must be undertaken.

It is said in hatha yoga that in this physical body there are hundreds and thousands of channels or flows of energy, and everywhere this energy is facing a blockage due to impurities. Through the practices of hatha yoga the body must be purified. When the body is purified, these *nadis* or channels of energy become free of obstruction and then the pranas flow freely, the consciousness flows freely. There is no blockage. Then you can experience perfect health, perfect state of mind, perfect understanding of yourself.

Why talk about the mind?

Throughout the world nowadays, people everywhere talk about their problems intellectually. Whether it is philosophy, religion, psychology or psychotherapy, people are just talking intellectually, but this does not solve the problems. If you have worries, you cannot get rid of them just by analysis, because your personality likes to worry. If you have fears, you cannot get rid of them by analysis, because the root of fear is in your personality and that cannot be resolved by an intellectual process. That is why nothing is improving.

How can you clean a plate with dirty water? How can you clean the mind with a dirty mind? How can a conflicting mind cure a conflicting mind? We are trying to solve the problems of the mind with a sick mind. You must have a strong, healthy, powerful, intelligent, enquiring and clear mind, then you will have no conflict.

Physical and mental diseases, lack of concentration, psychological and emotional problems should not be exaggerated. They are just material problems. If you are suffering from insomnia, practise a few asanas, a few pranayamas, a few minutes concentration and yoga nidra, and see what happens.

Emotional problems create a lot of difficulties in our lives and they have to be understood. Emotional problems occur because we have surplus emotions which we are not able to adjust. How to adjust these surplus emotions is a very important subject in yoga. But in short, I can tell you that in order to be happy, to be satisfied, to grow, you must do something to tap that inner reservoir or source.

The source of experience, of happiness, is not outside; it is inside. The external events of this world do not contribute to your happiness and unhappiness. If you are not satisfied with your husband or wife, I can assure you that there is nothing wrong with them; the mistake is with you. You are not able to explore the centre of happiness within you and therefore you are unhappy with him or with her.

You think the experience of unhappiness arises from external objects, external events and circumstances, but this is not correct. Unhappiness is a product of your own mind; happiness is a product of your own mind, but someone else becomes the scapegoat. You must realize this. You can live in the world as you want to, but in order to experience satisfaction, happiness, contentment and positive health, you will have to tap that source of energy sooner or later.

A master of accomplishment

Everybody wants to do something, to be an artist, painter, musician, writer, composer, translator, interpreter, trader, businessman or administrator. You want to be creative, to do something, and for that just thinking is not enough. Millions and millions of people have been born on this earth and they have all thought to do something, to be something, to become immortal, but only a few have succeeded.

Those few who have shone before us like the sun, moon and stars were people in control of their own forces. I'm not only talking about yogis, clairvoyants and liberated people. I am talking about average people: statesmen, musicians, painters, writers. They were able to accomplish many great things in their lives by the help of this special energy.

Therefore, if you want to be a master of creativity, of creative intelligence or the creative faculty, then you should not merely bank upon this limited mind which has fences and boundaries. You will have to practise something to transcend this limited mind, either bhakti yoga, raja yoga, karma yoga, kriya yoga, jnana yoga, mantra yoga or sannyasa yoga. There are many forms of yoga.

You should practise something in your daily life for some time, maybe six months, one year, two years or even three. It can even take ten years or more. By those practices you will have to try to contact that inner reservoir of your strength, of your force. You will have to awaken your chakras and nadis. You must awaken your kundalini shakti. Then you will become a master of accomplishment.

The forces of the mind

Many times when I read books about the accomplishments of people in various lands, especially during my childhood, I used to wonder, "How did they do it? Was it an accident? Did they become creative by chance?" Then gradually I came to understand that we have been squandering and misusing this great energy of the mind for small returns, whereas we can do anything with it.

You see, when solar energy is concentrated through a magnifying glass, it can burn paper or cloth. In the same way, when you concentrate the energies of the mind, it can create objects, events and effects. Concentration of the mind is so important. With all the forces of the mind and consciousness, you think of this and that, of various things throughout the day, for up to eighty years. Even when you go to a church or temple or to a guru, where is your mind? You say, "You are my father, you are my mother, you are my God," but you are thinking of something else all the time because you haven't got knowledge of the forces of the mind.

For modern man, the mind is a physiological substance, but for me, the mind is an energy substance. It has voltage: 220, 110. It has amperes. It can be registered and charged. It has frequencies and velocities, and it has a field. For me, a thought is a product of energy, like light in the bulb is a product of energy: positive and negative currents put together give light.

This is the basic philosophy of yoga and if you cannot master the process of thought and feeling, you can gain nothing in this life. You will leave this world like billions of people before you have done – eat, drink, enjoy and die. Are you satisfied with that way of life? If you are, then yoga is not meant for you. Don't talk about accomplishment and creative intelligence. Don't talk about health, peace, equanimity and tranquillity.

If you are that type of person, then I have nothing to say, but I do not believe you are like that. You want to understand the deeper forces of life, the deeper forces of the mind. However, there is a confusion and the confusion is this – whether that force is in heaven or that force is inherent in you. If that force is in heaven, I tell you, heaven is within you. It is a state of experience. You don't have to transcend this planet and go to some other planet to find a paradise or heaven. The experience is here, but you have to do the whole work yourself.

If you can, devote half an hour every day with absolute regularity to just one practice. One practice is not greater than another, please understand. If you are interested in hatha yoga, practise it. If you are interested in meditation, practise it. If you want to practise mantra, do so. If you don't want to practise any form of classical yoga but you want to grow and awaken your kundalini, then practise the most difficult yoga – karma yoga. Whatever yoga you choose, try to remember that it is a tool, a means for awakening the evolutionary energy within you. Then you will succeed, whatever you do. This is the basic philosophy of yoga.

35

The Supreme Yoga

Lillian Rock Ashram, Australia, 21 February 1984

Inner discipline is very important, not only for enlightenment, but also for the survival of humanity. We should not underestimate the value of discipline for the survival of the family, of the nation, of the government, of humanity. For greater accomplishment, for inner knowledge, for higher enlightenment and for happiness inside and outside, inner discipline is necessary and yoga talks about this.

Inner discipline has nothing to do with social, political and other forms of external discipline which you know. Some forms of discipline are very hard to practise and you don't want to follow them, but you have to. If you don't, you will be punished, but in yoga the discipline is grown as you grow flowers, from the seed state to the blossoming state. Discipline is grown, it is perfected, it becomes a part of your thinking, of your feeling, of your living. It becomes a part of your interaction with your friends, with your enemies, with the people who are good and who are not good. Therefore, we talk about yoga in the light of this inner discipline.

For most people discipline has a very limited meaning. If you go to a Catholic school there is a very good discipline. They teach you how to move, how to wink, how to sneeze, how to cough, how to stand, how to sit. These are forms of disciplines, but they are just exercises. You don't accept them, you do them, but you'd prefer it if they were not there because you want to live in freedom, to act in freedom, to feel free. This freedom without discipline is anarchy. Freedom with discipline creates a stable, peaceful and enduring society.

The yoga system
In yoga, we talk of both freedom and discipline at the same time, but freedom with discipline and discipline with freedom never come together unless you undergo proper training related to the laws of your body, of your mind, of your emotions, of your spirit, of your consciousness. Therefore, in yoga we have various branches which deal with all these aspects of your being. All the yogas are broadly classified into four main branches known as karma yoga, bhakti yoga, raja yoga and jnana yoga. Then, within these four main branches you have other forms of yoga like hatha yoga, kriya yoga, laya yoga, nada yoga, etc.

So, these four broad forms of yoga are related to your body, mind, intellect, emotions, passions, actions, interactions, manifestations and expressions. If your capacities, if the elements of your personality are not progressing, are not improving, are not evolving systematically, then there will be lopsided development. You may have too much intellectual growth, but emotionally you are stunted, therefore, it is advisable to have a synthesis of all the forms of yoga.

The Raja Yoga Sutras
Of all the yogas, there is one yoga which stands out and about which I will give you some idea. That yoga is known as *raja yoga*, the supreme yoga, the presiding yoga, or the yoga related to the secrets within yourself. Each of the yogas has an ancient classical text. These texts are written in the form of *sutras*, not in poetry or prose; they are just very short notes, we call them aphorisms. The whole raja yoga philosophy, the raja yoga system is contained within a collection of four hundred and ninety-five short sentences. In the same way every form of yoga has a classical text briefly expressed.

The raja yoga system was condensed into the form of yoga sutras by a great saint called Patanjali. Yoga did exist before him. He is not the founder of the yoga system, but he is one of the main expounders of the yoga system. He was a contemporary of Buddha, that is, he lived two thousand five hundred years ago. Sage Patanjali wrote the *Yoga Sutras*. It is a wonderful book and you should try to go through it at least once. I have written a commentary on this book, which is known as *Four Chapters on Freedom*.

The definition of yoga
What is the basic principle in raja yoga? What do you have to do and what do you have to accomplish? First of all the process of yoga and the various techniques of yoga are meant to block the modifications, the external manifestations of the mind during certain practices.

To explain it more clearly, the mind expresses itself in the form of modifications. What are these modifications? If you throw a pebble or a stone into a quiet and tranquil lake, the moment the pebble touches the water, ripples are formed and the ripples keep on moving outward in concentric patterns. In the same way, when an objective experience or an experience relating to a person, an object or an event takes place, ripples are formed in the mind, in the brain, in the consciousness. These are known as modifications, such as anger. When someone is creating a problem for you, then you become angry. This anger is a kind of ripple which is caused by the hit of an experience.

In the same way, every experience produces these circular ripples in you consciousness. They are a consequence of the interaction between your mind and the event. These ripples are continuously created throughout the day and night, either subjectively or objectively. You have to stop that process during meditation, and the purpose of yoga is this. This is the definition of yoga.

Therefore, in the *Raja Yoga Sutras* by Sage Patanjali, the first sutra is, "Yoga is blocking the modifications of the mind."

During meditation, when you are able to control, to block, to eliminate these circular motions which are taking place in your mind, then an experience arises. What is that experience? That is a non-dual experience.

In every experience there is a process of duality, the seer and the seen, the listener and the sound, the subject and the object, myself and my thought. There is always duality in the process of mental experience, but when you are able to control, to eliminate those circular patterns formed in your consciousness, then a non-dual experiences arises, which is called the total experience of yourself. That is also known as *samadhi*, *nirvana*, *kaivalya*, enlightenment. These are all synonymous terms, they are not different. There are many other expressions which are used by wise men to denote this highest experience in human life, which can be gained according to raja yoga by blocking the circular patterns.

What are the circular patterns?
Technically these circular patterns are known as *vrittis*. You can say modifications of the mind, patterns of consciousness. Here, one thing you must remember very well is that the mind and the vrittis are not the same thing. When you are controlling the vrittis, you are not controlling the mind. When you are blocking the created experience, you are blocking a particular experience in your mind, you are not blocking the mind. When you are suppressing an experience in your mind, you are not suppressing the mind, because mind and experience are not the same, they are two different things.

According to yoga, to modern psychology, to every philosophy and to every science, mind is a force. Mind is total awareness and this mind is a composition of elements. Twenty-four elements make up the mind. If you disintegrate, split and separate those elements, then the mind is destroyed. Otherwise the mind cannot be destroyed. So in the practices of yoga you are not suppressing the mind, you are not hurting the mind, you are not even dealing with the mind, but you are dealing with the formations of the mind.

Supposing you throw a pebble in the lake and circular patterns are created. How do you stop that? You stop throwing the pebbles, that's all. So these circular patterns are the same as the vrittis of the mind. There are many types of vrittis, which have been classified in raja yoga. It is very interesting to study them. It will not be possible for me to explain them here in detail, but I will give you a few examples.

I am speaking here about yoga, raja yoga or bhakti yoga, and you are listening to what I'm telling you. The knowledge is proceeding. What is that knowledge? That cognition, that process of knowledge taking place in you is one type of vritti, which is based on a concrete event. Here is a garland, and when you look at it, you see a garland. This experience taking place in you is real and that is called a vritti.

In the same way as you have experiences in the mind which are connected with a real object, there are also experiences or formations in the mind that are not related to something real. For example, if you go outside at night, you may feel that there is a ghost or a spirit lurking in the shadows. No spirit is there, but you imagine there is a spirit and you begin to see some formations created by fear and awe. These are the formations created in the mind by imagination.

So an experience in the mind can be created by a real object, by an imaginary object, by a false object and, in the same way, by memory and sleep. Sleep is also an experience. Now, when you are practising yoga and meditation, you are trying to achieve a state, an experience, an awareness where there is neither the sleep experience, nor the memory experience, nor the hypnotic experience, nor the imaginary experience, nor even experience of concrete objects which you know.

All these formations are ingrained; they are stored in you. They come from outside, but at the same time every experience which you have during your lifetime and which you have during meditation is already present in you. Since these things are present in you, what happens when you sit for meditation is that they begin to come up to the surface. So by practising the various forms of yoga, you are trying to separate the mind from these experiences, these formations, these patterns. How do you do it?

Abhyasa, repeated practice

In these *Raja Yoga Sutras*, there are two ways prescribed. One of the ways is constant, repeated practice, which in yogic terminology is called *abhyasa*. When we were in school and we made a mistake in spelling, the teacher would make us write out the word twenty times on the left side of the page. That is called abhyasa. To write it again and again, to repeat it again and again, to practise it again and again is called abhyasa.

Abhyasa is very important, even if you do not get any immediate result thereby, because it is able to fix your inner vrittis, your inner karma, your inner samskaras, the experiences which are already stored in you. Gradually, the practices which you do in your daily life, even if they do not show external results, will definitely produce an effect within the subconscious and unconscious mind.

We know that abhyasa is very difficult. There are many great obstacles in the path of repeated, constant practice. In the *Raja Yoga Sutras* they have detailed nine obstacles. You should read about them. One obstacle in your practice is physical disease and another is doubt. Another obstacle is irregularity, erratic practice. You practise two hours every day for one month and suddenly you drop it. Then another is that even if you decide to practise, you never do it. You think about it. There is a lot of enthusiasm. You promise yourself that you will do the practice every day, but when it comes to the point of actually practising, you just fail. You are not able to stick to your resolution. Like this, there are nine obstacles and you must know what they are.

In order to avoid these nine obstacles, there are certain prescribed ways. To overcome sickness, you must practise hatha yoga. In order to avoid doubting the quality and the result of your own practices, you must have satsang with the wise and you must have a relationship with the guru. You must study books written by wise men, which will again restore and resurrect your faith and belief in the practices. You have to find out how you are going to avoid these obstacles which can completely take you away from those practices of yoga to which you are committed, which you have resolved to do at any cost and which you know are very important for you.

So, in Sage Patanjali's *Yoga Sutras* it is said that abhyasa must be perfected first, then comes vairagya.

Vairagya, disidentifying oneself

Vairagya is a process of disidentification with the pleasant and unpleasant experiences which you are having in your day-to-day life, or which you have already had in the past. It is a fact that everyone who is born must have these conflicting experiences of life. You can't only have experiences of success, happiness, pleasure, love, contentment. No, it's not possible because this life is a creation of duality.

There is duality everywhere in this life. If you are happy, you are going to be unhappy; if you are born, you will die; if you succeed, you will fail; but you want only one side, isn't it? Nobody wants to be unhappy, to be sick, to fail, to die, to lose, to have enemies. So there is a problem. You don't want unhappiness, but it comes and you are finished; it hits you very hard. Because you don't want to accept a particular experience when it comes to you, it completely injures the whole psychological framework of the mind. Therefore, vairagya must be practised.

Vairagya is not renunciation of people, of relationships, of matter and object. No! Because you know, even if you renounce the matter and the object, still you can identify with happiness and unhappiness. So instead of renunciation, you have to practise vairagya, and what is vairagya? It is a process of disidentification of your own ego, from what is happening in life, by a very careful attitude. If you can practise this vairagya during meditation and outside of meditation, by proper thinking, by proper analysis, by trying to understand the laws of nature, by trying to understand the realities, then you will be able to disidentify yourself.

A Buddhist parable

One simple example of disidentification was given by Buddha. Maybe you know it. Once a young lady came to Buddha with her dead child in her lap. She heard that Buddha was a great wise man and that he was enlightened. So she came to him and said, "Lord, my child is dead. Please give him life." She was stricken with sorrow, great sorrow, utmost sorrow. Buddha said, "Okay, please go and bring some mustard seeds for me."

The lady was very happy because after all, it's not very difficult to get mustard seeds anywhere. But as she was going out, the Buddha said, "Remember one thing, you must get the mustard seed only from a house where nobody has died." The lady did not understand him because she was in complete distress. She was only thinking about her child, she could not see the reality.

So she went to one family and knocked on the door. The father came out and said, "What do you want?" She replied, "I want a few mustard seeds to give to Lord Buddha, so he will bring my child back to life." The man went inside and brought out a few mustard seeds, but when he was about to give them to her, she remembered to ask, "But did anyone die in you family?" The man replied, "Of course, my father died, my son died, my brother died."

Like this, the woman went from house to house, and by evening she was completely exhausted. She could not find even one family in which nobody had died. When she came to Buddha, he asked her to give him the mustard seeds. She said, "Lord, I could not get them. I did not find even one home which death had not visited." Buddha said, "Then are you going to be an exception?"

A subtle difference

This is the law, the *dharma*, the process. This is how he caused that disidentification, the vairagya, the realization of the truth regarding the experience which she was undergoing. It may be any other experience. It may be an experience of a fight within the family. It maybe a simple experience or an ever recurring experience which happens every now and again. Every time you make a promise, you repent, you forgive, you forget and every time it comes again and makes you unhappy. If you can understand the reality, then vairagya, disidentification, will come to you.

Then, when a fight is going on you will understand and it will not hit your consciousness so hard. It will not create a scar; there won't be any wound. You will only participate in the quarrel, that's all. Participation in a quarrel, in unhappiness, in failure, is one thing – and to experience it is another. There's a very subtle difference between the two. That is called vairagya and you will have to understand it more.

The eight steps of yoga

Sage Patanjali says that those who want to practise yoga must cultivate these two things – abhyasa and vairagya, regular and consistent practice and disidentification with various situations by a systematic approach. He has suggested the ways in which we can get into the mood of meditation and experience samadhi. He has explained what meditation is and what steps precede meditation. These are known as the eight steps of yoga, therefore, the raja yoga of Sage Patanjali is known as ashtanga yoga.

Ashtanga means eight, the eight steps of yoga. The first four steps are known as external practices and the latter four steps are known as inner practices. What are these eight steps? Let me just enumerate them for you:

1. *Yama*, discipline
2. *Niyama*, regulation
3. *Asana*, posture
4. *Pranayama*, breathing technique
5. *Pratyahara*, withdrawing the senses
6. *Dharana*, concentration
7. *Dhyana*, meditation
8. *Samadhi*, transcendental awareness.

These are the eight stepping stones to samadhi.

The first four steps are known as external preparations. What is yama? This is called discipline of the self. There are five yamas: *satya*, truth; *ahimsa*, non violence; *brahmacharya*, purity of sensuality; *asteya*, non-stealing; *aparigraha*, non-accumulation. These are the five self-disciplines which you have to practise according to your situation and your possibility. Side by side with these disciplines, there have to be some regulations. These are called niyama and they are also five in number.

The third step is asana or position. Asana does not mean those exercises which you are taught. *Asanas* are the positions intended for meditation, like padmasana and siddhasana. In these positions, the body is upright and the spine is straight. The flow of energy inside the body can move unobstructed and there is total relaxation of everything within the system. This is called asana.

The fourth step is pranayama. *Pranayama* means forcing the pranic energy, instilling the pranic force into every part of the body. There are certain pranayamas which accomplish this. When you practise pranayama, the nervous system, the brain and many other systems in the body begin to cooperate with one another, because many times what happens when you are trying to meditate is that the body is not cooperating. When there are impurities in the body the pranas are very low. So these are the first four steps. which lead to enlightenment or samadhi.

Now, coming to the last four: pratyahara, dharana, dhyana, samadhi. *Pratyahara* means withdrawing the experience through the senses. Every sense has something to experience: – sight, sound, smell, touch and taste. These create an experience and in the practice of pratyahara you try to withdraw them. How do you do it? Through the practice of mantra, of kirtan, or by concentration on a number of things which I will enumerate. You can concentrate on a light, on a sound, on an idea, on a particular feeling, on some saint or divine personality and so on. What happens when you concentrate on one particular thing? The neurosis of the mind is withdrawn for the time being.

Now, when concentration becomes deep, then what happens is that you lose touch with the ego. This is a very important accomplishment in yoga. In the *Raja Yoga Sutras*, this particular accomplishment is known as samyama. When concentration and meditation take place at once, without any effort, with absolute spontaneity, that is called *samyama*.

Psychic powers
What is the outcome of this samyama? Sage Patanjali has said that by achieving this great faculty of samyama, you can influence matter, events, the thought process and, if you know how, you can even influence the laws of nature. This particular result is known in yoga as *vibhooti* and also as a siddhi. *Siddhi* means psychic perfection. Telepathy is a siddhi, clairvoyance is a siddhi, mesmerism is a siddhi. Likewise, there are eight psychic achievements called the eight siddhis. These eight siddhis relate to the state of perfection of the mental force.

When the mental force is divided, when it is dissipated, then it is powerless, it has no strength. When the mental force is not divided, when it is not dissipated, but when all the mental force is united and directed towards one channel, then it creates a greater force and that force can be applied, that force can influence the event.

Of course, throughout the *Yoga Sutras* it is said that the psychic powers are obstacles in the path of enlightenment. They will come to everyone who is practising, but you must avoid them. You should not use them, you should not practise them. Do not experiment with psychic powers because it is clearly said that these do come at a particular level of evolution of the mind. At a certain point of union or unification of the mental forces, they come automatically to you. You can read others' thoughts, but don't do it. You can influence others' minds, but don't do it. You can even come to know what's going to happen in the future, but don't try to know.

This is a very important discipline in yoga. Because many yoga practitioners do not practise this, they lose their yoga practices and then they don't see the light. When you practise yoga for some time with sincerity, suddenly you develop a little power, you can read thoughts – that's all. You are puffed up. However, these siddhis are expressions or manifestations of the mind, not of the self. Therefore, you cannot hold them; they are bound to disappear.

There was a time, thirty years ago, when I could read everyone's thoughts. Of course I did not do it, but I lost that power. There was a time when whatever I spoke would happen. That was the siddhi of speech. Then automatically it went away. In the evolution of the forces of the mind, these things which you call psychic powers, which are responsible for the so-called miracles, do come in the life of every yogi, in the life of every spiritual aspirant, but you must not practise them.

That is the first thing, and it is for this reason that you need a guru. Every horse needs a master, every car needs a driver and every disciple needs a guru because guru is the controller, the master, the whip. He controls. He says, "No, don't do it." Many times I was tempted, but my guru said, "No, don't do it, because you have to invest this into the capital fund. Don't squander the spiritual gain."

Siddhi is the outcome of samyama. When you sit and concentrate on a particular object, suddenly everything is withdrawn and only the object remains there. The ego is withdrawn, the duality is withdrawn. Concentration on each and every object produces a different result. That is the contention of the *Raja Yoga Sutras* and Sage Patanjali has cited a few examples.

When you concentrate on ida or pingala nadi, on the sun or the moon, on the navel, on a star, on a flower, what is going to be the outcome? For the time being, your mind loses the absolute duality. It becomes just a one-pointed force, which can be channelled in one direction. But you have to avoid this achievement until the time when you are able to transcend the temptation of the siddhis. When you are able to avoid this temptation, then enlightenment comes.

Purusha and prakriti

Now, I am going to use the word *samadhi* instead of enlightenment. What is samadhi? In the *Raja Yoga Sutras* Sage Patanjali says, "Every experience, every form of awareness, every feeling, every form of knowledge, every understanding is an outcome of prakriti." This is a very important thing which you have to understand, because in the yoga system, in the Samkhya system, there are two things which are talked about every now and again – purusha and prakriti.

Purusha means consciousness and *prakriti* means nature. According to Samkhya, yoga and tantra, prakriti is the creative force. Purusha is not the creator; it is the witness. This is completely different to the idea of religion, where it is believed that God created the whole world. If you are religious, you will not be able to understand it, so for the time being that religious cosmology must be kept aside. We are not going to discuss how creation took place. We are only saying that in Samkhya, in yoga, they have talked about the existence of two universal forces, not one.

Therefore, yoga is considered to be a dualistic philosophy. It is not a monistic philosophy because in yoga, in Samkhya and in tantra, they say that there are two universal forces. One force is called nature, which is represented by the total matter. Not only the earth, the stars, the sun and the moon, but throughout the cosmos, all that is matter is represented by prakriti. This prakriti is called Nature with a capital N. This Nature is in a process of creation and the matter is constantly evolving, it is never static.

Of course those who have studied modern physics will understand it better. In physics also they talk about the laws of nature and how nature has been evolving from the invisible to the visible state, how nature has been evolving from one creation and that is destroyed, to another creation and that is destroyed. The yoga philosophy of purusha and prakriti is more or less along the same lines as the principles of matter and energy found in modern physics.

Separation and union

Now, this aspect of purusha in your body is called microcosmic and in the total universe it is called macrocosmic. Therefore, you are the replica of the cosmos, or the whole cosmos or the whole of creation is nothing but an extension of yourself. You are the microcosmic reality of the macrocosmic existence and there is absolutely no qualitative difference between the microcosmos and the macrocosmos. As it is in the microcosmos, so it is in the macrocosmos. In modern physics also they say the same thing.

This purusha and prakriti interact with each other like the butter in the milk, like the oil in the sesame seed, like nuclear energy in uranium. They are constantly interacting, so you can't see them separately. Purusha and prakriti are like Shiva and Shakti. You have seen the symbology of Shiva and Shakti in cosmic embrace? Matter and energy merge into each other; you can't separate them.

As long as purusha and prakriti are together there is creation, experience, objectivity, cognition, perception. If you want to transcend external experience, transcend duality, then what have you to do is separate purusha from prakriti. Shiva and Shakti are in each other's embrace. You have to separate both of them. So the raja yoga of Sage Patanjali isn't the union of purusha and prakriti but the separation, but ultimately in the yogic tradition, *yoga* means union. It doesn't mean separation.

This is an important thing which we have to understand. Unless you are able to dissociate your mind, to divert your mind from matter for some time, you can't have the experience of your true self. Experience of your true self and your true nature is called union.

So, there are three important things to remember: the first is purusha, the second is prakriti and the third is atma. *Atma* means my self: matter, energy and consciousness – three things. The practices of yoga relate in the first step to separation of matter from energy and then in the second step to union with consciousness. So, samadhi is experience of your infinite, eternal, true and enlightened nature.

What happens in samadhi? During that period the seed of dualistic experience is completely fried. During the moment of samadhi, what you experience I do not know and Sage Patanjali has also not said anything about it. He only said, and everybody who has experienced it has said, that this is an experience which cannot be shared, which cannot be explained, which cannot be categorized. This is an experience which you can have and you can share it with yourself.

36

How to Meditate

Healing Centre, Nimbin, Australia, 22 February 1984.

Everybody is aware of the efficacy of meditation. There are a lot of books on this subject available today and throughout the world scientists, psychologists and people working in every field are talking about meditation. In many countries they are experimenting on the effects of meditation and they have found that it is a powerful tool provided by nature, if only you know how to use it.

According to the philosophy of yoga and tantra, tranquillity of mind, peace of mind and relaxation do not represent passive states. Tranquillity and peace are active states of mind – this you must remember. Therefore, meditation is not a passive condition of mind. When meditation is practised passively, then it is hypnosis. Hypnosis creates passivity and meditation creates activity. Therefore, when I talk about meditation or dhyana yoga, I'm not talking about a way by which you can attain passivity of mind.

During meditation, when you replenish the lost energy, when you conserve the prana and when you give ample rest to your nervous system, then you are able to think better, you are able to feel better and to work better. But the important and difficult point is, how to meditate? This is what I am going to tell you here.

Suppressing the tendencies of the mind

There are various paths and techniques which are taught for acquiring good meditation. These methods and techniques are taught by various wise people and teachers throughout the world. In America there are thousands of institutions which teach meditation. For each class, each hour or half hour of meditation which you practise with them, you have to give half a week's salary – but the people are not foolish and the teachers are not cheats. Because meditation is helping them in their daily life, in their social life, in their business life, in their emotional life, in their personal life, in their spiritual life and even in their sexual life, so they go and learn.

However, most of the teachers teach meditation by controlling or suppressing the tendencies of the mind. It is one way. When you are trying to meditate on a particular point or object, you must think only about that. If something else comes into your mind, you must reject it. That is the system of meditation in which the non-meditational object is rejected, that wave is denied.

So, you are maintaining constant awareness of that particular object on which you have decided to meditate or concentrate. Any other thought which comes into your mind is a foreign thought or a vicious thought, because it is other than the thought of the particular object of meditation. This is the general way in which meditation is now being practised and taught throughout the world. I do not disagree with this way of practising meditation, but it is not fit for people with a restless mind. It is only fit for those who have acquired a high degree of serenity in their mind, who have crossed the borderlines of rajoguna and are already somewhere close to sattwa guna.

The three gunas

The mind, the consciousness or the personality is broadly classified into three qualities of nature. Some people are very quiet and peaceful. They can always adjust and understand. These people are called *sattwa gunis*. Then there are those who are restless, anxious, in a hurry, jumping up and down all the time for nothing. This is the nature of a particular type of people called *rajo gunis*. Then there is the third type of people who are inert by nature. They are like pythons. No matter what happens, the mind does not move – it sleeps. These people are called *tamo gunis*. They are always lethargic, procrastinating, postponing everything for tomorrow. That is the tamasic temperament.

So these are broadly the three qualifications or qualities of the mind and a combination of these three composes our personality. Some people are predominately tamasic, a little bit sattwic and a little bit rajasic. Some people are predominantly rajasic, partly tamasic and partly sattwic. Some people are predominantly sattwic, partly tamasic and partly rajasic. According to the combination of these qualities, the practices of meditation must be selected. If the practices are not selected according to the particular temperament or the combinations just described, then problems arise.

Many times when you practise meditation, you become introverted and you don't know how to relate with people. You feel that your behaviour with your wife or husband or with your children was much better before you started meditation, although your mind was restless. After meditation you get irritated and angry for nothing. Why? Not because of meditation, but because of the wrong dose of medicine you have taken. The prescription was wrong. Therefore, in yoga, the practices are done according to the evolutionary level of the mind.

Stages related to the mind
According to the yogic system, the mind is supposed to be undergoing a process of evolution. In the first stage you grow physically. A tree grows, a plant grows, a human body grows. First it's a baby, then it's a young man, then it's middle-aged, then it's an old man, then it dies. These are the stages related to the growth of the body. In the same way, the mind also grows, which means that the mind has various stages of development just like the body.

The primitive state of the mind is dullness. When the mind emerged from crude matter in the scale of evolution, it was dull. Then it evolved and became dissipated. Dissipated means broken mind. Monkeys have broken minds. They will take any object for a few seconds, look it up and down and then throw it away and forget it. That is called a broken mind. The mind breaks away from a particular sequence and then goes on to another, completely forgetting the last. That type of mind exists not only in monkeys but in us also and such people are often sent to the mental hospital.

The dull state of mind and the broken state of mind are unyogic stages. They are abnormal stages. If you have a dull mind or a broken mind, you have to go to the mental hospital, because these stages do not relate to the normal evolution of the human being. If a monkey has a broken mind or a python is dull, that is normal because its natural evolution is only up to that point.

Now, the yogic state of mind begins with an oscillating mind. An oscillating mind swings back and forth like a pendulum. It will move out but come back. It has an area or a path of movement. In an oscillating mind, when you are trying to concentrate on a particular object, the mind wanders and then comes back again to the same point. Therefore, in yoga, what we try to do is train the broken mind to oscillate, because the mind can't evolve directly. It can't become one-pointed all at once. It has to be brought to the oscillating state first and after that you can take it to the state of one-pointedness.

Three important controls
I am going to tell you a few practices which will help you. I will also tell you that in the science of yoga there are not just a few techniques, but a few hundred thousand techniques. For whom? For millions of people who are all slightly different from each other. We may belong to the same race, to the same religion, to the same nation, but according to the laws of evolution, we are all slightly different from each other.

Therefore, hundreds of thousands of practices of yoga have been propounded from the early human evolution up to this time. It is not necessary to learn all of these, but there are a few techniques which are very useful, because in my opinion, when you are trying to practise meditation, you should not only take the mind into your confidence, you must take the body also into your confidence. If you first take the body into your confidence, then mind will automatically come into confidence.

There are elements in the body which control the mind. The breath controls the mind. The hormonal secretions in the body control the mind. If you take ganja, what happens? It affects the mind. Of course, the effect is temporary, but it is there, you can't deny that. The body has three important internal controls: the hormonal secretions, the brainwaves and the breath. If you can coordinate the movement of all these three, then you don't have to deal with the thoughts, with the mental problems, with the worries and anxieties, which are drawing the mind out and disturbing it all the time.

The hormonal secretions

Now, of these three, the most difficult to control or to gain access to is the hormonal processes. You need a proper guide who understands how to regulate the ratio and the proportion of the different hormonal secretions such as adrenaline and thyroxin, so that they all combine together and create an influence on the mind. If you want to achieve meditation by coordinating or by creating a balance in the hormonal process of the body through the practices of hatha yoga, kriya yoga, etc., then it is important that the sexual habits and diet must be corrected.

There is one practice for example, khechari mudra, in which the tongue is elongated by so many techniques, and after elongating the tongue, it is inserted into the nasal passage. Then the breath is taken in and held. When the tip of the tongue is inserted into the back of the throat, it touches a particular centre at the posterior side of the nasal passage, if it can reach that far. Then that stimulus is transferred to a higher centre in the cranial passage of the brain where a tiny gland is situated.

According to yoga that point is known as the seat of nectar, ambrosia or *amrit*, which is a particularly powerful secretion, but the amount is very small. Now, that fluid has to be drawn down. How to do it? What they do is insert the tongue into the nasal passage as far back as possible and try to touch that posterior centre, what you call the contact switch. If they are able to do that, then the nectar which is stored there begins to flow down into the body.

When the secretion of that fluid takes place, suddenly the mind becomes quiet, the thoughts cease. You are looking at everything with your eyes open, but at the same time, the mental movement is not happening. The sensorial movement is happening, perception is taking place, but cognition is not taking place because the mind has become quiet. That is the effect of this particular secretion when it is absorbed by the body.

The bitter and the sweet

However, although this secretion is so fantastic and powerful, the rules for the practitioner are very severe. I will give you an example. Many years ago, when I was in Munger a mechanic from the railway workshop came to me. He had been practising khechari mudra for quite a few years. He was expecting that some day the nectar would come and when it came, the mind and body would become quiet and he would have the inner light, or enlightenment. Instead, what happened was that he started getting some bitter taste. Gradually the taste got more and more bitter, even more bitter than quinine. The man was terrified and he stopped the practice, but that bitter taste remained.

Someone informed him that I was living in Munger and perhaps I could advise him. So he came and told me what was happening. I asked him about his diet. He said, "I'm a householder and I eat what ever my wife cooks for me.'" Then

I asked him about his brahmacharya. He told me about it. I said, "Look here, if you want the sweet nectar, then you must listen to me, and if you want the bitter, you continue." Well what happened later is another matter.

When you want to take the body, the physical nature into your confidence and thereby help yourself in meditation, then there are certain rules and regulations which must be adhered to. For those who cannot follow those rules, there are many simpler methods which take more time – maybe one, two, three, four or five years.

The breath and the mind
Out of all those methods, the easiest are those which utilize the breath. I will tell you about one such practice called *ajapa japa*, which means awareness of your breath in the form of sound. It is awareness of your natural breath as if it were a particular sound. What is that sound? It is the mantra *Soham*.

In the course of time, you are able to adjust the flow of this natural breath and gradually it becomes reduced. In the beginning the rate of respiration is about fifteen per minute. That comes to about nine hundred per hour. As the mind becomes quieter and quieter, involving itself in the awareness of the ingoing and outgoing breath, with the awareness of *Soham*, the rate of breathing also becomes slower and slower.

Now, when you are practising *Soham* with the breath, you are not practising deep breathing. You are trying to be natural, but remember, as the mind becomes quieter and quieter, you'll find that this ratio of fifteen rounds per minute becomes ten rounds, eight rounds, six rounds per minute. You don't know it, but it's happening. Therefore, in the classical texts on hatha yoga it is said, "As the mind becomes one-pointed and the dissipations, oscillations, wanderings, movements and vibrations of the mind become quieter and quieter, the gap between the breath becomes greater."

In the case of nervous disturbance, for example, you can breathe as many as thirty to forty times a minute. Normally, you breathe about fifteen rounds a minute. In deep meditation, you breathe six rounds a minute and when samadhi takes place, maybe one round a minute, but you must not reduce the breathing rate by force. If you do, then there will be problems. It has to develop spontaneously because the mind and the breath are both influencing each other. If the breath is restless, the mind becomes restless, or vice versa. If there is peace of mind, then the breath also becomes peaceful.

Point of fixation

When you are trying to concentrate or to meditate, a centre of fixation is very important, otherwise the mind is disturbed by the rapid eye movements. During meditation the eyeballs keep on moving. All the time there is vibration and as they vibrate, they disturb the image and the awareness. It is a very subtle thing, but it is true. Therefore, the eyeball movement must be fixed before you can fix the mind, because the mind and body interact with each other in almost all cases.

When you become a yogi and have attuned yourself to a higher state, then the body and mind act independently, but in most cases the mind and body interact upon each other. Therefore, the eyeball movements do disturb the process of concentration on an image. So, you have to fix that as such. While you are practising your inner gaze, your mind should be fixed either at the tip of the nose or at the eyebrow centre. For some the eyebrow centre is easier and for others the nosetip is easier.

In India, all the ladies put some mark at the eyebrow centre. Of course, they consider this to be a cultural mark, but it is not. It is actually intended to maintain constant pressure at this point so that the awareness remains there and the eyeball movement is fixed. Therefore, if you look at the eyes of an Indian lady, you will see they are not jumping up and down. They are steady and still, not because they have been practising any yoga, but because of the pressure there.

As a result of that pressure at the mid-eyebrow centre, the eyeballs remain centred, one-pointed and still at all times. That is an important point. Therefore, either the eyebrow centre or the nosetip gaze must be perfected while you are practising awareness of the breath.

Coming to the point of concentration

In the first stage of ajapa japa, you practise mental repetition of the mantra *Soham* together with the breath. On inhalation you repeat *So* and on exhalation *Ham*. Then after some time, you change the circuit in the mind. Don't change the circuit in the prana; change the circuit in the consciousness. And what is it? Now, you say *Hamso*. There is no difference in the system of breathing or in the awareness of the breath, but the difference is that instead of the *Soham* circuit, you are now practising the *Hamso* circuit. *Soham* is the first circuit and *Hamso* is the second.

Now, when you practise this for some time, let us say ten minutes or even less than that, you will experience that your mind is gaining a kind of psychic equilibrium. The moment this stage is reached by you, there is an indication, just like a bell. The moment that indication appears, it means stop your ajapa japa and start concentration.

Up to now you are not practising concentration; you are trying to develop concentration. As soon as concentration develops and the psychic equilibrium takes place, there is an indication. You lose touch with the external and you begin to see something inside. It could be a flower, a colour, sunlight, moonlight, a donkey, a kangaroo. It can be anything. It need not be a divine being or your guru, but it is something in the psychic dimension which you are able to see as you see a dream. The moment that psychic expression, psychic balance or psychic equilibrium takes place, you should begin the practice of concentration.

Practise concentration on your symbol, on your guru, on your ishta devata or on any form which you have chosen for yourself. Supposing your symbol is the full moon. At that moment, you begin thinking about the full moon and you will succeed in seeing the full moon as if you are dreaming with your eyes open, as if you are dreaming with total consciousness.

The inner vision of the full moon takes place clearly for a few seconds, or maybe just for a split second. To be able to retain the experience of that concentration which I am talking about is not easy. Suddenly the mind breaks and you begin to see TV inside. You know that your mind is drifting but it is very hard to bring it back. In that process, you come out and once you come out, don't start again. Leave the practice and do your work.

You may remain in that psychic realm for half a minute, but not five or ten minutes. It is a very short period. Sometimes that experience is finished within twenty or thirty seconds, but it seems to last for hours together. That is because the time ratio in the mind and the time ratio outside are not the same. What is one second here could be an hour there.

Do you understand the time difference? I'm talking about the relative value, the relative context of time. They are not the same and therefore you may have been there for a few seconds or maybe one minute, but in that psychic realm it could be many hours. So it doesn't matter if you have been there for only ten seconds. Even one second is more than enough.

Pranayama as dynamic meditation

This is one way of meditation for people who can manage with the mind more easily. The other way is more for people who have very disobedient, arrogant, tough, sensual, pampered minds. In that case, it is better to choose a practice in which you are not involved with the mind at all, by which you keep the mind away. This is best achieved by the techniques of pranayama.

I'm not going to talk about all the pranayamas at this moment. I'm just taking one practice known as nadi shodhana. Breathe in through the left nostril, hold the breath by pressing both nostrils with the thumb and ring finger. Breathe out through the right nostril, hold the breath. Breathe in through the right nostril, hold the breath. Breathe out through the left nostril, hold the breath. That is one round. Practise five rounds, no more. Of course, this is just a brief outline of the practice; it is not the complete technique.

Before you go on with the practice of pranayama, you must learn the bandhas. *Bandha* means locking, binding or contracting. There are three bandhas, three locks, which must be perfected. One is called *jalandhara bandha*, the chin lock, another is *uddiyana bandha*, the abdominal lock, and the third is *moola bandha*, contraction of the perineum. All these three bandhas have a direct bearing on the nervous system and help to raise the pranic level in the body. Therefore, they must be mastered before you practise pranayama and meditation.

Now, when you have perfected the coordination between the breathing and the bandhas, then the third point comes – the ratio. This is very important because it is directly linked with the right and left hemispheres of the brain and with the sympathetic and parasympathetic nervous systems. There has to be a ratio in pranayama not so much for the sake of oxygenation, but in order to influence the brain, the nervous system, the heart and so forth.

The ideal ratio which will completely put the mind under control so that it can't move is 1:6:4:4, but you cannot do this right from the beginning. You must start with the minimum ratio, which is 1:2. Retention you may adjust, but the ratio of inhalation and exhalation has to be one to two. Later you can increase it to 1:3, 1:4, 1:5 1:6.

So you practise only five rounds of nadi shodhana, not more. In the beginning the five rounds will take you five minutes, but after you have been properly established in your practice, the five rounds will take you three hours. Then you don't need to practise five rounds, just one round is enough. When you have practised one round of this pranayama, then you are ready to start concentration.

Concentration with pranayama

Pranayama should not be practised without a proper break in between. You complete one round quietly, and what do you do in that time after the round? For a short period, concentrate on the symbol or the object which you have chosen. Here I'm not talking about psychic equilibrium.

Remember, psychic equilibrium, which we discussed in the first practice, comes as an indication. Here the indication will not come, it should not come. If the indication comes, your pranayama practice will fail because, as I said, this practice is meant for people with very rough, arrogant, disobedient, pampered and spoilt minds.

After completing one round of pranayama, close your eyes and stabilize the body. Start concentration, say on shivalingam or whatever your symbol is. Practise this for a short time, maybe a minute or two, not more than that, and then open your eyes again and start the second round accordingly. In between each round you practise concentration, so if you practise five rounds of pranayama, then you do five rounds of concentration.

Importance of meditation

These are the methods which I suggest to you. Of course, there are many more, but it is not possible to discuss more here. Before I close, I want to tell you that meditation is more important than food, it's more important than sleep, it's more important than any pleasure in life. And if you are able, somehow or other, accidentally or by good luck, grace or whatever, to step one foot, not even both, into meditation, you are not a human being, you are a superhuman being.

However, just because you have closed your eyes and stopped the mind and gone into the dream state doesn't mean that you have achieved meditation. Many times, instead of meditation you undergo an experience of hypnosis. Many people do it. They are not actually practising meditation; they are practising hypnosis, because they are trying to crush the mind, to trample the mind, just like you say to your children, "Oh, don't do this, don't do that." Then what happens? The children become calm and quiet, they don't say anything, they are very obedient.

If you can accept the importance of meditation, then definitely you are going to spare at least half an hour every day to practise it. Meditation can transform the quality of experience, not only divine experience, not only ideal experience, but even the quality of a most ordinary experience. It may be the experience of eating, drinking, sexual involvement or any kind of experience.

Meditation is able to transform the quality of a desirable experience and it is able to minimize the quality of a lower experience. If there is any unhappiness in the family, any tragedy in the family, the experience will be minimized; that is the effect of meditation and when there is happiness, it will flow.

QUESTIONS AND ANSWERS

What is the best way to measure the duration of the breath while practising the ratio in nadi shodhana pranayama?
In many yogic texts, they have suggested to clap one, snap one, but I have found this very disturbing and cumbersome. I have also found counting inaccurate. What I have found most accurate is mantra. Your personal mantra is not appropriate because it is not accurate. The mantra which is used for measuring the duration of the breath is known as Gayatri mantra.

Gayatri is a mantra of twenty-four syllables, and once you repeat the mantra mentally, you are completing one vital circle of the breath. Everybody has a different vital capacity. Some people take in less air and others take in more. There has to be a balance or a limit so that the psychic expression will take place, and Gayatri mantra is designed for this purpose.

Here are the twenty-four syllables of Gayatri mantra: *Om Bhurbhuvah suvah, Tatsaviturvarenyam, Bhargo Devasya Dhimahi, Dhiyo Yo Nah Prachodayaat*. Gayatri mantra is the length equal to the ideal vital capacity, so when you inhale, you mentally repeat one Gayatri mantra. When you retain the breath inside, repeat once or twice. When you exhale, repeat twice and when you retain the breath outside, repeat once.

Gayatri mantra is ideal, but it is not compulsory. You can use any other mantra. However it is very difficult to tell exactly how many repetitions will be equal to the vital capacity. You will have to decide for yourself. It could be two, three, four, five, six, seven, eight – I don't know. For this reason, in my opinion, you should learn Gayatri mantra.

Gayatri need not be your personal mantra and it is not a personal mantra. Gayatri mantra is intended for pranayama; it relates to the breath. It is said that Gayatri is the pranic force, the life force. So, if you want to utilize your prana for concentration and meditation, you should practise Gayatri mantra with pranayama.

Gayatri is the sound which makes your mind free from the clutches of the senses. You are not able to meditate because you are not able to make your mind free from the clutches of the senses. The greatest disturbing factor in meditation is the senses. Like a postman, every now and then, these senses bring the news and when they bring the news they disturb the mind. So you have to render your mind free from the clutches of the senses, and that is the role of Gayatri mantra.

When practising bandha with pranayama, how do you know which to perform first and which to release first?
Along with pranayama, you must practise the three bandhas in order to kick the energy. The practice of bandha relates to retention. When you retain the breath inside, you practise two bandhas: jalandhara bandha and moola bandha. When you retain the breath outside, then you practise the three bandhas: jalandhara bandha, then uddiyana bandha and then moola bandha. When you are releasing, first release moola bandha, then uddiyana bandha and then jalandhara bandha.

In the practice of ajapa japa, what is the meaning of Soham and Hamso, or are they just sounds?
The distinct sound of the breath which has been discovered and revealed by the wise men is *Soham*. *Soham* means 'I am That'. This is what the breath is trying to remind us of, to teach us, all the twenty-four hours of the day. It is making us repeat, 'I am That'; I am that infinite Consciousness, that transcendental Consciousness. I am that Consciousness – that

Consciousness is me. This is the knowledge that must dawn at the end of meditation.

Meditation must bring us to a higher experience wherein we identify ourself with something higher, not just the name, the race, the body, the circumstances we are living in. I have a body, I have a race, I have a nation, I have a caste, I have a sex, I am a man or a woman, but that's not me. What am I? I am That; and that Consciousness, with a capital C, is what meditation has to bring us to ultimately. This is the significance of the mantra *Soham*.

Now, when we reverse the order of awareness, without changing the order of the prana or the breath, we get the mantra *Hamso*. In yoga and in tantra, *hamsa* means 'replica of your individual consciousness'. It is not the body, not the mind, not the senses, not the karma, not the chances of life, not the success, not the victory, not the loss, not the birth or death. There is something in us which is the white bird – the swan.

The swan is a bird which has a special quality; all the mystics have spoken about it. It is able to separate milk and water. That is the quality, the mystic symbology of the swan, *hamsa*. Therefore, when you are practising *Hamso*, you are becoming aware of that white, pure bird, which is your self, which is able to separate this body from consciousness.

How can we know which quality or guna we belong to in order to select the proper practices?

You do not know, and nobody can know, exactly which quality you belong to – whether you are sattwic, rajasic or tamasic. Therefore, it is safe to presume that we are predominantly tamasic. Don't say, "I am predominantly sattwic." *Sattwic* means balanced, harmonious, serene, quiet. You must always go by the principle "I am predominantly *tamasic*, dull, inert, procrastinating, lacking in motivation."

Today we are lacking in motivation, especially in Western countries. Everything has become so easy. In India, my God, you have to work very hard. To build a house, to dig a well, to prepare a plot of land, to make an ashram, you have to sweat from top to toe, but in the West they can build ashram after ashram – easy. Where things come easy, however, struggle is lost and when struggle is lost, the mind begins to snore. Then tamo guna becomes predominant.

When tamo guna becomes predominant, then the appropriate yoga is hatha yoga and kirtan. These are the two basic forms of yoga for the humanity of today. Through these two forms of yoga you will be able to realize the highest form, the highest experience of your life.

37

Indirect Method of Meditation

Bellingen Ashram, Australia, 23 February 1984

There are many paths of yoga which are intended for spiritual growth. Out of all those paths I'm going to discuss a very important one, the path of meditation, because I feel that many people want to know how to practise it. This path is the ultimate path. It is a part of your own existence. Therefore, throughout the world, people have been searching for the technique, the way to practise meditation.

Not only in this century, but for thousands of years wise men have said that you must try to transcend the external experience. When you are able to transcend the external experience for a short time, then you will be able to receive another higher experience. You may call it spiritual experience, transcendental experience or experience of your own self, but the problem remains: how to transcend the external awareness? How to transcend the external feelings related to objects, related to the body, related to your own environment and also related to your own mind?

The drug experience
People have been trying to experience that state in various ways. During the late 1960s in America they tried LSD, because they thought that with the help of this drug they would be able to break through the barriers of outer consciousness

and go into deeper consciousness of their own self. Whether or not they succeeded is left entirely up to you to decide.

In the same way, many thousand of years ago during the vedic period in India, the wise men discovered a drink that was known as soma. When they used to drink soma, they were able to transcend the outer consciousness and unite with their inner being. They continued this for many centuries. What happened to that soma? We don't know anything about it. Today scholars have been trying to work out which creeper it is. They have identified it with many plants and herbs in India, South America and elsewhere, but they haven't found it yet, I'm sure.

The Indian mind rejected soma, not because it was unable to produce the desired result, but because it lacked one basic element. What was the basic element which it lacked? Soma did give fantastic inner experiences, like LSD gives. However, it lacked the basic process of yoga, which relates to the evolution of consciousness and not to a change in the quality of consciousness. Meditation, *dhyana yoga*, must come to you as a matter of evolution of consciousness. Just as your body is evolving, the matter is evolving, the mind is evolving, the consciousness is also evolving.

The prophets of dialectic materialism have been saying for hundreds of years that there is only one substance in creation, in the universe. That substance is called matter and matter is evolving. However, in the philosophy of yoga, matter, mind and consciousness are all evolving at the same time, and this evolution of consciousness gives you an experience. With the help of the practices of yoga and meditation, you can accelerate the pace of this evolution and so, in India, they went on rejecting the use of any external substance like soma.

In India they also experimented with another herb, which is known as ganja. You call it marijuana or cannabis indica. Indians have tried every possible method to destroy this outer shell of consciousness and go within; not only drugs and various practices of yoga and tantra, but ultimately, through their experiences over thousands of years, they have come to one conclusion. They have declared that, if you want to break that outer shell and see the light within you and experience the infinity of your nature, then you have to go through the practices of yoga and meditation.

The monkey mind

Even as the West has perfected science and technology, the Indian mind, for thousands of years, has concentrated on the evolution of consciousness. Who am I? What is the mind? What is the position of the body? What is waking awareness, dream awareness, sleep awareness, hallucination, imagination? All these matters and many more were the important issues for Indians, and therefore they have never abandoned this culture of yoga.

Out of all the forms of yoga, meditation is supreme. In order to achieve meditation the wise men have tackled the problems of the mind through psychological and psychobiological methods. They have decided that there cannot be one path or system of meditation which is suited for everybody because everybody does not stand on the same point of evolution. We are controlled by our mind and our mind is sometimes *sattwic*, harmonious, sometimes *rajasic*, restless, and sometimes *tamasic*, dull. These are the three broad qualities of the mind. Everyone's mind is a composition of these three *gunas* or qualities.

These three attributes control the quality, the behaviour and the expression of the mind. Sometimes we are so restless; at that time the attribute of rajas is predominating. Sometimes we are peaceful, integrated and tranquil; then sattwa is predominating. Sometimes we are very dull and inert, without motivation; at that time the mind is under the sway of tamas. These three gunas are the qualities of nature. They are not only the qualities of the mind, they are the qualities of everything that is existing in this world.

According to the predominance of these qualities within you, the path of meditation, the technique has to be chosen. Therefore, one technique or one way of meditation does not suit the temperament of all. The human mind is like a monkey; it is never constant. It will hold an object for a period of time and then forget about it completely. For those people who do not have a constant flow of mind, success in meditation does not come through one particular technique, because their mind breaks.

This monkey, which is restless by nature, was stung by a scorpion and the monkey began to jump up and down. Finally somebody came and said, "This monkey is suffering. Let us give him a peg or two of whisky." So they gave him a few pegs of whisky and then he stopped jumping. This is the condition of the human mind which is stung by the events, tragedies and fears of life. What should the practice of meditation be for this restless mind which isn't able to stabilize itself for a moment?

You can just sit quietly, close your eyes and try to concentrate your mind on one object. If you are enthusiastic you may be able to do it for some time, but then the mind is not able to maintain consistency. It breaks and when it breaks, the meditation is lost. That is precisely the reason why so many people today who are truthful and sincere are not able to evolve in the path of meditation.

Therefore, I want to suggest one system of meditation, which I call psycho-biological, versus the other system which is purely psychological. When you are trying to tackle the mind through the mind, it is called psychological. When you are trying to tackle the mind through the processes inherent in the body, it is called biological or psycho-biological.

Tantric methods

In yoga and in tantra, they have direct and indirect systems of meditation. The direct system is to sit down quietly, close your eyes, concentrate on an object. That is called the direct method. The indirect method can be induced by the help of pranayama, kriya yoga, trataka, nada yoga, ajapa japa and other techniques. There are not just a few hundred techniques, but a few hundred thousand. Several years ago when I was writing the book *Meditation from the Tantras*, I had quite a number of these techniques in my mind because I knew that most people could not practise direct meditation, but indirect meditation was possible.

Direct meditation, which is practised through the psychological process, is very difficult because when you are trying to tackle the mind with the mind, you are creating a split in your personality. Therefore, we teach the tantric methods whereby you can experience meditation indirectly by working through the physical body. What are these methods? I can give you one example.

The nectar of the gods

In tantra and in yoga, there is a practice known as *khechari mudra*. That practice relates to elongating the tongue and then folding it back. First you press the bottom of the tongue against the upper palate. Then you push it back as far as possible into the upper nasal orifice, the upper part of the epiglottis. In the course of time, the tip of the tongue presses a particular centre on the posterior side of the nasal passage. That is a stimulating centre or a connecting point for a particular process which takes place in the brain.

At the top back of the brain there is a centre known as bindu visarga. *Bindu* means 'drop' and *bindu visarga* is the place from where the drop falls. In this centre a small amount of very important fluid is stored and when the tongue presses the connecting point in the posterior part of the nasal passage, then the stimulus is conducted to that centre in the brain. It begins to secrete that particular fluid which, in yoga, is known as amrit.

Amrit means nectar or ambrosia and when that fluid is secreted into the body and absorbed, then the quality of experience changes. Restlessness disappears. The body becomes stable; the breath becomes regular. The physiological processes in the body which were responsible for disturbances are all balanced. The rapid eyeball movements are stabilized; the eyes become one-pointed.

What happens to the mind? The mind becomes steady, and that particular experience called stopping the mind, which you have been working for your whole life, which you have been striving for lifetime after lifetime, is achieved just by one simple physiological process which is already inherent in you. This is the primary hypothesis of the yogic texts.

There are many other practices in yoga and tantra. They are just simple practices, physical practices, but the effects of those practices are so deep that they can create a change in the energy cycles in the body. They can create a balance in the endocrine secretions.

Pranayama and consciousness
I'll give you another example. In yoga they talk a lot about pranayama. Pranayama is not breathing exercise; it has been wrongly translated. *Pranayama* is a practice which involves inhalation, retention and exhalation of the breath. This is called pranayama. When you inhale, retain and exhale, what happens?

In the last few years leading scientists have worked on this subject and they have come to the conclusion that when you inhale and exhale through the nostrils, great changes, great events are taking place, not only in your lungs but in your brain. That is what yogis told us thousands of years ago. When you breathe, you are not only exercising your lungs. It is not just a process of oxygenation; it is more than that.

The breath which you inhale through the right and left nostrils has an immediate effect on the two hemispheres of the brain. Therefore, please remember, when you are breathing all the twenty-four hours, it is not only for the sake of oxygen, not only for the sake of the heart, but for the sake of your consciousness.

38

The Systems of Yoga

Newcastle Ashram, Australia, 25 February 1984

You can find Chinese restaurants in every city throughout the world. Similarly every culture has developed certain arts and skills related to man's needs in life. Western countries developed the art of technology and ancient civilizations, Romans, Greeks, Babylonians and Egyptians, developed their own skills, arts, culture and philosophy. Great indeed has been the contribution of these civilizations in the past; we cannot underestimate them. However, none of these cultures has understood the total man. They have understood only the external man.

How the philosophy of yoga developed

Since the dawn of civilization, the Indian mind has been thinking about man's existence. What is man, what is he composed of and what is his destiny and far future? What possible depth of knowledge can he gain? What knowledge can he acquire about the universe, reality and himself? The Indian mind did not think so much about how to grow food, although they did think a little about it. They did not think so much how to kill people in warfare although they did face war.

The one subject which has kept Indian minds busy for thousands and thousands of years, much before the Babylonians, Egyptians, Romans, Greeks or any civilization, is: What is man? Is he this physical body or is he something more than that? They went on thinking about why man is unhappy. Does he take another birth in order to work out his desires and fulfil his wishes? Is there an unending process of evolution or is man just born and then he will die? Is this the first time he has been born and the last time he will die? Finally, they came to one conclusion and the conclusion was that nobody, no book, no scripture, no prophet, no avatar can answer these questions for you. Any question related to the depths of life can only be answered by you.

Therefore, each and every individual must increase or expand his consciousness, because the answer you arrive at is according to the quality of your mind. The concept of God, soul, life after death and many other secret elements in life can only be understood by you according to the quality of your mind. Some people believe in one way and others believe in another because of the differences in the quality of the mind. The billions of people who inhabit this planet do not have the same quality of consciousness, the same quality of mind or the same quality of understanding. Everybody has a different understanding and according to this, they develop a philosophy and give a reply.

My conclusions cannot be your conclusions. Your conclusions cannot be mine, because any conclusions which you arrive at through the mind are not absolute. They are relative because your mind is relative and your mind is relative because it is bound by time and space. As long as the mind is bound by time and space, it is relative and when it becomes free from time and space boundaries, then it becomes absolute. When your mind becomes absolute, then the reply is final and correct.

It is in this particular context that they discovered a science many thousands of years ago, which all of you know today. Yoga! This particular science of yoga covered every aspect of human existence, because after realizing who man was, what the components of man's existence and personality were, they divided him into various dimensions. In order to develop a particular area of human life, they prescribed one form of yoga.

A science, not a system

Today, throughout the world, there is a resurgence of yoga in many fields of social life. Some people feel that when you practise yoga, you can relax very well. Others feel that if you practise yoga, you develop psychic powers like extrasensory perception, that you become intuitive and that your capabilities are enhanced. There are those people who believe that through the practices of yoga the incurable diseases like blood pressure, insomnia, arthritis, rheumatism, peptic ulcer and others can be cured. Like this, people throughout the world have discovered one or more forms of yoga for themselves.

According to your understanding of the condition of your life, you understand yoga. I ask many people, "What, do you practise yoga?" They say, "Ah, yes, I practise yoga and it has done me a lot of good." They do not say that they have only practised one form of yoga. If you see what they are doing, you find they are practising a few postures. For them, that is yoga.

Yoga is not a particular system or faculty. Just as medicine is a general term and you must say aspirin, panadol, cortisone or this or that to be more specific, in exactly the same way, the word yoga is a general expression for various systems. When you talk about science, what do you mean? Do you mean chemistry, biology, physics? Just as the terms medicine and science are general expressions and not specific ones, in the same way, yoga is a general term for various systems related to the human personality.

According to the science of yoga, the human being is a composition of many elements. This philosophy of yoga says that the physical body is one dimension, the emotional body is another dimension, the mental body is another dimension and the intellectual body is yet another dimension. Like this, the physical, emotional, mental, intellectual, psychic and spiritual dimensions all assembled together are known as human life or human existence.

If you are trying to cater to the needs of these different bodies, which particular form of yoga will you take up? In a car there are so many parts and each part is an item by itself, different from the other; if you have an electrical fault in your car, you bring an electrician; a simple mechanic will not do. In the same way, when you talk about this physical body, the emotions or the mind, etc., you are talking about them very broadly. The body is a broad expression. You will have to analyze it.

Hatha yoga relates to the energy fields
This structure which you know as the body is made up of flesh, blood, bone, marrow, skin, cells, nerves and so many other things which you learn about through your studies, but yoga has gone a little further than what modern science has so far achieved in its discoveries. Of course, in the last few years, the scientists have been coming to the same discoveries which the yogis indicated many thousands of years ago.

We do agree that man has a physical body – 50 kg, 60 kg, 70 kg, which is the gross total weight of your bones, blood, muscle, etc., but behind this visible body which weighs 70 kg, there are energy fields. These energy fields are the subject matter of hatha yoga. I am not going to talk about the energy fields in detail here, because that is a very defined system. I am only hinting that in the yoga system the energy fields relate to and control the physical and mental functions.

Your physical functions, motor activities and mental functions are controlled by these energies and if there is any defect or obstruction in the field of this energy in the physical body, then it can be rectified by the practices of hatha yoga, the yoga postures, which most people throughout the world are conversant with. Therefore, hatha yoga is one form of yoga which concerns your complicated, intricate and complex systems in this physical body and it is a very interesting subject.

Hatha yoga is not just physical exercise
In the last few years, when the scientists in the Western countries were exposed to the existence of a yoga system in India, first of all they were very critical and sceptical. They thought, "Oh, it is another type of Indian mysticism!" But when they began to conduct experiments on various yoga postures and breathing techniques, they found that certain unexpected and positive changes take place in the body, in the respiratory system, circulatory system and nervous system.

Again and again these wise men tried to understand what happens to the body, what changes take place in the endocrine secretions and in the brainwaves. At first they thought that yoga exercises were like any other exercises. Many years ago, the Directorate of Physical Education in Czechoslovakia invited me to attend and address their annual seminar in Prague. I refused to go. I said, "First of all find out scientifically what yoga is."

Just because you see a person doing the headstand pose or some sort of physical feats, you can't put it under the category of physical education. You will have to find out what hatha yoga is. In order to find out, there are two ways of deciding this question. One way is to ask an expert on the science like me. I'll tell you what it is. If you don't have faith that what I am telling you is true, then you can ask your scientists, doctors and laboratories to do the research. Then they will tell you that hatha yoga is not just physical exercise.

Hatha yoga is a system which the Indians discovered thousands of years ago to control, direct and connect the energy circuits in this physical body. Whereas in acupuncture you control the energies in the physical body by pressing needles into certain points along the meridians or channels of energy, in yoga the energy blocks can be cleared through hatha yoga practices. You can direct the flow of energy from any junction to any junction, not intellectually, but just by maintaining a certain posture.

I also wrote to the people in Prague, "I do not agree with your definition of pranayama as breathing exercises.

Pranayama is not just breathing exercises." There are thousands of books published throughout the world which say pranayama is breathing in more oxygen; it is true, but pranayama does not mean that.

There are two sets of nervous systems in this physical body, the sympathetic and parasympathetic nervous systems. Each has a definite role to play. One is connected to the physical aspect and the other to the mental aspect of your personality. Through the practice of pranayama you are not just inhaling oxygen. The effect of the breath which you inhale and retain directly affects your nervous system and your brain.

This has been proved and approved, experimented and concluded by eminent scientists through their hard labour. They say that when you are breathing through the left or right nostril or both nostrils, or when you are retaining the breath, certain vital and significant changes take place in the functioning of both the brain and the brainwaves. If you want to understand how the breath affects the brain, I have written a book called *Swara Yoga* about this ancient science of brain breathing and it contains a very old text which I have translated and commented upon.

When you practise pranayama, activities take place in the brainwaves, hormonal secretions and the physical functioning of the brain, and later on these are passed to various areas of the physical body. This is called hatha yoga and it relates to your body and brain, but it is not all about hatha yoga. I am just giving you a glimpse into this important system of yoga.

Bhakti yoga, the supreme form of yoga

When you practise hatha yoga, you are able to correct your energy flows and control the brainwaves, but is that all there is in life? What happens to your emotions? You may have a healthy body, everything is well with you, but one negative emotion can make you a criminal, can make you commit suicide or become violent. One negative emotion can bring about depression in your nervous system. What you have gained through the hatha yoga practices which you do, you can lose in one minute, one second or a fraction of a second, if you have not got a strong and healthy emotional body.

Therefore, in yoga there is another system which relates to the emotional body. This emotional body is man's very important body. If you can understand and handle it, if you can create a total balance in your emotional body, in the excited, upsurging emotions, in the depleted or surplus emotions, in the conflicting and confused emotions which you have, if you can centre them properly, then your feelings and emotions will be very healthy.

As I told you, emotions play the most important role in man's life. They play an important part in your expression of feelings such as love, hatred, joy, elation, sorrow and suffering. As a matter of fact, ninety percent of your external life, your day-to-day life, is controlled by your emotional body, but you have not taken care of it.

Everybody wants to experience love and joy. Nobody wants to feel hatred and sorrow. Everybody wants to receive a happy message; everybody wants to be praised. Nobody wants the other side. So what happens? In the absence of training, if you get a shock, bad news or something which you don't want, which is undesirable, at once the emotional body falls flat. Just as there is physical heart failure, in the same way there is another kind of emotional heart failure, and both heart failures can be connected at some point or the other. Breakdown in emotion affects the heart.

So, there is a form of yoga known as bhakti yoga. Wise men and yogis say it is the supreme form of yoga. They do not say that hatha yoga is the supreme form of yoga, although most people nowadays think that hatha yoga is the only form of yoga. I am not criticizing hatha yoga; I teach it every day, but I must make it clear that bhakti yoga is the supreme form of yoga. It is the easiest, safest, quickest, cheapest and best of all, because through the practice of *bhakti yoga* you are trying to express your noble emotions, surplus emotions, confused emotions, complicated emotions and emotions of various kinds. You are getting rid of them.

When you are feeling guilt in your mind, that is an emotion. When you are repenting, necessarily or unnecessarily, that is an emotion. When you pray or choose a guru for yourself, that is an emotion. Therefore, I came to the conclusion that bhakti yoga should be considered as the supreme form of yoga though, of course, it is not the only form of yoga.

Raja yoga, an interdisciplinary system

Now, besides this, the modern psychologists, especially after the advent of Dr Sigmund Freud, have been saying that our personality, behaviour, social interactions, subjective feelings or collective relationships, right and wrong, are all related to the deeper forces of the mind. That is right. So there is another form of yoga, known as raja yoga, which relates to your mind through which you understand and retain the impressions within yourself.

This mind, this consciousness, is operating on three dimension: the conscious level, subconscious level and unconscious level. You are able to control and discipline your conscious mind somehow, but what about that interdiscipline? You are not able to control your subconscious mind and you know nothing about the unconscious mind. It has been said by Freud that the mind is like an iceberg, only a little of it is seen, the rest is submerged. In the same way, almost the whole of your mind is beyond your perception. You know nothing about your mind; you only know about the modifications of the mind.

When you are angry, you know you are angry; when you are sorry, you know you are sorry; when you are happy, you know you are happy. That much you know. These are not the mind, but the modifications of the mind. They are patterns of the mind: anger, jealousy, hatred, greed, passion, ambition, love, compassion, mercy and so forth. They are not the mind and therefore just knowing these is not enough. Then, what is mind?

In order to understand and realize the total mind there are practices known as raja yoga. What is *raja yoga*? In short, it is a yoga which is a collective expression of withdrawal, concentration and meditation. This is the shortest definition of raja yoga. In order to know the mind, the whole mind, the mind which is on the top, in the middle and at the base, the total mind, you will have to withdraw yourself from the knowledge of external objects.

External objects relate to five types of experience and these experiences relate to form, sound, smell, touch and taste. As long as you are aware of these sensory experiences you can't withdraw, you can't go inside. However, the moment you are able to withdraw yourself from these five types of sensory experiences, you begin to go into the depths of your mind. This is called the path of dhyana yoga, meditation, the third path. Raja yoga is particularly concerned with knowing the mind and creating a system of interdiscipline.

After Sigmund Freud, the father of modern psychology, there was another great man in that field, Carl Jung, who came in touch with yoga. Freud never made mention of yoga and tantra. Either he did not know about it or he was not honest, because what he talks about in modern psychology, what he says about sex, about free thought flow and hypnosis is nothing but tantra. Any scientist, to be honest, should quote the source. Freud did not quote the source.

Jung, on the other hand, did quote the source and he was in absolute contact with yoga philosophy. He has given certain references to and opinions on the fact that every individual can control his mind without the help of an external agency, because in the mind there is another factor, another event or effect, which is called the guiding effect. If your mind is going wrong, if it is sick or abnormal, there is at the same time a guiding element within the mind. You know you are going wrong, don't you? That one who knows that you are going wrong is the disciplinary mind, the guiding mind.

Therefore, everybody has the mind which goes wrong and the mind which knows that it is going wrong. That particular interdisciplinary relationship is something which the yogis in the past also discovered. When you are angry, you are out of control. You can do anything at that time, but after fifteen minutes, one hour or two hours, if I ask you or you ask yourself, "Did you do the right thing?" you will never say it was right. Ordinary people refer to this as the conscience. In yoga we say it is the interdisciplinary element, which is a part of man's erring mind. It goes with the errors, the mistakes that we make.

This interdisciplinary element was discovered by the yogis in the past and accordingly they said, "Look here, you should try to withdraw your mind every day." You say, "But it is very difficult. Withdraw where?" They said, "Withdraw your mind into the mind, withdraw your mind into the consciousness." You say, "Where is consciousness?" The yogis said, "Consciousness is an experience. It is neither in the body nor outside the body. It is a completely different field of existence."

You can't say that the mind is here or there. Mind is a field, consciousness is a field, like a radioactive field, an electromagnetic field. There are many fields which you talk about in science. Those of you who have studied science understand what I mean when I say field. What is a unified field, can you explain it? Where is it? Mind relates to a particular field in this physical body and this field can be unified. According to this, raja yoga goes hand in hand with the modern unified field theory and the theories of science related to matter.

Meditation, which is the most important part, the final section of raja yoga, is going in with the help of the mind and transcending the external senses and becoming aware of one point. You have to decide on some point for yourself and when you are trying to become aware of that point, then you begin to know the mind. This is raja yoga.

Karma yoga, a dynamic system

However, the most important and vital thing is day-to-day life – your creed, ambitions, family, successes and failures. From the time you become aware of this life to the time of death, you are facing so many things and, at that time, you don't know how to balance yourself, how to control yourself. Then you become abnormal, your mind becomes sick. There is one form of yoga for this, which is known as karma yoga, a dynamic system which associates man with his day-to-day experiences, total experience.

Your relationships with your total experience are covered by karma yoga. This science relates to the daily activities which you do from morning until night and those activities which you do from time to time. It also relates to your involvement with actions done for a selfish motive. All the actions, all the performances and every accomplishment related to your selfish motivation, your occasional obligations and daily obligations are covered by the philosophy of karma yoga.

In karma yoga there is a way of living life. I have not come across any other classical book on this except for the *Bhagavad Gita*. This is a very small book and the theme is simple. It has eighteen chapters and the title of each is a different yoga. The first chapter is entitled 'The Yoga of Despondency'. You have heard about hatha yoga, laya yoga, kriya yoga, nada yoga, raja yoga, siddha yoga, karma yoga, but have you ever heard about the yoga of despondency?

When you are dejected and frustrated, when everything in your life is broken, what is the state of your mind at that time? What is the state of your mind when everything is against you, when you are facing conflict, when you are facing indecisiveness in life, when you don't know what to do? What is the situation of your mind at that time? That state of mind is called 'despondency yoga'.

So, how to come out of these disappointments and frustrations? When you are having a nervous breakdown, your body trembles, your palms sweat, you can't talk. When negative elements hover in your mind, you think you are going to die, your wife is going to leave you, your property is going to the dogs and everything bad is going to happen. You see only the inauspiciousness, everything is dark. What yoga will help you?

The *Bhagavad Gita* says, start with karma yoga. The despondent, dejected, depressed and low state of mind you are going through can be cured by the practice of karma yoga. What is karma yoga? You do work every day. You are a doctor, trader, factory worker, housewife. This is not karma yoga; this is karma. *Karma yoga* is a form of yoga in which there is a certain philosophy. It is a form of yoga in which you are incessantly participating in every aspect of life but, at the same time, you are only acting, you are not involving yourself. This is a very subtle point.

Herbs and drugs
I have given you an idea about bhakti yoga, raja yoga, hatha yoga and karma yoga. Beside these, there are other forms of yoga related to the deeper man in man. The forms of yoga which I am talking about now are related to the man who is fighting an external life. He wants a healthy body, mind and emotions, but what about the man behind the man? Have you ever thought about it? What about the mind behind the mind?

Yoga, yogis and sages say that behind this apparent physical structure, beyond this mind, within you, there is an effulgent centre. There is a point and man must connect himself with that particular radiant point. There is no name for that point. You can call it *bindu*, centre, nucleus: *atma*, the self; *jyoti*, light; *shoonya*, void. You can give it any name you like. You can say A, B, C or X, Y, Z. That is the centre from which you have sprung, that is the ultimate field and that is the ultimate experience.

People have tried to experience their radiant point by many ways in the past. Many thousands of years ago Hindus used to drink soma. This drink soma was made out of creepers. After drinking soma they tried to go in and experience their radiant point, but suddenly the soma disappeared. Today many scientists and researchers are trying to find out what soma was. Some equate it with a creeper found in the Himalayas, but they have not come to a conclusion.

Soma seemed to withdraw the external senses and make that radiant centre one-pointed but, as I said, it disappeared. Then came another drug called cannabis indica. You smoke it, sit down and forget everything, drop in and drop out! It has not disappeared in India. Some Indians still take it, but very few are interested in this. They say, "Why take it? I tried it because I wanted to have some experience, but when I had that experience, I knew that it was not adequate or true." So they gave it up.

Like this, Indians have tried many methods to tap or discover that radiant central point behind man's existence and all the methods were finally rejected. There are not only these two herbs in India, we know of hundreds. You just take them and you can't move. Then they came to a conclusion regarding a method known as kriya yoga. They said practise kriya yoga and what you want to achieve from these external herbs, drink and drugs is not necessary.

The effect which you create by drugs or soma or this or that herb can be created just by a process of thinking, of feeling. You don't have to take these external things inside the body. In *kriya yoga* the restless mind, the non-cooperative mind, the dull mind, the excited or disobedient mind can be brought into perfect quietude for a certain period of time, say fifteen to twenty minutes, under absolute control. It can't budge even a small point.

The innermost experience

Now, yoga talks about the body and suggests a system of practices, about the emotions and suggests a form of practice, about the psyche and suggests a few practices. But ultimately yoga believes that these forms of yoga are disciplining your body, mind and emotions so that you may be able to accomplish that innermost experience for which man is born. The ultimate destiny of man's incarnation, of his birth and of his appearance in this form, is to acquire the inner experience.

That inner experience is another dimension of experience. You are not supposed to be there all the twenty-four hours of the day. You don't have to have this experience thirty days in a month or three hundred and sixty-five days in a year – it's not possible! Even if you are able to have the glimpse of that inner experience for a fraction of a second in your eighty years of life, you are fortunate; you have fulfilled your spiritual obligations and can go and retire from this life completely.

This inner experience comes to you within a fraction of a second – like lightning! It comes and before you are able to understand it, it goes away, but at that time you are not this body. You are nameless, formless, beyond duality, with no knowledge of time, space or this empirical, gross, physical, mundane existence. You have nothing to do with your religion, whether Hindu, Muslim or Christian; nothing to do with nationality, Australian, Indian, Chinese, Philippino. You have nothing to do with anything at that time. You are dead to this world!

The Christian St John of the Cross wrote, "By God I swear I die every night." That is not physical death. You do not have to be afraid of this death. For one fraction of a second you experience light, the supreme lightning. I can't tell you what that experience is, even if I have had it. It flashes through the mind, through the area of your experience and after that, you have fulfilled the purpose of yoga.

39

Yoga Research and Meditation

Taree Ashram, Australia, February 24 1984

I first came to Australia in 1968 and since then I have been visiting very often, so I'm not new to this country. I know the people very well. The mere fact that we have twenty-six well established yoga ashrams and schools and a few thousand dedicated yoga teachers all over Australia proves that I understand what Australians need from yoga.

Not only in Australia, but throughout the world, wherever I have been, I have felt that people were waiting for yoga. Millions of people have heard about yoga, but the system of teaching and the practical methods of yoga were not known to them. They thought that it was an obscure practice which was intended for mystics, renunciates and hermits who wanted to abandon their relationship with day-to-day life.

When I came into the arena, I told the people that yoga was intended to bring about coordination, harmony, positive health and a deeper understanding of one's own self. At first they did not understand. They thought I was playing a publicity stunt in order to spread yoga. It was very difficult for me to convince most people, especially the scientists and doctors, intellectuals and deep-rooted religious people, that yoga had something to offer them.

Effects of yoga on coronary diseases

Then I decided to start experimenting on the effects of yoga on the body and mind. The first research I conducted in India with the financial assistance of the central government. The subject was the effects of yoga in coronary diseases. For five years this medical research was done. Many cardiologists in India participated and coordinated their results. We came to the conclusion that the practices of yoga have a very positive effect on those people who suffer from coronary problems. That was an astounding research.

Later, this research was referred to the medical fraternity in France and I was invited twice by the medical scientists in Paris to address the medical men on the effects of yoga on the cardiovascular system. A document of that discussion with the medical doctors in Paris has been published. The name of that document is *Yoga and Cardiovascular Management*. It is a very technical discussion between a cardiac specialist and myself, a specialist in yoga.

Psychic research

Since that time and even before that, hundreds of researches have been done in Japan, India, Poland, Russia, France and America. The scientists in various countries have adopted one of the many aspects of yoga and conducted their research on that. For example, in USSR, they did research on the effects of yoga on psychic abilities. Two volumes were published in the West, one is called *Psychic Discoveries Behind the Iron Curtain* and the other is called *Probability of the Impossible*.

These documents show that the effects of breathing, the effects of concentration of mind and many other practices of yoga were investigated with different subjects and it was found that by practising various forms of yoga, the psychic ability of the subject was greatly enhanced. This is the substance of both the documents related to the researches in the Soviet Union.

I can give you one example which will be of very great interest to you. Two subjects were asked to communicate with each other on the mental plane. At first, the distance was one metre. Then the concentration was deepened and as they were able to deepen their concentration, these two subjects were able to communicate with each other through the mind at a greater distance. Finally, they were able to communicate on mental frequencies at a distance of sixteen hundred miles.

After achieving this, one of the subjects was enclosed in a Faraday's cage, which was placed at the bottom of the ocean. It is impossible for electrical waves, radio waves, electromagnetic waves, sound waves or any other types of waves to penetrate, but the mental waves could still penetrate through the water and through the Faraday's cage. This is one example of the research they did in the Soviet Union.

The effect of sirshasana

In Poland another type of research was done by a team of scientists under the supervision of Prof Julian Alexandrowicz, Director of the Third Clinic of Medicine in Cracow. With the approval of the medical fraternity, which is necessary in socialist countries, they conducted research for six months on the effect of *sirshasana*, the headstand pose. In that inverted posture, the centre of gravity is shifted from the feet to the top of the head and all the organs are inverted – heart, lungs, abdominal organs, muscles, arteries, veins, as a matter of fact, the whole body is inverted. If you don't know this practice, please ask your teacher to tell you what sirshasana is and what it is good for. Is it just a gymnastic exercise or a type of acrobatics, or has it got any deeper effect on the entire system? This was worked on by the Polish scientists.

At the end of the research, they came to the conclusion that the practice of sirshasana was particularly beneficial for what you call habitual hypertension, those people who think to much, who worry over nothing. It is beneficial for those people who suffer from improper consumption of oxygen in the body, that is, the body is somehow not capable of conserving, using and absorbing oxygen. When you are not able to absorb oxygen, then you feel fatigued, lethargic, depressed and maybe you get angry too.

Anger, irritation, lethargy, procrastination, lack of motivation could all be due to improper absorption or the absence of absorption of oxygen. They found that during the practice of headstand pose, the body achieves total equilibrium. The acid secretions, the rate of respiration, the consumption of oxygen, the ventilation in the brain are all absolutely ideal.

Effects of yoga on the brain

In America, they have been doing hundreds of researches and many institutions are engaged in trying to understand how the practices of pranayama create a change in the processes of the physical body, like blood pressure, kidney reactions, cardiovascular reactions, the behaviour of the lungs and the response of the sympathetic and parasympathetic nervous systems. Then they went further than this. They found that during the practice of pranayama, in moments of concentration and meditation, and when you are practising *yoga nidra* or yogic relaxation, the electroencephalogram shows that the brainwaves are normalizing their frequencies.

There are four types of brainwaves, known as beta, alpha, delta and theta, which rise and fall according to pressure created in the brain. Sometimes there is pressure in the brain when you are thinking or worrying too much, then beta waves are intensified. When you are tranquil and composed and when your thoughts are moving with very soft speed, at that time the alpha waves attain intensity.

Now, when alpha waves are intensified in the brain, the pressure is at once released from the heart. If you are suffering from blood pressure, if your heart is palpitating too much, if you are feeling scared or nervous on account of anything, or if you are very angry, at that time if you can somehow develop the alpha rhythm in the brain, the behaviour of the heart will at once become normal. The blood pressure will come down. It may be 220, but within five minutes it can drop down to 160.

Of course, it may not stay like that, afterwards it may again go up to 220, but with continued practice of that particular yoga technique or system, you can develop the habit of normalizing your own blood pressure. We have seen that in many cases.

The American scientists have gone even further than this. They say that by the practice of mantra, the repetition of a certain sound for ten, fifteen, or twenty minutes, you can change the brainwaves within that period. They have tested this. When subjects practising a mantra like *Om*, were exposed to ECG, EEG and other machines which register what is happening in the body, they found at the end of the practice that the brainwaves had shifted from beta to alpha and that the heart, the lungs, the nervous system and the brain as a whole showed a very normal, healthy picture.

Inner peace
Beyond this, they have found something else of great importance. They found that during the practice of pranayama, the two portions of the autonomous nervous system, that is the sympathetic and parasympathetic nervous systems, are harmonized. When the sympathetic and parasympathetic nervous systems are in balance, you have a clear mind, good memory, good control over yourself. You have positive thinking and not only that, you have creative thinking, excellent thinking and peaceful thinking, which is more important – peace of mind.

This peace of mind is so important for us because prosperity, property, friendship, money, children, job, success can give us everything except inner peace. This inner peace cannot be bought in any of the supermarkets. Of course, sometimes you may find one packet labelled 'Inner peace', but that cannot be real inner peace because inner peace cannot be had from outside. Inner peace is an expression of what is already in you – your inner being, your centre, your nucleus, your point.

There is a reservoir of peace within us. It is not an idea or a philosophy I am talking about. There is some place, some point, some spot in us where there is a reservoir and we should be able to tap that reservoir. But how to tap it? Because we are not able to go there, we are not able to lay our hands on it. However, it is possible to tap that reservoir when we practise yoga and there is a balance in the sympathetic and parasympathetic nervous systems. Then the mind can function at a higher level.

The best form of yoga
In India, for thousand of years sannyasins and swamis, saints and sages, renunciates and householders have been doing the same kind of research, but the research was done within the laboratory of the human body and mind. In Russia, Poland, Japan, America and elsewhere, the researches were done with the help of other machines, but in India the research was done in this human machine.

When you practise asana, pranayama and meditation, you begin to feel that your personal experience is the result of that research. Therefore, I have come to tell you that yoga has many things to offer all of us. Whether you want spiritual light, psychic abilities, perfect physical health, a peaceful mind or inner happiness, the practices of yoga can give you all that, but I consider the best form of yoga is meditation. I won't say meditation alone is the definition of yoga.

There are various forms of yoga which everyone can practise according to their ability, need, situation and limitations, but meditation is one form of yoga where there are no limitations. Everyone cannot practise yoga. You may not be able to practise pranayama because you drink too much. You may not be able to do some form of yoga because you eat meat, fish and eggs, but there is one form of yoga which everybody can practise. If you can think, you can practise meditation, sure and certain!

Meditation is known as *dhyana yoga*. This is part of the ancient culture of India. Over two thousand five hundred years ago, Lord Buddha used to teach dhyana yoga to thousands of disciples and his teachings spread all over the world. His disciples carried the practical aspects of dhyana yoga all over the world because that was the central teaching of Buddha.

His disciples went to China and the science of dhyana yoga was established there. Now the Chinese call it chan, because that is how they pronounce it. Then it went to Japan where it was known as jhana and then shortened to Zen. Dhyana, chan, Zen, meditation, total attention, total awareness – it is all the same thing.

When you are able to transcend the world of the senses, when you are able to transcend the world of experiences for a short period, when you are able to transcend the memories of the past, the anticipations of the future and the anxieties of the present, when you are able to forget for the time being, your name and form, your placement, your position, your environment and, when you are able to become aware of something inside yourself – that is called meditation.

Difference between meditation and sleep

I'll explain it again. What happens when you sleep in the night after a hard day of work? You forget all about your name, don't you? You transcend name, form, environment, past, present, future. In sleep you are able to transcend all that, and in dhyana you also transcend, but in dhyana there is something else which is not there in sleep.

In sleep, you transcend everything for four, five, six, seven hours. Some brave people transcend for twelve hours. That is exactly the quality you need in meditation. That means you can meditate for twelve hours, not just ten minutes. If you understand how to do it, you can meditate for as long as you have been sleeping. Because meditation and sleep have something in common, but everything is not the same.

There is one important factor in dhyana which is not there in sleep. In dhyana, when you have transcended everything, when you have forgotten everything as you do in sleep, at that time you should become aware of one symbol within you. It can be anything – a blue lotus, the symbol *Om*, full moon, shining sun, candle flame, twinkling star. There are thousands and thousands of symbols out of which you have to pick up one for yourself.

If you are not aware of that symbol, that form, then your meditation is equal to sleep. If you are able to visualize that twinkling little star when you are deeply asleep, when you are in profound meditation, when the world is completely dead for you, when you are not even aware of your own existence, it is at that moment – even if you can think of that little shining star for only a fraction of a second, for a few seconds, for one or two minutes – that is called dhyana.

So, dhyana does not mean unconsciousness. Dhyana means innermost, total consciousness. *Dhyana* is a Sanskrit word which means attention, awareness, complete awareness; not divided awareness, not dissipated awareness, not split awareness, not broken awareness, not wavering awareness, but one-pointed awareness! When your mind is thinking, aware, seeing, conceiving, experiencing just one object, just one thing, just one item, and everything else is dead, this is called dhyana.

Dhyana yoga is a system within the yogic science containing not just a few hundred or a few thousand techniques, but a few hundred thousand techniques. If you were to sit here for ten days, I could go on telling you about those thousands of techniques. That means in meditation there is not just one door, one way, one method, one technique. There are as many techniques as there are people to practise them. Maybe there are three billion techniques for three billion people and out of all of them, you must find out one for yourself.

What should that practice accomplish for you? It should accomplish two things. One of them you already know – how to transcend. Every night you transcend, you don't have to be taught that. Nature has taught you how to transcend form, how to transcend name, how to forget your environment, yourself, your bed, your room, your people, your likes and dislikes, your friends and enemies, every time you go to sleep. Yoga doesn't have to teach you that. But there is one important thing which you will have to learn – how to maintain constant, unflickering, unbroken, undivided awareness. For this purpose you will have to practise two things every day, one is mantra and the other is concentration on the symbol.

Mantra meditation

How to practise the mantra is very simple. There is no trick, no technique, no special way. Just as a farmer sows the seed, he does not inspect whether the seed has fallen rightly or wrongly, whether the seed is upside down or not, or whether it is horizontal or perpendicular. He doesn't care and it's of no use; whichever way the seed falls, it will germinate.

The same principle applies in mantra. Whichever way you practise the mantra, it will produce results. Your mind is the soil, the mantra is like the seed and you practise it every day in the morning, or if it is not possible to practise in the morning, then you practise in the night. If it is not possible to practise either in the morning or at night, you can practise it anytime during the day – after lunch, before lunch, after dinner, before dinner. You can practise anywhere, but not when you are driving a car, of course.

Practise your mantra for a full ten minutes. Start with your eyes closed and your body still like a statue. Your mind can be focused at the eyebrow centre, at the lotus of the heart, at the navel, on the breath or wherever you like, but the point of focus should remain the same throughout the practice. After fixing your mind at one of those centres, then start thinking about the mantra mentally. Try to feel it, just like you feel the rhythm of the pulse. Just as you feel the palpitation of the heart, tuk, tuk, tuk, you can also feel the mantra there in exactly the same way.

The mantra has to be practised rhythmically, not very fast – *Om, Om, Om,* and then very slow – *Om . . . Om . . . Om . . .* Repetition of the mantra has to be a rhythmic movement and then the mental resonance of that mantra will vibrate throughout the body. If you don't believe me, try it and see for yourself. It's up to you.

The efficacy of mantra

When you think about hatred, when you think about love, when you think about passion, does it vibrate through and through your body or does it not? Even a sound can disturb you. If you are walking along the road and somebody shouts, "Hey, you dirty rascal," that's enough. It disturbs you so much that you are not able to sleep the whole night. If a thought can vibrate through and through your body, through and through your emotions, through and through your feelings, through and through your personality, then why not this mantra? This is the logic.

You can't say that mantra is useless. When you are practising mantra, it becomes a part of your mind, a part of your consciousness, a part of yourself. How can you say it is ineffective, how can you say it is futile? Anything that becomes a part of your mind, of your consciousness, is not futile. It is going to have some effect on you.

Sound is the potential form of energy and matter. You know about matter. In physics they talk about matter and energy, but I'm talking about matter, energy and sound. Sound is the first, not the second. Sound means *mantra*. In the Bible, at the very outset, they speak about the Word, "In the beginning was the Word and the Word was with God." I say sound, it's all the same.

Word means shabda in Sanskrit; in yoga they call it nada. The inner sound, the unheard sound is *nada*. The spoken sound is *shabda*. I am talking; this sound is called shabda because I am pronouncing the words. It has a low frequency. However, the source of this sound is an inner sound. That inner sound is the basis of creation, the basis of matter, the basis of energy.

Matter is not the first manifestation. This universe, this solar galaxy, this earth, was not created first. Creation is not first, creator is first. And who is the creator? Sound. In the Vedas it is written that *Om* is the first sound and from this sound all creation started.

I'm talking to you about the efficacy of the mantra in meditation. Therefore, all of you must understand that sound is the beginning of the yogic practices of meditation and if you practise that sound you are creating energy, you are creating vibration, you are creating frequency.

Consolidation of energies

Now, this sound creates frequencies and then what happens? Beautiful experiences begin to come. When these beautiful experiences, these deeper, mystical experiences begin to come, at that time you must concentrate in your mind on one form. That form is called the symbol. That form is known as *mandala*.

The word mandala is used in yoga very often. It is also used in modern psychology by Dr Carl Jung and by many others. This mandala is important for the consolidation or crystallization of the mental energies. Crystallization is a process in which first you hang a crystal inside a sugar liquid or a salt liquid. That crystal gradually collects all the salt or all the sugar. That is called crystallization.

When you concentrate on the mantra, the symbol or the mandala, it will crystallize all the energy forms, all the forms of nervous energy, emotional energy, physical energy, muscular energy, spiritual energy and whatever else is there in you. They will all be crystallized on that and that crystallization of various forms of energy is called spiritual experience.

40

Satsang

Perth Ashram, Australia, 10 March 1984

I am married with three children and although I've got a reasonably compatible relationship with my family, I have felt something lacking. So I have turned to the practice of yoga for a higher quality of experience in my life. My question is: am I to be denied that experience because I do not wish to give up my present life and become a swami? If I cannot have this experience without becoming a swami, then what is the point of practising yoga as a householder?

Human life is a stepping stone which ultimately leads one to higher consciousness. When we are born as human beings, we are definitely linked with the past and with the future. This chain or link is known as evolution.

Evolution, as we understand it scientifically, concerns progress, growth, change, transformation and metamorphosis. The outcome of that evolution is the finest experience – the experience of one's nucleus, *bindu*, the centre. What we have studied in modern science is the theory of natural evolution, how life evolves, the body changes, cells multiply. This is what we study about the evolution of matter in this universe, in this creation and more particularly on this earth.

According to this scientific theory of evolution, everything in nature is part of that progress. All beings, whether mineral, vegetable, animal or human, are interconnected. They are not different from each other. They all contain the possibility of evolution within them. According to that possibility, we have evolved to the stage of human beings today. In this long chain of evolution of matter, what we find is that every stage of manifestation is a stepping stone to a higher existence, but science does not talk about the evolution of mind.

When Charles Darwin wrote about his theory of natural evolution, the whole West was shaken; they were not prepared to accept it. Western thinking, philosophy and religion are so designed that there is practically no scope for the theory of evolution. This is a very important point and a very dangerous point too. In the theory of natural evolution there is no creator – and where there is a creator there is no evolution. Therefore, the theory of natural evolution was a bombshell for the idea of an absolute creator, an absolute controller, which they call God.

God is everything in the philosophical, mystical, theological and religious currents, particularly in the West. He creates the earth, the water, the sun, the moon and he does all things. He does the work of everybody. He does not need anyone. He's absolute, total and almighty. However, after Charles Darwin had lived in Ecuador for some time and had begun to ponder over this philosophy, he came to realize that in the whole spectrum of life, in the total manifestation of life, all forms exist in relationship to one another.

For example, you have a cotton plant. You remove the cotton and make a thread. You take the thread and make a piece of cloth. You take the cloth and make a shirt. The cotton has changed form many times since it was on the plant, but it is not separate from the shirt. Therefore, your shirt can definitely be linked with the cotton from which it was made. In the same way, every stage in this creation is a stepping stone to the next.

This concerns physical evolution, but what about mental and spiritual evolution, which the scientists, thinkers and psychologists throughout the world are still quiet about? In India they have spoken about this, not just in the recent past, but perhaps much before the world knew anything about civilization. They thought about the evolution of the mind, body and consciousness as one whole.

In this particular sense they classified the whole span of human life into four stages. They were regarded as the four broad classifications of human consciousness, mind, emotions, feelings, ambitions, passions and all that the mind is. They also made it very clear that this particular classification of the whole span of life into four divisions was ultimately intended to experience the inner light. That was the purpose.

For thousands of years, or since man began to think, Indian philosophers have made one thing very clear. That is, the fundamental and basic philosophy, the purpose of the human incarnation is to evolve to higher experience. This is the destiny of every being. Therefore, when the lifespan was classified into four divisions, it was done in such a way that the process of evolution could go on harmoniously and at optimum speed.

Now, these four classifications were known as *ashramas*. The first was *brahmacharya ashrama*, the life of celibacy before marriage, which included education. Second was *grihastha ashrama*, what you call householder life. Third was *vanaprastha ashrama*, which was known as the life of a recluse or hermit, but I call it *karma sannyasa*. Fourth was *sannyasa*, the life of a swami or renunciate. These were the four broad divisions or classifications of the whole lifespan intended to facilitate the process of higher experience while, at the same time, going through the experience of the empirical, objective and lower life.

According to this classification, the life of a *brahmachari* or a student was planned very well. Today, unfortunately, it is not because the purpose of education in our present structure is not to make us free from ignorance; it is job-oriented education. The education we receive is not real education. It is injection. Education literally means the expression of the knowledge which is already in you. Education is not injecting the knowledge or information from outside; but it is creating an atmosphere in which you will be able to express the knowledge which is already in you.

In the life of a brahmachari, the education must be designed in such a way that it can serve both purposes. The first purpose is to enlighten the intellect, to purify the emotions and to improve the quality of social awareness, of inter-relational awareness. The second purpose is to awaken and express the inner knowledge. That is called vidya. *Vidya* means knowledge. Therefore, in India, education is known as vidya.

After completing his education the person was married. The purpose of marriage was also specified. Marriage was the bringing together of two souls to participate in this long and strenuous ritual of life called evolution. Then the householder had to go through all the experiences of life, whatever they may be, marital, family, economic and so forth. That is an entirely different picture to what we see happening today. Now, householders feel that spiritual enlightenment cannot be attained unless they do away with their household life.

This is particularly so in the Western countries because basically there is some sort of guilt or inferiority complex, which has been deeply ingrained in the subconscious mind of the entire community. Society demands that people have family and children and yet deep down inside they feel guilty about it. When they become serious, when they think earnestly, honestly and truthfully about inner experience, then they develop some sort of complex in themselves about their own status in life, or the life of a householder.

As a householder they feel that everything they do is detrimental to their progress in spiritual life. This is the first thing which has to be corrected. If a householder is to have the deeper, greater, inner experience, first of all he will have to correct the definition, the impression and the opinion about his own status in life. The life of a householder is a stepping stone. It is not detrimental, it is not a deviation, it is not a path which will lead you away from or against or opposite to the real experience.

However, just to be a householder is not enough. There is a very important factor which has to be considered and experienced in the life of a householder, and what is that? Here I would like to introduce to you the teaching of *Bhagavad Gita*. It is not a religious book. It is in the form of a dialogue between Sri Krishna, the guru, and Arjuna, the disciple. The theme of the dialogue is whether through action, through involvement, through the process of participation in one's day-to-day life, relationships, persons and events, one can realize the ultimate experience, and if so, then why does one not realize it?

Sri Krishna says there are two ways of participating in life. One, you participate in life as a part of it. The other way is you participate as an actor. So there are two theories very clearly laid down. One is the theory of action in inaction; the other is the theory of inaction in action. Even while you are acting, you can still be indifferent. You can still be out of it. You can still remain untainted by the blocks of karma and at the same time, even if you are not involved in karma, even if you are not involved in life, still you can remain affected.

Therefore, a householder must step out of the deep neurosis he is undergoing. Everything he is experiencing, everything he is understanding, everything he is living with does become a part of his consciousness, and so it becomes the cause of neurosis and psychosis. As long as one is suffering from neurosis and psychosis, one cannot have true knowledge.

What is this neurosis and psychosis? We are so attached to each and every thing which goes through our life, each and every experience, each and every act, each and every person. Each and every feeling goes so deep into our consciousness that we are not able to get out of it. This is precisely the reason for all the mental problems in the Western countries, which psychoanalysis and psychotherapy cannot and has not been able to solve, because the crux of the problem is man's deeper consciousness.

Each and every experience which you go through in your life every day does not merely pass through your eyes, ears, mind, intellect. Each and every experience which you have been undergoing for the last twenty, thirty, forty, fifty and sixty years has become part of your consciousness, a part of your personality. Those experiences are absolutely in you, not only from the time you began to think, but from the time when you were conceived by your mother.

Everything which you were receiving from her during the nine months in the womb and later when you grew up, from the outside environment, each and every experience is absolutely, immutably, immortally registered in your consciousness as in a tape recorder. Those experiences are not only in thousands, millions or billions; they are trillions! These experiences make up the whole structure of your consciousness, of your thinking, and that structure is not capable of experiencing the ultimate experience.

That is the problem and many spiritual seekers feel it. They don't know how to get out of this dimension of consciousness, at least for the time being, and go to another dimension for some time, say ten minutes or so. They don't know how to jump out of this state into another and then come back again. When they try to jump, some of them are very sincere and bold, but others are afraid of losing their identity, this 'I'. There is so much attachment to this I, and finally we realize that this I is a mythological I and not the real I.

When you get up in the morning, the I is there. In the night when you dream, the I is there. This I has been created by the rotation or the movement of thousands and thousands and thousands of experiences. I am, I am, I am – the stress is always on I. When you sit for meditation, the I is there. When you do your worship, the I is there. Even when you go to church and pray, the I is there. You are not there.

This I, which is called *ahamkara* in yogic terminology, is the root cause of all the problems in the psychological, psychic and mental fields. Therefore, the most important thing for a householder is to create a true philosophy within oneself, a true approach, a true understanding of oneself in relation to all mankind.

There is a story about a swami who had a very beautiful cow. Next to his kutir there lived a Muslim and he had a beautiful goat. The swami and the Muslim were very good friends. One evening the swami heard the Muslim gentleman crying and crying the whole night. So finally he went to his hut and asked, "My good friend, why are you crying and what has happened to you?" The Muslim said, "My goat is dead and I'm very sorry about it because she was my true friend." The swami said, "Yes, the goat was a true friend but, after all, relationships are not self-created, they are man-made, psychological, emotional and an outcome of man's narcissistic complex." In this way he was able to give some consolation to his friend, who thereafter recovered psychologically and emotionally.

It so happened that after a year or so, the cow of the swami also died and the swami did not come out for many days. Then the Muslim gentleman went to him and asked, "What has happened to you?" The swami replied, "My cow is dead and I'm very sorry about it." The Muslim said, "But when my goat died, you said it was nothing but an outcome of the manifestation of man's narcissistic complex, the soul is immortal and so on." The swami replied, "Yes, that was right for you, but it is not right for me." The Muslim asked, "How is that?" The swami said, "Because the goat belonged to you and the cow belonged to me."

This is a very peculiar way of dealing with the total problems of the human mind and personality. The goat or the cow – nothing belongs to you, but you have created a sort of relationship with the objects, with the events, with the tragedies and comedies. You have created a kind of relationship because it gives you some sort of recognition.

Householders can realize the ultimate experience, but they will have to step out – not of participation, not of manifestation – they will have to step out of their own little nest which they have created for themselves within their own selves. This process of stepping out can take place by imposing upon oneself a sort of idea, which they call rishi.

In India there is an ancient tradition of rishis. *Rishi* means 'seer', the seer of the self, the seer of reality, the seer of inner experience. Such a person is known as a rishi. This rishi is not a celibate, a brahmachari, a recluse, or a renunciate. No. He has a family, children, responsibilities, commitments, a large society, political involvement. So the lifestyle of a rishi has to be related to all aspects of life. As a householder, one can definitely become a rishi. And what is this path? It is called *karma sannyasa*. I have initiated thousands of householders into karma sannyasa over the last few years. These householders are committed to the practice of yoga techniques, spiritual techniques, to spiritual enlightenment.

They do not have to change their vocation; they do not have to change anything else in their life because external change does not mean anything, but at the same time I have made them aware of something which they do not experience in life. I have made them aware of the insufficiency of their philosophical outlook on life. These householders are now treading upon the spiritual path in thousands throughout the world. The relationship which they have with me reminds them every now and then that they have to keep walking on this unknown, great, infinite spiritual path, which is within us all.

There is a great controversy over the practice and benefits of mantra. Can you explain the meaning, source and relevance of mantra in the life of an aspirant who is a householder?

The practice of mantra is very powerful and it is the most scientific of all the practices. For some time people did think that mantra was related to certain religious deities, but now it has been understood that mantra relates to the sound principle. This sound principle is again to be understood to be the form of sound energy.

Sound is like nuclear energy, radioactive energy and all other forms of energy. Sound is the principal form of energy. If it can be exploded, it can work on the external plane too. Sound waves have their own frequencies and they can become a very powerful source of transmission of energy, but I'm not talking about the external sound; I am talking about the inner sound.

Inner sound is mantra. What is the meaning of mantra? In many books, mantra is translated as 'the holy syllable', but this is not correct. *Mantra* is a Sanskrit word, and etymologically it means 'by the repetition of which the mind becomes free from the external experiences'. This is the literal meaning of mantra.

So the mantra is a tool which you can utilize for making the mind free from the external experiences which keep on disturbing you during the moments of your silent meditation. Before you go into yourself, before you experience your inner self, the total silence, the totality, it is important that the mind must remain undisturbed. The mind is disturbed all the time now by the external experiences which are brought through the medium of the senses.

The five senses or *indriyas* continually bring impulses, experiences, to the mind and they disturb the mind. It has been seen in scientific observations that when you are meditating in a quiet room, say on a form, then the machine shows one kind of brainwaves. As soon as you make a sound in the room, tap, tap, tap, the sound is heard through the ears and transported to the brain. Then the electrical impulses which are being shown on the screen show the change.

Each and every experience through the ears, eyes, nose, tongue, skin, passes to the brain and there it alters or disturbs the quality of one-pointedness. This disturbance has to stop, that is the first thing. If you do not stop it, then meditation cannot be one-pointed. No matter how deep you go, the sounds from outside will keep on disturbing you because the mind is connected with the senses. You will have to cut off the telephone line if you do not want the telephone to ring.

Now, how to isolate the mind? How to isolate the brain? Or how to separate the senses? These senses are so keen that sometimes even if the sympathetic and parasympathetic nervous systems are at rest, they can receive an experience without any physical medium. Without any physical vehicle they receive the message.

You can train the mind to function, to experience, to see, to think, without having any relationship with the senses. That is, the mind becomes completely free from the sense relationships, from the objective relationships, from the experiences of the external world. After that, even if there is a big sound, even if there is a big transmission taking place in the room, it will not get into the brain. It will not get into the mind, because now the mind has not only been isolated, it has been fortified.

The consciousness should be completely insulated. This is very important. Many people do not understand it and if you study the yoga philosophy in depth, if you study the teaching of Buddha in depth, then you will come across one important element. Just by closing the mind, by trying to concentrate, you do not experience the inner thing. No. Because the moment the mind is concentrated, it becomes very sharp.

As and when the concentration takes place and your mind begins to focus itself, and for the time being you think you have transcended the external experiences and you are one hundred percent one-pointed, your mind becomes so sensitive that it begins to experience the external things independently. It does not need eyes, it does not need skin. It begins to see things, to feel things, in the room, outside the room, in the toilet, behind the walls.

Now, what are you going to do? That is the problem which people do not even understand. At this time, many people develop the ability called ESP (extrasensory perception). This is direct perception without the help of the senses. It is called direct knowledge, psychic knowledge or extrasensorial cognition. They begin to use it for some time, but it does not last because again the mind is disturbed.

The law is that when the mind is concentrated, it becomes sensitive. When is becomes sensitive, it can cognize without any external agency, but when it is able to cognize without any external agency, again it is disturbed. Once it is disturbed, the independent cognition is finished. Therefore, the Buddhist, yogic and tantric philosophies talk about one thing; it is not only concentration which is important, but total insulation of the mind.

When your mind becomes one-pointed and sensitive, at that time it should not be able to cognize the external object through its own efficiency. That is one problem they have tried to solve. For that purpose they say practise mantra, because when you practise mantra, then gradually you are giving a training to the mind.

Then there is a second problem, which occurs when the mind becomes concentrated and it is able to have independent cognition, direct cognition, extrasensorial cognition. Supposing you are able to control that somehow, then another problem comes up. The mind begins to dive deep into its past experiences, which are stored in millions and billions and trillions. This particular tendency of the mind to dive deep into its own subjective experiences makes the mind experience what we call mystical experiences.

These mystical experiences which people have are nothing but the cognition of the mind of its content of past experiences. In modern terminology it is called realization of archetypes. These archetypes are the seed forms of your past experiences from the womb, from childhood, and as an adult. All these experiences are reduced into seed forms, symbolic forms. They are symbols. If you experience happiness or tragedy, this entire process of experience is reduced to one microscopic symbol in you.

It remains there – and during concentration this little seed, this little archetype is blown up, it becomes magnified. This magnification is called mystical experience, which is what many people are seeking. These mystical experiences lure them for months and months together and they are very happy. They see heaven and earth, sun and moon, this and that. They talk in rhetorical language, they write poems – and we are very impressed by that.

However, they are not able to have the experience which we have been talking about for thousands of years – the inner experience, which is far beyond mystical experiences. I'm not trying to underrate the value of mystical experiences, please don't misunderstand me. I'm only trying to point out the difference between mystical experiences and *the* experience, because everybody must go through the stage of mystical experiences. But how to do it?

When you are practising your mantra, whichever it is, this sound attains a very high frequency in the mind. Just as you put a satellite onto a rocket, which takes off at a speed of thirty thousand miles per hour and then it is detached, in the same way, we have the relationship between mind and mantra. First we use the mind and we place the mantra in it. Then we go on practising the mantra and gradually, in the course of time, the mind assumes greater frequency. When the mind attains greater frequency, at that time, the experiences come out.

First of all you begin to think of all the things around you. Gradually you transcend them and then you have experiences – mystical experiences. First they are of a very ordinary quality. Later they are of greater quality, then they are of a beautiful quality, they are of absolute quality. You can have all kinds of mystical experiences, not only beautiful experiences. You can have frightening experiences. You can experience death and birth. You can experience beautiful flowers.

All the experiences that you have by the practice of mantra are a process of re-expression. I will explain what re-expression means. When you eat food and then eliminate it, this is re-expression. You eat food and then re-express it. In the same way, you experience some object through your senses, you take it in, but how do you pass it out? This is called psychic elimination and this re-expression is so important for working out the karma. You can't work out the karma unless the mind is made free from the totality of experiences.

Now, the mantra is related to one's own personality. Everybody has his own mantra; the same mantra does not work on all. According to the science of mantra, sounds are divided first of all into five *tattwas* or elements: ether, *akasha*; air, *vayu*; fire, *agni*; water, *apas*; and earth, *prithvi*. These are the five primordial elements and when they permute and combine with each other, creation takes place. These five elements are again related to sound. Sound has colour according to the quality of the tattwa or element. Each and every sound has a colour and this colour represents its nature, its frequency and its symbology.

Sound has form and sound is formless also. I hope you understand what I mean when I say that sound has form. Supposing I produce the sound ka. Ka is written k-a, but that is not the form I am talking about. Every sound has its own form and that form is called *yantra*. At the same time, there is a form associated with the mantra, which is called *devata*. This form is the pictorial representation of the mantra; it is also known as *mandala*.

Form and sound are inseparable. By concentrating on the form, you are concentrating on the sound or by concentrating on the sound, you are concentrating on the form. It is much easier to conceive a sound, to understand a sound, to handle the concept of the sound through the mind. It is very difficult to conceive the form of a sound. When you are practising mantra, the form of the sound gradually evolves from that.

A few years ago, when I was in France, I saw a book by a French artist. It was a very old book printed in the nineteenth century. The author of that book talked about the shape of the sounds and it interested me very much because this is my subject. So I went on reading the book. I was simply amazed! He had a wonderful concept and he made line drawings of the forms of the sounds. One of the things that struck me was that in most of the sounds he had drawn the lotus, not the rose – lotus and snake. In kundalini yoga the snake represents *kundalini*, the serpent power and the lotus represents the *chakras* or psychic centres. These are the formations of the sound movement, the sound principle or the sound energy.

Therefore, the mantra should not be misunderstood as a holy word or as a religious practice. We will have to understand the force of sound in a very scientific sense. There was a great scientist, Itzak Bentov, who wrote a beautiful book called *Stalking the Wild Pendulum*. That book concerns these matters which we are discussing – mantra, kundalini, shakti, the power of the mind and concentration. He writes as a swami, not as a materialist.

In one of his essays he talks about the energy of sound. He says that when you produce a sound, you have already postulated a form for it, that is the problem. At once it brought to my mind one of my illiterate disciples in an Indian village. I gave him the mantra *Om Namah Shivaya*. After a few months he came to me and narrated his experiences. I gave the same mantra to someone else as well, but the other man was literate. For him the form of the mantra was the letters which he could understand and write in Sanskrit or Devanagari.

The literate man had a preconceived form of knowledge about the form of the sound in his mind. He couldn't get out of it, but the illiterate man had no barriers which he had created for himself. For him, the sound was always unmanifest, so when he started practising *Om Namah Shivaya*, he began from the unmanifest level. Whereas when the other man started practising, he began right from the earth level and he could not rise above it. The gravity of that prepostulated hypothesis of contact of the sound was so deeply ingrained in him that he could not get out of it.

O-m is *Om* for us. Can you catch the sound of *Om Namah Shivaya*, as it is? The illiterate disciple could do it. This is what the scientist was writing about in his book. He said the sound in its primordial form, in its true form is one form of sound. The sound which you hear through the ears is another form of sound. The sound which you think in your mind is yet another form of sound.

Therefore, according to the science of mantra, there are four levels of sound, which are: audible, murmuring, whispering and mental sound. When I am talking to you, this is one level of sound, but I can say the same thing to you in your meditation. You can hear exactly the same thing, but that is another level of sound, another dimension of sound. That dimension of sound relates to the inner sound and to the inner dimension of your mind as well.

If your mind has not changed the dimension, then the experience also cannot change. Once upon a time, many years ago, I heard a beautiful song. I was lying down in a room with my eyes closed. I began to hear every instrument, all the raga and ragini and alapa. It was beautiful. I don't know how long it went on, but all that was happening within me. That is one dimension of sound.

Therefore, in my opinion, the mantra sadhana, the mantra philosophy is unprecedented. It is one of the most important and most powerful tools for a richer and higher spiritual experience.

41

Karma Sannyasa Initiation

Auckland Country Ashram, New Zealand, 17 March 1984

Today you are being initiated into karma sannyasa. It is a very important initiation. Karma sannyasa is much more difficult than full sannyasa, because you have to maintain a very careful balance between the external life and the inner inspiration without rejecting anything. Therefore, the balance that you have to maintain between the external life and the inner life becomes a very important philosophy for you.

For most people, the difficulties, the problems in life are either punishments of nature or the fruits of one's bad karma. For a karma sannyasin, every experience in life is a stepping stone; it is complementary and not contradictory. This point and this philosophy have to become very clear for a karma sannyasin, then only whatever you are, whatever you do or whatever you experience in life will help you to have inner experience.

If you think that this external life is harmful, that it is not good and it is anti-spiritual, then you will create a conflict between the inner and outer life. As a karma sannyasin, you are trying to unite both the forms of life. This is a very important aspect of karma sannyasa. When you are trying to unite or to fuse the external things of your day-to-day life, your job, your family, your children, with the inner experience, then you will have to create a very definite and clear-cut relationship between the two.

How is your external life to which you are committed every day? Is it related to an inner experience? Is it related to spiritual life, and how is it related? Now, in this particular respect you must remember that any experience which you have in your day-to-day life: quarrels, unhappiness, success, jubilation, joy, anger, frustration or even physical sickness, is leading you to inner experience; it is not disturbing your inner experience.

However, most of us do not think like that and we are angry, we are sorry, we repent and we don't want to have it any more. When we are unhappy and frustrated, we don't want that experience. That is the psychology of most people, but in karma sannyasa any experience which nature has provided for you is helpful for the spiritual experience and for the growth of spiritual life.

Three things are very important for a karma sannyasin. One is his daily practice, which he must decide for himself and do every day. The second is to involve himself in the spirit of karma yoga. The spirit of karma yoga is the fulfilment of all obligations without attachment. When you are unaffected by what happens in your daily life, that is called *karma yoga*. The third thing is relationship with guru, not on the physical plane, mental plane, intellectual plane or emotional plane, but on the spiritual plane. To experience the relationship between guru and disciple on the spiritual plane, it will become necessary for you to go a bit deeper into the mind. When you go deeper into the mind, then you begin to realize the spiritual relationship. When you are not deep in the mind, when you are outside, then you realize the physical relationship, emotional relationship or intellectual relationship.

However, there is something called the spiritual relationship, which I will not be able to explain to you now, but which you will experience only when you have been able to go a bit deeper into your mind. As you dive deeper into the mind there comes the awareness of a link between guru and disciple. So, karma yoga, your spiritual sadhana and your relationship with guru are the three most important factors in the life of a karma sannyasin.

There are quite a few books you should read on karma sannyasa. One book published by me entitled *Karma Sannyasa* contains the philosophy, doctrine and practices of karma sannyasa. It will give you a very clear idea and answer many questions on the subject.

The second is a very important old and classical text known as the *Bhagavad Gita*. It is a small book in which you can read about the difficulties which a karma sannyasin encounters in day-to-day life and how he has to deal with his problems, with his inner life and with various aspects of his life. You should read it from time to time. That will give you a philosophical approach and understanding of karma sannyasa.

42

Methods for Awakening Higher Consciousness

Auckland Country Ashram, New Zealand, 18 March 1984

The science of tantra is very ancient. It is not, and it has never been, confined to any one culture or period of history. Even when man lived in a primitive state, tantra was known from time to time in every society. Especially in the olden days, people living in communities or villages found someone having special abilities like healing, reading thoughts, controlling the weather or predicting coming events.

Such people were found in every community, in every time and period in history. These people did not practise any yoga. They somehow jumped over the fence, or maybe the generative combination in them meant they were born with a particular ability unrelated to the logical combination of mind, object and senses.

The source of man's psychic abilities

Our experiences in day-to-day life depend upon coordination between the mind, the senses and the object. If this coordination is not there, then there is no experience, but in those cases which I am referring to, knowledge and experience did take place without any coordination between object, mind and senses.

In the communities of primitive ages, these people were known as psychics, witches, hermits or ascetics. They were given various names according to the quality of the culture, and at the same time their ability was attributed to different causes. Some people said a spirit had entered them and so the spirit was doing it. Others said that those abilities had developed due to drugs. Still others said that they had been blessed by God, some divinity, angel or deva and so he was doing this. Various explanations were given for these psychic abilities.

In India, they tried to find the exact source of man's psychic abilities, whether it was due to an external spirit, devil or demon or if it was due to a spontaneous evolution in the system – maybe psychological, maybe genetic. In this research, this experimentation, this discovery, they came to realize that all that was happening in these people was on account of expansion of mind, expansion of consciousness, expansion of awareness.

This expansion of awareness, which took place in these people spontaneously, by an accidental genetic combination, created what we call a fresh release of energy. Here you come to the secret. When you are able to expand the mind, you release energy. Releasing energy means liberating energy, emancipating energy. What is this liberation, what is this emancipation and what is this word freedom?

The process of fission and fusion
Let me explain this in the tantric sense. When you churn milk, the butter is released; butter is freed or liberated. In the same way, when you separate the elements in matter, say uranium, then the energy is released – nuclear energy. In all matter there is a certain amount of energy. According to the tantric science, matter is a gross form of energy. The matter does not contain energy, matter is a gross form of energy and, therefore, matter is nothing but energy. As such, matter can be completely converted into energy and energy can be converted into matter totally.

Matter and energy are not two separate things. Matter in one state, when converted, equals energy. However, when we are talking about a process of conversion, then we come to the conclusion that the energy has to become free from matter and to release the energy, a certain process has to be initiated. In nuclear science there are two processes. One is called fission and the other is called fusion. These two processes are utilized in the nuclear release.

The same fission and fusion process is also used in releasing, in liberating one's personal energy. When we say fission we mean that you will have to separate the idea and experience from the experiencer. He is called the seer, the one who sees, experiencer who experiences, witness who witnesses. What does he see? He sees an object. What does he think? He thinks a thought. What does he witness? He witnesses an event.

There is an experiencer in us. And that experiencer is experiencing, is witnessing, is seeing each and every process, but these two things, the experiencer and the experience, are both so mixed with each other, like tea and sugar, so interspersed and entangled with each other, that we philosophers, logicians, intellectuals know them as two, but we can't see them as two. We can't separate the seer and the seen. This separation is called fission. You have to separate both seer and seen, and when you are separating the seer from the object, the witness from the event, at that time what happens is called yoga – separation.

Now, in the Samkhya system, which is the basic philosophy behind yoga and tantra, they don't say seer and seen, witness and event. They use the terms purusha and prakriti. The consciousness is called purusha and the experiences or the events are called prakriti.

It is very difficult to translate these two terms exactly. *Prakriti* means nature, not just in the relative sense, but in the total sense. It refers to all creation, everything that is in existence. *Purusha* is the consciousness, the seer of time, the seer of space, the seer of all events, the seer of past, present and future, the seer of everything.

You are that, but you cannot experience yourself in the pure purusha state because whenever you try to experience yourself, you are experiencing yourself in time and space. There is no pure awareness of the self, of the consciousness, and this has to be established, accomplished first. That is called fusion. What is fusion?

In fusion, when you are concentrating on a particular point, object, idea or substance, at that time the whole of your mental consciousness must fuse with that object, so that for the time being you lose self-awareness – 'I am that'. These two processes have to be established. In one you become aware of yourself and also of the experiences. That is called fission – separation. In the other, you lose self-consciousness and merge with the experience. That process is called fusion. This is tantra.

The beginning of psychic research
In tantra they say very clearly that the mind is the tool of awareness and knowledge in every sphere. This mind can function without limitation, but in order to make it function beyond limitation you will have to train it. The mind is limited. If an object is here, you can see it; if an object is not here, you can't see it. If music is played here, you can hear it; if music is not played here, you can't hear it. That is the limited scope of the mind.

Now, what is expansion of mind? When the mind can experience something without the aid of an object, without the aid of the senses, then it is called expansion of mind. If you sit down quietly somewhere and spontaneously begin to listen within yourself to a theme of music or a song, or you begin to see within yourself something beautiful or horrible, something pleasant or unpleasant, that is called expansion of mind, because your mind is able to perceive without any external basis.

At this time a certain amount of energy is released and the release of this energy is called awakening. It is in this context that tantra has established the processes of yoga: hatha yoga, kriya yoga, mantra yoga. These are all branches of tantra; they are not different from tantra. Yoga is the practical side of tantra.

In this tantric system innumerable experiments have been conducted for thousands of years. Of course, many of these experiments are unsuitable today, although the scholars who write the books on tantra never fail to mention all those frightening practices and then the people try to utilize them. These practices are unsuitable, because in each and every age the techniques of yoga and tantra have to be adapted to the particular culture and taught in the framework of that culture. That is the way the practices have to be done.

In the olden days, sometimes people tried to awaken their consciousness through the drinking of soma, but later it was stopped because they found that it was not adequate for perennial spiritual experience. They also realized that after the drinking of soma, if the expansion of mind did take place and energy was released, they were not able to handle that experience. Later on, many other drugs were tried in the course of history. They tried cannabis indica and hashish, which the West is trying now, and finally they rejected it.

Early tribes used many things in their quest for consciousness expansion. Here in the museum you have ancient tribal symbols called tikis. Now the origin of these symbols has been forgotten, but they were once intended to influence the psychic framework, the psychic dimension of the mind. That is why they used to keep these things for ceremonials and dance around them and sing and sing. Thereby, the practice was obviously able to trigger off the higher consciousness.

Many ancient tribes all over the world in Africa, South America, India, Persia, the Middle East, Scandinavia, Slavonic countries, Japan and China had symbols of psychic culture. These symbols were considered to be idols or to represent some form of divinity, and they were intended to stimulate, to blow, to detonate, to explode that energy within us.

They also tried the method which releases energy through sexual interaction. In tantra, this is called the *pancha makara*, which involves the use of the five *tattwas* or elements: wine, woman, flesh, fish and grain. Throughout the world, even today, scholars who write about tantra never fail to mention this practice, not because it is relevant today, but in order to expose this aspect of tantra.

People did try that aspect of tantra as well, but they found that all these practices had their own limitations, either cultural, moral, religious or even spiritual. If you keep taking hashish or cannabis indica for many, many years, your memory will definitely be shattered along with your lungs. If you try to practise this pancha makara ceremony, you are going to create moral anarchy. There will be problems everywhere throughout the country.

In addition to these practices, Sage Patanjali's *Yoga Sutras* gave five traditional ways of awakening. If you want to perfect your consciousness, to raise your energies and to improve the quality of your awareness, then these five ways are suggested:
1. birth
2. mantra
3. austerity
4. herbs
5. concentration.

Awakening by birth

Out of these five methods the first, which is by birth, is impossible for us in this lifetime. We have missed the bus, but you can utilize the opportunity of being householders to produce awakened offspring, who have a psychic genetic constitution. By your deep thought, by your willpower, by the quality of your psychic imagination, by the power of the vibrating transmissions of the mind, by controlling the passions, it is possible that you can create a genetic combination in the womb of a woman, which will produce a psychic person.

In recent years there has been a lot of talk about genetic engineering. This subject which the scientists have been talking about was also in the minds of the yogis. In the *Bhagavad Gita* it is clearly written that those who have not completed the practices of yoga, those who have not attained the destined result of yoga, those who have not achieved the highest point of yoga in this life are reborn in favourable circumstances so that they can continue the practice of yoga.

Either they are born into the family of a yogi who has higher consciousness and then they resume the practice of yoga from the point where they left off in their previous life. Or they are born into a devoted, clean and prosperous family, where they can continue their raja yoga as a householder. If they are born in the family of a yogi, that means their consciousness is very high. They can just leave family life and practise yoga; they don't have to remain in the family.

Now, this means the tantric scientists were very aware of the possibility of willing the quality of children you want to bear. Your progeny should not just be an expression of your passion. If you produce lemon trees, peach trees, mango trees or avocado trees, is it only for show? No. You are trying to produce the best quality of fruit, which will give the most vitamins and nutrition. If you can try to produce a fruit of higher quality, more natural and more nutritious, then why not your children?

However, most of us do not think about the quality of children we are producing. We only want to produce children whom we can love, as if they are the object of our narcissism. A yogi is very clear in this respect. Either he does not produce any progeny or he produces them only with an absolute combination, so that the child is born with developed and evolved psychic and spiritual abilities.

That method is called awakening by birth and there are many more points about it which you will understand later. This method of awakening is very important for the evolution of the human race, because in order to change the world you don't need to have religions or governments – you must have a higher calibre of people. Good laws, good police and good religion do not make a better humanity. A higher quality of mind and consciousness has to be produced.

By mantra

The second method of awakening is by mantra. Even though you may not have any psychic experience, even though the mantra may not be able to give you concentration, even though you may not like the mantra, this mantra which you practise every day with regularity, ultimately causes the energy to awaken, to explode. This is an important way because it can be utilized by all, no matter what their situation or status in life.

By tapasya

The third way of awakening is by *tapasya* or disciplined austerity. Tapasya means a process of purification by burning or destroying the undesirable elements of your personality. We know that there are undesirable elements in our personality. Through the disciplined practice of tapasya, by the gradual pursuance of tapasya, it is possible that these negative elements of our personality can be burned and destroyed. Then what will happen?

When the impurities of the mind are destroyed, the mind becomes healthy. When the impurities of the body are burned out, the body becomes healthy. When the impurities of the emotions are burned out, the emotions become healthy. In order to have a healthy body, a healthy mind and healthy emotions, what we need to do is burn the undesirable elements. If this room is shabby, then you want to clean it, fix the furniture and then get the electrical wiring fixed up; that is the principle of tapasya.

Tapasya, austerity or penance is practised in many ways. There is physical austerity and mental austerity. There is austerity related to speech. There is sattwic austerity, rajasic austerity and tamasic austerity. In tamasic austerity, you try to impose pain on the body. The mind and the body both have to undergo a lot of pain. In rajasic austerity, you do one day fasting and two days feasting. Go to India, no smoking, no drinking – nothing! Come home and compensate. That is called rajasic austerity.

Sattwic austerity is very serene, very disciplined. You proceed according to the ability of the body, mind and emotions, and that is related not only to fasting, not only to feasting, not only to one thing or the other. There are many kinds of austerity and you can read about them in the *Bhagavad Gita*.

By herbs
The fourth method of awakening is by herbs. These herbs are not known by anyone, I can tell you frankly. Gurus, especially the tantrics, have always been very careful about revealing them. These herbs are neither hashish nor peyote nor soma. They are the herbs which do create stability of mind and inner awareness, and are only to be taken under the guidance of a guru.

These herbs are not growing only in the most remote places. In India we use them in our everyday life from time to time, so you don't have to go to the Himalayas, the Alps or the Andes in order to find them. You can just grow them in your garden, but then you must know how to use them, the proper time and the proper combinations and preparations. That is the method of herbs.

By the practice of concentration
The fifth method of awakening, which is very important, is called concentration. Sage Patanjali's *Yoga Sutras* have spoken in detail about this. It says that when concentration and meditation take place at the same time, there is total consummation of consciousness. That is called samyama.

Samyama means spontaneous, on the spot, concentration on the symbol, meditation and becoming one with it. Supposing you are concentrating on a flame of fire. When you concentrate on the flame you are trying to hold that image in your mind. That is called concentration, and suddenly you forget yourself. You forget that you are concentrating or meditating and only the fire flame is present. The meditator, the process of meditation, everything is lost and there is only one-pointed awareness of the fire flame. That is called samyama.

In order to achieve samyama you have to utilize various techniques, because one technique is not suitable for all. One way of practising concentration is pranayama. That is a very powerful method of concentration, meditation and samadhi. According to hatha yoga, mind and prana affect each other. When prana is disturbed, the mind is disturbed and when the prana is in harmony, mind is also in harmony. If you can concentrate the mind, you can control the pranas thereby. This is called raja yoga. However, in hatha yoga, first you control the prana, then the mind will automatically be controlled.